Ancient Psychoactive Substances

UNIVERSITY PRESS OF FLORIDA

Florida A&M University, Tallahassee
Florida Atlantic University, Boca Raton
Florida Gulf Coast University, Ft. Myers
Florida International University, Miami
Florida State University, Tallahassee
New College of Florida, Sarasota
University of Central Florida, Orlando
University of Florida, Gainesville
University of North Florida, Jacksonville
University of South Florida, Tampa
University of West Florida, Pensacola

ANCIENT PSYCHOACTIVE SUBSTANCES

Edited by

SCOTT M. FITZPATRICK

University Press of Florida

Gainesville · Tallahassee · Tampa · Boca Raton

Pensacola · Orlando · Miami · Jacksonville · Ft. Myers · Sarasota

Published in the United States of America

This book may be available in an electronic edition.

First cloth printing, 2018
First paperback printing, 2020

25 24 23 22 21 20 6 5 4 3 2 1

Library of Congress Cataloging-in-Publication Data
Names: Fitzpatrick, Scott M., editor.
Title: Ancient psychoactive substances / edited by Scott M. Fitzpatrick.
Description: Gainesville : University Press of Florida, 2018. | Includes bibliographical references and index.
Identifiers: LCCN 2017032192 | ISBN 9780813056708 (cloth : alk. paper)
ISBN 9780813068183 (pbk.)
Subjects: LCSH: Psychotropic drugs—History. | Hallucinogenic drugs—History. | Altered states of consciousness—History. | Hallucinogenic drugs and religious experience—History. | Drug abuse—History. | Alcoholism—History.
Classification: LCC RM315 .A58 2018 | DDC 615.7/883—dc23
LC record available at https://lccn.loc.gov/2017032192

The University Press of Florida is the scholarly publishing agency for the State University System of Florida, comprising Florida A&M University, Florida Atlantic University, Florida Gulf Coast University, Florida International University, Florida State University, New College of Florida, University of Central Florida, University of Florida, University of North Florida, University of South Florida, and University of West Florida.

University Press of Florida
2046 NE Waldo Road
Suite 2100
Gainesville, FL 32609
http://upress.ufl.edu

CONTENTS

ILLUSTRATIONS

TABLE

FIGURES

ACKNOWLEDGMENTS

I thank each of the authors for their extraordinary patience as the volume came together over the past few years. Matthew Napolitano deserves special recognition for helping to format the text, produce or modify figures used in the book, and tie up various loose ends. Mark Merlin, one of the world's leading authorities on a number of psychoactive substances and the author or coauthor of three chapters in this book, was especially helpful in clarifying many issues that arose and has become a welcome and inspiring colleague. Special recognition goes to Meredith Babb at the University Press of Florida for guiding the volume through the various stages of review and production. And to my family and friends for their long-term support of this and other research-related activities that have occasionally taken much longer than expected. Finally, I would like to acknowledge my uncle, David Fitzpatrick, who benefitted greatly in the last years of his life from the Oregon Medical Marijuana Program to alleviate suffering from brain cancer and related treatments. This initiative and many others like it are positively affecting thousands of lives. They are also a strong testament to the need for conducting further scientific inquiry into the wide array of psychoactive substances known worldwide so that their medicinal, nutritional, mind-altering, and other properties can be more thoroughly investigated and understood. As this volume clearly illustrates, the effects and benefits of entheogens—recognized by our ancestors millennia ago—continue to dramatically structure and influence our daily lives.

Introduction

Drugs from a Deep Time Perspective

SCOTT M. FITZPATRICK AND MARK D. MERLIN

It is often said that history repeats itself and that necessity is the mother of invention. While these two well-known maxims could equally apply to any number of contexts and situations across space and time, we would argue that they are perhaps at their most appropriate when describing the need for humans on a global scale to alter their reality. More often than not, this is achieved through the use of psychoactive substances.

The term *psychoactive* can be defined as "of or pertaining to a substance having a profound or significant effect on mental processes." Broadly construed, this covers a range of compounds found in an enormous variety of different biological organisms that alter perceptions of the user. The widespread use of legal (e.g., coffee, tea, betel nuts, tobacco, alcohol) and illicit drugs (e.g., heroin, cocaine, many hallucinogens) in modern society, and the subsequent problems they can create, is a strong testament to how pervasive and sometimes dangerous it is for humans to seek out and succumb to the vagaries of both natural and synthetic substances. It is a near-universal phenomenon and one that many have argued has roots that extend deep into our ancient evolutionary past (Clarke and Merlin 2013; Dobkin 1990; Furst 1972; Guzmán 1983; Merlin 1984, 2003; Schultes and Hofmann 1980; Schultes et al. 2001; Torres 1999, 2001).

There are many different types of psychoactive substances that are often grouped into four major categories: inebriants (e.g., alcohol), stimulants (e.g., betel nuts, caffeine, nicotine, cocaine, ephedrine), opiates and other narcotics (e.g., opium and its derivatives, such as heroin), and hallucinogens (e.g., mescaline, psilocybin, and synthetics such as LSD). Many of the known, naturally occurring psychoactive substances produced by certain flowering plants and fungi, which can cause "alteration in perception, cognition, and mood as [their] primary psychobiological actions in the presence of an otherwise clear sensorium" (Abraham et al. 1996: 287), have often been classified as hallucinogenic species. However, their potent, mind-altering plant substances generally do not produce dependence or become addictive (Nicols 2004: 131). In recent decades, these substances have been the focus of abundant research in the social and natural sciences (e.g., Brawley and Duffield 1972; Clarke and Merlin 2013; Devereux 1997; Dobkin de Rios 1990; Grinspoon and Bakalar 1979; Lee and Roth 2012; Martin and Sloan 1977; Merlin 2003; Nicols 2004; Rivier 1994; Sankar 1975; Schultes and Hofmann 1980; Schultes et al. 2001; Siegel 1989; Strassman 1984; Torres 2001). Most of these mind-altering substances are bitter alkaloids, which seem to have evolved naturally as defense mechanisms against herbivores (e.g., see Abraham et al. 1996: 285–86).

Numerous scholars, however, have questioned the sweeping use of the term *hallucinogen* to categorize some of these diverse substances, especially in light of their traditional applications and the cognitive interpretations of their significance. An alternative term, *entheogen*, has been offered as a more appropriate classification because peoples who have long used these traditional psychoactive substances have perceived their effects as generating a deity or supernatural forces within those who consume them, thus supporting the concept that these substances are products of the "plants of the gods" (e.g., Schultes et al. 2001; also see Griffiths et. al. 2006; Ruck et al. 1979). While the term *hallucinogen* is still often used in scholarly and scientific literature, as past research has shown, and as chapters in this volume demonstrate, entheogens are not just psychedelics or hallucinogenic but encompass a broad range of substances that are technically classified as inebriants, stimulants, opiates, or narcotics.

Ancient Psychoactive Substances

Societies in the ancient past used dozens of psychoactive substances, including many hallucinogens (e.g., see Schultes et al. 2001 for an extensive list). However, among those hallucinogens used most commonly in traditional contexts were lysergic acid amides, mescaline, psilocybin, *iboga*, harmine, and dimethyltryptamine (DMT), though some are not very visible or well-documented archaeologically.

Many potent mind-altering substances have a serotonergic basis and are composed of components that fall within a narrow group of chemical classes described by Schultes and Hofmann (1980) that include ibogaindoles, ergolines, beta-carbolines, tryptamines, isoquinolones, phenylethylamines, quinolizidines, tropanes, isoxazoles, dibenzopyrans, and phenylpropenes. Aghajanian and Marek (1999: 16S) report that there "is now converging evidence from biochemical, electrophysiological, and behavioral studies that the two major classes of psychedelic hallucinogens, the indoleamines (tryptamines) (e.g., LSD) and the phenethylamines (e.g., mescaline)[,] have a common site of action as partial agonists at 5-HT2A and other 5HT2 serotonergic receptors in the central nervous system." Nicols (2004: 135) suggests, however, that there should probably be two subsets of tryptamines: the simple tryptamines (e.g., DMT, 5-methoxy-DMT [5-MeO-DMT]) and psilocybin, "which possess considerable conformational flexibility"; and the ergolines (e.g., LSD), which are "relatively rigid analogues."

In any case, precisely when psychoactive substances first came into use prehistorically via their plant or fungus sources is not entirely clear, because much of the evidence comes from indirect indications in the form of artifacts or iconographic imagery and is often challenging to anchor chronologically. Schultes and colleagues (2001) offer some very useful, albeit occasionally vague, historical references for the antiquity of many of the known hallucinogens (their sources, chemistry, and uses), some of which are discussed in this volume in the context of their biotic and cultural diversity (also see Merlin 2003 for an archaeobotanical and archaeological review of ancient psychoactive drug plant use in the Old World). This introduction briefly evaluates some of the major psychoactive plants found in both the Old and the New World to provide basic biological and archaeological context and to highlight those chapters in the present volume that discuss them in more detail.

THE OLD WORLD

Although anatomically modern humans (AMHs) are generally believed to have originated in sub-Saharan Africa and radiated out from the continent tens of thousands of years ago, only one relatively well-known documented psychoactive species is native to this immense region, apart from the widely popular coffee plant (Genera: *Coffea*; primarily *C. canephora* and *C. arabica*), which is generally referred to as iboga (*Tabernanthe iboga* Ballion). There is little or no archaeobotanical or archaeological evidence of the ancient use of this native African species or any others, such as the tropical African kola nut tree species (*Cola* spp.), which produce fruits that contain caffeine, and the evergreen khat (or qat) shrub or small tree (*Catha edulis* Forsk) with stimulant leaves, although there is some evidence for the cultural introduction and use of *Cannabis* dating back many centuries in the region (e.g., see Clarke and Merlin 2013; Merlin 2003).

The iboga plant (*T. iboga*), also referred by the Fang group in Gabon as *eboka* (Fernandez 1972), is a shrub native to the tropical forests of West-Central Africa that is often used as a decorative bush in Fang villages associated with the Bwiti Cult. Although the root bark was earlier said to contain three alkaloids (tabernatheine, ibogamine, and iboluteine), today it is known to have at least a dozen (Schultes et al. 2001), with the primary psychoactive agent being the indole alkaloid ibogaine (12-methoxyibogamine). The ibogaine alkaloid is recognized as a stimulant similar to amphetamines and comparable to cocaine (Dobkin de Rios 1990: 163), as well as being hallucinogenic (for a personal account of ingesting iboga, see Pinchbeck 2002: 25–32). Ibogaine acts as a "choline-esterase inhibitor, causing some hypotension and stimulation of digestion and appetite," and is also found in other plants of the Apocynaceae, or dogbane family, including *Tabernaemontana undulate* Vahl and *Voacanga africana* Stapf (Stafford 1992: 361). *Tabernanthe iboga* is widely used and particularly well-known in Gabon and other parts of the Congo region. In these areas, iboga has been especially important in religious ceremonies at least since it became prominent in the Bwiti religious cult, which dates to the end of the nineteenth century.

Several other important psychoactive substances found in both the Old World and the New World are not well-known archaeologically, apart from mostly iconographic representation, but were quite common and recorded historically. These include mushrooms such as various species in the genus *Psilocybe*, which, along with many other mind-altering fungi genera, appear to have a very widespread, long-term association with humans. These hallucinogenic *Psilocybe* fungi contain the indole alkaloids psilocybin (O-phosphoryl-4-hydroxy-N,N-dimethyltryptamine = indocybine) and psilocin (3-(2-dimethylamino-ethyl)indol-4-ol = psilocin) the contents of which vary between species. Both alkaloids are tryptamine derivatives and are known to cause intense auditory and visual hallucinations during which a dreamlike state becomes or is interpreted cognitively as reality (Guzmán 2008a, 2008b; Letcher 2006; Schultes et al. 2001).

Two other species native to the drier central regions of Asia where

AMHs arrived approximately 35,000 years ago (and where people probably encountered them early on) are two resource-rich plant genera: *Cannabis* and *Ephedra*. As Merlin and Clarke note in chapter 1 in their discussion of ancient *Cannabis* remains, and Merlin notes in his discussion of ancient *Ephedra* use in chapter 3, humans developed very long and ancient relationships with plants in these genera across much of Eurasia (and, in the case of *Ephedra*, in some arid temperate areas of North and South America as well) for a variety of uses, including those often categorized as psychoactive and/or medicinal. Like some other species with psychoactive properties, *Cannabis* plants have been used for many traditional purposes over thousands of years as sources of fiber, oil, food, medicine, ritual, and recreation (for an up-to-date, comprehensive review and discussion of the natural and cultural history of *Cannabis*, see Clarke and Merlin 2013). Emerging archaeological evidence for *Cannabis* is demonstrating that this plant was used for thousands of years by humans in Central Eurasia and eventually began to spread out quite rapidly, becoming one of the most commonly used psychoactive plants in the world today. As Merlin in chapter 3 discusses, the term *Ephedra* normally refers to the gymnosperm plant *Ephedra sinica* Stapf, with its epithet indicating its biogeographical association with China, where it is known as *ma huang* (pinyin: *má huáng*, literally translated as "yellow hemp," e.g., see Lee 2011). *E. sinica* has been used in East Asia for thousands of years (Zhao and Xiao 2009), but it is not the only species in its genus with a long history of medicinal and psychoactive use.

While the Old World has comparatively fewer known psychoactive species than the New World, ergot fungi (*Claviceps purpurea* [Fr.] Tul.) and the opium poppy (*Papaver somniferum* L.) have a rich history of use in Western Eurasia, though the former is virtually unknown archaeologically. There are at least ten species of ergot fungi in the genus *Claviceps*, of which *C. purpurea* is the most common. This phytopathogen is a parasite on rye, other cultivated grains, and many wild grasses. Similar to other ergot species, *C. purpurea* produces ergoline and lysergic acid derivatives; some of these alkaloids are physically toxic while others are remarkably psychoactive. Ergot was well-known in Europe during the Middle Ages as an "herbal" medicine used by midwives for control of postpartum bleeding and other purposes. However, ergot poisoning has sometimes affected small to larger numbers of people who inadvertently ingested parts of the fungus that invaded cultivated rye or other grain crops, usually when the infected grain was baked into bread. The disease associated with this poisonous malady became known as St. Anthony's fire (e.g.,

Schultes et al. 2001). Gabbai and colleagues (1951) described a supposed "outbreak" of ergot poisoning at Pont St. Esprit in southern France in the middle of the previous century, and more recently, Albarelli (2009) and Samuel (2010) referred to a more sinister, but not widely accepted, explanation for this mass poisoning event.

The opium poppy, discussed by Chovanec in chapter 2, is quite well-known archaeologically from iconographic representations, artifacts, historical reports, and archaeobotanical remains (Merlin 1984, 2003). The poppy belongs to the family Papaveraceae, which is characterized by the production of watery or milky latex. Careful incisions of the unripe opium poppy fruit capsule releases this latex (opium) onto the surface, where it congeals and can be collected for processing into various psychoactive substances. In fact, the opium poppy is one of the most useful psychoactive plants and is well-known in the modern world for its pain-mitigating medicinal properties as well as its seeds and oil, which are common ingredients in many foods. The opium poppy was widely used in the ancient European world for millennia as the source of one of the first and most important anesthetic medicines, while the dried latex and its main alkaloid, morphine (along with its chemical derivatives, particularly heroin), have been the cause of major drug wars in China and Afghanistan over the past 150 years (e.g., see Beeching 1975; Goodhand 2005). As is well known, natural and semisynthetic substances derived from or chemically based on its potent latex morphine were problematic for peoples in the past and continue to be so for modern society, given their propensity for addiction and abuse. The first known recorded "opium addict" was the Roman emperor Marcus Aurelius (AD 161–180), as reported by his personal physician, Galen (e.g., see Africa 1961; Merlin 1984).

The primary psychoactive agents of opium derive from two main alkaloid groups: isoquinolines (e.g., papaverine and noscapine), which do not affect the central nervous system, and phenanthrenes (e.g., codeine, thebaine, and morphine), which have many uses but can cause high levels of addiction (Tetenyi 1997). Morphine ((5α,6α)-7,8-didehydro-4,5-epoxy-17-methylmorphinan-3,6-diol) is the most important of the psychoactive substances derived from opium given its potency as an analgesic that appears to mimic endogenous opioids commonly used for relieving severe pain. Opium has a long history of use in the Old World for its superlative anesthetic qualities and variety of other uses, especially those involving its seeds, which are tasty and produce edible oil.

One of the most commonly used psychoactive substances in the world is the betel nut or areca nut (*Areca catechu* L., e.g., see Marshall 1987;

Strickland 2002; Winstock 2002), although it is still virtually unknown in the Western Hemisphere. The betel nut is technically a drupe about the size of a walnut and is borne on a member of the palm family Arecaceae (syn. Palmae). It is cultivated today throughout much of South and Southeast Asia, insular Oceania, particularly Melanesia and western Micronesia, and coastal areas of East Africa and Madagascar. Its parasympathetic properties are known to produce euphoria, reduce appetite, and counteract fatigue. Betel nuts are typically chewed or sucked on along with a leaf of the pepper vine *Piper betle* L. and slaked lime in the buccal cheek cavity. The combination of these ingredients creates a psychoactive effect similar to that of nicotine. The addition of the *P. betle* leaf to the quid contributes to its aromatic scent and pungent taste because of the phenols contained in the leaf (Rooney 1995); the *P. betle* leaf also has the effect of turning the saliva reddish brown. Over time, the teeth of habitual users become permanently stained.

There are several major alkaloids found in the betel nut, including arecoline (arecaidine; $C_8H_{13}NO_2$ [or $C_7H_{11}NO_2 + H_2O$]), guvacine, and guvacoline. Arecaidine (n-methylguvacine, the active principle) is crystalline and isomeric (the former converts to arecoline with the introduction of the methyl group), and chemically, arecaidine is methyl-tetrahydronicotinic acid. The effects of arecoline (methyl-arecaidine) are said to resemble pilocarpine, a "cholinergic" drug used to treat or control dryness of the mouth or lack of saliva (xerostomia), glaucoma, and production of fluid in the eyes. Betel nut is also an analgesic and psychoactive stimulant but requires the addition of slaked lime (calcium hydroxide [$Ca(OH)_2$]), which converts the stimulating alkaloids into free base and renders the compound active. Very early archaeological evidence for *Areca catechu* appears to come from Spirit Cave in northwestern Thailand that was occupied as early as 12,000 years BP for about five millennia and contained a level with areca fruit petioles dated to 8776 BP (95% CI 8196 ±9356) (Gorman 1970; also see Gorman 1971).

The only psychoactive species known to be native to Remote Oceania is kava (*Piper methysticum* Forst. f.), a shrub belonging to the pepper family, Piperaceae. It is known in much of the South Pacific as kava or kava kava, or *'awa* in Hawai'i, *yagona* in Fiji, and *sakau* and *seka* respectively on the eastern Caroline Islands of Pohnpei and Kosrae in central Micronesia. This pepper shrub is native to some islands in Melanesia and was probably first domesticated in Vanuatu (Crowley 1994: 92; Lebot and Lévesque 1989; Lebot et al. 1992: 51–53). Kava has been used as a traditional remedy for numerous ailments, including rheumatism, menstrual cramps, venereal disease, tuberculosis, and leprosy; it is also said to induce abortions if the leaves are inserted into the vaginal canal. Traditionally, kava use had profound spiritual associations in many Oceanic societies before colonizing Western missionaries banned its use because of their perceptions about its connections with "pagan" beliefs (e.g., see Lebot et al. 1992). Archaeologically, kava has been observed in the form of macrobotanical remains and artifacts used to process the roots or consume the beverage, such as wooden bowls and pounding stones.

THE NEW WORLD

There are numerous psychoactive species that early peoples appear to have first encountered in the New World after they arrived, as early as perhaps 15,000 years ago, and dispersed through the vast, formerly unoccupied Western Hemisphere. These New World species include psilocybin mushrooms, tobacco, certain cacti, and a series of other flowering plant species with hallucinogenic (entheogenic) and/or stimulant effects that long ago became important resources for spiritual, ceremonial, and healing activities (see the review by Rafferty in chapter 4).

In addition, and certainly not unique to the New World exclusively, is alcohol (ethanol), which can be produced from a wide variety of plants and involves yeasts and the conversion of simple sugars to carbon dioxide and ethanol through the process of fermentation. The evidence for alcohol production archaeologically, historically, and ethnographically is robust, with innumerable examples that are too lengthy to list here. Suffice to say, the natural fermentation of fruits and other plants may have been the impetus for humans to develop and refine the process of alcohol production, especially beer and wine early on, but also distilled spirts. As several chapters in this volume describe (chapter 7 by Seinfeld, chapter 8 by Loughmiller-Cardinal, and chapter 11 by Jennings and Valdez), alcoholic beverages made from primarily maize (*Zea mays* L.) or manioc (cassava; *Manihot esculenta* Crantz) were an important and integral part of feasting and ritual by peoples in the New World, particularly Mesoamerica and South America.

The New World is also home to many different hallucinogens, including several psychoactive cacti. There is limited archaeological evidence for these, which include peyote (*Lophophora williamsii* [Lemaire ex Salm-Dyck] J.M. Coult.), San Pedro cactus (*Trichocereus pachanoi* Britton & Rose, syn. *Echinopsis pachanoi* [Britton & Rose] H. Friedrich and G.D. Rowley), and the Peruvian torch (*Trichocereus peruvianus* Britton & Rose, syn. *E. peruviana* [Britton & Rose] H. Friedrich & G.D. Rowley). All contain the highly potent, mind-altering substance mescaline (3,4,5-trimethoxyphenethylamine), an alkaloid known almost exclusively from these cacti. San Pedro mescaline is also found in very small amounts in some beans such as those produced by *Acacia berlandieri* Benth. Of these species, peyote contains the highest percentage of mescaline (about 1–6 percent of dried content). Ingestion of peyote induces an altered state of consciousness perceived as profound metaphysical or spiritual introspection, often coupled with intense visual and/or auditory effects. Peyote has been used ritualistically and medicinally for thousands of years within its natural range in the desert scrub environments of Mexico and small areas of southern Texas.

The earliest archaeological evidence for mescaline use comes from peyote discovered at two sites in southwestern Texas and Coahuila, Mexico. El-Seedi and colleagues (2005) dated peyote caps from Shumla in Texas (presumably Cave No. 5) to 3780–3660 BC (1σ), while another study by Terry and colleagues (2006) dated several specimens from the same site to 4045–3960 BC (2σ mean of three dates), which differed slightly from an earlier archaeological dating of two of the same specimens (Bruhn et al. 2002). In Mexico, ancient peyote specimens were recovered from another site at Cuatro Cienagas that has been dated to AD 1070–1280 (2σ; for a discussion of archaeobotanical remains in the northeastern Mexico and Trans-Pecos region that suggest changes in preferred ritual psychoactive plant sources over a long time depth, see Adovasio and Fry 1976).

Ayahuasca (*Banisteriopsis* spp.), extracted from South American vines (primarily *Banisteriopsis caapi* [Spruce ex Griseb.] C.V. Morton but also *B. inebrians* Morton), contains harmine (7-methoxy-β-carbolines), a beta-carboline alkaloid that acts as a monoamine oxidase inhibitor (MAOI), which, when mixed with other substances, allows the powerfully psychoactive dimethyltryptamine (DMT) alkaloid derived from another plant, predominantly *chacruna* (*Psychotria viridis* Ruiz & Pav.), to become orally active. As Torres discusses in chapter 9, the desired mind-altering effects are produced by combining these two ingredients, harmine and DMT, in a special brew.

Referred to as the "magic drink of the Amazon" (Schultes et al. 2001: 124–36), the use of ayahuasca (also known as yagé [or yaje], caapi, and various other indigenous names) among native groups in northern South America has been well studied. Although there is an abundance of ethnographic evidence of the use of ayahuasca, archaeological evidence is still rare. However, in areas under the control of the Tiwanaku empire (in Bolivia and Chile) circa AD 500–1000, grave goods (e.g., snuffing kits, along with powdered residue from a snuffing tablet) were found in the Solcor-3 cemetery (Tomb 112 at San Pedro de Atacama). These are indicative of the presence of *Anadenanthera colubrina* (Vell.) Brenan (Torres et al. 1991: 643), probably derived from its crushed seeds, which contain potent psychoactive alkaloids of dimethyltryptamine and suggest the ancient use of psychoactive substances.

Dimethyltryptamine (DMT), a powerful mind-altering substance, is found in various South American plants such as chacruna (*Psychotria viridis*), as well as in the seeds of *Anadenanthera colubrina* and *A. peregrina* (L.) Speg. var. *falcate* (Benth.) Atschul (commonly known as cohoba [or *cojoba*], *vilca*, cebil [or *cebíl*], and *yopo*). DMT is also found in the bark or other parts of additional plants, including *Virola* spp., sometimes used in conjunction with *Banisteriopsis* and *Acacia* spp. (*Anadenanthera* and *Acacia* belong to Fabaceae, the bean family, while *Psychotria* belongs to Rubiaceae, the coffee family, and *Virola* belongs to Myristicaceae, the nutmeg family).

A. peregrina is the most northerly distributed species of the genus *Anadenanthera*, and it became widely known as cohoba from Brazil up through the Antilles chain of islands in the Caribbean after it was introduced prehistorically by migrants from somewhere in northern South America. The first documentation of *A. peregrina* being used by native Amerindians was shortly after European contact in the Caribbean islands by both Ramón Pané (1999) and Bartolomé de Las Casas (1999), who remarked on the use of paraphernalia such as snuffing tubes and spouted bowls to inhale powder from ground cohoba beans. As Kaye notes in chapter 6, a variety of other objects—including *duho*s (ornate wooden stools), effigy figures, and vomit spatulas—were also associated with the cohoba ritual.

A. colubrina is known in Peru as vilca (or *builca*) and in northwestern Argentina as cebíl (Torres 1995: 295), and it is discussed in more detail by Sayre in chapter 10 as it pertains to the Chavín de Huántar site in Peru. According to Schultes and colleagues (2001), cebíl was first mentioned by Cristóbal de Albornoz, a Spanish chronicler who worked in the southern Andean region. Again, both direct and indirect archaeological evidence for the use of *A. colubrina* are much more extensive than for most other psychoactive substances known from South America (e.g., see Torres and Repke 2006). The use of vilca has been identified from powdered residue on snuffing trays, including those found in tombs associated with the Tiwanaku civilization (Ogalde et al. 2009) dated to circa AD 500–1000, and is inferred from trays and other snuffing paraphernalia.

An interesting addition to the family of psychoactive plants in North America is *Ilex vomitoria* Aiton, commonly known as yaupon or yaupon holly. Yaupon is an evergreen shrub native to the southeastern United States in Aquifoliaceae, the holly family. This species contains high levels of caffeine and grows to a height of 5–9 meters tall, producing small red berries; it is the only native North American plant that is known to contain caffeine. The active constituents are the bitter alkaloid theobromine (3,7-dimethyl-1H-purine-2,6-dione) (also found in cacao) and the crystalline xanthine alkaloid caffeine (1,3,7-trimethyl-1H-purine-2,6(3H,7H)-dione; 3,7-dihydro-1,3,7-trimethyl-1H-purine-2,6-dione), which is a stimulant (Reginatto et al. 1999).

Historically, *I. vomitoria* is known primarily for its use in the "black drink" prepared by Native Americans in the southeastern United States, using the leaves and stems to brew a "tea" for rituals involving purification (Fairbanks 1979; Merrill 1979). True to its Latin binomial epithet, yaupon is a purgative, likely as a result of overconsumption during periods of feasting. Recent microbotanical analysis identified holly (*Ilex* sp.) pollen from deposits dated to circa 900 BC–AD 200 at Fort Center, Florida; these microfossils could have come from *I. vomitoria*, which is known to have been used by the Calusa people of southwestern Florida in ceremonies (Austin 2006: 412), as discussed by Thompson and Pluckhahn in chapter 5.

Some of the most common and widespread psychoactive plants in the New World were tobaccos (*Nicotiana rustica* L. and *N. tabacum* L.), traditionally used for purification, association with the divine, and recreation. Tobacco has had a long, central role in shamanism across the Americas (see Wilbert 1987 for South America; Elferink 1983 and Robicsek 1978 for Mesoamerica; and Linton 1924, von Gernet 1992, and Winter 2000 for North America).

Approximately sixty-five species of "tobaccos" are known in the genus *Nicotiana*, which belongs to Solanaceae, the tobacco or deadly nightshade family. Most are found in the New World, but only a few of these species (or hybrids) had widespread use prehistorically, and they were frequently referred to by early Spanish chroniclers in the New World (e.g., Monardes 1565; Oviedo y Valdes 1535). Tobacco plant parts or concoctions made with them were administered through chewing, smoking, snuffing, drinking, or enemas or were applied to the skin as an ointment.

Coca (*Erythroxylum coca* Lam. and *Erythroxylum novogranatense* [D. Morris] Hieron.) are two closely related psychoactive plant species native to the Andean highlands of South America. Each of these two recognized species of cultivated cocas have two recognized varieties: (1) *E. coca* var. *coca* (Bolivian or Huánuco coca) and *E. coca* var. *ipadu* (Amazonian coca); and (2) *E. novogranatense* var. *novogranatense* (Colombian coca) and *E. novogranatense* var. *truxillense* (Trujillo coca) (Cortella et al. 2001: 792; Plowman 1984). These two *Erythroxylum* species belong to the family Erythroxylaceae, which comprises about 250 species of shrubs and medium-sized trees. The leaves of these two coca species, with the addition of slaked lime, are masticated for their stimulating effects, which are produced principally by the cocaine alkaloid (methyl (1R,2R,3S,5S)-3-(benzoyloxy)-8-methyl-8-azabicyclo[3.2.1]octane-2-carboxylate). In addition to the cocaine alkaloid, coca leaves are rich in vitamins, protein, calcium, iron, and fiber. The major effect of chewing these leaves is the reduction of fatigue, hunger, and thirst. Coca also counters the symptoms of oxygen deprivation, important for surviving in higher altitudes like the Andes. Coca was not only for "chewing," however; it also served as "a symbol of social status and ethnic identity and an element of oracles and rituals" (Dillehay et al. 2010; see Plowman 1984). Coca leaves thus appear to have been used for religious and other purposes for millennia in parts of South America.

As described above, there are numerous psychoactive species with ancient roots in human culture. But these are only a sample of the much larger number of mind-altering plant and fungi species that humans encountered during their early dispersal into many regions of the world and that were incorporated into cultural traditions through time. Although this survey is limited, readers should hopefully have gained a better understanding of the geographical breadth and antiquity of psychoactive substances on a global scale and the importance they had for humans across a spectrum of social, medicinal, political, and economic systems.

Archaeological Perspectives

Exactly when the first humans chose to ingest a mind-altering substance will likely never be known. In part, this is the curse of archaeology: many materials, especially organic ones, simply do not preserve well over time except under exceptional circumstances. The depositional context must be constant and ideally anaerobic or extremely arid over time. If the environment fluctuates too much—from cold to warm, wet to dry, and many conditions in between—bones, leaves, wood, and other remnants of plants and animals decay rapidly and are lost to the vagaries of time. But in those rare instances where a tomb is sealed, a ship is sunk, or a layer of sediment is laid quickly on top of something once living, archaeologists have the unique opportunity to extract information hundreds or even thousands of years old that can be used to say something meaningful about the people who left them behind.

As chapters in this volume illustrate, the ability of archaeologists to recover, identify, and analyze psychoactive substances and their related paraphernalia has grown exponentially in recent years. This is in large part due to advances in the natural sciences, such as chemistry, geology, and biology, but also because of the increasingly refined methods used in archaeology to record and examine stratigraphic deposits, artifacts, archaeobotanical data, other ancient environmental parameters, and human skeletal remains. Archaeologists are now able to ask questions regarding human health and behavior that would have been unthinkable even a decade ago. The ability to couple archaeological data with these new lines of scientific inquiry, along with existing ethnohistoric descriptions and ethnographic accounts, provides a powerful matrix of inquiry that is dramatically changing how we think of past human use of psychoactive substances through the ages.

The need to change or modify one's reality through the use of mind-altering substances is not relegated to the past few centuries in nondescript places: this is a phenomenon that goes back millennia and reaches to nearly every corner of the globe. Archaeological evidence, in fact, demonstrates that psychoactive substances—and the various other ingredients, technologies, and paraphernalia used to harness their mind-altering power—have been a part of daily and/or ritual life for many cultures and has, in many ways, led to profound effects on those individuals and societies. This is not necessarily surprising, given that we have been hunters and gatherers for 99 percent of human history and would have come into contact with, consumed, and experimented with a wide array of plants. Continued scientific research is now demonstrating that those taxa with psychotropic properties have helped fuel social cohesion, led to the development of religious ideologies, and become the latticework in which social complexity arises. From the smaller hunter-gatherer bands that roamed Africa and Eurasia eons ago to the shamans of the southwestern United States, Egyptian pharaohs, Mayan kings and queens, and many more, psychoactive substances for these and many other human groups were an integral part of living, surviving, and ruling.

Much has been written in the past few decades by ethnobotanists and anthropologists on how traditional cultures have acquired and imbibed psychoactive substances, particularly hallucinogens and stimulants. But over the past twenty years or so, numerous advances in analytical techniques such as gas chromatography/mass spectrometry and radiocarbon dating now provide a much stronger framework for examining the role that psychoactive substances played in ancient societies. What is becoming clearer is that the use of mind-altering materials—plants in particular—is not relegated to a shallow period of time but goes deep into the ancient past. Archaeology, archaeobotany, and many related subfields are opening new doors to understanding how humans actively sought out ways to alter their individual and collective behavior.

While many of the chapters included in this volume attest to the intensity and expansiveness of psychoactive substance use through a variety of methodological, theoretical, and cultural perspectives, the current volume is by no means complete. The extent of the antiquity and geographical distribution of many of these substances, their associated paraphernalia, and other representations in the archaeological record is both greater and more complex than we had ever imagined, and current evidence suggests that we are only beginning to understand the depth of human use of these substances in the past. So while this volume cannot hope to satisfactorily address the rich mosaic of mind-altering drugs used across the whole of human prehistory, it is the first attempt to conceptualize in a single volume how archaeological research can contribute to this fascinating area of study. This book essentially offers ways in which these avenues of ancient study can highlight when and how humans have—for so long—sought to partake of mind-altering substances.

Summary and Future Research

The worldwide chronology, biological diversity, and geographical range of human use of psychoactive drug plants are neither complete nor unchangeable. While there clearly is a great antiquity to the use of particular fungi, vines, cacti, and other plants by peoples around the world for their medicinal and mind-altering properties, many of these species and regions in which they are found are still under-researched and require initial or additional investigation. Many scholars would believe it safe to assume that most psychoactive plants have a longer history of use than that recorded here, and archaeological evidence will likely continue to push back their use into the deeper past, particularly as existing analytical techniques are defined and new ones are developed. In any case, we hope that the research presented here can at least serve as a starting point in synthesizing the antiquity of many of the world's best-known and most widely used psychoactive substances from which other scholars and students may build upon. With a critical application of archaeology, paleobotany, anthropology, cultural geography, history, botany, and other research disciplines to the study of mind-altering substances, our knowledge of their use in deep time will be significantly expanded, and as a result, the picture of their importance to human groups worldwide will become much more complete.

Most of the chapters contained in this volume were originally papers presented at the 2012 Society for American Archaeology conference in Memphis, Tennessee, and their authors include many of the world's leading junior and senior scholars in archaeology and paleoethnobotany. These researchers and many others are paving the way to more completely describing and recording the integral role that psychoactive substances played in ancient societies. We thank everyone who presented at the conference and shared their research, all of whom made a concerted effort to bring this book to publication.

References Cited

Abraham, D. A., A. M. Aldridge, and P. Gogia. 1996. The Psychopharmacology of Hallucinogens. *Neuropsychopharmacology* 14 (4): 285–98.

Adovasio, J. M., and G. F. Fry. 1976. Prehistoric Psychotropic Drug Use in Northeastern Mexico and Trans-Pecos Texas. *Economic Botany* 30: 94–96.

Africa, T. W. 1961. The Opium Addiction of Marcus Aurelius. *Journal of the History of Ideas* 22: 97–102.

Aghajanian, G. K., and G. J. Marek. 1999. Serotonin and Hallucinogens. *Neuropsychopharmacology* 21: 165–235.

Albarelli, H. P., Jr. 2009. *A Terrible Mistake: The Murder of Frank Olson and the CIA's Secret Cold War Experiments*. Walterville, Ore.: Trine Day.

Austin, D. F. 2006. *Florida Ethnobotany*. Boca Raton, Fla.: CRC Press.

Beeching, J. 1975. *The Chinese Opium Wars*. London: Hutchinson.

Brawley, P., and J. C. Duffield. 1972. The Pharmacology of Hallucinogens. *Pharmacological Review* 24: 31–66.

Bruhn, J. G., P.A.G.M. De Smet, H. R. El-Seedi, and O. Beck. 2002. Mescaline Use for 5700 Years. *Lancet* 359: 1866.

Clarke, R., and M. Merlin. 2013. *Cannabis: Evolution and Ethnobotany*. Berkeley: University of California Press.

Cortella, A. R., M. L. Pochettino, A. Manzo, and G. Ravina. 2001. *Erythroxylum coca*: Microscopical Identification in Powdered and Carbonized Archaeological Material. *Journal of Archaeological Science* 28: 787–94.

Crowley, T. 1994. Proto-Who Drank Kava? In *Austronesian Terminologies: Continuity and Change*, ed. A. K. Pawley and M. D. Ross, 87–100. Canberra: Department of Linguistics, Research School of Pacific and Asian Studies, Australian National University.

Devereux, P. 1997. *The Long Trip: A Prehistory of Psychedelia*. New York: Penguin Putnam.

Dillehay, T. D., J. Rossen, D. Ugent, A. Karathanasis, V. Vasquez, and P. J. Netherly. 2010. Early Holocene Coca Chewing in Northern Peru. *Antiquity* 84 (326): 939–53.

Dobkin de Rios, M. 1990. *Hallucinogens: Cross-Cultural Perspectives*. Prospect Heights, Ill.: Waveland Press.

Elferink, J.G.R. 1983. The Narcotic and Hallucinogenic Use of Tobacco in Pre-Columbian Central America. *Journal of Ethnopharmacology* 7: 11–122.

El-Seedi, H. R., P.A.G.M. De Smet, O. Beck, G. Possnert, and J. G. Bruhn. 2005. Prehistoric Peyote Use: Alkaloid Analysis and Radiocarbon Dating of Archaeological Specimens of *Lophophora* from Texas. *Journal of Ethnopharmacology* 101: 238–42.

Fairbanks, C. H. 1979. The Function of Black Drink among the Creeks. In *Black Drink: A Native American Tea*, ed. C. M. Hudson, 120–49. Athens: University of Georgia Press.

Fernandez, J. W. 1972. *Tabernanthe iboga*: Narcotic Ecstasis and the Work of the Ancestors. In *Flesh of the Gods: The Ritual Use of Hallucinogens*, ed. P. Furst, 237–60. Prospect Heights, Ill.: Waveland Press, Inc.

Furst, P. T. 1972. *Flesh of the Gods: The Ritual Use of Hallucinogens*. Prospect Heights, Ill.: Waveland Press.

Gabbai, Lisbonne, and Pourquier. 1951. Ergot Poisoning at Pont St. Esprit. *British Medical Journal* 2 (4732): 650–51.

Goodhand, J. 2005. Frontiers and Wars: The Opium Economy in Afghanistan. *Journal of Agrarian Change* 5 (2): 191–216.

Gorman, C. F. 1970. Excavations at Spirit Cave, North Thailand: Some Interim Interpretations. *Asian Perspectives* 13: 79–108.

Gorman, C. F. 1971. The Hoabinhian and After: Subsistence Patterns in Southeast Asia during the Latest Pleistocene and Early Recent Periods. *World Archaeology* 2: 300–320.

Griffiths, R.R.W., A. Richards, U. McCann, and R. Jesse. 2006. Psilocybin Can Occasion Mystical-Type Experiences Having Substantial and Sustained Personal Meaning and Spiritual Significance. *Psychopharmacology* 187 (3): 268–83.

Grinspoon, L., and J. Bakalar. 1979. *Psychedelic Drugs Reconsidered*. New York: Basic Books.

Guzmán, G. 1983. *The Genus* Psilocybe*: A Systematic Revision of the Known Species Including the History, Distribution and Chemistry of the Hallucinogenic Species*. Nova Hedwigia Beihefte 74. Berlin: J. Cramer.

Guzmán, G. 2008a. Diversity and Use of Traditional Mexican Medicinal Fungi: A Review. *International Journal of Medicinal Mushrooms* 10 (3): 209–17.

Guzmán, G. 2008b. Hallucinogenic Mushrooms in Mexico: An Overview. *Economic Botany* 62: 404–12.

Las Casas, B. de. 1999. Appendix C. In *An Account of the Antiquities of the Indians*, by R. Pané, 54–67. Ed. J. J. Arrom, trans. S. C. Griswold. Durham, N.C.: Duke University Press.
Lebot, V., and J. Lévesque. 1989. The Origin and Distribution of Kava (*Piper methysticum* Forst. f., Piperaceae): A Phytochemical Approach. *Allertonia* 5 (2): 223–81.
Lebot, V., M. Merlin, and L. Lindstrom. 1992. *Kava: The Pacific Drug*. New Haven, Conn.: Yale University Press.
Lee, H.-M., and B. L. Roth. 2012. Hallucinogen Actions on Human Brain Revealed. *Proceeding of the National Academy of Sciences* 109 (6): 1820–21.
Lee, M. R. 2011. The History of *Ephedra* (*Ma-Huang*). *Journal of the Royal College of Physicians, Edinburgh* 41: 78–84.
Letcher, A. 2006. *Shroom: A Cultural History of the Magic Mushroom*. London: Faber and Faber.
Linton, R. 1924. *Use of Tobacco among North American Indians*. Anthropology Leaflet 15. Chicago: Field Museum of Natural History.
Marshall, M. 1987. An Overview of Drugs in Oceania. In *Drugs in Western Pacific Societies: Relations of Substance*, ed. L. Lindstrom, 1–49. ASAO Monograph 11. Boston: University Press of America.
Martin, W., and J. Sloan. 1977. Pharmacology and Classification of LSD-Like Hallucinogens. In *Drug Addiction II*, ed. W. Martin, 305–68. Berlin: Springer-Verlag.
Merlin, M. D. 1984. *On the Trail of the Ancient Opium Poppy*. London: Associated University Presses.
Merlin, M. D. 2003. Archaeological Evidence for the Tradition of Psychoactive Plant Use in the Old World. *Economic Botany* 57 (3): 295–323.
Merrill, W. L. 1979. The Beloved Tree: *Ilex vomitoria* among the Indians of the Southeast and Adjacent Regions. In *Black Drink: A Native American Tea*, ed. C. M. Hudson, 40–82. Athens: University of Georgia Press.
Monardes, N. B. 1565. *Historia medicinal de las cosas que se traen de nuestras Indias Occidentales*. Seville: Sebastian Trugillo.
Nicols, D. E. 2004. Hallucinogens. *Pharmacology and Therapeutics* 101: 131–81.
Ogalde, J. P., B. T. Arriaza, and E. C. Soto. 2009. Identification of Psychoactive Alkaloids in Ancient Andean Human Hair by Gas Chromatography/Mass Spectrometry. *Journal of Archaeological Science* 36 (2): 467–72.
Oviedo y Valdes, F. G. de. 1535. *Historia general de las Indias*. Seville: Juan Cromberger.
Pané, R. 1999. *An Account of the Antiquities of the Indians*. Ed. J. J. Arrom, trans. S. C. Griswold. Durham, N.C.: Duke University Press.
Pinchbeck, D. 2002. *Breaking Open the Head: A Psychedelic Journal into the Heart of Contemporary Shamanism*. New York: Broadway Books.
Plowman, T. 1984. The Origin, Evolution and Diffusion of Coca (*Erythroxylum* spp.) in South and Central America. In *Pre-Columbian Plant Migration*, ed. D. Stone, 125–63. Papers of the Peabody Museum of Archaeology and Ethnology 76. Cambridge, Mass.: Harvard University.
Reginatto, F. H., M. L. Athayde, G. Gosmann, and E. P. Schenkel. 1999. Methylxanthines Accumulation in *Ilex* species—Caffeine and Theobromine in Erva-Mate

(*Ilex paraguariensis*) and Other *Ilex* Species. *Journal of the Brazilian Chemical Society* 10: 443–46.

Rivier, L. 1994. Ethnopharmacology of LSD and Related Compounds. In *Fifty Years of LSD: Current Status and Perspectives of Hallucinogens*, ed. A. Pletscher and D. Ladewig, 43–55. New York: Parthenon.

Robicsek, F. 1978. *The Smoking Gods.* Norman: University of Oklahoma Press.

Rooney, D. F. 1995. Betel Chewing in South-East Asia. Paper prepared for the Centre National de la Recherche Scientifique (CNRS) in Lyon, France, August 1995. http://rooneyarchive.net/lectures/lec_betel_chewing_in_south-east_asia.htm.

Ruck, C.A.P., J. Bigwood, D. Staples, J. Ott, and R. G. Wasson. 1979. Entheogens. *Journal of Psychedelic Drugs* 11 (1–2): 145–46.

Samuel, H. 2010. French Bread Spiked with LSD in CIA Experiment. *The Telegraph* (London), March 11.

Sankar, D. 1975. *LSD, A Total Study.* Westbury, N.Y.: PJD Publications.

Schultes, R., and A. Hofmann. 1980. *The Botany and Chemistry of Hallucinogens.* Springfield, Ill.: Thomas.

Schultes, R. E., A. Hofmann, and C. Rätsch. 2001. *Plants of the Gods: Their Sacred, Healing, and Hallucinogenic Powers.* Rochester, N.Y.: Healing Arts Press.

Siegel, R. K. 1989. *Intoxication: Life in Pursuit of Artificial Paradise.* New York: E. P. Dutton.

Stafford, P. 1992. *Psychedelics Encyclopedia.* 3rd ed. Berkeley, Calif.: Ronin Publishing.

Strassman, R. J. 1984. Adverse Reactions to Psychedelic Drugs: A Review of the Literature. *Journal of Nervous and Mental Disorders* 172: 577–95.

Strickland, S. S. 2002. Anthropological Perspectives on Use of the *Areca* Nut. *Addiction Biology* 7 (1): 85–97.

Terry, M., K. L. Steelman, T. Guilderson, P. Dering, and M. W. Rowe. 2006. Lower Pecos and Coahuila Peyote: New Radiocarbon Dates. *Journal of Archaeological Science* 33: 1017–21.

Tetenyi, P. 1997. Opium Poppy (*Papaver somniferum*): Botany and Horticulture. In *Horticultural Reviews*, vol. 19, ed. J. Janick, 373–408. New York: John Wiley and Sons.

Torres, C. M. 1995. Archaeological Evidence for the Antiquity of Psychoactive Plant Use in the Central Andes. *Annual de Museum Civilisation Rovereto* 11: 291–326.

Torres, C. M. 1999. Psychoactive Substances in the Archaeology of Northern Chile and NW Argentina. *Chungara* (Arica, Chile) 30: 49–63.

Torres, C. M. 2001. Shamanic Inebriants in South America Archaeology: Recent Investigations. *Eleusis*, n.s., 5: 3–12.

Torres, C. M., and D. Repke. 2006. *Anadenanthera: Visionary Plant of Ancient South America.* New York: Haworth Herbal Press.

Torres, C. M., D. Repke, K. Chan, D. McKenna, A. Llagostera, and R. E. Shultes. 1991. Snuff Powders from Pre-Hispanic San Pedro de Atacama: Chemical and Contextual Analysis. *Current Anthropology* 32: 640–49.

von Gernet, A. D. 1992. Hallucinogens and the Origins of the Iroquoian Pipe/Tobacco/Smoking Complex. In *Proceedings of the 1989 Smoking Pipe Conference: Selected Papers*, ed. C. F. Hayes III, 171–85. Research Records 22. Rochester, N.Y.: Rochester Museum and Science Center.

Wilbert, J. 1987. *Tobacco and Shamanism in South America*. New Haven, Conn.: Yale University Press.
Winstock, A. 2002. Areca Nut-Abuse Liability, Dependence and Public Health. *Addiction Biology* 7: 133–38.
Winter, J., ed. 2000. *Tobacco Use by Native Americans: Sacred Smoke and Silent Killer*. Norman: University of Oklahoma Press.
Zhao Z. and Xiao P. 2009. Mahuang (*Ephedra*). In *Encyclopedia of Medicinal Plants*, 342–45. Shanghai: Shanghai World Publishing.

1

Cannabis in Ancient Central Eurasian Burials

MARK D. MERLIN AND ROBERT C. CLARKE

Over the vast time span within which humans have known and used *Cannabis* for many purposes, it has been heralded as one of our supreme resources and cursed as one of our utmost burdens. Today the consumption of mind-altering *Cannabis* plant material for recreational or medicinal reasons is widely known. However, the original and early use of psychoactive *Cannabis* may have been principally for ritualistic religious purposes (for a comprehensive discussion of the evolutionary biology and ethnobotanical history of the genus *Cannabis*, see Clarke and Merlin 2013; also see Duvall 2015; Small 2015).

The natural origin area of *Cannabis* was most likely the central steppe and forest zones of Eurasia. Early modern humans probably first encountered and utilized one or more of the products of this annual, herbaceous genus in its native biogeographical range. Remarkable early twentieth- and twenty-first-century discoveries of archaeobotanical remains in ancient burials confirm the nonfood and nonfiber use of *Cannabis* in Central Eurasia at least by the first millennium BCE. In these cases, *Cannabis* appears to have been used for mind-altering ceremonial, purification, or therapeutic purposes. This chapter focuses on the presence and putative uses of psychoactive *Cannabis* in ancient burials that are well over two thousand years old and found in southeastern Russia and western China.

Today, *Cannabis* remains a controversial yet remarkably multipurpose genus with a very ancient history of diverse human-plant relationships. As an introduction, we offer some biological and theoretical background to indicate the importance and special context of the archaeobotanical evidence discussed in detail below. First, we describe the special botanical and ecological aspects of *Cannabis* that initially attracted people and eventually became accentuated by human use over time; then we focus on ancient burial sites in Central Eurasia found over the past century that confirm the great time depth of human ceremonial association with psychoactive *Cannabis*.

Some scholars, such as Beckwith (2009), argue for a major reconsideration of the function of Central Eurasia in world history. Hanks (2012: 469) focused on the "Eurasian steppe" and presented an informative general review of the archaeology of this region and Mongolia, arguing that "steppe prehistory must come to play a more significant role in developing more comprehensive understandings of world prehistory." This is relevant here in light of the evidence for a presumably important spiritual and/or medicinal function of mind-altering *Cannabis* during a key period in cultural innovation and exchange in Central Eurasia and well beyond this region: "To some extent, the history of Eurasia as a whole from its beginnings to the present day can be viewed as the successive movements of Central Eurasians and Central Eurasian cultures into the periphery and of peripheral peoples and their cultures into Central Eurasia" (Beckwith 2009: xxi).

Some Botanical and Ecological Aspects of *Cannabis*

Cannabis plants have an annual life cycle and under natural conditions develop into medium to tall erect herbs. However, ecological influences and artificial selection on these populations throughout their geographical range have had strong effects on their growth habits and the potential products available to humans. *Cannabis*, adapted to continental temperate climate zones, can grow into large, well-branched plants reaching maximum heights of about 5 meters (approximately 15 feet) or more within a four- to six-month growing season in open sunlit environments that have rich permeable soils and sufficient water. Ideal habitats for *Cannabis* include exposed banks of waterways as well as disturbed areas near human habitation and agricultural lands because they usually provide abundant sunshine, moist but well-drained soil, and plentiful nutrients. When grown in relatively dry locations with limited soil nutrients, *Cannabis* develops negligible foliage and can mature and produce a few seeds when it reaches only 20 centimeters (8 inches) in height.

In contrast, if cultivated in dense stands on rich soil, which is standard farming procedure during fiber hemp cultivation, plants develop tall, slender, straight stalks devoid of branches and can increase in height by as much as 10 centimeters (4 inches) per day. The quickly lengthening stalks generate a sturdy bast (bark) fiber long used as a source for cordage and woven textile production. If a plant is cultivated for seed or psychoactive drug production, more space is given between individual plants, and as a result, limbs bearing plentiful flowers are produced from diminutive axial meristems (growing points) positioned at the nodes (intersections of the petioles or leaf stalks) along the main stalk.

Cannabis is normally dioecious, with unisexual male or female flowers produced on separate plants; however, monoecious examples with both sexes produced on one plant sometimes develop. *Cannabis* is wind pollinated and therefore relies mainly on air currents to transmit pollen grains from male plants to fertilize receptive female plants that form seeds.

The growth of flowering *Cannabis* differs greatly between the sexes. Female plants produce many inflorescences made up of numerous pairs of small flowers with a bract about 2–8 millimeters (1/12–1/3 inches) long and with a leaflet beneath; these parts are all closely packed within upright, dense clusters. Each female flower consists of two long white, yellowish, or pinkish stigmas (female sexual organs) that are receptive to pollen. These are attached to the single ovule and extend beyond the bract (modified leaflike structure) tightly surrounding each ovule. Male plants develop fewer, smaller leaves along elongated limbs, and flowers (about 5 millimeters [1/5 inch] long) are suspended from multibranched, lax clusters, promoting dissemination of pollen by air currents.

The female bracts are covered with a multitude of secretory plant hairs (glandular trichomes). Theoretically, the resinous secretions of these glands offer protection for the ovule and developing seed by reducing plant water loss (transpiration) and may also fend off pests. This aromatic resin contains the psychoactive and/or medicinal properties that have attracted human attention for millennia (Merlin 1972; Clarke 1981, 1998a, 1998b; Pollan 2001; Russo 2007; Clarke and Merlin 2013; Small 2015).

The mature seed (achene fruit) of *Cannabis* is somewhat elongated and flattened, 2–6 millimeters (1/12–1/4 inch) in length and 1–4 millimeters (1/24–1/6 inch) at its greatest width. The seeds have a lengthy history of utilization as an edible grain and a source of useful oil. In fact, *Cannabis* seeds are a first-rate dietary resource, containing easily digestible protein and essential fatty acids, but they are not psychoactive (e.g., see Deferne and Pate 1996).

Early Human Contact with *Cannabis* in Central Eurasia

Initial human contact with *Cannabis* and the subsequent discovery and application of its useful resources likely took place during the distant past in one of the more temperate and well-watered areas of ancient Central Eurasia (e.g., see Merlin 1972; Clarke and Merlin 2013; Small 2015). In this broad region, the ancient burial sites highlighted in this study were constructed thousands of years later, in the first millennium BCE. In the following discussion, we outline the hypothetical, very ancient and widespread cultural-historical predisposition of people to induce spiritual experiences through the use of psychoactive drug plants, including certain biotypes of *Cannabis*. This provides the framework from which we can interpret the relatively recent discoveries of ancient ritualistic funerary use of *Cannabis* in Eurasia discussed below.

In contemporary modern societies, direct personal revelations or mental images ascribed to religious inspiration are often dismissed as figments of the imagination or hallucinations, and yearnings to experience direct communion with a deity are frequently construed as a symptom of mental illness or even insanity. Nonetheless, some scholars and scientists believe that such revelations and contacts with the supernatural, very often via the use of psychoactive plant substances, are basically the result of age-old, ongoing cultural traditions (La Barre 1970, 1977, 1980; Kramer and Merlin 1983; Smith 2000; Schultes et al. 2001; Merlin 2003). We believe that throughout much of human history, and certainly during much of the Holocene, people of various Eurasian cultures have practiced traditions involving the use of mind-altering *Cannabis*, often motivated by a desire to produce cognitively profound, essentially religious experiences that supported their particular spiritual beliefs. During earlier as well as modern times, societies often evaluated the societal significance of psychoactive *Cannabis* use in conflicting ways, to a large extent based on a society's interest in using or preventing the use of plants in this genus (Farnsworth 1968; Dikötter et al. 2004).

In the early 1970s, a systematic review of the world's ethnographic literature indicated that approximately 90 percent of human societies have integrated "culturally patterned forms of an altered state of consciousness" (Bourguignon 1973: 11). A major percentage of these reported altered states resulted via ingestion of drug plants. This supports the hypothesis that the common use of psychoactive plants in traditional societies should not be doubted, just as the disposition of people in industrial societies is generally known to be mediated by a balance of mind-altering substances such as caffeine, nicotine, alcohol, and others (Sherratt 1995a).

Customary consumption of most psychoactive drug plants throughout human history appears to have been connected predominantly with ritualistic and often spiritual activity. Indeed, before modern times, the incentives for ingestion of mind-altering, organic substances, especially those classified as hallucinogens or entheogens—which includes psychoactively potent *Cannabis*—were mainly inspired by religious or therapeutic necessities (the term *entheogen* refers to a substance that can, from a cognitive perspective, generate a god or deity within and as such is less pejorative than *hallucinogen*, which refers to a substance that produces a false sense of reality). Nevertheless, contemporary use of these substances in many cultures, especially in those regions affected by Western civilization, is frequently inspired by individual "recreational" motivations to induce relaxation, contentment, or exhilaration and often is encouraged by social incentives. *Cannabis* can generate diverse altered states of awareness depending on the quality and quantity of plant parts ingested, as well as the psychological mind-set of the user and the social-environmental setting in which it is consumed; the altered states of *Cannabis* ingestion are also affected by the mode of consumption (e.g., oral ingestion versus breathing vapors or smoking [see Earleywine 2002; Julien et al. 2011]). In the discussion that follows, we draw attention to selected archaeobotanical discoveries of extraordinary ancient burials in the late twentieth and early twenty-first centuries that verify human association with *Cannabis* in Central Eurasia thousands of years ago.

Psychoactive Use of *Cannabis* among Ancient Eurasian Cultures

During the middle of the fifth century before the birth of Christ, at or near the apogee of the Classical Greek era, the historian Herodotus described the use of *Cannabis* by peoples whose territory was located beyond the Hellenic realm. In a well-known section of the fourth book of his *Histories*, Herodotus referred to the "Scythians," describing them as people alien to the Greeks who lived to the northeast, and noted that they burned the seeds of *Cannabis* in a vessel (censer) as a part of their funeral ritual. The following is a translation of Herodotus' description of this funerary purification ritual, which we suggest had shamanistic or ecstatic religious importance: "They make a booth by fixing in the ground three sticks inclined towards one another, and stretching around them woolen felts which they arrange so as to fit as close as possible: inside the booth a dish is placed upon the ground into which they put a number of red hot stones and then add some hemp seed . . . immediately it smokes, and gives out such a vapor as no Grecian vapor-bath can exceed; and the Scythians, delighted, shout for joy" (Hyams 1971: 100; also see Eliade 1964; Sélincourt 1965; Bremmer 2001). (The issue of whether hemp seed alone or as part of the inflorescence of *Cannabis* was placed upon a fire or heated stones is addressed below.)

The Scythians were an Iranian nomadic confederacy referred to variously as Indo-Scythians, Indo-Iranian Sakas, or Sakas; these people were members of a culturally unified group of widespread tribes that occupied a vast region of the Great Eurasian Steppes. The Scythians, as Herodotus described them, were "barbaric" people located, more or less, on the Pontic steppe in the westernmost region of Central Eurasia. According to Beckwith (2009: xxii–xxiii), the "sensationalistic" stereotyping of these people by "Herodotus and other early historians" as barbarians was a "Greco-Roman idea, or fantasy," that failed to recognize the Central Eurasian cultures as agropastoralists or as a general mix of nomadic pastoralists, farmers in oases, and even urban merchants making up "complex societies." The western Scythians that Herodotus referred to were a somewhat heterogeneous tribal group that appear to have initially entered into the intermediary area between Central Eurasia and eastern Europe extending from the Carpathian Mountains to the Don River in the second millennium BCE.

In his notable essay on Scythica, Meuli (1935) relied to some degree on Herodotus' funeral ceremony description referred to above. In Meuli's view, the Scythian "shamans" were channeling the souls of dead persons to their place in the afterlife while simultaneously purifying their homes or burial places; in the process, these "shamans" were also protecting people from the deceased returning as ghosts of the dead (also see Dodds 1951; Eliade 1964; Burkert 1972; Margreth 1993; Ginzburg 2012). According to Meuli's interpretation, the screaming and howling by the Scythians in their funeral ritual was the customary strident communication of shamans in an ecstatic trance state, and *Cannabis* seeds heated on glowing embers in censers probably induced their rapturous state (for another view, which suggests ecstatic use of *Cannabis* in the "vapour-bath" ceremony but possibly not involving classic shamanism, see Zhmud 1997; Bremmer 2001). (Note that *Cannabis* seeds are not psychoactive.)

The Massagetae (Great Getae) were another nomadic Iranian Central Asian tribe living on the Caspian steppe in the first millennium BCE. The

Massagetae are commonly believed to have been related to the Scythians, and they reportedly used a particular plant species for mind-altering purposes. Herodotus (*Histories* 1.202) noted that the Massagetae were well aware of the psychoactive "fruit" of this species (probably the seeds along with the inflorescences of female *Cannabis*), which had "a very odd property" and was described as the product of a "tree" (perhaps tall female *Cannabis* plants). Herodotus also tells us that when the Massagetae "have parties and sit round a fire, they throw some [*Cannabis*] 'fruit' into the flames, and as it burns it smokes like incense, and the smell of it makes them drunk just as wine does us; and they get more and more intoxicated as more fruit is thrown on, until they jump up and start dancing and singing" (Sélincourt 1965: 95). Some believe that Herodotus' reference to this plant's "fruit[s]" and their strange and powerful effects (when consumed) is a somewhat muddled allusion to the psychoactive use of *Cannabis* (e.g., see Bremmer 2001; also see Duvall 2015 for an alternative but minor view).

During Herodotus' time, at least one of the ancient Thracian (Getae) tribes living in Dacia, an area north of the Danube and west of the Dniester River in the Carpathian basin, participated in a curious mystical "shaman" cult known as the "Kapnobatai." Eliade (1964: 394–95) elaborates on the use of psychoactive "hemp" (*Cannabis*) among the Getae with reference to more than one ancient Greek source, including Herodotus:

> The Getae were described by Herodotus as the most valiant and law-abiding of the Thracian tribes. What chiefly impressed the Greeks was their belief in the immortality of the soul. They were expert in the use of the bow and arrow while on horseback. Their name first appears in connection with the expedition of Darius Hystaspes against the Scythians (515 BCE). They were conquered briefly by the Romans, but regained their independence. Only one document appears to indicate the existence of Getic shamanism: it is Strabo's account of the Mysian Kapnobatai, a name that has been translated, by analogy with Aristophanes' Aerobates, as "those who walk in clouds," but which should be translated as "those who walk in smoke." Presumably the smoke is hemp smoke, a rudimentary means of ecstasy known to both the Thracians and the Scythians. The Kapnobatai would seem to be Getic dancers and sorcerers who used hemp [*Cannabis*] smoke for their ecstatic trances. (Also see Emboden 1972, which refers to Strabo 7.3.3, quoting Posidonius; Eliade 1972; Eliade and Trask 1972)

Following from Meuli (1935), Eliade states that the goal of the Scythian "cult of the dead" funerary purification rite involving the use of *Cannabis* "could only be ecstasy" (in the Greek sense, *ecstasis* essentially means a release of the mind from the body into a spiritual state of bliss consciousness).

> In this connection Meuli cites the Altaic [referring to the Altai Mountains where the ritual ensemble described by Herodotus was uncovered in a tomb near Pazyryk described below] séance described by Radlov (1884, 1893–1911), in which the shaman guided to the underworld the soul of a woman who had been dead forty days. The shaman-psychopomp is not found in Herodotus' description; he speaks only of purifications following a funeral. But among a number of Turko-Tatar peoples such purifications coincide with the shaman's escorting the deceased to his new home, in the nether regions. . . . One fact, at least, is certain: shamanism and ecstatic intoxication produced by hemp smoke were known to the Scythians. As we shall see, the use of hemp for ecstatic purposes is also attested among the Iranians, and it is the Iranian word for hemp that is employed to designate mystical intoxication in Central and North Asia. (Eliade 1964: 190–97)

The ancient reference by Herodotus to *Cannabis* use by peoples to the north and northwest of Greece has been supported by the now relatively well-known, but somewhat controversial, discovery of *Cannabis* seeds and related ritual paraphernalia in several remarkable frozen tumulus-shaped graves, or "kurgans," located in the Pazyryk Valley of the Ukok Plateau in the Altai Mountains of Siberian Russia, approximately 200 kilometers (124 miles) north of the Chinese border and 150 kilometers (93 miles) west of Mongolia. The tomb in Barrow 2 was originally exposed and excavated under the direction of Sergei Rudenko in 1947 and was later dated to the Iron Age (ca. 430 BCE). Rudenko's account of the occurrence of *Cannabis* seeds and their use in ritual "purification" in the tomb has been referred to often, even though a good deal of it is decidedly hypothetical. According to Rudenko (1970: 285),

> in Barrow 2, two smoking sets were found: vessels containing stones that had been in the fire and hemp seeds; above them were shelters supported on six rods, in one case covered with a leather hanging and in the other case probably with a felt hanging, large pieces of which were found in the southwest corner of the tomb. Finally, there was a [leather]

"flask" containing hemp seeds fixed to one of the legs of a hexapod stand. Consequently, we have the full set of articles for carrying out the purification ritual, about which Herodotus wrote in such detail in his description of the Black Sea Scyths. There had been sets for smoking hemp in all the Pazyryk barrows; the sticks for the stand survived in each barrow although the censers and cloth covers had all been stolen except in Barrow 2.

Rudenko (1970:285) further described the *Cannabis* seeds and related equipment for their ritualistic use:

> In each vessel besides the stones . . . there was a small quantity of seeds of hemp (*Cannabis sativa* L. of the variety *C. rideralis* [*sic*] Janisch. [probably *Cannabis indica* Lam.; see Hillig 2005a, 2005b; Clarke and Merlin 2013]). Burning hot stones had been placed in the censer and part of the hemp seeds had been charred. Furthermore, the handle of the cauldron censer had been bound round with birch bark, evidently because the heat of the stones was such that its handle had become too hot to hold in the bare hands.

Rudenko's supposition regarding the "smoking" of *Cannabis* by Iron Age Scythians, based largely on Herodotus' accounts, has led to many claims that the Scythians laid *Cannabis* inflorescences on the red-hot stones and inhaled the smoke to both purify themselves and facilitate communication with their ancestral spirits. However, all that we know with certainty is that *Cannabis* seeds were found in a ritual context in the Pazyryk tombs.

Herodotus' description refers to only the burning of *Cannabis* seeds; he did not clearly indicate that Scythians placed the psychoactive plant's flowers on the hot rocks in the censers. Most interpretations of Herodotus' descriptions of the funeral ritual assumed that he confused *Cannabis* seeds with inflorescences containing seeds and thus presumed that bunches of female *Cannabis* flowers must have been burned to cause the Scythians' cries of joy.

Although it is rarely acknowledged, seeds of coriander (*Coriandrum sativum* L.), also known as cilantro or Chinese parsley, were also recovered from the Pazyryk burials. Coriander is not native to the Pazyryk region, and therefore its seeds must have been imported from "Asia Minor," or the Near East region of Eurasia (Rudenko 1970). In any case, we should not dismiss the suggestion that mind-altering resinous parts of *Cannabis*, together with its seeds, were burned in the censers. It is also possible that seeds of both *Cannabis* and coriander were dropped on the heated rocks to produce a fragrant, if not also inebriating, smoke for ritual purification; if so, the smoke could have pervaded the tomb where the dead bodies were placed and thus served as a deodorant. In addition, it is worth noting here that linalool, the main aromatic oil component of coriander seeds, is pharmacologically active. In fact, linalool can relieve pain and inflammation and has possible synergistic affects with tetrahydrocannabinol (THC) and cannabidiol (CBD), compounds produced only by *Cannabis* (e.g., see Russo 2011).

Before we continue with our discussion of mind-altering ceremonial, purification, and therapeutic use of *Cannabis* in Central Eurasia, we briefly focus on its ancient presence and use in the Near East, where unique and relevant evidence for medicinal and/or ritual utilization was discovered in Israel in the 1990s. In this case, *Cannabis* was found in a tomb from the Late Roman period (315–392 CE) located in Beit Shemesh, an urban area about 30 kilometers (19 miles) west of Jerusalem with a cultural history that goes back to prebiblical times. Israeli researchers discovered carbonized material in connection with the corpse of a young female dated to approximately 1600 BP, based on bronze coins also recovered from this tomb. Initial microscopic analysis indicated that the carbonized material resulted from burning a mixture of *Cannabis* and other plants, and subsequent chemical investigation revealed the presence of Δ^8-THC, another compound unique to *Cannabis.* Researchers concluded that *Cannabis* had been burned to facilitate the birth process (Zias et al. 1993), an early medicinal use of plants in this genus. Russo (2007: 1634) provides the following discussion of this remarkable discovery in the ancient burial tomb: "the skeleton of a 14-year-old girl was found along with 4th century [CE] bronze coins. Contained in her pelvic area was the skeleton of a term fetus, of a size that would disallow a successful vaginal delivery. In her abdominal area, gray carbonized material was noted and analyzed, yielding TLC and NMR spectroscopy evidence of Δ^8-THC, a more stable trace component of cannabis. It was surmised that the cannabis had been burned in an unsuccessful attempt at delivery of the fetus, perhaps paralleling the ancient Egyptian usage."

The hypothesis that the Scythians of the Eurasian steppe region "smoked" *Cannabis* has been referred to not only as the earliest suspected case of *Cannabis* smoke inhalation but also as one of the few examples of "smoking" generally in all of Eurasia prior to the discovery of tobacco smoking in the New World. Although Liebenberg (1990) tells us that people may have begun inhaling smoke emitted by the burning of certain plant materials many thousands of years ago, with traces of such use going back to the early use of fire, the ultimate origins of the use of such substances are still unclear. Nevertheless, conscious inhalation of smoke is most likely a very ancient custom and "may even be as old as the human control of fire" (Rudgley 1999: 142; see Duvall 2015 for a strong case arguing that smoking in various parts of Africa started centuries before the so-called Columbian Exchange that began in 1492). In the case of Scythian "smoking," as alluded to by Herodotus, the inhalation of smoke or vapors can be differentiated from true smoking. By definition, "smoking" is the inhalation of smoke through a device that contains burning plant material and provides a pathway to deliver the smoke to the respiratory system. This definition assumes that the breathing of smoke from the air is not true smoking but simply intentional inhalation. Metal censers, wooden rods, and felt or leather covers, along with the partially charred seeds, could be the earliest evidence of deliberate inhaling of *Cannabis* smoke, and they definitely predate any contact with the New World by nearly two thousand years. If the ancient Pazyryk *Cannabis* evidence could be further confirmed by the discovery of deposits of mind-altering cannabinoids (compounds unique to *Cannabis*), it would stand as a significant verification of the ritual breathing of smoke in the Old World.

Before we focus on the remarkable discovery of about 0.8 kilograms (almost 2 pounds) of *Cannabis* stems with leaves as well as female flowers and seeds in another first-millennium BCE tomb (this one located southwest of the Pazyryk kurgan sites in northwestern China), some other relevant ancient Eurasian archaeological sites where hemp seeds have been found in ritual vessels should be addressed.

For example, "pipe-cup," "polypod," or "footed" ceramic vessels somewhat similar in shape to those found in the Pazyryk tomb have been discovered containing *Cannabis* seeds in two, much more ancient, western Eurasian archaeological sites. One of these vessels was in a kurgan pit grave at Gurbanesti near Bucharest in Romania and the other was in an Early Bronze Age site situated in the northern Caucasus Mountains; both have been dated back six thousand years or more (Ecsedy 1979). Furthermore, numerous equivalent bowls found without ancient *Cannabis* seeds or other parts of the plant in them have been discovered in several sites of about the same age. Are these vessels indicative of ancient, widespread cult use of *Cannabis* for psychoactive, spiritual, or purification purposes? In light of Herodotus' description of the Scythian "vapor bath" ritual involving *Cannabis* and hemp seed discoveries in widely separated locations from the Altai Mountains of central to western Eurasia and into parts of eastern Europe, Sherratt (1991: 61–62) postulated that "the practice of burning *Cannabis* as a narcotic [*sic*] is a tradition which goes back in this area some five or six thousand years and was the focus of the social and religious rituals of the pastoral peoples of central Eurasia in prehistoric and early historic times."

An earlier analysis of associated artifacts by Sherratt (1987) presented a hypothesis for the cordage impressions on many of these ancient Eurasian ritual bowls. He suggested that these impressions were made with twisted hemp (*Cannabis*) fibers by peoples belonging to a cultural complex spread over a huge area of the Eurasian steppes from eastern Europe to western China by the third millennium BCE. Sherratt argued that these peoples had widely dispersed an alcohol-based hospitality or "social lubricant" culture, and he also proposed that *Cannabis*, likely long cultivated for its fiber by this time, was also "enjoyed" by steppe peoples, well beyond the range of the drinking complex. In Sherratt's view, psychoactive *Cannabis* was added to their alcoholic beverages, and the vessels containing these infusions have surface impressions formed with the use of hemp cordage as a way of indicating the vessels' contents (also see Sherratt 1991, 1995a, 1995b, 1997). Furthermore, the corded ware vessels might have been held in reserve for ceremonies instead of being used commonly (for a minority view, see the critical review of Sherratt's and other scholars' interpretations of ritual smoking or other forms of ingestion of psychoactive *Cannabis* in ancient Eurasia by Duvall 2015).

Although Herodotus described the ritual use of *Cannabis* by ancient nomadic tribes in western Central Eurasia in some detail, only a relatively small amount of historical evidence for early ritual and/or medicinal use of *Cannabis* from eastern Central Eurasia has been identified. This has been particularly the case for northwestern China, where shamanistic activities were either not commonly practiced or at least were not overtly revealed to any substantial degree in available ancient Chinese texts (see, e.g., Li 1974a, 1974b, 1975, 1977; Touw 1981). However, new evidence of ancient practical, symbolic, and even psychological or spiritual significance of *Cannabis* use in northwestern China has recently been uncovered at other archaeological sites in this region.

Ancient *Cannabis* in a Yanghai Tomb

We know that the Chinese have had a very long and complex relationship with *Cannabis* (Clarke and Merlin 2013); although they utilized it for thousands of years as an important source of bast fiber, edible seeds, oil, and medicine, its use for psychoactive ritualistic or recreational purposes has been frowned upon at least since the influence of Confucius became widespread in East Asia starting about 2,200 years ago (e.g., Li 1974a, 1974b, 1975, 1977; Weiming 2000).

Nonetheless, before the rise of the Confucian philosophical and ethical system, the use of *Cannabis* to alter consciousness and for medicinal purposes was probably widespread among people living in the vast area now known as China, at least by shamans and herbalists. This utilization remains significant today in parts of western China and includes psychoactive uses that are, in most cases, not strictly religious or ritualistic.

The *Hou Hanshu*, or *Book of the Later Han* (an early Chinese historical manuscript attributed to Fan Ye and dated to the fifth century CE), refers to China's "Western Regions" during the period 25–220 CE. According to the *Hou Hanshu*, these regions were noted for their fertility and valuable production of several crops, including rice, millet, wheat, beans, mulberries, grapes, and hemp (*Cannabis*); as a result of this prolific agricultural potential, the Han Chinese waged a relentless struggle with the non-Han Central Asian cultures for control (Hill 2003). As the reader might suspect, based on what is noted above, the Han Chinese (widely influenced by Confucianism) have had dissimilar associations with *Cannabis* than the strongly nomadic-based people of the Central Eurasian cultural complex, who formed alliances that repeatedly challenged the primarily sedentary, agriculture-based Chinese empires.

These long-held differences in relationships with psychoactive *Cannabis* are still manifest today with limited to no mind-altering use of *Cannabis* in the traditionally Han culture areas of China, as opposed to continued indulgence by the descendants of the Central Eurasian cultural complex based in western China. One contemporary people related to this cultural complex and now occupying the Tarim basin are known as the Uighurs. According to Dikötter and his colleagues (2004), with the exception of the Uighurs (and perhaps some other local ethnolinguistic groups), the people in China, especially those belonging to the Han culture, have a strongly held opinion that the smell of smoked *Cannabis* is objectionable and that this common perception hindered the spread (or continuation) of its use as a euphoric substance. According to Rudgley (1999), the Han Chinese still perceive the local Muslim peoples of Xinjiang province today, mostly Uighurs, as consumers of psychoactive *Cannabis*, especially in the form of hashish, and recent use of this mind-altering substance by Uighurs has been documented for some of those residing in large Chinese urban areas such as Beijing and Shanghai (e.g., see Labrousse and Laniel 2001). The negative mind-set regarding the psychoactive use of *Cannabis* among most Chinese has existed for many hundreds, if not thousands, of years, but as suggested above, this unenthusiastic attitude was probably quite different before the rise of the Han and the ascendancy of Confucianism.

The recent discovery of remarkably well preserved remains of psychoactive *Cannabis* in one of the Yanghai Tombs (M90) provides physical evidence of its very old cultural importance in this western Chinese area of Central Eurasia for shamanic and probably psychoactive or medicinal purposes (Jiang et al. 2006). The Yanghai Tombs consist of a large number of ancient graves recognized as belonging to the early Gushi culture (also referred to as the Subeixi culture [see Jiang et al. 2007]). The people of this culture were likely speakers of a Tokarian language. The Yanghai Tombs are situated in a rocky arid region of the Turpan basin of China's Xinjiang province, which was known earlier as Eastern Turkestan and more recently as Chinese Turkestan. The first literary reference to the Gushi people can be found in the *Hou Hanshu*. In this written account we find them defined as blue-eyed Caucasian nomads with light-colored hair who spoke an Indo-European language; they reportedly herded horses and other grazing animals, cultivated some crops, and were known to be experts with bows and arrows, much like their Eurasian steppe ancestors (Russo et al. 2008; also see Ma and Sun 1994; Mallory and Mair 2000; Karpowicz and Selby 2010). The probable migration of the Gushi people (or their ancestors) from the eastern Eurasian steppes of what is now southern Russia into western China began thousands of years ago.

Positioned in the Turpan basin, roughly in the middle of the Eurasian landmass, the Yanghai Tombs were constructed in one of the lowest areas on earth; in one of the many Yanghai graves (M90), which is about 2,700 years old, the remains of female *Cannabis* and skeletal remnants of a high-ranking Caucasoid male were discovered. These were later studied by two collaborative research teams (Jiang et al. 2006; Russo et al. 2008; also see Xinjiang Institute of Cultural Relics and Archaeology 2004; Academia Turfanica 2006). The ancient man found in this Yanghai grave appears to have been about forty-five years old when he passed away, and he was discovered as a disarticulated skeleton rather than as a mummified body, which is more often the case in the Yanghai Tombs. Russo and his colleagues (2008) believe that this is an indication that the man most likely died in the uplands of the Tian Shan, or "Heavenly Mountains," and later his bones were moved to Yanghai, where they were buried; these researchers also pointed out that contemporary Uighur herders undertake a comparable yearly migration to summer grazing territory about 60–80 kilometers (36–48 miles) away from the burial sites.

Grave gifts found with the skeleton in this tomb included implements associated with horsemanship, along with a bow, arrows, and a musical instrument known as a *kong gou* harp; these and other artifacts, which are more elaborate than others found within the greater Yanghai tomb complex, have led to the conclusion that the man buried in Yanghai grave M90 was a "shaman." Most importantly, a relatively large, lidless "leather" basket and a "wooden bowl" were found near the head and foot of the corpse, respectively, and these contained a total of 789 grams (nearly 2 pounds!) of female *Cannabis* inflorescences and seeds, seemingly within close reach of the deceased in the afterlife. Although this remarkably preserved plant material was first believed to be coriander, which could have served as a deodorizer in the burial tomb, following careful botanical scrutiny it has been positively identified as *Cannabis* (in the authors' estimation, *C. indica*, not *C. sativa*, as originally reported in Jiang et al. 2006). The first radiocarbon dating of this ancient *Cannabis* determined it to be approximately 2,500 years old, but with a thorough comparative study of the early equestrian artifacts and tree-ring correlation between wooden relics in the tomb and other ancient Chinese timber, the date has been "corrected to a calibrated figure of 2700 BP" (Russo et al. 2008: 4173).

The wooden bowl found in the tomb has a smoothed inner surface and is perforated on one side, evidence of its protracted utilization as a mortar, apparently to grind *Cannabis* flowers and/or mix them with other ingredients before their use for psychoactive or medicinal purposes. The remains, including the *Cannabis*, from the Yanghai burial are very well preserved because of three combined factors: the tomb's depth (2 meters, or approximately 6 feet or more), the exceptionally arid climate with very modest or no rainfall (averaging about 16 millimeters, or about 2/3 inch, per year), and the alkaline soils with a high pH of 8.6 to 9.1. As a consequence, the *Cannabis* remains from this burial include intact and ground-up leaves, stems, seeds, and bracts with nonglandular and glandular trichomes, essentially undamaged after their deposition in the tomb more than two and a half millennia ago.

The *Cannabis* flowers, seeds, stems, and leaves in the ancient containers could have been a gift for the deceased "shaman," but why would he need them in the afterlife? According to Jiang and colleagues (2006: 420), "If they were meant as a cereal or for oil extraction, the leaves and shoots would have been removed; if fiber production was intended, only the stems needed to be saved. In this connection it is significant that no hemp textiles have been unearthed in the Yanghai Tombs."

The lack of evidence demonstrating use of *Cannabis* for food, seed oil, or fiber at the Yanghai Tombs is noteworthy. However, the placement of female inflorescences, the most potent portion of the plant, in containers close to the dead "shaman" is a robust indication that the deceased had been well aware of the plant's psychoactive and/or medicinal properties.

Ancient therapeutic, ritualistic, and psychoactive uses of *Cannabis* are often difficult to separate (Sherratt 1991; Merlin 2003). We do know that shamans of the nomadic tribes of Siberia and Central Eurasia frequently served as general practitioners of healing arts as well as rituals; in these contexts, they probably utilized the mind-altering properties of *Cannabis* in shamanic practices related to purification and curative ceremonies, at least to some extent comparable to the ceremonial use of hemp fiber throughout much of Eurasia during the early twentieth century (Touw 1981; Clarke and Merlin 2013). In any case, the first international team of scientists that studied Yanghai Tomb M90 generally concluded that there was a spiritual connection between the "shaman" and the *Cannabis* contents in the ancient basket and bowl. This research group suggested that the "gift of *Cannabis*" given to the dead shaman was most likely offered as a ritualistic means of connecting the deceased with the spirit world, enabling him "to continue his profession in the afterlife" (Jiang et al. 2006: 421).

Another, more recent, international, interdisciplinary research team (Mukherjee et al. 2008) combined "botanical examination, phytochemical investigation, and genetic deoxyribonucleic acid [DNA] analysis by polymerase chain reaction [PCR]" to reveal that the ancient *Cannabis* material contained "tetrahydrocannabinol [THC]" and that this very old organic chemical material was found along with "its oxidative degradation product, cannabinol, other metabolites, and its synthetic enzyme, tetrahydrocannabinolic acid [THCA] synthase, as well as a novel genetic variant with two single nucleotide polymorphisms." On the basis of these findings, the team of researchers suggested that the Yanghai *Cannabis* was probably used "as a medicinal or psychoactive agent, or an aid to divination." What is more, genetic analysis suggests that this ancient *Cannabis* belonged to a cultivated variety rather than a truly wild or weedy biotype (see Mukherjee et al. 2008). Even though no evidence of smoking paraphernalia was discovered at Yanghai, *Cannabis* probably would have been directly ingested in the form of a baked preparation or placed in a fire to produce fumes. This hoard of *Cannabis* is not the oldest example of early use of this genus, but it certainly is among the best studied. In any case, the ancient Yanghai evidence embodies the earliest tangible record of *Cannabis* use "as a pharmacologically active agent" and thus is an important addition to the documentation of medicinal, if not psychoactive, use by the Gushi people (Russo et al. 2008: 4171). More-recent discoveries of ancient seeds (Chen et al. 2012), fiber (Chen et al. 2014), and even relatively intact, nearly whole plants (Jiang et al. 2016), as well as more deposits of female inflorescences of *Cannabis* in tombs of other ancient cemeteries in the Turpan basin area of Xinjiang province in western China, further support the ancient presence and strong symbolic, ritualistic, and cultural associations of *Cannabis* in this region.

Especially noteworthy are the thirteen nearly whole female plants of *Cannabis* recently discovered in a tomb in the Jiayi cemetery of Turpan in Xinjiang province of northwestern China (see Jiang et al. 2016). These remarkably well preserved *Cannabis* plants have been radiometrically dated to be approximately 2,400–2,800 years old, and they appear to have been locally produced and purposefully arranged into a burial shroud or funeral bouquet that was placed on a male corpse. Both morphological and anatomical features of these ancient plant remains support their identification as *Cannabis*. This unique discovery provides extraordinary further insight into the ritualistic, possibly purification and curative ceremonial, use of *Cannabis* in prehistoric Central Eurasia. In addition to these remains, the fragmented female flowering parts (infructescences) discovered in other tombs of the Jiayi cemetery, together with *Cannabis* remains recovered from the contemporary Yanghai Tombs in the Turpan basin, as well as those found in the Altai Mountains region, all strongly suggest that *Cannabis* was used by the local Central Eurasian people for ritual and/or medicinal purposes in the first millennium BCE.

Summary and Conclusions

The early history of *Cannabis* as a mind-altering commodity was a period of great expansion of the plants in this genus into new climates and cultures in Eurasia, each with its own selective pressures, setting the stage for its geographically localized and isolated evolution at the hands of humans. New drug *Cannabis* varieties arose through artificial selections directed by choice of preferred end product and type of effects, accompanied by natural ecological constraints imposed by respective geographical areas. Throughout the cultural dispersal of drug *Cannabis*, countless opportunities arose in terms of when and where it benefited humans, and subsequently its proliferation was encouraged. *Cannabis* could not have achieved nearly worldwide distribution had it not been favored by at least some human groups time and time again (e.g., see Benet 1975; Abel 1980; Grinspoon and Bakalar 1997; Clarke 1998a; Pollan 2001; Booth 2003; Clarke and Merlin 2013; Duvall 2015).

Most likely the earliest mind-altering use of *Cannabis* occurred near the origin of psychoactive variants of the genus in Central or East Asia. Well before contact with modern humans during the early Holocene, *Cannabis* was already present in several regions of Eurasia. Perhaps previous to, and certainly during, migrations by nomadic peoples from Central Asia, the knowledge of *Cannabis* use as a powerful tool in shamanic ritual was spread east, west, and south. Knowledge of the uses of psychoactive *Cannabis*, as well as seeds of selected variants with increased potency, was carried beyond Eurasia by later traders. In some areas, the inebriating properties of *Cannabis* were exploited later than its fiber and food uses, especially in some parts of Europe and East Asia and more recently in North America.

Apart from ritualistic inhalation of vapors, until tobacco was introduced from the New World, *Cannabis* was largely eaten along with food and drink in Eurasia. Once people began to smoke rather than eat the products of *Cannabis* inflorescences, for example, in large parts of Africa (see du Toit 1980; Duvall 2015) and in areas of South Asia (e.g., see Clarke and Merlin 2013), many more began to use *Cannabis* for its mind-altering effects.

Of the myriad effects *Cannabis* has exerted on the evolution of human culture, its ability to alter our consciousness is arguably the most profound. From a traditional, historical point of view, consumption of entheogens such as *Cannabis* through the ages has allowed humans to cognitively recognize the god within and facilitate communication with their spirit world. *Cannabis* was certainly used by shamans, and its increasing ritual use may have influenced aspects of worship adopted by the major religions of settled peoples around two thousand years ago. Many of the cultural traditions of Eurasia were influenced by *Cannabis* consumption during their formation and evolution. Today, the psychoactive use of *Cannabis* is more widespread than at any time in history, and it is said to be the most frequently used illicit drug in the world (e.g., Richardson

2010). If we are to accept the importance of *Cannabis* in molding our past and its certain influence on our present societies, then we should expect that it may well influence human cultural evolution in the future.

Acknowledgments

We would like to acknowledge the following for their major contributions to this research: Hong-En Jiang, Ethan Russo, Andrew Sherratt, Richard Evans Schultes, many other scientists from various disciplines, and of course Herodotus. In addition, we offer our special gratitude to the Chinese Academy of Sciences for their support, and to Scott Fitzpatrick for inviting Mark Merlin to present this paper in a special symposium on psychoactive substances in ancient societies at the annual meetings of the Society for American Archaeology in Memphis in April 2012.

References Cited

Abel, E. L. 1980. *Marihuana: The First Twelve Thousand Years.* New York: Plenum Press.

Academia Turfanica. 2006. *Selected Treasures of the Turfan Relics.* Turpan, China: Academia Turfanica.

Beckwith, C. I. 2009. *Empires of the Silk Road: A History of Central Eurasia from the Bronze Age to the Present.* Princeton: Princeton University Press.

Benet, S. 1975. Early Diffusion and Folk Uses of Hemp. In *Cannabis and Culture,* ed. V. Rubin, 39–49. The Hague: Mouton.

Booth, M. 2003. *Cannabis: A History.* New York: St. Martin's Press.

Bourguignon, E., ed. 1973. *Religion, Altered States of Consciousness, and Social Change.* Columbus: Ohio University Press.

Bremmer, J. N. 2001. *The Rise and Fall of the Afterlife: The 1995 Read-Tuckwell Lectures at the University of Bristol.* London: Routledge.

Burkert, W. 1972. *Lore and Science in Ancient Pythagoreanism.* Trans. E. L. Minar Jr. Cambridge, Mass.: Harvard University Press.

Chen, T., Y. Wu, Y. Zhang, B. Wang, Y. Hu, C. Wang, and H.-E. Jiang. 2012. Archaeobotanical Study of Ancient Food and Cereal Remains at the Astana Cemeteries, Xinjiang, China. *PLoS ONE* 7 (9): e45137.

Chen, T., S. Yao, M. Merlin, H. Mai, Z. Qiu, Y. Hu, B. Wang, C. Wang, and H.-E. Jiang. 2014. Identification of *Cannabis* Fiber from the Astana Cemeteries, Xinjiang, China, with Reference to Its Unique Decorative Utilization. *Economic Botany* 68 (1): 59–66.

Clarke, R. C. 1981. *Marijuana Botany.* Berkeley, Calif.: And/Or Press.

Clarke, R. C. 1998a. *Hashish!* Los Angeles: Red Eye Press.

Clarke, R. C. 1998b. Botany of the Genus *Cannabis.* In *Advances in Hemp Research,* ed. P. Ranalli, 1–20. Binghamton, N.Y.: Haworth Press.

Clarke, R. C., and M. Merlin. 2013. *Cannabis: Evolution and Ethnobotany*. Berkeley: University of California Press.
Deferne, J. L., and D. W. Pate. 1996. Hemp Seed Oil: A Source of Valuable Essential Fatty Acids. *Journal of the International Hemp Association* 3 (1): 1, 4–7.
Dikötter, F., L. Laamann, and Z. Xun. 2004. *Narcotic Culture: A History of Drugs in China*. Chicago: University of Chicago Press.
Dodds, E. R. 1951. *The Greeks and the Irrational*. Berkeley: University of California Press.
Du Toit, B. 1980. *Cannabis in Africa*. Rotterdam: A. A. Balkema.
Duvall, C. 2015. *Cannabis*. London: Reaktion Books.
Earleywine, M. 2002. *Understanding Marijuana: A New Look at the Scientific Evidence*. Oxford: Oxford University Press.
Ecsedy, I. 1979. *The People of the Pit-Grave Kurgans in Eastern Hungary*. Budapest: Akadémiai Kiadó.
Eliade, M. 1964. *Shamanism: Archaic Techniques of Ecstasy*. New York: Pantheon.
Eliade, M. 1972. *Zalmoxis, the Vanishing God*. Trans. W. R. Trask. Chicago: University of Chicago Press.
Eliade, M., and W. R. Trask. 1972. Zalmoxis. *History of Religions* 11 (3): 257–302.
Emboden, W. 1972. Ritual Use of *Cannabis sativa* L: A Historical-Ethnographic Survey. In *Flesh of the Gods: The Ritual Use of Hallucinogens*, ed. P. T. Furst, 214–36. New York: Praeger.
Farnsworth, N. R. 1968. Hallucinogenic Plants. *Science* 162: 1086.
Ginzburg, C. 2012. *Threads and Traces*. Trans. A. C. Tedeschi and J. Tedeschi. Berkeley: University of California Press.
Grinspoon, L., and J. Bakalar. 1997. *Marihuana, the Forbidden Medicine*. New Haven, Conn.: Yale University Press.
Hanks, B. 2012. Archaeology of the Eurasian Steppes and Mongolia. *Annual Review of Anthropology* 39: 469–86.
Herodotus. 1921. *The Persian Wars*. Vol. 2, bks. 3 and 4. Trans. A. D. Godley. Loeb Classical Library 118. Cambridge, Mass.: Harvard University Press.
Hill, J. E., trans. 2003. The Western Regions According to the Hou Hanshu. The Xiyu Juan "Chapter on the Western Regions" from *Hou Hanshu* 88.
Hillig, K. W. 2005a. A Systematic Investigation of *Cannabis*. PhD diss., Indiana University, Bloomington.
Hillig, K. W. 2005b. Genetic Evidence for Speciation in *Cannabis* (Cannabaceae). *Genetic Research and Crop Evolution* 52 (2): 161–80.
Hyams, E. 1971. *Plants in the Service of Man: 10,000 Years of Domestication*. Philadelphia: J. B. Lippincott.
Jiang, H.-E., X. Li, Y. X. Zhao, D. K. Ferguson, F. Hueber, S. Bera, Y. F. Wang, L. C. Zhao, C. J. Liu, and C. S. Li. 2006. A New Insight into *Cannabis sativa* L. (Cannabaceae) Utilization from 2500-Year-Old Yanghai Tombs, Xinjiang, China. *Journal of Ethnopharmacology* 108 (3): 414–22.
Jiang, H.-E., X. Li, and C. S. Li. 2007. Cereal Remains from Yanghai Tomb in Turpan, Xinjiang and Their Palaeoenvironmental Significance. *Journal of Palaeogeography* 9: 551–58.

Jiang, H., L. Wang, M. D. Merlin, R. C. Clarke, Y. Pan, Y. Zhang, G. Xiao, and X. Ding. 2016. Ancient *Cannabis* Burial Shroud in a Central Eurasian Cemetery. *Economic Botany* 70 (3): 213–21.

Julien, R. M., C. D. Advokat, and J. Comaty. 2011. *A Primer of Drug Action: A Concise, Nontechnical Guide to the Effects of Psychoactive Drugs*. London: Worth Publishers.

Karpowicz, A., and S. Selby. 2010. Scythian Bow from Xinjiang. *Journal of the Society of Archer-Antiquaries* 53: 94–102.

Kramer, J. C., and M. Merlin. 1983. The Use of Psychoactive Drugs in the Ancient Old World. In *Discoveries in Pharmacology*, vol. 1, *Psycho- and Neuro-pharmacology*, ed. M. J. Parnham and J. Bruinvels, 23–48. Amsterdam: Elsevier Science Publishers.

La Barre, W. 1970. Old and New World Narcotics: A Statistical Question and an Ethnological Reply. *Economic Botany* 24 (1): 73–80.

La Barre, W. 1977. Anthropological Views of *Cannabis*. *Reviews in Anthropology* 4 (3): 237–50.

La Barre, W. 1980. History and Ethnography of *Cannabis*. In *Culture and Context: Selected Writings of Weston La Barre*, ed. W. La Barre, 93–107. Durham, N.C.: Duke University Press.

Labrousse, A., and L. Laniel. 2001. *The World Geopolitics of Drugs, 1998/1999*. Dordrecht: Kluwer Academic Publishers.

Li, H. L. 1974a. The Origin and Use of *Cannabis* in East Asia: Linguistic and Cultural Implications. *Economic Botany* 28 (2): 293–301.

Li, H. L. 1974b. An Archeological and Historical Account of *Cannabis* in China. *Economic Botany* 28 (4): 437–48.

Li, H. L. 1975. The Origin and Use of Cannabis in Eastern Asia. In *Cannabis and Culture*, ed. V. Rubin, 51–62. Paris: Mouton.

Li, H. L. 1977. Hallucinogenic Plants in Chinese Herbals. *Harvard University Botanical and Museum Leaflets* 25 (6): 161–81.

Liebenberg, L. 1990. *The Art of Tracking: The Origin of Science*. Claremont, South Africa: David Philip.

Ma, Y., and Y. Sun. 1994. The Western Regions under the Hsiung-Nu and the Han. In *History of Civilizations of Central Asia*, vol. 2, *The Development of Sedentary and Nomadic Civilizations: 700 BC to AD 250*, ed. J. Harmatta, B. N. Puri, and G. F. Etamadi, 227–46. Delhi: Motilal Banarsidass Publishers.

Mallory, J. P., and V. H. Mair. 2000. *The Tarim Mummies: Ancient China and the Mystery of the Earliest Peoples from the West*. New York: Thames and Hudson.

Margreth, D. 1993. *Skythische Schamanen? Die Nachrichten über Enarees-Anarieis bei Herodot und Hippokrates*. PhD thesis, Philosophical University of Zurich. Schaffhausen, Switzerland: Meier und Cie.

Merlin, M. D. 1972. *Man and Marijuana: Some Aspects of Their Ancient Relationship*. Rutherford, N.J.: Fairleigh Dickinson University Press.

Merlin, M. D. 2003. Archeological Evidence for the Tradition of Psychoactive Plant Use in the Old World. *Economic Botany* 57 (3): 295–323.

Meuli, K. 1935. Scythica. *Hermes* 70: 121–76.

Mukherjee, A., S. C. Roy, S. De Bera, H.-E. Jiang, X. Li, C. Li, and S. Bera. 2008. Results of Molecular Analysis of an Archaeological Hemp (*Cannabis sativa* L.) DNA Sample from North West China. *Genetic Resources and Crop Evolution* 55 (4): 481–85.

Pollan, M. 2001. *The Botany of Desire*. New York: Random House.

Radlov, V. V. 1884. *Aus Sibirien*. Leipzig: T. O. Weige.

Radlov, V. V. 1893–1911. *Opyt slovarja tjurkskix narečij: Versuch eines Wörterbuches der Türk-Dialekte*. 4 vols. St. Petersburg: Asiatic Museum.

Richardson, T. H. 2010. Cannabis Use and Mental Health: A Review of Recent Epidemiological Research. *International Journal of Pharmacology* 6: 796–807.

Rudenko, S. I. 1970. *Frozen Tombs of Siberia: The Pazyryk Burials of Iron Age Horsemen*. Berkeley: University of California Press.

Rudgley, R. 1999. *The Lost Civilizations of the Stone Age*. New York: Touchstone.

Russo, E. B. 2007. History of Cannabis and Its Preparations in Saga, Science, and Sobriquet. *Chemistry and Biodiversity* 4: 1614–48.

Russo, E. B. 2011. Taming THC: Potential Cannabis Synergy and Phytocannabinoid-Terpenoid Entourage Effects. *British Journal of Pharmacology* 63 (7): 1344–64.

Russo, E. B., H.-E. Jiang, X. Li, A. Sutton, A. Carboni, F. Del Bianco, G. Mandolino, et al. 2008. Phytochemical and Genetic Analyses of Ancient Cannabis from Central Asia. *Journal of Experimental Botany* 59 (15): 4171–82.

Schultes, R. E., A. Hofmann, and C. Rätch. 2001. *Plants of the Gods: Their Sacred, Healing and Hallucinogenic Powers*. Rochester, Vt.: Healing Arts Press.

Sélincourt, A. de, trans. 1965. *Herodotus: The Histories*. Penguin Classics. Reprint, Harmondsworth, U.K.: Penguin Books. Originally published 1954.

Sherratt, A. G. 1987. Cups that Cheered: The Introduction of Alcohol to Prehistoric Europe. In *Bell Beakers of the Western Mediterranean*, vol. 1, ed. W. H. Waldren and R. C. Kennard, 81–114. BAR International Series 331. Oxford: British Archaeological Reports.

Sherratt, A. G. 1991. Sacred and Profane Substances: The Ritual Use of Narcotics in Later Neolithic Europe. In *Sacred and Profane: Proceedings of a conference on Archaeology, Ritual and Religion*, ed. P. Garwood, D. Jennings, R. Skeates, and J. Toms, 50–64. Oxford University Committee for Archaeology Monographs 32. Oxford, U.K. Reprinted 1997 in Sherratt, *Economy and Society in Prehistoric Europe: Changing Perspectives*, 403–30 (Princeton University Press).

Sherratt, A. G. 1995a. Introduction: Peculiar Substances. In *Consuming Habits: Drugs in History and Anthropology*, ed. J. Goodman, P. E. Lovejoy, and A. Sherratt, 1–10. London: Routledge.

Sherratt, A. G. 1995b. Alcohol and Its Alternatives: Symbol and Substance in Preindustrial Cultures. In *Consuming Habits: Drugs in History and Anthropology*, ed. J. Goodman, P. E. Lovejoy, and A. Sherratt, 11–46. London: Routledge.

Sherratt, A. G. 1997. *Economy and Society in Prehistoric Europe: Changing Perspectives*. Princeton: Princeton University Press.

Small, E. 2015. Evolution and Classification of *Cannabis sativa* (Marijuana, Hemp) in Relation to Human Utilization. *Botanical Reviews* 81 (3): 189–294.

Smith, H. 2000. *Cleansing the Doors of Perception: The Religious Significance of Entheogenic Plants and Chemicals*. New York: Tarcher/Putnam.

Touw, M. 1981. The Religious and Medicinal Use of *Cannabis* in China, India and Tibet. *Journal of Psychoactive Drugs* 13 (1): 23–34.
Weiming, T. 2000. Implications of the Rise of "Confucian" East Asia. *Daedalus* 129 (1): 195–218.
Xinjiang Institute of Cultural Relics and Archaeology. 2004. Tu lu fan kao gu xin shou huo: Shanshan Xian Yanghai mu di fa jue jian bao (New results of archaeological work in Turpan: Excavation of the Yanghai Graveyard). *Tu lu fan Xue yan jiu* (Turfanological Research) 1: 1–66.
Zhmud, L. 1997. *Wissenschaft, Philosophie und Religion im frühen Pythagoreismus.* Berlin: Akademie Verlag.
Zias, J., H. Stark, J. Sellgman, R. Levy, E. Werker, A. Breuer, and R. Mechoulam. 1993. Early Medical Use of *Cannabis. Nature* 363: 215.

2

Intoxication on the Wine Dark Sea

Investigating Psychoactive Substances in the Eastern Mediterranean

ZUZANA CHOVANEC

For the past three decades, archaeologists have emphasized the advantages of incorporating organic residue analysis into archaeological research with the aim of addressing questions that are minimally approachable using traditional methods (Evershed 2000: 204–7; Loy 1993: 44; Pollard and Heron 2008: 9–11). One such area concerns the range of psychoactive products that were used by ancient peoples, the ways in which they were prepared and consumed, and the social importance attributed to them. As the range of chapters in this volume demonstrates, the archaeological examination of the use of psychoactive substances has largely centered on New World societies. La Barre (1970: 73–75, 1972) and Schultes (1969: 245) suggested that a far greater number of such substances were utilized in New World societies in comparison to their Old World counterparts based on limited knowledge, both folk and scientific in nature, of the global distribution of flora. In the 1970s, this difference was viewed as a New World predisposition for the pursuit of intoxicating substances. Explanations for this proposed lack of Old World psychoactive plants have centered on the development of agriculture (La Barre 1970: 78, 1972; Merlin 1984: 100–105, 204–9, 219–21; Schultes 1969, 1990, 1998: 6). It has since been acknowledged that the disparity in the use of intoxicants is partly the result of the breadth of anthropological and ethnobotanical documentation of New World societies in the recent past (Fericgla 1996; Merlin 2003: 296–97). Despite this acknowledgment, the investigation of Old World intoxicants has predominantly focused on the use of fermented beverages, especially in the circum-Mediterranean region where the production and consumption of alcohol is well documented (Badler et al. 1990; Barnard et al. 2011; Grace 1979; Guerra-Doce 2015; Hadjisavvas 2009; Hamilakis 1999; Joffe 1998; McGovern 2003, 2009; McGovern et al. 2004, 2009).

The centrality of alcohol use in the more recent past often renders the discussion ahistoric. In the Mediterranean, analogies based on Classical writings abound and in some respects are the convention. The dangers of using historic analogies have been discussed by Wylie (1985, 1988) and many others (Feinman 1997; Lyman and O'Brien 2001; Stahl 1993) and will not be repeated here. However, implicit assumptions are particularly misleading when considering the development and proliferation of a substance that has come to be consumed on a global scale, for which there are various lines of evidence, and with which humans have maintained a long and complex relationship (Fericgla 1996; McGovern 2003, 2009; McGovern et al. 2004; Ott 1993: 156).

Patrick McGovern has been instrumental in elucidating the history of this relationship. In his 2009 volume, he frames alcohol production and consumption in historical context and highlights that the grape wines and grain beers discussed in ancient texts likely represent specialized products that progressively focused on individual ingredients (McGovern 2009: 103). This suggests that prior to the emergence of complex society, there would have been much greater variety in the types of beverages consumed and the ingredients utilized in their production (McGovern 2009: 95). Thus, we might expect local varieties of psychoactive substances to have been produced from a wider range of local ingredients.

This emphasis on the local is key in that knowledge of the specific ingredients utilized in the production of psychoactive substances further highlights aspects of broader economic production as well as the social contexts of consumption. The preparation and consumption of psychoactive substances often constitute highly significant events with specific religious, economic, and political outcomes, making it inappropriate to assume that the same substances were being consumed in the same contexts with the same ideological implications (Dietler 2006: 231–33; Hamilakis 1999; Hayden 2001: 58–59; Locke and Kelly 1985: 13, 15–17; Sherratt 1987: 389–91, 1991: 50–52; Steel 2002, 2004a, 2004b). Such assumptions do not serve us in our aim to document the role of specific psychoactive substances in the past. While the anthropological value of ancient texts cannot be denied, similarities in the substances being produced and the social contexts of their consumption must be demonstrated materially, rather than simply presuming continuity.

In this chapter, I discuss literary evidence for the use of psychoactive substances in the Mediterranean and the challenges that have been encountered in associating names and descriptions with specific botanical species. I argue that the incorporation of chemical analysis has the potential to identify such substances in prehistoric contexts and in cases in which traditional archaeological and literary methods are insufficient.

Psychoactive Substances in the Mediterranean

Literary sources in the Mediterranean region contain numerous references to psychoactive substances. In many cases, however, they are not explicitly named; because of the issues raised earlier, they were presumed to be wine or beer. A typical example comes from *The Odyssey*, in which Circe ushered her guests into a hall, where she "prepared them a mixture of cheese, barley-meal, and yellow honey flavored with Pramnian wine. But into this dish she introduced a powerful drug to make them lose all memory of their native land" (Seltman 1957: 43). In other references to this mixture, it is described as being "spiced with baneful drugs" (Totelin 2009: 92), but the source of the drugs is not identified.

Elsewhere, the name of a drug is mentioned but is not translatable. One such example is the euphoric *nepenthes* that Helen of Troy added to a special wine to allay Telemachus' grief (Ott 1993: 156; Ruck 2008a: 15). The "strong drink" that the Hebrews referred to as *shekar* was distinguished from two wines of variable strength, *yayin* and *tirosh* (Ott 1993: 157). The terms *rosh* and *la'ana* are mentioned numerous times in the Old Testament and refer to bitter and/or poisonous plants that have been suggested to be the opium poppy (*Papaver somniferum*), white wormwood (*Artemisia herba-alba*), poison hemlock (*Conium maculatum*), and the thorn-apple (*Datura inoxia*) (Amar 2006: 113–4; Ayalon 2006: 8; Kapoor 1995: 7; Merrillees [1989] 2003: 180–81; Zohary 1982: 185–86). While the Hebrew examples have limited analytical evidence for these identifications,[1] the sacred Egyptian drink *shedeh* was determined to be a red grape wine based on the presence of pigments characteristic of red grapes (Guash-Jané et al. 2006: 99–100). In other cases, the plant or substance is unknown, such as in several references in the Ebers Papyrus, a medical text written in the reign of Amenophis I in 1536 BC (Carpenter

1 Results published by Chovanec and colleagues (2015) in the *Journal of Mediterranean Archaeology and Archaeometry* discuss the analysis of three Base Ring I juglets from Late Bronze Age levels at Tel Beth-Shemesh, Israel. One of the juglets may have contained a species of wormwood.

et al. 1998: 3). For example, the *ibw* plant from Upper Egypt was listed as a tree sacred to Horus, but the name—and, therefore, the botanical identify of the tree—is untranslatable (Budge 1978 in Carpenter et al. 1998: 18 Rubric No. 282, Column 50, Line 13). Merlin (1984, 2003) detailed similar issues in his attempts to associate botanical representations in the archaeological record with specific plant species, such as the opium poppy.

In other cases, it may be a matter of generalization. A prime example comes from references to the cult of Dionysus, whose female devotees were documented to have "periodic bouts of . . . frenzy" (Seltman 1957: 101). Ruck (2008a: 14) highlighted that the vine that was so venerated by Dionysus may not have simply been the grape vine and points to the symbol of the *thyrsus*, "a fennel stalk stuffed with ivy leaves." The stalk was commonly used to gather wild herbs, and the ivy, also sacred to Dionysus, was said to have psychoactive properties. While there is no question that "in wine, Dionysus found his greatest blessing" and the commonly held association with this substance is accurate, there is ample suggestive evidence that "ancient wine . . . did not contain alcohol as its sole inebriant but was ordinarily a variable infusion of herbal toxins in a vinous liquid" (Ruck 2008a: 15).

Harner (1973), Ott (1993), and Wasson (1990, 2008) emphasized the experience and behaviors associated with the consumption of hallucinogens, which function to alter experience, the perception of reality, time, space, and consciousness itself, as opposed to psychotropic substances, which "act normally only to calm or stimulate" (Schultes 1990: 4). A review of such observations in the context of ancient Mediterranean texts further suggests that in *some* cases, an intoxication other than alcohol inebriation may be indicated (Ott 1993: 156–57).

From the Ebers Papyrus, the translation of the recipe for a medicine for "correcting the urine (in the) diseased pubic region (at) the first occurrence of suffering" (Carpenter et al. 1998: 19, Rubric No. 283, Column 50, Line 16) suggests the presence of two bitter-tasting plants. The first was proposed to be *Ricinus communis*, the castor oil plant, but is more accurately translated as "plant with a bitter taste" (Budge 1978 in Carpenter et al. 1998: 20). The second is a reference to bryony, which is in the cucumber family and some varieties of which are known to have toxins (Manvi and Garg 2011: 107–8).

While scholars like Patrick McGovern (2003, 2009; McGovern et al. 2004, 2009), Andrew Sherratt (1987, 1991), and Michael Dietler (2006) have done much to illuminate the diversity of fermented beverages and to historicize their usage, less attention has been given to other psychoactive substances indigenous to this region.

A key exception to the overwhelming focus on alcohol in the region is the attention given to the opium poppy, *Papaver somniferum* L., the human use of which has been discussed by Bernáth (1998), Chovanec and colleagues (2012), Collard (2011), Kapoor (1995), Merlin (1984, 2003), Merrillees ([1962] 2003, [1979] 2003, [1989] 2003), and others. While a variety of uses are documented, the medicinal and psychoactive properties of the plant, afforded by the more than forty alkaloids it synthesizes, make it remarkable (Hesse 1981: 2; Rafferty 2007: 179). The chief alkaloids found in the opium poppy include morphine, codeine, papaverine, thebaine, and noscapine.

Archaeological evidence from the eastern Mediterranean for the exploitation of the opium poppy for its narcotic principles comes from the island of Cyprus and is specifically associated with a particular pottery vessel, the Base Ring juglet, which was manufactured during the Protohistoric Bronze Age (circa 1700–1400 BC). The high quality, distinctive shape and decoration, and wide distribution of the vessels throughout the eastern Mediterranean led Robert Merrillees to suggest that the juglets were made to emulate the shape of a poppy capsule and served as specialized containers for the transport of opium throughout the region (Åström 1972: 137, 173–74; Bisset et al. 1994: 104; Chovanec 2013: 21–22; Merlin 1984, 2003). The implication for the distribution of a psychoactive substance on such a scale would be immense. Moreover, textual evidence for this suggested opium trade is at best anecdotal and at worst based on *presumed* form-function relationships.

To further the discussion of the use of psychoactive substances in the Mediterranean and elsewhere, the presentation of specific material evidence for the organic ingredients utilized is necessary.

Methodology

As part of the investigation of the potential intoxicating substances used in the circum-Mediterranean region, an organic residue analysis program was undertaken centered on the molecular characterization of a range of psychoactive plants known to be indigenous to the region. Methodologically, identifying intoxicants in the archaeological record requires a chemical analysis of organic residues that targets alkaloids, the chemical compounds found in psychoactive substances that serve to calm, stimulate, intoxicate, and alter consciousness, as well as other biomarkers that have a limited distribution and can be associated with specific botanical sources (Evershed 2008: 897–98; Rafferty 2007: 197; Waterman 1998: 87–88).

The necessary chemical characterization was accomplished by obtaining reference samples of a range of plants and alkaloids, extracting their constituent compounds with a combination of organic solvents, and analyzing them by gas chromatography/mass spectrometry (GC/MS). GC/MS is an analytical technique effective in this avenue of research because it is based on the separation and identification of chemical compounds within a mixture. Organic chemical compounds found in botanical samples and other natural products that may have been absorbed into ancient pottery are extracted using a combination of organic solvents that are heated and concentrated. Following this extraction, a sample is injected into the GC, which separates volatile chemical components and identifies them as peaks[2] based on how long it takes them to emerge from the system (Barnard et al. 2007: 48; Evershed 2000: 196; Heron and Evershed 1993: 265; Kitson et al. 1996: 3–6; Pollard and Heron 2008: 61–63; Rafferty 2002: 899). After injection into the instrument, the sample is separated into individual chemical constituents by the GC and measured, according to their component ions, by the MS.[3] The final output is a total ion current (TIC) graph that plots all of the molecules that were detected in the sample based on their retention time (RT), or the time it takes for a chemical compound to emerge from the GC (Barnard et al. 2007: 51; Pollard and Heron 2008: 62; Rafferty 2002: 900). The TIC plots all of the molecules detected in a sample with the most abundant molecule being set to 100 percent and all other molecules being plotted relative to that.

A variety of ancient products have been identified using this analytical technique, including turpentine, cannabis, various fermented beverages, beeswax, tobacco, ayahuasca, and many others (Derham 2005; McGovern 2003, 2009; McGovern et al. 2004; Mills and White 1989; Ogalde et al. 2007; Rafferty 2002; Regert et al. 2001).

---

2 Each peak has a mass spectrum, representing a series of ions based on the intensity of their mass-to-charge ratio (m/z); the distribution of these ions is characteristic of particular compounds.

3 The mass spectrum is linked to a mass spectral database (NIST02.L) that reports the probability that the detected mass spectrum matches a known compound.

By one of two methods, the chemical constituents of the following psychoactive substances indigenous to the region were characterized:

- opium poppy (*Papaver somniferum*);
- Syrian rue (*Peganum harmala*);
- ephedra (*Ephedra* sp.);
- a series of plants containing tropane alkaloids, including deadly nightshade (*Atropa belladonna*) and henbane (*Hyoscyamus niger*);
- two plants containing the terpenoid thujone, including a species of sage (*Salvia* sp.) and wormwood (*Artemisia* sp.);
- wine; and
- beer.

The first extraction method involved heating pulverized plant samples in a mixture of ethanol and methanol (25 milliliters, 1:1 [volume/volume]) in a reflux apparatus for three hours. The solution was subsequently filtered and concentrated to a volume of 1 milliliter under a controlled stream of nitrogen gas. In the second method, a sample in 5–10 milliliters of dichloromethane:methanol (2:1 [volume/volume]) was placed into a bath ultrasonicator for two hours and left to settle for twenty-four hours. When necessary, the solution was filtered and/or centrifuged for five minutes and then concentrated to 1–2 milliliters under nitrogen gas.

All samples, regardless of sample type or extraction method, were analyzed using a Hewlett Packard 6890 gas chromatograph used in tandem with a 5972 selective mass detector equipped with a 1 microliter autoinjector and fitted with an HP-5 capillary column measuring 30 meters in length and 250 micrometers in diameter with 5 percent phenylmethylsiloxane and a film thickness of 0.25 micrometers. Two sets of analytical parameters were used in the analysis of the samples. In the first, an initial temperature of 150°C was held for 1 minute and then ramped up to 280°C at 15°C per minute and held for 3 minutes, making a total run time of 12.67 minutes. There was a splitless interface to the quadrupole mass selective detector with a 2-minute solvent delay and a mass range from 50 to 500. In the second, an initial temperature of 75°C was held for 2 minutes and then ramped up to 280°C at 15°C per minute and held for 30 minutes, making a total method run time of 45.00 minutes. There was a splitless interface to the quadrupole mass selective detector with a 3-minute solvent delay and with a mass range from 50 to 500. The same procedures were applied to ancient pottery samples from archaeological contexts.

For quality control, all glassware used in the analysis was cleaned and sterilized and solvent blanks were run prior to any reference or archaeological samples to ensure that chemical constituents were in fact inherent in the sample. Data interpretation involved comparison of the chemical compounds identified in reference samples with those present in archaeological residues.

Ancient Cyprus

The eastern Mediterranean island of Cyprus has been the target of interest in isolating cultural processes on more than one occasion (Falconer et al. 2005; Fall et al. 2008; Frankel et al. 1995). While the characterization of islands as cultural laboratories may be questionable (Fitzpatrick 2004), the fact that Cyprus is the only island in the eastern Mediterranean, has a long record of occupation, and has a trajectory of cultural development that differs dramatically from its mainland counterparts makes it an interesting case for examining prehistoric intoxication (Keswani 1994, 1996; Knapp 1993, 2008: 13–21; Peltenburg 1996: 23–24) (see figure 2.1).

As elsewhere in the circum-Mediterranean region, the appearance of fine, highly decorated containers in Cyprus during the Chalcolithic period (3900–2400 cal BC) and Bronze Age (2500–1000 BC) has been taken as evidence for the production of alcoholic beverages—in particular, beer

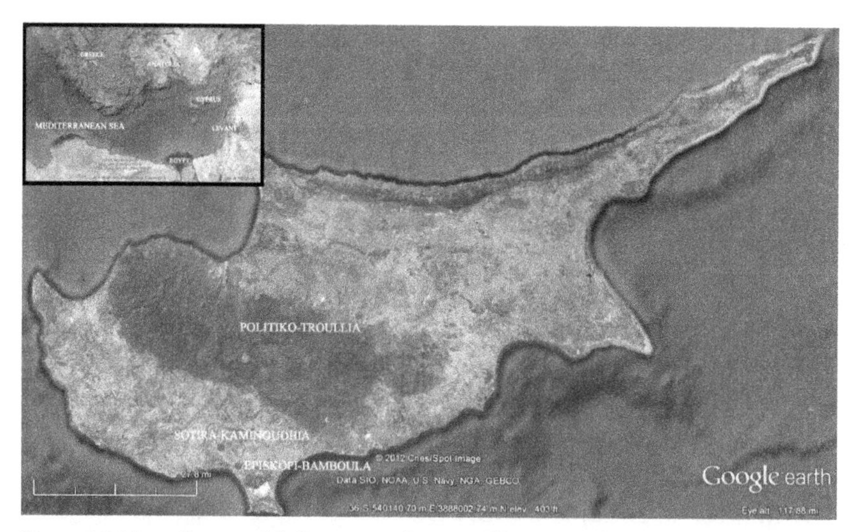

Figure 2.1. Map of eastern Mediterranean basin and location of archaeological sites on Cyprus. (Map by Google Earth: Eastern Mediterranean, Southwest Asia, Northern Africa [Mountain View, Calif.: Google, 2012].)

(Knapp 1993: 90; 2008: 70; Steel 2004a: 13). Steel (2002: 107–8; 2004a: 113; 2004b: 282) and Manning (1993: 45) point to a novel range of containers that included spouted vessels, bowls, jugs, flasks, and bottles as ideal shapes for drinking alcohol and reiterate Sherratt's (1987) emphasis on the integral role that fermented beverages played in the development of social complexity in European and Near Eastern societies. Others suggest that this individualized equipment designed for mixing and pouring signals the development of communal rituals in which alcoholic beverages, especially beer, would have become increasingly important (Herscher 1997 cited in Steel 2002: 108; Manning 1993: 45; Peltenburg 1996: 23; Webb and Frankel 2008: 289–90; 2010: 197). While the consumption of fermented beverages is likely, there is little in the way of analytical chemical evidence for their production with the exception of Beck and colleagues' (2004: 18) suggestion that the presence of pine resin in a series of White Slip bowls may indicate a retsina, or a pine-flavored wine.

The presence of liquid containers in a range of sizes does not necessarily preclude the production of other specialized products, such as perfumes, unguents, medicines, and other beverages containing psychoactive products. Regarding the latter category, the nonalcoholic psychoactive substance that has received the greatest attention in Cyprus is the opium poppy. As mentioned above, Merrillees ([1962] 2003: 2–3; [1979] 2003: 123–24) first proposed that the Base Ring juglet was utilized in the storage and transport of opium from Cyprus to destinations throughout the eastern Mediterranean. He suggested that the juglet's shape was consistent with that of an inverted poppy capsule and that its decoration resembled the incision method that is used to extract opium from the poppy capsule (Åström 1972; Bisset et al. 1996; Koschel 1996: 159–60; Merlin 1984: 251–56; 2003: 309; Merrillees [1962] 2003: 2–3; [1979] 2003: 123–24) (see figure 2.2).

Several scholars have attempted to chemically analyze these vessels to determine whether they in fact served as specialized containers for opium. These analyses include the following:

- an early twentieth-century colorimetric test of a residue preserved in a Base Ring juglet from an Egyptian tomb (Schiaparelli, Muzio in Bisset et al. 1994: 100);
- the analysis of two Base Ring sherds from the Institute of Archaeology and the Rockfeller Collection in Jerusalem, respectively, with the former reported by John Evans (in Merrillees [1989] 2003: 185–86) as containing opium and olive oil;

- the identification of five opium alkaloids in a Base Ring I juglet from the Martin von Wagner Museum in Germany by Klaus Koschel (1996) and Norman Bisset's (1996) research group;
- the analysis of two sealed Base Ring juglets from the British Museum by Dr. Rebecca Stacey (e-mail, April 14, 2008);
- David Collard's (2010, 2011) attempts, though lacking results for opium, which were noteworthy for collecting in situ samples; and
- the analysis of three Base Ring I juglets from Late Bronze Age levels at Tel Beth-Shemesh, Israel, by Chovanec and colleagues (2015), which showed no trace of opium but indicated the presence of aromatic oils that may have had medicinal or cosmetic applications.

Figure 2.2. Base Ring I juglet. (Reprinted courtesy of the Semitic Museum, Harvard University, Cambridge, Mass.)

For reasons I have detailed elsewhere (Chovanec 2013; Chovanec et al. 2012), the nature of opium use in the eastern Mediterranean during the Bronze Age remains unclear. What is evident, given the diversity of highly decorated ceramic containers designed for the storage of liquids, is that there was a great emphasis on the production and use of prestigious liquid substances. The question that remains to be answered is whether these prestigious substances were psychoactive substances, perfumed oils, or medicinal concoctions.

To that end, a sample of 113 pottery vessels from three curated museum collections and six stratified archaeological sites spanning the Bronze Age were analyzed by GC/MS with the aim of identifying prestigious products, such as psychoactive substances, perfumes, and medicines. While all three types of products are represented, only results suggesting the presence of psychoactive substances are discussed below.

Results

Evidence from seven vessels suggests the presence of three types of substances with psychoactive properties: fermented beverages, opium, and wormwood. The presence of fermented beverages was determined based on the identification of compounds associated with fermentation (malic, succinic, butyric, and butanoic acids and their derivatives). It should be noted that tartaric acid, which is typically found in ancient grape wines, was not identified (Guash-Jané et al. 2006: 98; McGovern et al. 2004: 17596–97; Michel et al. 1993: 411–12). Evidence for the presence of opium is based on the presence of noscapine, one of the chief alkaloids found in opium. In addition, three samples indicated the presence of a psychoactive substance other than alcohol or opium based on the presence of terpenoids.

Opium

As noted above, a recurring question has been whether opium was known in ancient Cyprus, particularly in connection with the Base Ring juglets. Interestingly, there was no chemical evidence in any of the Base Ring vessels analyzed that indicated the presence of opium. However, the opium alkaloid noscapine was identified in one Red Polished vessel from the Middle Bronze Age site of Politiko-Troullia, a deeply stratified village excavated by Dr. Steven Falconer from Arizona State University from 2007 to 2012. The village is situated in close proximity to the copper-rich foothills of the Troodos Mountains and consists of four architectural phases,

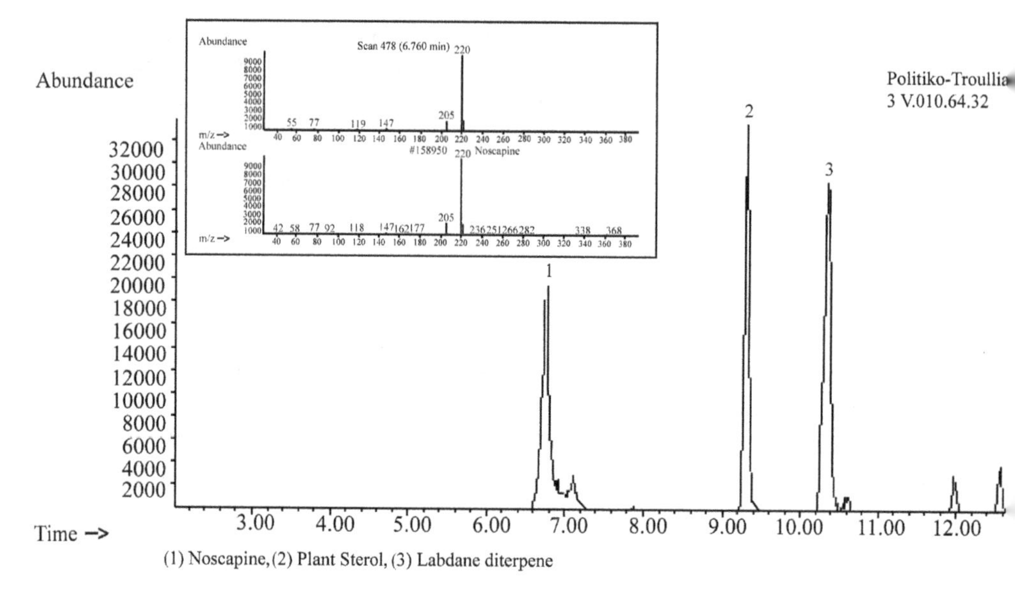

Figure 2.3. Chromatogram of Red Polished spouted vessel with chemical compounds detected indicated and a comparison of the detected mass spectrum with the mass spectrum of noscapine.

with two courtyards positioned on a north-south axis and surrounded by domestic spaces and one alleyway (Falconer and Fall 2013; Falconer et al. 2005; Fall et al. 2012).

Noscapine ((3S)-6,7-dimethoxy-3-[(5R)-5,6,7,8-tetrahydro 4-methoxy -6-methyl-1,3-dioxolo(4,5g)isoquinolin-5-yl]-1(3H)-isobenzofuranone) was identified (see figure 2.3) in the remains of a spouted vessel (see figure 2.4) recovered from the northeastern corner of the central courtyard at Politiko-Troullia. In addition to noscapine, a plant sterol (cycloartenol) and a labdane diterpene, labda-8(20),12,14-trien-19-oic acid, methyl ester, (E)-(1-naphthalenepropanol, .alpha. -ethenyldecahydro-5-(hydroxymethyl)-.alpha.,5,8a-trimethyl-2-methylene-[1S-[1.alpha.(R*),4a.beta.,5.beta., 8a.alpha.]]-) were present. The labdane diterpene was identified in botanical reference samples of sage (*Salvia* sp.) and pink rockrose (*Cistus incanus*), both of which are local varieties obtained from Cyprus. The resin of the latter is known as labdanum and was highly prized in antiquity for its aromatic qualities and its ability to fix scents (Angelopoulou et al. 2001: 167, 169–70; Bolster 2002: 42–43; Oritani 1998; Zohary 1982: 194). According to Miller and Miller (1990: 38), labdanum continues to be esteemed in the modern-day perfume industry because it serves as one of the alternatives to animal-derived fixatives. This suggests that the

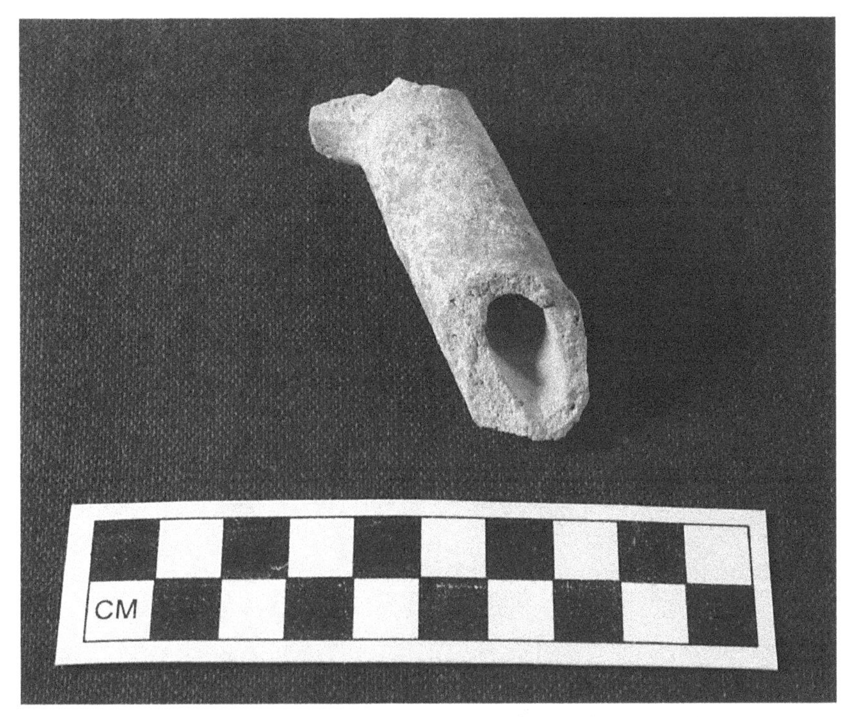

Figure 2.4. Fragmentary Red Polished spouted vessel from Politiko-Troullia (3 V.010.64.32).

contents of the vessel included an aromatic, intoxicating mixture containing opium and the resin of pink rockrose flowers or sage. However, other constituents of these plants were not identified. The presence of noscapine is intriguing because this alkaloid was shown by Chovanec and colleagues (2012) to dissociate readily into a series of derivative compounds (meconic acid, hydrocotarnine, cotarnine, and opianic acid). A question for future research would be whether the pink rockrose or sage provides an antioxidant effect, thereby slowing the process of chemical degradation.

FERMENTED BEVERAGES

In one of the domestic spaces (Area P) at the north end of Politiko-Troullia, malic acid (2-hydroxybutanedioic acid), a compound associated with grape wine fermentation, was identified in a small Red Polished bowl that was found in situ with the base of a jug exhibiting the kind of visible attrition that has been shown to be associated with fermentation (Arthur 2003: 522–24; Kunkee 1977: 62–63; Wansbrough 1998) (see figure 2.5). The jug also showed the presence of malic acid and another compound,

Figure 2.5. Small Red Polished bowl (*upper*) and Red Polished IV jug base (*lower*) from Politiko-Troullia (41 P.004.40.1 and 42 P.004.41.2, respectively).

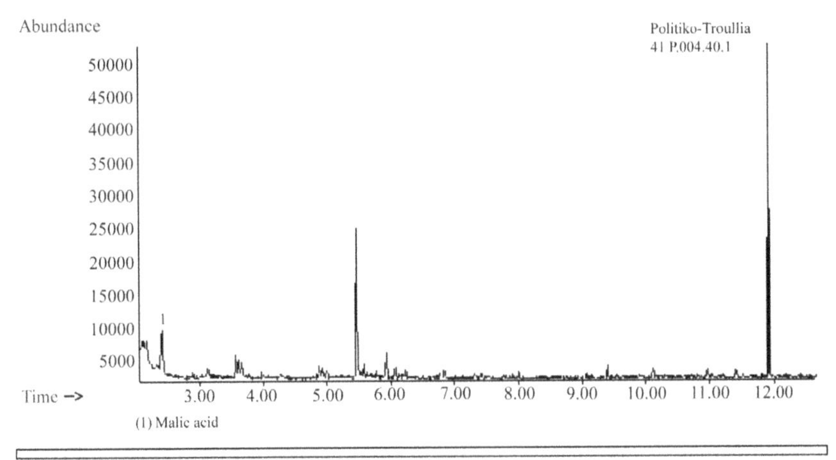

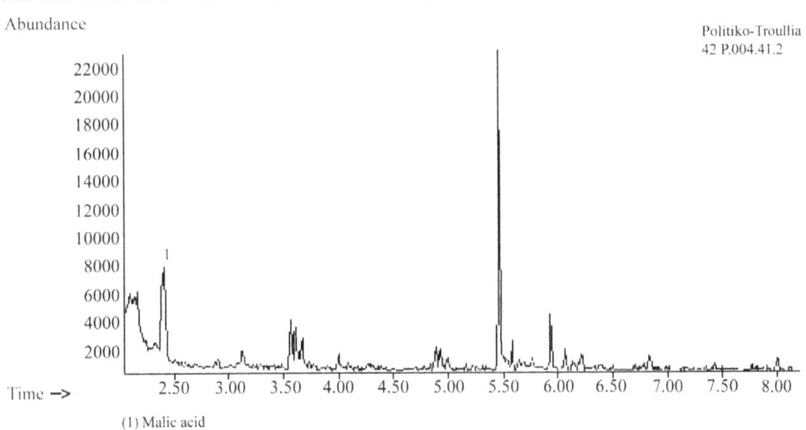

Figure 2.6. Chromatogram of small Red Polished bowl with chemical compounds detected indicated (*above*); chromatogram of Red Polished IV jug with visible attrition (*below*).

longipinene epoxide, which is a constituent in Taurus cedar (*Cedrus libani*) (Başer and Demirçakmak 1995: 17) (see figure 2.6). Because small jugs and bowls have been found in conjunction with each other in other Middle Bronze Age contexts on the island (see below), the two may represent a drinking set that was used for the consumption of an alcoholic beverage that included grapes and cedar resin.

A third vessel from Politiko-Troullia, a Red Polished bowl with incised decoration (see figure 2.7) recovered from a room (Area Z) at the south end of the site, also indicated the presence of malic acid. Although the incidence of this compound may suggest that the vessel contained a fermented substance, Garnier and Valamoti (2016: 202) suggest that it is a biomarker for dark, teinturier grapes. Tartaric acid and syringic acid

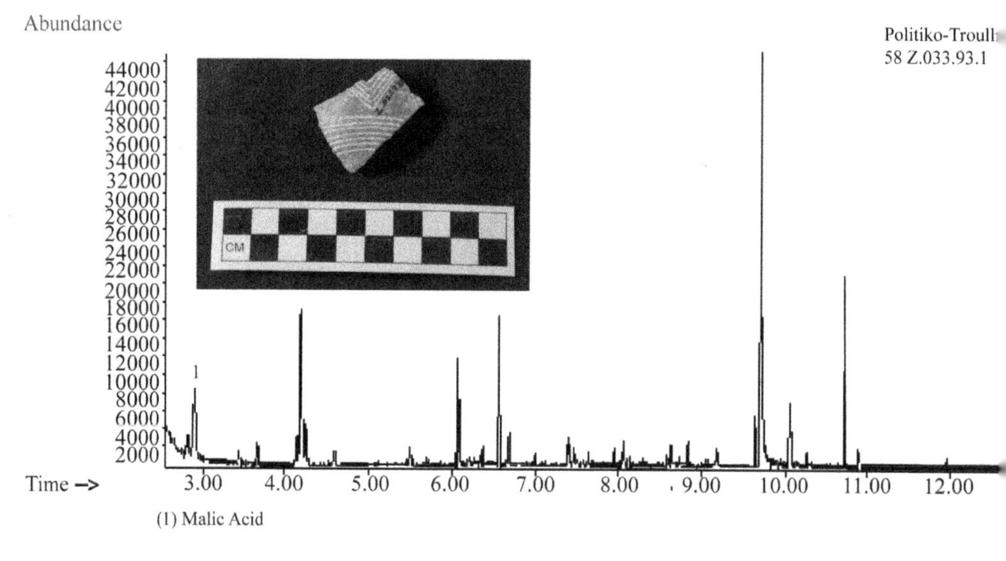

Figure 2.7. Chromatogram of Red Polished bowl (*inset photograph*) with incised decoration from Politiko-Troullia with chemical compounds detected indicated.

are generally considered more direct biomarkers of grape wine (Koh et al. 2014; McGovern et al. 2009). However, Mariti (1984: 70) indicates that Cypriot wine made with traditional methods never produces tartar, which may suggest that a different set of chemical biomarkers may need to be identified. Although neither tartaric nor syringic acid was identified in reference samples of Cypriot wine, however, this should not be taken to suggest that these compounds do not occur in Cypriot wines; rather, it indicates that more research is needed into the chemical composition of local wine varieties. Moreover, in light of Garnier and Valamoti's (2016: 201) recent experimental study, which details optimized parameters for the identification of biomarkers of ancient wine, more robust extraction procedures may be required for the detection of syringic acid in absorbed residues.

OTHER PSYCHOACTIVE SUBSTANCES

The Middle Bronze Age site of Alambra-Mouttes represents a key example of the use of various bowls and jugs in sets, as discussed above. This settlement was excavated by Cornell University in the 1980s and consisted of seven buildings that largely documented domestic activities. The exception was Building IV, which had a series of unusual architectural features, a different layout, and variable distribution of artifacts, which suggested a feasting function (Coleman et al. 1996: 75–89; Crewe and

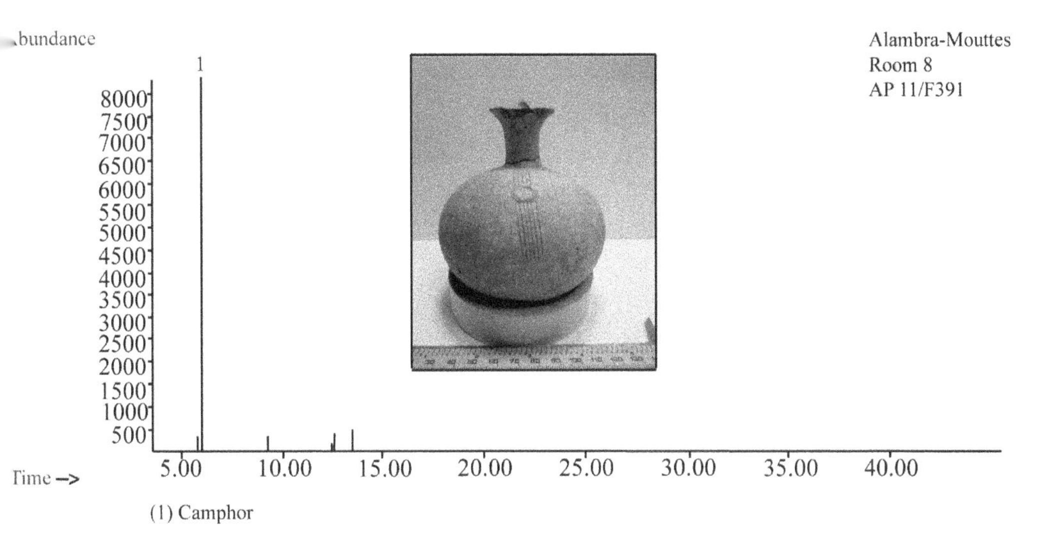

Figure 2.8. Chromatogram of juglet with unique decoration (*inset photograph*) from Alambra-Mouttes with chemical compounds detected indicated.

Hill 2012: 224; Knapp 2008: 75, 80). Rooms 8 and 13 were particularly significant in this regard in that they contained an assemblage of twenty-eight nearly complete vessels that lay concentrated along a shared party wall. The assemblage consisted of fourteen juglets, thirteen small bowls, and one large bowl and may represent a series of drinking sets that were used communally (Coleman et al. 1996: 77–78, 85–89; Crewe and Hill 2012: 224).

Samples from thirteen juglets underwent the analytical procedure outlined above with only one exhibiting evidence for a preserved residue.[4] A small vessel with unique decoration that fits in the palm of one's hand (approximately 10 centimeters in width) (see figure 2.8) showed the presence of a single compound, camphor (1,7,7-trimethylbicyclo[2.2.1] heptan-2-one). The poor analytical results were perhaps due to additional chemical degradation that occurred over the thirty years since they were excavated.

Camphor was known in antiquity as a remedy for coughs and as a fever reducer and was used to soothe the gums (Aboelsoud 2010; Pliny [AD 77] 2006). The camphor that was known to ancient authors derived

4 Sampling consisted of taking scrapings from the interiors of these vessels, which were curated at the Cyprus Archaeological Museum in Nicosia, Cyprus. Sampling was not permitted for the accompanying bowls because scraping would have damaged the visible interior surface.

from the camphor laurel (*Cinnamomum camphora*), which is not a plant indigenous to Cyprus (Meikle 1977, 1985). During the Middle Bronze Age, Cypriot society largely consisted of small agricultural villages that would have exploited plants that were locally available. Camphor is also a constituent in a series of other aromatic plants indigenous to the island, including rosemary, oregano, wild fennel, tansy, coriander, three species of wormwood—absinthe (*Artemisia absinthium*), annual (*Artemisia annua*), and white wormwood (*Artemisia herba-alba*)—basil (*Ocimum basilicum*), thyme (*Thymus sp.*), and lavender (*Lavandula sp.*) (Fasseas et al. 2007: 1191; Ferreira et al. 1997: 347–48; Lee et al. 2005: 134; Nezhadali et al. 2008: 557, 559–60; Piccaglia and Marotti 2001: 241; Radulović and Blagojević 2010: 1117–19; Teixeira da Silva 2004: 707–10, 712–13; Veličkovič et al. 2003: 17, 19–20). The data are insufficient to associate the contents of the vessel with a psychoactive substance, even though a mildly psychotropic substance such as wormwood is possible. More importantly, this result highlights that a much wider range of substances was in use, namely, aromatic oils with medicinal benefits.

A better indicator of a psychotropic substance is the identification of the terpenoid thujone ((1*S*,4*R*,5*R*)-4-methyl-1-(propan-2-yl)bicyclo[3.1.0]hexan-3-one) and its derivatives as biomarkers of different species of wormwood. *Artemisia absinthium* was the species used in the production of various absinthe liquors that were popular in nineteenth-century Europe (Emmert et al. 2004: 352; Höld et al. 2001: 589–90; Ott 1993: 157, 389–93; Parry 1922: 56–58). While this species of wormwood is present in the region, there are other local varieties, such as white wormwood (*A. herba-alba*) and annual wormwood (*A. annua*) (Zohary 1982: 184). As discussed above, *rosh* and *la'ana* are mentioned in the Old Testament as bitter or poisonous plants. Zohary (1982: 184) suggested that white wormwood may be the botanical counterpart. Furthering the case for this identification is the fact that the Greek term for *la'ana* is *apsinthos*.

Like Politiko-Troullia, the site of Marki-Alonia is a settlement located in the foothills of the Troodos Mountains, but it was occupied in the Early Bronze Age (Frankel and Webb 2006: 1–3). Architecturally, the settlement consisted of a series of domestic units of two to three rooms with little indication of spaces that may have served special functions, such as at Alambra-Mouttes (Frankel and Webb 2006: 12–21, 37–40). Eight pottery samples from four depositional contexts underwent the analytical procedure outlined above.

One vessel, a large Red Polished pyxis (see figure 2.9), suggests the presence of a species of wormwood based on the identification of artemiseole

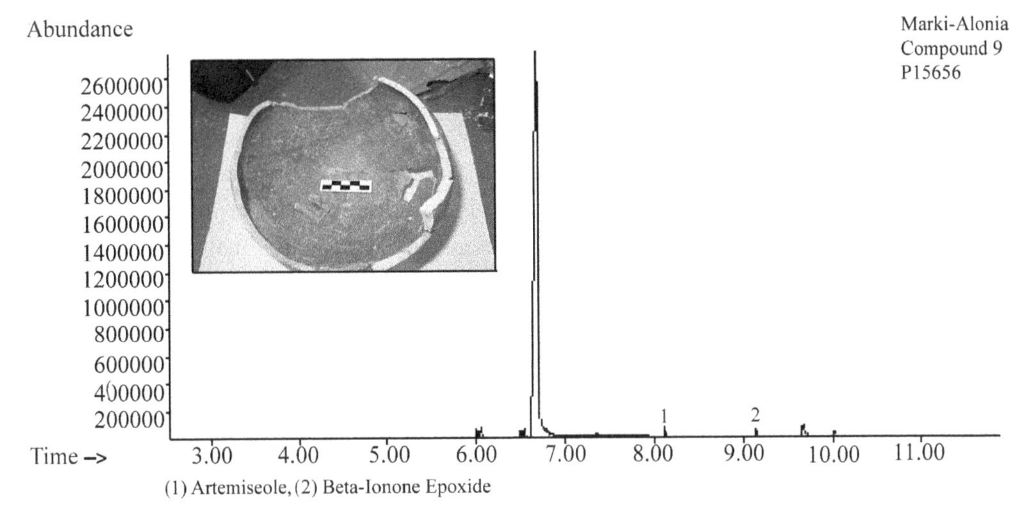

Figure 2.9. Chromatogram of Red Polished pyxis from Marki-Alonia with chemical compounds detected indicated.

(1,6,6-trimethyl-4-ethenyl-exo-2-oxabicyclo[3.1.0]hexane), which also occurred in a reference sample of wormwood. Preliminary data analysis also suggested the presence of cis-sabinene (cis-5-isopropyl-2-methyl-bicyclo[3.1.0]hexan-2-ol), which is structurally related to thujone and is a constituent of absinthe wormwood (Emmert et al. 2004: 352–54; Parry 1922: 56–58). However, this identification could not be confirmed. A second compound, beta-ionone epoxide (4-(2,2,6-trimethyl-7-oxabicyclo[4.1.0]heptan-1-yl)but-3-en-2-one), represents a decomposition product of ionone, one of the major constituents in rose, as well as two species of rockrose (Angelopoulou et al. 2001: 167–70; Van Ouwerker et al. 1977). As with the spouted vessel from Politiko-Troullia, the pyxis from Marki-Alonia also suggests the mixture of a potentially psychoactive substance with an aromatic oil. However, caution should be exercised in attributing a strict psychoactive use to this case, given the size and shape of the vessel and its domestic depositional context. Additional analytical results also suggest the presence of thujone or related compounds but require further study.

Discussion and Conclusions

These results indicate that a broad range of products were being prepared and consumed on the island of Cyprus during the Bronze Age. Fermented beverages were likely being consumed in Cyprus as they were elsewhere in the Mediterranean. However, not all liquid-dispensing containers should be assumed to have been used for this purpose, as there is ample evidence that aromatic oils and medicinal substances were also used widely. As for other types of psychoactive substances, opium has long been suggested to have been known on the island; what was unexpected was the potential use of opium in conjunction with aromatic substances. However, it is increasingly evident that during the Bronze Age on Cyprus, a variety of local plants were being utilized in the production of a wide range of substances, including herbal mixtures and perfumed oils, as well as those psychoactive in nature.

We should, however, exercise caution in interpreting such findings and heed the warning once given to Wasson, to not see intoxicants everywhere. Moreover, these substances likely crossed ancient categories and may not have been viewed as psychoactive but instead as substances that filled multiple social, economic, and religious roles. And finally, we do not know the extent of the intoxication produced by these substances, because they are often in complex mixtures in which the psychoactive ingredients may have played only a minor role.

It should be noted that this research is based entirely on the analysis of residues that would have been absorbed into the ceramic wall of fragmentary vessels, rather than visible residues preserved inside complete vessels. This issue of preservation may have implications for conclusions about the type of substance that a vessel may have contained. Specifically, the compounds identified here may tend to preserve more readily than others. To further our understanding of how processes of preservation and degradation affect chemical compounds in archaeological contexts, a series of experimental studies have been conducted on lipids (Dudd et al. 1998; Malainey et al. 1999), tobacco (Rafferty 2002; Rafferty et al. 2012; chapter 4, this volume), opium (Chovanec et al. 2012), and grape wine (Garnier and Valamoti 2016). For alkaloids, the benefit of such studies is determining which compounds to target in future chemical analyses. However, the case is less clear for plant substances that have a wider distribution, such as essential oils, and would be a useful direction for future research.

Acknowledgments

This essay was presented in a session on psychoactive substances at the 77th Annual Meeting of the Society for American Archaeology in Memphis, Tennessee. The research discussed here was supported by National

Science Foundation (NSF) Grant 0822493, awarded to Dr. Sean M. Rafferty, Dr. Stuart Swiny, and Dr. Igor Lednev at the University at Albany, State University of New York. The analysis of ceramic samples from Politiko-Troullia, Marki-Alonia, and Alambra-Mouttes was funded as part of NSF Grant 1031527, awarded to principal investigators Steven Falconer and Patricia Fall, the Swiny Fellowship, the American Schools of Oriental Research (ASOR), Sigma Xi, and the University at Albany Graduate Student Organization. Thanks are extended to Dr. Maria Hadjicosti and Dr. Pavlos Flourenztos at the Department of Antiquities in Cyprus and the excavation directors (Jane Barlow, Dr. John Coleman, Dr. David Frankel, Dr. Jennifer Webb, Dr. Steven Falconer, and Dr. Patricia Fall) for permission to export and analyze pottery samples. Recognition is also extended to the staff of the University at Albany Chemistry Department and Forensics Laboratory who provided access to facilities and assistance without which this study would not have been possible.

References Cited

Aboelsoud, N. H. 2010. Review: Herbal Medicine in Ancient Egypt. *Journal of Medicinal Plants Research* 4 (2): 8286. Electronic document, www.academicjournals.org/jmpr/pdf/pdf2010/18Jan/Aboelsoud.pdf.

Amar, Z. 2006. Use of the Cultivated Poppy in the Land of Israel and the Surrounding Region up to the New Era. In *Forbidden Fields: The Poppy and Opium from Ancient Times until Today*, ed. E. Ayalon and C. Sorek, 108–21. Tel Aviv: Eretz Israel Museum.

Angelopoulou, D., C. Demetzos, C. Dimas, D. Perdetzoglou, and A. Loukis. 2001. Essential Oils and Hexane Extracts from Leaves and Fruits of *Cistus monspeliensis*: Cytotoxic Activity of Ent-13-epi-manoyl Oxide and Its Isomers. *Planta Medica* 67 (2): 167–71.

Arthur, J. W. 2003. Brewing Beer: Status, Wealth and Ceramic Use Alteration among the Gamo of South-Western Ethiopia. *World Archaeology* 34 (3): 516–28.

Åström, P. 1972. *The Late Cypriote Bronze Age Architecture and Pottery: The Swedish Cyprus Expedition.* Vol. 4, part IC. Lund: Swedish Cyprus Expedition.

Ayalon, E. 2006. The Poppy and Opium from Ancient Times till Today. In *Forbidden Fields: The Poppy and Opium from Ancient Times until Today*, ed. E. Ayalon and C. Sorek, 8–81. Tel Aviv: Eretz Israel Museum.

Badler, V. R., P. E. McGovern, and R. H. Michel. 1990. Drink and Be Merry! Infrared Spectroscopy and Ancient Near Eastern Wine. In *Masca Research Papers in Science and Archaeology: Organic Contents of Ancient Vessels: Material Analysis and Archaeological Investigation*, ed. W. Biers and P. E. McGovern, 25–37. Philadelphia: University of Pennsylvania.

Barnard, H., A. N. Dooley, and K. F. Faull. 2007. An Introduction to Archaeological Lipid Analysis by Combined Gas Chromatography Mass Spectrometry (GC/MS).

In *Theory and Practice of Archaeological Residue Analysis*, ed. H. Barnard and J. W. Eerkens, 42–60. British Archaeological Reports International Series 1650. Oxford: Archaeopress.

Barnard, H., A. N. Dooley, G. Areshian, B. Gasparyan, and K. F. Faull. 2011. Chemical Evidence for Wine Production around 4000 BCE in the Late Chalcolithic Near Eastern highlands. *Journal of Archaeological Science* 38: 977–84.

Başer, K.H.C., and B. Demirçakmak. 1995. The Essential Oil of Taurus Cedar (*Cedrus libani* A. Rich): Recent Results. *Chemistry of Natural Compounds* 31 (1): 16–20.

Beck, C. W., E. C. Stout, K. M. Wovkulich, V. Karageorghis, and E. Aloupi. 2004. The Uses of Cypriote White-Slip Ware Inferred from Organic Residue Analysis. *Ägypten und Levante* 14: 13–43.

Bernáth, J. 1998. Introduction. In *Poppy: The Genus* Papaver, ed. J. Bernáth, 1–6. Amsterdam: Harwood Academic Publishers.

Bisset, N. G., J. G. Bruhn, S. Curto, B. Holmstedt, U. Nyman, and M. H. Zenk. 1994. Was Opium Known in 18th Dynasty Ancient Egypt? An Examination of Materials from the Tombs of the Chief Royal Architect Kha. *Journal of Ethnopharmacology* 41: 99–114.

Bisset, N. G., J. G. Bruhn, and M. H. Zenk. 1996. The Presence of Opium in a 3,500 Year Old Cypriot Base-Ring Juglet. *Ägypten und Levante* 6: 203–4.

Bolster, M. G. 2002. *Ambergris Fragrance Compounds from Labdanolic Acid and Larixol.* Wageningen, Netherlands: Wageningen Universiteit.

Carpenter, S., M. Rigaud, M. Barile, T. J. Priest, L. Perez, and J. B. Ferguson. 1998. *An Interlinear Transliteration and English Translation of Portions of the Ebers Papyrus Possibly Having to Do with Diabetes Mellitus.* Annandale on Hudson, N.Y.: Bard College.

Chovanec, Z. 2013. Products of Social Distinction: Organic Residue Analysis of Specialized Products in Bronze Age Cyprus. PhD diss., State University of New York, Albany.

Chovanec, Z., S. M. Rafferty, and S. Swiny. 2012. Opium for the Masses: An Experimental Archaeological Approach in Determining the Antiquity of the Opium Poppy. *Journal of Ethnoarchaeology* 4 (1): 5–35.

Chovanec, Z., S. Bunimovitz, and Z. Lederman. 2015. Is There Opium Here? Analysis of Cypriot Base Ring Juglets from Tel Beth-Shemesh, Israel. *Journal of Mediterranean Archaeology and Archaeometry* 15 (2): 175–89.

Coleman, J. E., J. A. Barlow, M. K. Mogelonsky, and K. W. Schaar. 1996. *Alambra, a Middle Bronze Age Settlement in Cyprus: Archaeological Investigations by Cornell University, 1974–1985.* Studies in Mediterranean Archaeology, vol. 118. Jonsered, Sweden: Paul Åströms Förlag.

Collard, D. 2010. Tombs, Temples, and Transcendence: Altered States of Consciousness and Bronze Age Cypriote Ritual Practice. Paper presented at the annual meeting for the American Schools of Oriental Research in Atlanta, Georgia.

Collard, D. 2011. Altered States of Consciousness and Ritual in Late Bronze Age Cyprus. PhD diss., University of Nottingham, Nottingham.

Crewe, L., and I. Hill. 2012. Finding Beer in the Archaeological Record: A Case Study from Kissonerga-Skalia on Bronze Age Cyprus. *Levant* 44: 205–37.

Derham, B. 2005. Archaeological and Ethnographic Toxins in Museum Collections.

In *Impact of the Environment on Human Migration in Eurasia*, ed. E. M. Scott, A. Y. Alekseev, and G. Zaitseva, 185–97. NATO Science Series 4, Earth and Environmental Sciences 42. Dordrecht, Netherlands: Kluwer Academic.

Dietler, M. 2006. Alcohol: Anthropological/Archaeological Perspectives. *Annual Review of Anthropology* 35: 229–49.

Dudd, S. N., M. Regert, and R. P. Evershed. 1998. Assessing Microbial Lipid Contributions during Laboratory Degradations of Fats and Oils and Pure Triacylglycerols Absorbed in Ceramic Potsherds. *Organic Geochemistry* 29 (5–7): 1345–54.

Emmert, J., G. Sartor, F. Sporer, and J. Gummersbach. 2004. Determination of Alpha/Beta Thujone and Related Terpenes in Absinthe Using Solid Phase Extraction and Gas Chromatography. *Deutsche Lebensmittel Rundschau* 100 (9): 352–56.

Evershed, R. P. 2000. Biomolecular Analysis by Organic Mass Spectrometry. In *Modern Analytical Methods in Art and Archaeology*, vol. 155, ed. E. Ciliberto and G. Spoto, 177–240. Toronto: John Wiley and Sons.

Evershed, R. P. 2008. Organic Residue Analysis in Archaeology: The Archaeological Biomarker Revolution. *Archaeometry* 50 (6): 895–924.

Falconer, S. E., and P. L. Fall. 2013. Spatial Patterns, Households and Community Behavior at Bronze Age Politiko-Troullia, Cyprus. *Journal of Field Archaeology* 38 (2): 101–19.

Falconer, S. E., P. L. Fall, T. W. Davis, M. T. Horowitz, and J. Hunt. 2005. *Initial Archaeological Investigations at Politiko-Troullia, 2004*, 70–85. Report of the Department of Antiquities. Cyprus.

Fall, P. L., S. E. Falconer, M. Horowitz, J. Hunt, M. C. Metzger, and D. Ryter. 2008. *Bronze Age Settlement and Landscape of Politiko-Troullia, 2005–2007*, 183–208. Report of the Department of Antiquities. Cyprus.

Fall, P. L., S. E. Falconer, C. Galletti, T. Schirmang, E. Ridder, and J. Klinge. 2012. Long-Term Agrarian Landscapes in the Troodos Foothills, Cyprus. *Journal of Archaeological Science* 39: 2335–47.

Fasseas, M. K., K. C. Mountzouris, P. A. Tarantalis, M. Polissiou, and G. Zervas. 2007. Antioxidant Activity in Meat Treated with Oregano and Sage Essential Oils. *Food Chemistry* 106: 1188–94.

Feinman, G. M. 1997. Thoughts on New Approaches to Combining the Archaeological and Historical Records. *Journal of Archaeological Method and Theory* 4 (3–4): 367–77.

Fericgla, J. M. 1996. Traditional Ethneogenic and Intoxicating Substances in the Mediterranean Area. Paper presented at International Conference on Entheogenic Substances, November 10, San Francisco, California.

Ferreira, F. S., J. E. Simon, and J. Janick. 1997. *Artemisia annua*: Botany, Horticultura, Pharmacology. In *Horticulture Review*, vol. 19, ed. J. Janick, 319–72. New York: John Wiley and Sons.

Fitzpatrick, S. M. 2004. Synthesizing Island Archaeology. In *Voyages of Discovery: The Archaeology of Islands*, ed. S. M. Fitzpatrick, 3–18. Westport, Conn.: Praeger.

Frankel, D., and J. M. Webb. 2006. *Marki Alonia, an Early and Middle Bronze Age Settlement in Cyprus: Excavations, 1995–2000*. Studies in Mediterranean Archaeology 123, no. 2. Sävedalen, Sweden: Astrom Editions.

Frankel, D., C. Eslick, and J. M. Webb. 1995. Anatolia and Cyprus in the Third Millennium B.C.E.: A Speculative Model of Interaction. *Abr-Nahrain*, suppl. 5: 37–50.

Garnier, N., and S. M. Valamoti. 2016. Prehistoric Wine-Making at Dikili Tash (Northern Greece): Integrating Residue Analysis and Archaeobotany. *Journal of Archaeological Science* 74: 195–206.

Grace, V. R. 1979. *Amphoras and the Ancient Wine Trade: Excavations at the Athenian Agora*. Picture Book no. 6. Princeton, N.J.: American School of Classical Studies at Athens.

Guash-Jané, M. R., C. Andrés Lacueva, O. Jáuregui, and R. M. Lamuela-Raventós. 2006. The Origin of the Ancient Egyptian Drink *Shedeh* Revealed Using LC/MS/MS. *Journal of Archaeological Science* 33: 98–101.

Guerra-Doce, E. 2015. The Origins of Inebriation: Archaeological Evidence of the Consumption of Fermented Beverages and Drugs in Prehistoric Eurasia. *Journal of Archaeological Method and Theory* 22 (3): 751–82.

Hadjisavvas, S. 2009. Wine for the Elite, Olive for the Masses: Some Aspects of Early Agricultural Technology in Cyprus. In *Exploring the Long Duree: Essays in Honor of Lawrence E. Stager*, ed. J. D. Schloen, 141–49. Winona Lake, Ind.: Eisenbrauns.

Hamilakis, Y. 1999. Food Technologies/Technologies of the Body: The Social Context of Wine and Oil Production and Consumption in Bronze Age Crete. *World Archaeology* 31 (1): 38–54.

Harner, M. J., ed. 1973. *Hallucinogens and Shamanism*. New York: Oxford University Press.

Hayden, B. 2001. Fabulous Feasts: A Prolegomenon to the Importance of Feasts. In *Feasts: Archaeological and Ethnographic Perspectives on Food, Politics, and Power*, ed. M. Dietler and B. Hayden, 23–64. Washington, D.C.: Smithsonian Institution Press.

Heron, C., and R. P. Evershed. 1993. The Analysis of Organic Residues and the Study of Pottery Use. In *Archaeological Method and Theory*, vol. 5, ed. M. B. Schiffer, 247–84. Tucson: University of Arizona Press.

Hesse, M. 1981. *Alkaloid Chemistry*. Trans. I. Ralph and C. Bick. Zurich: John Wiley and Sons.

Höld, K. M., N. S. Sirisoma, and J. E. Casida. 2001. Detoxification of Alpha- and Beta-Thujones (the Active Ingredients of Absinthe): Site Specificity and Species Differences in Cytochrome P450 Oxidation in Vitro and in Vivo. *Chemical Research in Toxicology* 14 (5): 589–95.

Joffe, A. H. 1998. Alcohol and Social Complexity in Ancient Western Asia. *Current Anthropology* 39 (3): 297–322.

Kapoor, L. D. 1995. *Opium Poppy: Botany, Chemistry, and Pharmacology*. New York: Haworth Press.

Keswani, P. S. 1994. The Social Context of Animal Husbandry in Early Agricultural Societies: Ethnographic Insights and an Archaeological Example from Cyprus. *Journal of Anthropological Archaeology* 13: 255–77.

Keswani, P. S. 1996. Hierarchies, Heterarchies, and Urbanization Processes: The View from Bronze Age Cyprus. *Journal of Mediterranean Archaeology* 9 (2): 211–50.

Kitson, F. G., B. S. Larsen, and C. N. McEwen. 1996. *Gas Chromatography and Mass Spectrometry*. San Diego, Calif.: Academic Press.

Knapp, A. B. 1993. Social Complexity: Incipience, Emergence, and Development on Prehistoric Cyprus. *Bulletin of the American Schools of Oriental Research* 292, Perspectives on Cypriot Social Complexity (Nov.): 85–106.

Knapp, A. B. 2008. *Prehistoric and Protohistoric Cyprus: Identity, Insularity, and Connectivity*. Oxford: Oxford University Press.

Koh, A. J., A. Yasur-Landau, and E. H. Cline. 2014. Characterizing a Middle Bronze Palatial Wine Cellar from Tel Kabri, Israel. *PLoS ONE* 9 (8): e106406.

Koschel, K. 1996. Opium Alkaloids in a Cypriote Base Ring I Vessel (Bilbil) of the Middle Bronze Age from Egypt. *Äegypten und Levante* 6: 159–66.

Kunkee, R. E. 1977. Some Roles of Malic Acid in the Malolactic Fermentation in Wine Making. *FEMS Microbiology Letters* 88 (1): 55–72.

La Barre, W. 1970. Old and New World Narcotics: A Statistical Question and Ethnobiological Reply. *Economic Botany* 24: 73–80.

La Barre, W. 1972. Hallucinogens and the Shamanic Origins of Religion. In *Flesh of the Gods: The Ritual use of Hallucinogens*, ed. P. T. Furst, 267–78. New York: Praeger.

Lee, S., K. Umano, T. Shibamoto, and K. Lee. 2005. Identification of Volatile Components in Basil (*Ocimum basilicum* L.) and Thyme Leaves (*Thymus vulgaris* L.) and Their Antioxidant Properties. *Food Chemistry* 91: 131–37.

Locke, R. G., and E. F. Kelly. 1985. A Preliminary Model for the Cross-Cultural Analysis of Altered States of Consciousness. *Ethos* 13 (1): 3–55.

Loy, T. H. 1993. The Artifact as Site: An Example of the Biomolecular Analysis of Organic Residues on Prehistoric Tools. *World Archaeology: Biomolecular Archaeology* 25 (1): 44–63.

Lyman, R. L., and M. J. O'Brien. 2001. The Direct Historical Approach, Analogical Reasoning, and Theory in Americanist Archaeology. *Journal of Archaeological Method and Theory* 8 (4): 303–42.

Malainey, M. E., R. Przybylski, and B. L. Sherriff. 1999. The Effects of Thermal and Oxidative Degradation on the Fatty Acid Composition of Food Plants and Animals of Western Canada: Implications for the Identification of Archaeological Vessel Residues. *Journal of Archaeological Science* 26: 95–103.

Manning, S. W. 1993. Prestige, Distinction, and Competition: The Anatomy of Socioeconomic Complexity in Fourth to Second Millennium B.C.E. *Bulletin of the American Schools of Oriental Research* 292, Perspectives on Cypriot Social Complexity (Nov.): 35–58.

Manvi, F. V., and G. P. Garg. 2011. Evaluation of Pharmacognostical Parameters and Hepatoprotective Activity in *Bryonia alba* Linn. *Journal of Chemical and Pharmaceutical Research* 3 (6): 99–109.

Mariti, G. 1984. *Wines of Cyprus: Wine Planting to Harvesting, Wine Making to Marketing.* Athens: Nicolas Books.

McGovern, P. E. 2003. *Ancient Wine: The Search for the Origins of Viniculture*. Princeton: Princeton University Press.

McGovern, P. E. 2009. *Uncorking the Past: The Quest for Wine, Beer, and Other Alcoholic Beverages*. Berkeley: University of California Press.

McGovern, P. E., J. Zhang, J. Tang, Z. Zhang, G. R. Hall, R. A. Moreau, A. Nuñez, et al. 2004. Fermented Beverages of Pre- and Proto-historic China. *Proceedings of the National Academy of Sciences* 101 (51): 17593–98.

McGovern, P. E., A. Mizolan, and G. R. Hall. 2009. Ancient Egyptian Herbal Wines. *Proceedings of the National Academy of Sciences* 106 (18): 7361–66.

Meikle, R. D. 1977. *Flora of Cyprus*. Vol. 1. Kew, U.K.: Bentham-Moxon Trust, Royal Botanical Gardens.

Meikle, R. D. 1985. *Flora of Cyprus*. Vol. 2. Kew, U.K.: Bentham-Moxon Trust, Royal Botanical Gardens.

Merlin, M. D. 1984. *On the Trail of the Ancient Opium Poppy: Natural and Early Cultural History of* Papaver somniferum. East Brunswick, N.J.: Associated University Presses.

Merlin, M. D. 2003. Archaeological Evidence for the Tradition of Psychoactive Plant Use in the Old World. *Economic Botany* 57 (3): 295–323.

Merrillees, R. S. (1962) 2003. Opium Trade in the Bronze Age Levant. In *On Opium, Pots, People, and Places: An Honorary Volume for Robert S. Merrillees*, 2–9. Sävedalen, Sweden: Paul Åström Förlag.

Merrillees, R. S. (1979) 2003. Opium Again in Antiquity. In *On Opium, Pots, People, and Places: An Honorary Volume for Robert S. Merrillees*, 121–28. Sävedalen, Sweden: Paul Åström Förlag.

Merrillees, R. S. (1989) 2003. Highs and Lows in the Holy Land: Opium in Biblical Times. In *On Opium, Pots, People, and Places: An Honorary Volume for Robert S. Merrillees*, 180–86. Sävedalen, Sweden: Paul Åström Förlag.

Michel, R. H., P. E. McGovern, and V. R. Badler. 1993. The First Wine and Beer: Chemical Detection of Ancient Fermented Beverages. *Analytical Chemistry* 65 (8): 408–13.

Miller, R. A., and I. Miller. 1990. Kether = Ambergris. In *The Magical and Ritual Use of Perfumes*, 37–39. Rochester, N.Y.: Destiny Books.

Mills, J. S., and R. White. 1989. The Identity of the Resins from the Late Bronze Age Shipwreck at Ulu Burun (Kaş). *Archaeometry* 31 (1): 37–44.

Nezhadali, A., M. Akbarpour, and B. Zarrabi Shirvan. 2008. Chemical Composition of the Essential Oil from the Aerial Parts of *Artemisia Herba*. *E-Journal of Chemistry* 5 (3): 557–61.

Ogalde, J. P., B. T. Arriaza, and E. C. Soto. 2007. Prehistoric Psychotropic Consumption in Andean Chilean Mummies. *Nature Proceedings* 1368 (1): 467–72.

Oritani, T. 1998. Synthesis of Ambergris-Fragrances and (+)-Ambreine. In *Abstracts of Plenary and Invited Lectures*, p. 9. Novosibirsk Institute of Organic Chemistry. Russia.

Ott, J. 1993. *Pharmacotheon: Entheogenic Drugs, Their Plant Sources and History*. Kennewick, Wash.: Natural Products.

Parry, E. J. 1922. *The Chemistry of Essential Oils and Artificial Perfumes*. Vol. 2. London: Scott, Greenwood and Son.

Peltenburg, E. 1996. From Isolation to State Formation in Cyprus, c. 3500–1500 BC. In *The Development of the Cypriot Economy: From the Prehistoric Period to the Present Day*, ed. V. Karageorghis and D. Michaelides, 17–37. Nicosia, Cyprus: Lithographica.

Piccaglia, R., and M. Marotti. 2001. Characterization of Some Italian Types of Wild Fennel (*Foeniculum vulgare* Mill.). *Journal of Agriculture and Food Chemistry* 49: 239–44.

Pliny. (AD 77) 2006. *The natural history*, 13.2.7–8. Ed. John Bostock, Henry T. Riley, and Karl Friedrich Theodor Mayhoff. Somerville, Mass.: Perseus Digital Library. http://www.perseus.tufts.edu/cgi-bin/ptext?lookup=Plin.+Nat.+toc.

Pollard, A. M., and C. Heron. 2008. *Archaeological Chemistry*. 2nd ed. Cambridge, U.K.: RSC Publishing.

Radulović, N., and P. Blagojević. 2010. Volatile Profiles of *Artemisia alba* from Contrasting Serpentine and Calcareous Habitats. *Natural Product Communications* 5 (7): 1117–22.

Rafferty, S. M. 2002. Identification of Nicotine by Gas Chromatography/Mass Spectroscopy Analysis of Smoking Pipe Residue. *Journal of Archaeological Science* 29: 897–907.

Rafferty, S. M. 2007. The Archaeology of Alkaloids. In *Theory and Practice in Archaeological Residue Analysis*, ed. H. Barnard and J. W. Eerkens, 179–88. British Archaeological Reports International Series 1650. Oxford: Archaeopress.

Rafferty, S. M., I. Lednev, K. Virkler, and Z. Chovanec. 2012. Current Research on Smoking Pipe Residues. *Journal of Archaeological Science* 39: 1951–59.

Regert, M., S. Colinart, L. Degrand, and O. Decavallas. 2001. Chemical Alteration and Use of Beeswax through Time: Accelerated Ageing Tests and Analysis of Archaeological Samples from Various Environmental Contexts. *Archaeometry* 43 (4): 549–69.

Ruck, C.A.P. 2008a. Hindsight. In *The Road to Eleusis: Unveiling the Secret of the Mysteries*, ed. R. G. Wasson, A. Hofmann, and C.A.P. Ruck, 11–18. Berkeley, Calif.: North Atlantic Books.

Ruck, C.A.P. 2008b. Solving the Eleusinian Mystery. In *The Road to Eleusis: Unveiling the Secret of the Mysteries*, ed. R. G. Wasson, A. Hofmann, and C.A.P. Ruck, 45–60. Berkeley, Calif.: North Atlantic Books.

Schultes, R. E. 1969. Hallucinogens of Plant Origin. *Science*, n.s., 163 (3864): 245–54.

Schultes, R. E. 1990. An Overview of Hallucinogens in the Western Hemisphere. In *Flesh of Gods: The Ritual Use of Hallucinogens*, ed. P. Furst, 3–54. Long Grove, Ill.: Waveland Press.

Schultes, R. E. 1998. Antiquity of the Use of New World Hallucinogens. *Heffter Review of Psychedelic Research* 1: 1–7.

Seltman, C. 1957. *Wine in the Ancient World*. London: Routledge and Kegan Paul.

Sherratt, A. 1987. Cups that Cheered: The Introduction of Alcohol to Prehistoric Europe. In *Economy and Society in Prehistoric Europe: Changing Perspectives*, ed. A. Sherratt, 376–402. Princeton: Princeton University Press.

Sherratt, A. 1991. Sacred and Profane Substances: The Ritual Use of Narcotics in Later Neolithic Europe. In *Sacred and Profane: Proceedings of a Conference on Archaeology, Ritual and Religion*, ed. P. Garwood, D. Jennings, R. Skeates, and J. Toms, 50–64. Oxford University Committee for Archaeology Monographs 32. Oxford.

Stahl, A. B. 1993. Concepts of Time and Approaches to Analogical Reasoning in Historical Perspective. *American Antiquity* 58 (2): 235–60.

Steel, L. 2002. Wine, Women, and Song: Drinking Ritual in Cyprus during the Late Bronze Age. In *Engendering Aphrodite: Women and Archaeology in Ancient Cyprus*, ed. D. Bolger and N. Serwint, 105–19. ASOR Archaeological Reports 7, CAARI Monographs 3. Boston: American Schools of Oriental Research.

Steel, L. 2004a. *Cyprus before History: From the Earliest Settlers to the End of the Bronze Age.* London: Duckworth.
Steel, L. 2004b. A Goodly Feast . . . A Cup of Mellow Wine: Feasting in Bronze Age Cyprus. *Hesperia: The Mycenaean Feast* 73 (2): 281–300.
Teixeira da Silva, J. A. 2004. Mining the Essential Oils of the Anthemideae. *African Journal of Biotechnology* 3 (12): 706–20.
Totelin, L.M.V. 2009. *Hippocratic Recipes: Oral and Written Transmission of Pharmacological Knowledge in Fifth- and Fourth-Century Greece.* Leiden, Netherlands: Brill.
Van Ouwerker, A., B. J. Chant, and A. L. Lieberman. 1977. Novel Fragrance Compositions Containing 2,6,6-Trimethyl-1-cyclohexen-1-yl Acetaldehyde and Phenyl C_6 Ketone. US Patent 4,028,279, filed August 4, 1975, and issued June 7, 1977.
Veličkovič, D. T., N. V. Randjelovic, M. S. Ristic, A. S. Veličkovič, and A. A. Smelcerovic. 2003. Chemical Constituents and Antimicrobial Activity of the Ethanol Extracts Obtained from the Flower, Leaf and Stem of *Salvia officinalis* L. *Journal of the Serbian Chemical Society* 68 (1): 17–24.
Wansbrough, H. 1998. *Chemistry in Winemaking.* Christchurch: New Zealand Institute of Chemistry. http://nzic.org.nz/ChemProcesses/food/6B.pdf.
Wasson, R. G. 1990. What Was the Soma of the Aryans? In *Flesh of Gods: The Ritual Use of Hallucinogens,* ed. P. Furst, 201–13. Long Grove, Ill.: Waveland Press.
Wasson, R. G. 2008. The Wasson Road to Eleusis. In *The Road to Eleusis: Unveiling the Secret of the Mysteries,* ed. R. G. Wasson, A. Hofmann, and C.A.P. Ruck, 21–34. Berkeley, Calif.: North Atlantic Books.
Waterman, P. G. 1998. Chemical Taxonomy of Alkaloids. In *Alkaloids: Biochemistry, Ecology and Medical Applications,* ed. M. F. Roberts and M. Wink, 87–106. New York: Plenum Press.
Webb, J. M., and D. Frankel. 2008. Fine Ware Ceramics, Consumption and Commensality, Mechanisms of Horizontal and Vertical Integration. In *DAIS: The Aegean Feast,* 287–95. Proceedings of the 12th International Aegean Conference, University of Melbourne. Liege: Universite de Liege, Historie.
Webb, J. M., and D. Frankel. 2010. Social Strategies, Ritual and Cosmology in Early Bronze Age Cyprus: An Investigation of Burial Data from the North Coast. *Levant* 42 (2): 185–209.
Wylie, A. 1985. The Reaction against Analogy. In *Advances in Archaeological Method and Theory,* vol. 8, ed. M. B. Schiffer, 63–111. New York: Academic Press.
Wylie, A. 1988. "Simple" Analogy and the Role of Relevance Assumptions: Implications of Archaeological Practice. *International Studies in the Philosophy of Science* 2 (2): 134–50.
Zohary, M. 1982. *Plants of the Bible: A Complete Handbook.* Cambridge: Cambridge University Press.

3

Ancient Use of *Ephedra* in Eurasia and the Western Hemisphere

MARK D. MERLIN

Anatomically modern humans are now believed to have arrived in Eurasia as much as 80,000–120,000 years ago (e.g., see Callaway 2015), and in bands of hunters and gatherers these early people moved east and west progressively across this massive landmass. In the process of spreading out over this vast continental region, they developed very ancient and long-lasting paleoethnobotanical relationships with numerous species; the more significant of these prehistoric relationships in Eurasia included medicinally and psychoactively important genera such as *Cannabis*, *Papaver*, and *Ephedra* (for *Cannabis*, see chapter 1 in this volume; for *Papaver somniferum* L., the opium poppy, see chapter 2). In the case of *Ephedra*, species in this genus appear to have been used very early on in some regions of both the Old and New World beginning many thousands of years ago.

Ephedra plants are often closely associated with *Ephedra sinica* Stapf (figure 3.1). The epithet *sinica* refers to the geographical range of this species within China, where it is known as Chinese *Ephedra* or *ma huang* (which can be literally translated as "yellow hemp" or "yellow *Cannabis*" [e.g., see Bensky and Gamble 1993; Lee 2011]). *E. sinica* has been used therapeutically and ritually in East Asia for thousands of years (Zhao and Xiao 2009; also see Chen 1974; Blumenthal and King 1995; Blumenthal 2003; Lee 2011), but it is not the only species in its genus with a long history of medicinal and others uses, including as a source of psychoactivity, and it is not the only species referred to as *ma huang*. In the discussion that follows, I first provide some botanical, ecological, and biogeographic background for the genus *Ephedra* and then review the ethnobotanical

Figure 3.1. *Ephedra sinica* Stapf, commonly known as *ma huang*; *E. sinica* has been used therapeutically and ritually in East Asia for thousands of years. (*A*, *Ephedra_sinica_alexlomas.jpg*, licensed under Creative Commons Attribution 2.0 generic license; *B*, courtesy of Chinese National Herbarium, Beijing, specimen no. 1750423, *E. sinica*, from Shanxi province.)

diversity, antiquity, and importance of selected *Ephedra* species with native distributions in the Western Hemisphere and Eurasia. Later in this chapter, I return to a discussion of the antiquity and significance of the use of *Ephedra* species, including *E. sinica*, in East Asia.

The genus *Ephedra* is the type and sole genus in the family Ephedraceae, an unusual and ancient plant family of gymnosperms, the open seed-producing species that includes conifers, cycads, ginkgo, and Gnetales. Today, *Ephedra* species are ecologically distributed in a variety of warm-temperate to subtropical environments and are adapted to dry, rocky, or sandy semiarid and arid regions, with a few species occurring in grasslands. Geographically, these species are found in parts of North America, Mexico, South America, Europe, Asia, and North and East Africa, including the Canary Islands (figure 3.2) (e.g., Kubitzki 1990; Stevenson 1993; Fu et al. 1999; Yang 2010).

The life-form or growth habit of *Ephedra* species varies significantly and includes small trees, shrubs, subshrubs, and, infrequently, lianas or

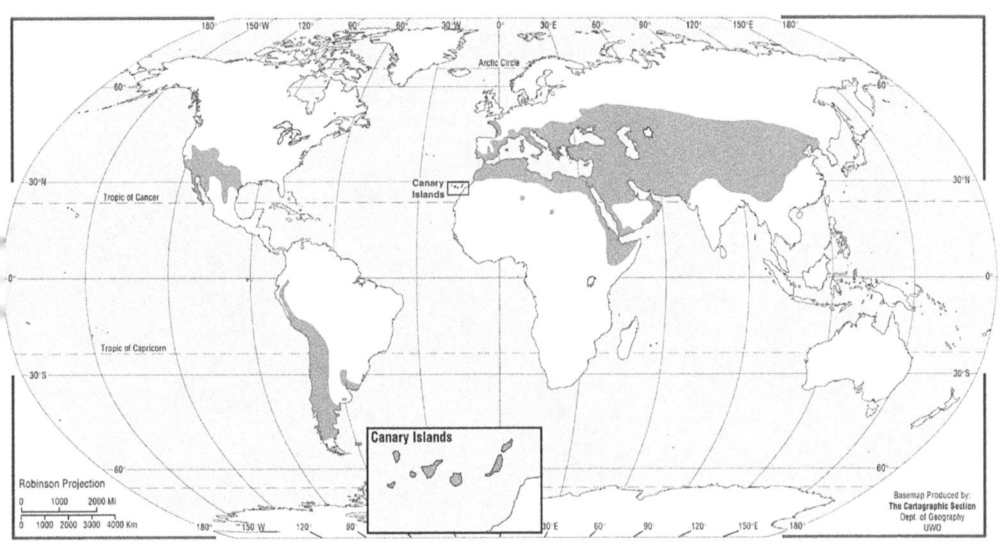

Figure 3.2. World distribution of *Ephedra*. Shaded areas depict regions where *Ephedra* species are found, based on data from Hunziker 1949; Freitag and Maier-Stolte 1989, 1996; Zhang et al. 1989; and Stevenson 1993. (Map based on map from Caveney et al. 2001 [reproduced with permission from *American Journal of Botany*].)

vine-like shrubs; regardless of its life-form, the stems of the diverse species are generally branched profusely, producing green branchlets arranged opposite or in whorls at the nodes. Other key characteristics of the *Ephedra* species are their greatly reduced leaves, resembling bracts, and their evergreen, relatively thin, broom-like photosynthetic stems. In addition, *Ephedra* plants are usually dioecious (male and female flowers on separate individual plants) and only rarely monoecious. One of the most common English names for many *Ephedra* species is "jointfir," because of the long, slender branches of plants in this genus and the tiny, scalelike leaves at their nodes (figure 3.3). Overall, the various species of *Ephedra* are more or less similar in general appearance; therefore, exact species identification requires careful determination. As a result, the number of recognized species in *Ephedra* is unclear, with totals ranging from approximately thirty-five to almost seventy (e.g., see Stapf 1889; Kubitzki 1990; Stevenson 1993; Price 1996; Huang and Price 2003; Huang et al. 2005; Yang et al. 2005; Ickert-Bond et al. 2009; Rydin and Korall 2009; Sharma et al. 2010); this ambiguity is especially pronounced in the Old World species (Yang 2010). I now focus on the archaeological, ethnohistorical, and ethnobotanical evidence for long-term traditional use of selected *Ephedra* species.

Figure 3.3. *Ephedra distachya* L. (syn. *E. vulgaris*) reaches 25–50 centimeters in height. It occurs in a wide area, ranging from Spain and western France through the Alps and along the northern Mediterranean coast to eastern Europe and the Near East and continuing to western Central Asia and southwestern Siberia (Freitag and Maier-Stolte 1994; Kakiuchi et al. 2011). *A*, Drawing of *E. distachya* from *Flora von Deutschland*, by Dr. Otto Wilhelm Thomé (1885); *B*, *Ephedra distachya* in the botanical garden of Osnabrück, Germany. (Photograph by Carsten Niehaus, licensed under Creative Commons Attribution–Share Alike 1.0 generic license.)

The Putative Neanderthal *Ephedra* Evidence from Shanidar Cave

The antiquity of *Ephedra* use for both medicinal and psychoactive purposes is evident in both the Old and the New World. In Eurasia, very ancient pollen of *Ephedra* was discovered in the Shanidar IV Neanderthal burial cave site in the Zagros Mountains of northern Iraq, which dates back more than 50,000 years (figure 3.4) (Solecki 1975; also see Lietava 1992; Merlin 2003). If the evidence is valid and interpreted correctly, it would represent the earliest known human use of *Ephedra* for medicinal, ritualistic, or other purposes (Lietava 1992; Solecki 1975; also see Shipley and Kindscher 2016 for a review of paleoethnobotanical evidence associated with Neanderthals).

The pollen of *Ephedra* (e.g., see Leroi-Gourhan 1975; Solecki 1971) found at Shanidar Cave was recovered from samples that yielded a large amount of pollen grains from a variety of plant species, which still occur naturally in the surrounding region of the cave site. "This evidence has

Figure 3.4. The exterior of the Shanidar IV Neanderthal burial cave site in the Zagros Mountains of northern Iraq. The photograph was taken during the summer of 2005; for scale, note the two squatting men in front of the cave. (*Erbil_governorate_shanidar_cave.jpg* [https://commons.wikimedia.org/w/index.php?curid=1445491], licensed under Creative Commons Attribution–Share Alike 3.0 unported license.)

been used to support the hypothesis that the hominid body was deliberately, and perhaps ritualistically buried on a bed of woody branches and flowers sometime between May and July, when the flowers of many of the species were in bloom" (Leroi-Gourhan 1975). Pollen examination recognized many different species, including "*Achillea*-type, *Centaurea solstitialis*, *Senecio*-type, *Muscari*-type, *Althea*-type, *Ephedra altissima* [*E. distachya* L.?]," and others (Leroi-Gourhan 1975); this analysis was followed by a pharmacological assessment of the healing potential of the plants represented by the pollen. The subsequent study (Lietava 1992) supported the hypothesis that these species possess objective therapeutic potential (for relevant newer evidence [some of which is discussed below] about Neanderthal symbolic thought and the use of medicinal plants, see Langley et al. 2008; Hardy et al. 2012; Monnier 2012). The medical utility of these plants could have stimulated the deliberate use of these species by the Paleolithic Shanidar Neanderthals. Because *E. altissima* yields ephedrine, an alkaloid that produces sympathomimetic and amphetamine-like effects, as well as euphoria (Teuscher 1979; Wenke 1986), it may have served as an entheogen (spiritually stimulating plant) for ritualistic, spiritual, and/or medicinal purposes. Solecki (1975) went so far as to speculate that the man in this Neanderthal burial "was not only a very important man, a leader, but also may have been a kind of medicine man or shaman in his group" (see Shipley and Kindscher 2016). The pollen of *Ephedra* may also have become deposited in this burial as the result of its woody branches along with parts of other plants being laid down as bedding (Leroi-Gourhan 1975).

Some scientists and scholars have challenged the hypothesis that the placement of the flowering plant offerings at the burial site was a conscious choice of the Neanderthals; instead, they suggest that the ancient pollen might have become lodged in the soil around the ancient Neanderthal burial through the activity of the burrowing "Persian jird" (*Meriones persicus* Blanford). This rodent species is known to have occurred in the area contemporaneously with Neanderthals and is also known to store in its burrows large amounts of seeds and flowers such those from the species identified via the pollen remains (e.g., see Sommer 1999; also see Nadel et al. 2013; Guerra-Doce 2014). In any case, the tantalizing evidence of possibly very ancient medicinal or even ritualistic psychoactive use by our Neanderthal relatives about 50,000 years ago demands further study.

Be that as it may, there are indications that Neanderthals had developed some degree of symbolic thought, which became more common after about 60,000 years ago (e.g., see Langley et al. 2008). This included the utilization of mineral pigments, the burials themselves, and additional evidence of behavioral complexity, "suggesting that [this and] . . . symbolic thought may have emerged as a component of Neanderthal adaptations towards the end of their existence as a species" (Monnier 2012). Furthermore, recent evidence of plant microfossils entangled in dental calculus from five Neanderthal individuals from the northern Spanish site of El Sidrón supports the hypothesis that the Neanderthal diet was not necessarily only or predominantly based on meat but also included plants (Hardy et al. 2012; also see Hardy et al. 2013; Weyrich et al. 2015), with perhaps at least some vegetation ingested or used for medicinal purposes (Callaway 2017). This evidence has been provided by a large, multinational research team, which "combined sequential thermal desorption–gas chromatography–mass spectrometry (TD-GC-MS) and pyrolysis–gas chromatography–mass spectrometry (Py-GC-MS) . . . with morphological analysis of plant microfossils to identify material entrapped in dental calculus" (Hardy et al. 2012: 617). This study provides the initial molecular evidence for wood-fire and fossil fuel smoke inhalation, consumption of various cooked plant foods, as well as "the first evidence for the use of medicinal plants by a Neanderthal individual." This suggests that "the Neanderthal occupants of El Sidrón had a sophisticated knowledge of their natural surroundings which included the ability to select and use certain plants." When this new molecular archaeological evidence is combined with previous research that demonstrated the presence of the "bitter taste perception gene" in the ancient Neanderthals found in the El Sidrón site, it leads to the conclusion that at least one individual had ingested bitter-tasting plants, most likely as a form of self-medication (see Hardy et al. 2012: 617–26). Further supporting evidence from more recent investigation of the dental calculus found at El Sidrón includes small pieces of inedible, and noncharred, conifer wood tissue in the plaque extracted from some of the Neanderthal teeth from El Sidrón. The most probable basic explanation is that these Neanderthals were placing toothpicks or wooden tools in their mouths (see Radini et al. 2016: 290–301).

This new dental calculus evidence tends to support earlier suppositions about the use of medicinal, or at least hygienic, if not spiritually motivated, psychoactive plants by Neanderthals well back into the Pleistocene. In the opinion of Solecki (1975: 880–81), "it is extremely likely that, as practicing naturalists (and early-day ecologists?), the Neanderthals must have known and appreciated all of their environment, since their very existence depended on it." Hardy and colleagues (2013: 875) argued that care "is needed in the selection and ingestion of plants so as to exclude noxious secondary compounds [that are] essential for survival and requires methods of knowledge transfer," and as such, positive and negative "experiences with various plants would have been passed down as part of Neanderthal ecological knowledge" (Shipley and Kindscher 2016; also see Solecki 1975). Given the evidence and the perspectives offered above, it seems safe to assume that Neanderthals "had a sophisticated knowledge of their natural surroundings, and were able to recognize both the nutritional and the medicinal value of certain plants" (Hardy et al. 2012: 624).

The possible identification of "*Ephedra distachya*" (not *E. altissima*, the *Ephedra* species found in association with the Neanderthal burial at the Shanidar IV cave), along with its long-term significance in the ancient and ongoing Zoroastrian religious practice, and its association with its ancient healing system, which "is based on Haoma or Hom," is discussed from a traditional Zoroastrian perspective by Eduljee (2014):

> While some of the plants associated with the pollen found beside Shanidar IV (perhaps we may be forgiven for calling him "Herb") may have pretty flowers, others such as the ephedra are not known so much for their flower value as they are for their herbal value. Ralph Solecki in *Shanidar, the First Flower People* (1971) at page 177 states, "We do not know if the Shanidar Neanderthals were aware of the medicinal properties as well as the ornamental properties of flowers, but it is likely that as working naturalists they must have given all living plants a taste during some time in their long existence. Until we know a little more about flowers in antiquity, it would be asking too much to believe that the Neanderthals were cognizant of the medicinal properties of flowers." What we do know is that almost all the plants whose pollen was found besides "Herb's" skeleton have recognized health giving and medicinal purposes. These include Ephedra distachya (otherwise known as Joint Pine or Woody Horsetail), Yarrow, Cornflower, Bachelor's Button, St. Barnaby's Thistle, Ragwort or Groundsel, Grape Hyacinth, and Hollyhock—plants known for their diuretic, stimulant, astringent and anti-inflammatory properties.
>
> The healing or medicinal use of ephedra either on its own or in combination with other plants is particularly significant for Zoroastrians whose ancient healing system is based on Haoma or Hom. . . . *Hom* is the Iranian name for the ephedra plant.

Eduljee (2014) sums up the hypothetical aspects of religious implications associated with the putative conscious Neanderthal offering of *Ephedra* in the Shanidar cave but also underscores the medicinal-spiritual Zoroastrian traditional use of these potent plants:

> Ephedra is reputed to be the world's oldest medicine and has reportedly been found buried in a 60,000 year old Middle Eastern Neolithic grave in Shanidar (Iraqi Kurdistan). . . . If the plant was intentionally placed in the grave, that might indicate a familiarity with its health uses and that the people of that time may have ascribed to ephedra spiritual properties that could assist the dead. This is speculative. What we do know, is that in Zoroastrian texts the method of haoma preparation imparts to the extract spiritual properties in addition to its healing properties.

Before I turn my attention to additional putative as well as documented ancient evidence of *Ephedra* species use in the Old World, I review the spatial and temporal extent of traditional use of *Ephedra* species in the

New World; indeed, some of the oldest botanical evidence for the use of these species in archaeological contexts has been found in New World sites, in both North and South America.

Evidence of Traditional and Early Use of *Ephedra* Species in the Western Hemisphere

There is extensive documentation for medicinal, food, fuel, and/or ritual use of many *Ephedra* species in the Western Hemisphere. A brief survey of such use across this huge range is presented below. Curiously, while all Old World *Ephedra* species appear to contain variable amounts of ephedrine, this potent alkaloid is reportedly not present in the New World *Ephedra* species (e.g., see Caveney et al. 2001). However, the data pertaining to the presence of ephedrine and other alkaloids in *Ephedra* species are contradictory, possibly due at least in part to the actual botanical identity of the species under study, as well as the sensitivity of the analysis used to determine alkaloidal content (e.g., see EFSA 2013). In fact, the psychotropic and medicinal properties ascribed to several of the native *Ephedra* species in the Western Hemisphere, such as *E. viridis* Coville, a species found in the arid Great Basin of western North America (figure 3.5), are still not fully understood, even though this species and various others in the New World have lengthy oral and written histories referring to their use to make therapeutic and/or stimulating teas known to have been imbibed by Native Americans, as well as by Mormons and other pioneers. These New World, stimulating, *Ephedra*-based beverages are variously known in English as "Indian tea," "Mormon tea," "Brigham tea," "cowboy tea," "whorehouse tea," "squaw tea," or "canyon tea."

A key hypothesis explaining the therapeutic but nonspiritualistic associations of the use of *Ephedra* species native to the Western Hemisphere apparently involves the lack of the powerful ephedrine alkaloids outside of Eurasia (e.g., see Trujillo and Sorenson 2003; Adams and Garcia 2006; EFSA 2013). Nevertheless, although ephedrine alkaloids are reportedly not detectable in New World species of *Ephedra,* these plants do produce "other nitrogen-containing secondary metabolites with known neuropharmacological activity" (for example, pseudoephedrine; see Caveney et al. 2001: 1199), as do the Eurasian species. Various acknowledged traditional uses for *Ephedra* species include the treatment of intestinal pains and symptoms of common colds, as well as problems affecting the urinary tract, curtailing diarrhea, and providing symptomatic relief from venereal

Figure 3.5. *Ephedra viridis* Coville in bloom. This *Ephedra* species is found in the Great Basin of North America, where it has a long history of use by Native Americans and some European settlers for medicine and an invigorating tea. (BLM_ephedra_epvi_017_php, courtesy USDA, PLANTS Database [http://plants.usda.gov, Feb. 6, 2016], National Plant Data Team, Greensboro, N.C., BLM photographer.)

disease (e.g., Steibel 1997; Rapoport et al. 2003; Ladio and Lozada 2009). A variety of *Ephedra* species also have long histories of the customary uses among native peoples in the New World, in some cases supported by documented archaeobotanical and archaeological evidence. Examples below refer to evidence from the North American Southwest and the southern region of South America.

In the central Mesa Verde region of Colorado, a single piece of *Ephedra* charcoal (likely *E. viridis*) dating to the Pueblo II period (AD 900–1150) was recovered from a hearth at the large, multicomponent Anasazi archaeological site of Shield Pueblo (figure 3.6) (Dunk 2006). However, the rarity of archaeobotanical remains of *Ephedra* charcoal in the region of this archaeological site corresponds with historic accounts, which indicate that *Ephedra* was not a commonly used hearth fuel. The main use of this plant was apparently as medicine; thus, the relatively unique *Ephedra* charcoal recovered from the ancient Anasazi hearth at Shield Pueblo may possibly have been burned for ritual purposes.

Archaeological evidence for the ancient presence if not the human use of *Ephedra* from the southwestern region of the United States has also been clearly documented through the study of pollen concentrations in human coprolites. For example, in the lower Pecos region of southwestern Texas, Sobolik (1988) studied the pollen concentration values from thirty-eight coprolites discovered in Baker Cave, Val Verde County, to determine the subsistence and diet of ancient hunter-gatherers who utilized the cave around AD 900. Sobolik (1988: 211) reported that *Ephedra* was a "possible economic pollen type generally found at low frequencies" but also "observed at a high frequency of 15%" in one of the samples; Sobolik also noted here that *Ephedra* was "found to be used in the Amistad Basin (of the Lower Pecos Canyonlands) as a flour (Story and Bryant, 1966) and as a possible diarrhetic at Caldwell Cave (Holloway 1983)." More recently, Sobolik and Gerick (1992) also found pollen evidence from coprolites recovered from Caldwell Cave, suggesting a strong use of *Ephedra* tea to help alleviate chronic diarrhea, one of the major medicinal uses of *Ephedra* from ancient to modern times (see Kiple and Ornelas 2000 for several references indicating such use).

Reinhard and colleagues (1991) documented use of *Ephedra* among the prehistoric dwellers in the stratified dry shelter of Bighorn Cave in the Black Mountains of western Arizona dated to AD 600–900 and from Granado Cave and Caldwell Shelter 1, located in the Rustler Hills of far western Texas; the latter site has "cultural deposits" ranging between AD 200 and AD 1400. Reinhard and colleagues (2002) completed a more recent analysis of the coprolites from the Bighorn Cave site, confirming the use of an *Ephedra* species during the Archaic period in that area. Although these authors and others may interpret such human ingestion of *Ephedra* as medicinal, it could have served as food or fuel or could even have been motivated by religious purposes (for a critical review of coprolite pollen presences and concentration values in relation to inferred human use, see Miranda Chaves and Reinhard 2006).

Several Native American groups in southern California reportedly have long traditions of using *Ephedra* for a variety of purposes. For example, packets of *Ephedra* have been reported in cave hoards in Chumash territory (Timbrook 2007), which suggests that *Ephedra* was a significant plant in the prehistoric period. Cooley and Barrie (2004) carried out archaeological excavation at the prehistoric village of Pa'mu, in the Ramona Valley of San Diego County, California, with a focus on prehistoric environment and plant use; they referred to the evidence of the ancient use of *Ephedra* in the form of pollen on four ancient stone pounders reportedly used prehistorically in the local southern California area for food or

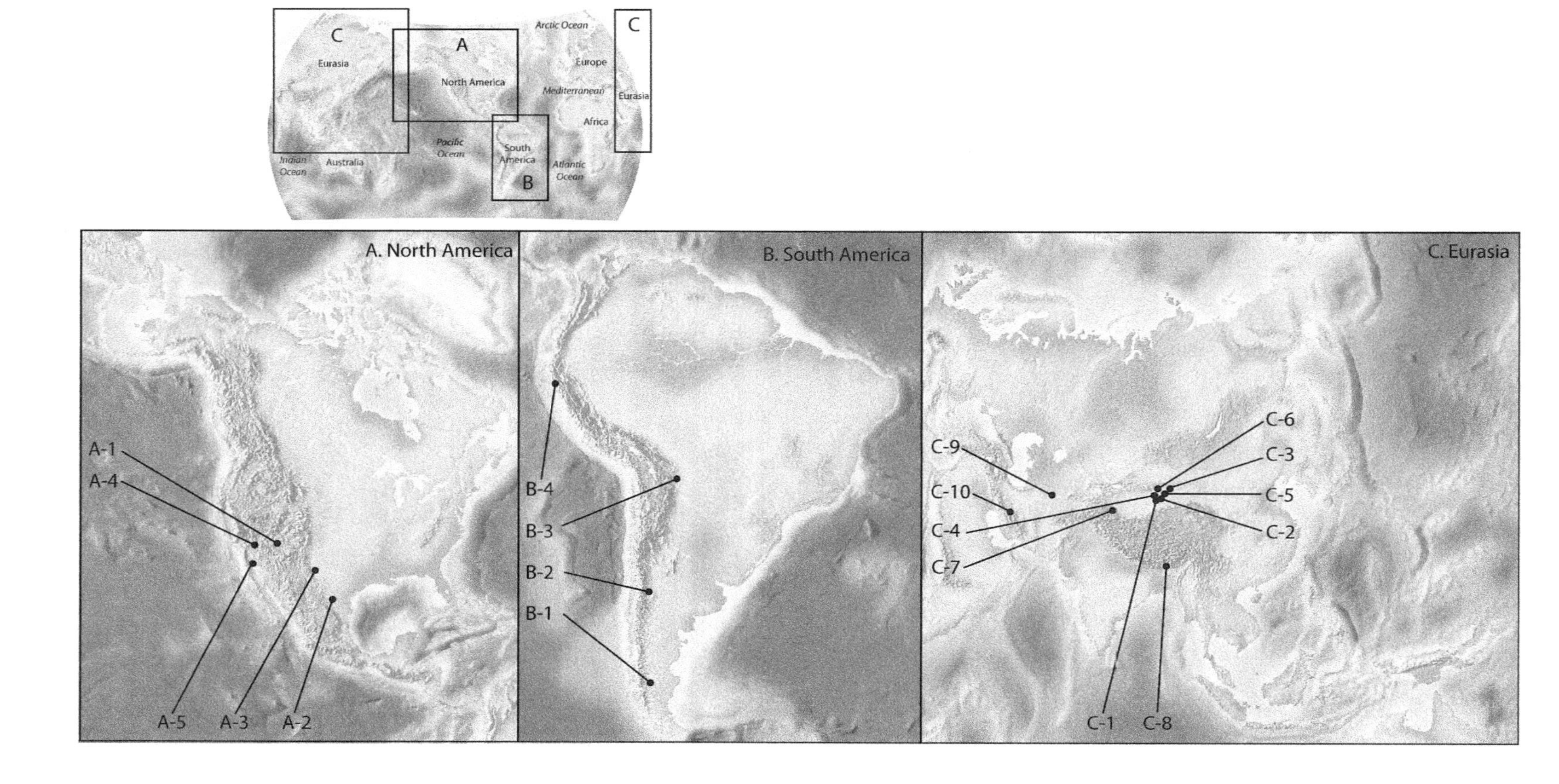

C
A
C
Arctic Ocean
Eurasia
North America
Europe
Mediterranean
Eurasia
Africa
Pacific Ocean
South America
Indian Ocean
Australia
Atlantic Ocean
B
A. North America
A-1
A-4
A-5
A-3
A-2
B. South America
B-4
B-3
B-2
B-1
C. Eurasia
C-9
C-10
C-4
C-7
C-6
C-3
C-5
C-2
C-1
C-8

Figure 3.6. Composite of three maps showing locations of archaeological sites with evidence of *Ephedra* referred to in this chapter: (*A*) North America, (*B*) South America, and (*C*) a large part of Eurasia. Key for site locations: A-1, Anasazi archaeological site of Shield Pueblo in southwestern Colorado (see Dunk 2006); A-2, Baker Cave, Val Verde County, in the lower Pecos region of southwestern Texas (see Sobolik 1988); A-3, Caldwell Cave in Culberson County, west Texas (see Sobolik and Gerick 1992); A-4, Bighorn Cave in the Black Mountains of western Arizona (see Reinhard et al. 1991, 2002); A-5, Kumeyaay village of Paʻmu in the Ramona Valley of San Diego County, California (see Cooley and Barrie 2004); B-1, Cerro Casa de Piedra, Cueva 7 site, province of Santa Cruz, Argentina (see Tosto et al. 2016); B-2, *Ephedra* species traditionally used for many thousands of years in the Argentine Monte region (see Ladio and Lozada 2009); B-3, Apillapampa in the Bolivian Andes (see Thomas 2008); B-4, Cajamarca, Peru (see Bussman et al. 2008); C-1, ancient burials with *Ephedra* discovered in Lop Nur desert of Xinjiang province (see Stein 1931); C-2, *Ephedra* associated with burial remains at Loulan City (see Jiang et al. 2007); C-3, *Ephedra* associated with burial remains in Yanghai Tombs (see Jiang et al. 2007); C-4, *Ephedra* remains found in the Xiaohe cemetery, dated circa 3980 to 3540 BP (Li et al. 2013); C-5, *Ephedra* remains found in the Gumugou cemetery, dated circa 3800 BP (see Wang 1993; Xie et al. 2013); C-6, *Ephedra* remains found at the Yuergou site, dated circa 2400–2300 BP (see Jiang et al. 2013); C-7, *Ephedra* remains found at Ladahk (Leh), Jammu and Kashmir, India (see Angmo et al. 2012); C-8, *E. gerardiana*, traditionally used in the Bhutan areas Lingshi, Bumthang, and Dagala (see Wangchuk et al. 2008); C-9, *Ephedra* remains found at Gonur Depe site complex, centered in the Kara Kum desert of Turkmenistan (see Sarianidi 1994); C-10, Zoroastrians of Yazd, Iran, use various *Ephedra* species for cult purposes (see Taillieu and Boyce 2003). (Maps by Scott Fitzpatrick and Mark Merlin.)

medicine. Wilken (2012: 82) referred to reports of at least some native peoples in California traditionally "gathering and grinding the seeds of *Ephedra* to make a pinole or mush" (e.g., see Bean and Saubel 1987; Roberts 1989; Hodgson 2001).

Whether *Ephedra* was being used only for food, for fuel, or for medicine and not for ritualistic or spiritual purposes remains to be determined, although as noted above, New World *Ephedra* species lack significant amounts of ephedrine, a stimulant used in the treatment of allergies and asthma; instead, natural ephedrine is more commonly found in Old World *Ephedra* species (e.g., see Ibragic and Sofić 2015). In any case, in addition to the widespread traditional medicinal use of *E. viridis*, most if not all of the other twelve or so *Ephedra* species known from various western regions of North America (Hollander and Vander Wall 2009) have long histories of traditional use among native peoples in the New World.

Although various peoples, including miners and other immigrants, brewed *Ephedra californica* S. Watson stems in more recent times to make a pleasant-tasting and medicinally effective wine-colored tea—which has been popular in all of the areas where it grows—Native Californians also have long considered it an effective remedy for kidney and urinary system disorders and sexually transmitted diseases, as well as useful for purifying the blood (Bean and Saubel 1987; Cortés Rodríguez 1988; Roberts 1989).

In the more arid regions of South America, Native American groups also had traditional and, in some cases, very ancient relationships with *Ephedra* species. For example, early Holocene evidence of *Ephedra* use was recently uncovered in the archaeobotanical study of coprolites discovered in Patagonia that are indicators of diet, cultural practices, and spatial use; according to Tosto and colleagues (2016: 204–9), the microscopic study of these coprolite samples revealed epidermal fragments of *Ephedra* species. These researchers argue that the identification of *Ephedra* allowed them to infer that plants of this species were used as medicine and fuel, if not as psychoactive agents as well:

> *Ephedra* sp. stem remains found in the coprolite dated to 11,025 cal BP could indicate the use of this taxon to cure a disease. Several species of this genus contain ephedrine, a phyto-composition characterized by its antitussive, cardiac stimulating, bronchodilating and vasopressing properties (Duke 1985). Furthermore, it has also been cited for the Patagonian region as a diuretic and as having properties against urinary tract disorders (Rapoport et al. 2003). Information by Harrington

(1968) reports that boiled *Ephedra ochreata* root was used to treat diarrhoea.

This evidence of very ancient associations of *Ephedra* and humans in southern South America is remarkable and should be considered along with the evidence of extensive ethnohistorical evidence of multiple traditional uses of *Ephedra* species in various parts of South America. For example, in the vastness of the Argentinean Monte, diverse aboriginal groups hunted and gathered for approximately 10,000 years before the arrival of Europeans (Bárcena 2001). In their study of resilience and ecological knowledge associated with human ecology, ethnobotany, and traditional practices in rural societies inhabiting the vast dry Argentinean Monte region, Ladio and Lozada (2009: 225) refer to the traditional uses of *Ephedra* species (e.g., *Ephedra ochreata* Miers and *Ephedra triandra* Tul. emend. J. H. Hunz) for "edible (fruit), fodder, medicinal (stems)" by such human groups as the Ranqueles, Techuelches, and Mapuches: "The ethnobotanical knowledge of greatest cultural and nutritional significance includes the use of many wild plants such as *Prosopis* spp., *Schinus* spp., *Ephedra* spp., *Condalia* and *Larrea* spp., among others. Since ancestral times, these xeric species have been utilized as edible, medicinal, tinctorial, fodder and fuel resources" (Ladio and Lozada 2009: 222; also see Steibel 1997; Jardín Botánico de la Patagonia Extra-Andina 2002; Rapoport et al. 2003). According to Ladio and Lozada (2009), among the wild plant materials traditionally used in this huge dry Monte region are the "solupe" fruit (*E. ochreata*).

Other South American regions where *Ephedra* species are known to have lengthy ethnobotanical relationships such as medicinal usage include the Bolivian Andes, where Thomas and colleagues (Thomas 2008) studied a community of Quechua subsistence farmers in the surroundings of Apillapampa, in the Bolivian Andes. They recorded the use of *Ephedra americana* Humb. & Bonpl. ex Willd. and *Ephedra rupestris* Benth. for a variety of purposes including social customs, medicine, fuel, and food for both humans and their animals. Macía and colleagues (2005: 348) studied commercialized marketing of *E. americana* and *E. rupestris* for medicinal use in La Paz and El Alto, Bolivia, noting that *Ephedra* plants "are well-known medicinal plants in South America or the Old World" and are still widely used by native "Kallawaya healers in Bolivia" (e.g., also see Bastien 1987; Vandebroek et al. 2004). These native therapists have had a long-lasting series of medicinal and spiritual influences over a vast range of South America: "The Kallawaya tradition is several hundred years old and interweaves the maintenance of health, the treatment of sickness, the fostering of spirituality, and the facilitation of social and environmental relationships" (Krippner and Glenney 1997: 212; also see Janni and Bastien 2004). The Kallawaya healers are seen by some not only as efficient doctors and physical therapists but also as shamanic ritual and psychological and ceremonial health providers in the Andean world; for example, Callahan (2011: 1) commented on their recognized historical and traditional expertise: "In November 2003, UNESCO named the 'Kallawaya Culture' of Bolivia, famed for the number and skill of its traditional healers, an 'Intangible Cultural Heritage of Humanity.' Overnight, Kallawaya medicine went from being viewed by many as a species of *brujeria* (witchery) without effect to a globally valued and scientifically legitimate cultural tradition."

Additional notable references to the traditional therapeutic use of *Ephedra* species in South America can be found in the work of Goleniowski and colleagues (2006: 325), who, over a twenty-six-year period, studied the traditional use of plants among the Comechingones, one of the few remaining folk cultures that persists in central Argentina. These researchers recorded *E. americana* as a "fairly abundant" species whose stems are used in traditional medicine as a diuretic; they pointed out that in spite of many clinical agents developed by the pharmaceutical industry, in their study area, "traditional indigenous phytotherapy is still practiced in many rural areas, using treatments handed down from generation to generation." Furthermore, Bussman and colleagues (2008: 358) listed *E. americana* as a native medicinal species sold in the market of Cajamarca, Peru, under the local name of "Diego Lopez."

My focus now returns to the Old World to review the ancient use of *Ephedra* species in Eurasia using historical and archaeological evidence to shed light on similar and different ancient traditional uses of *Ephedra* in this huge continental region.

Traditional and Early Use of *Ephedra* in Some Areas of Eurasia

The oral and written history in China provides special insight into the ancient relationships between *Ephedra* and humans in Central Asia and northern regions of East Asia. This type of evidence is supported by recent archaeological discoveries in western China. Many of the twelve to fourteen or more *Ephedra* species native to China appear to have been used medicinally for hundreds, even thousands, of years in the regions where they grow. The most ethnobotanically important of these species, *ma huang* (*E. sinica*), is a shrub, 30–50 centimeters in height, native to East Asia.

A well-known oral tradition in China, dating back to approximately 2800 BC, is associated with the legendary Chinese herbalist or shaman Shennong (or Shennung). This famous, fabled Chinese healer probably lived sometime between 3494 and 2857 BC (Chang 1962) and is traditionally credited with inventing agriculture and introducing many medicines into Chinese or East Asian culture. He has also been credited with compiling the oldest known medical text, which contained descriptions of hundreds of medicines from natural sources, including *ma huang*. This legendary collection of traditional Chinese herbal treatments by Shennong was eventually written down. Flaws (1998) tells us that the first written record of *ma huang* use in Chinese literature can be found in the ancient text entitled *Shennong Bencao Jing* (Divine Farmer's Materia Medica), which dates back to the first century AD (approximately at the end of the Han dynasty). This early scholarly treatise is supposedly based on the medicinal tradition of Shennong; it is a compilation of the greater part of all the knowledge about herbal medicine before the rise of the Han dynasty and describes the uses of 365 ancient medicinal plants, including *ma huang*.

Shennong is said to have referred to the medicinal use of the dried stems of *ma huang* to cure multiple ailments such as the common cold, coughs, asthma, headaches, and hay fever. That *ma huang* has long been used to treat bronchial asthma and hay fever, as well as both a spinal anesthesia and an analeptic agent, in East Asia is well-known (Chen 1974). According to Lee (2011: 78), more recently, in the sixteenth century AD, Li Shih-Chen described *ma huang* (*E. sinica*) as "a circulatory stimulant, a diaphoretic and an antipyretic," which was considered to be effective in the treatment of cough; and as a result, historically, the stem of this *Ephedra* species "became an important ingredient of many antitussive preparations."

In the early part of the twentieth century, Sir Aurel Stein discovered burials in the Lop Nur desert (Tarim basin), where the extreme dryness of the climate preserved some organic items as well as the remains of the deceased. Among these objects were fibrous sacks containing twigs of an *Ephedra* species (Stein 1931). However, Stein did not draw any definitive conclusions on the significance of this discovery, even though the presence of *Ephedra* "at the burial site could indicate that it was used for its cultic and religious qualities or as an embalming plant" (Abdullaev 2010:

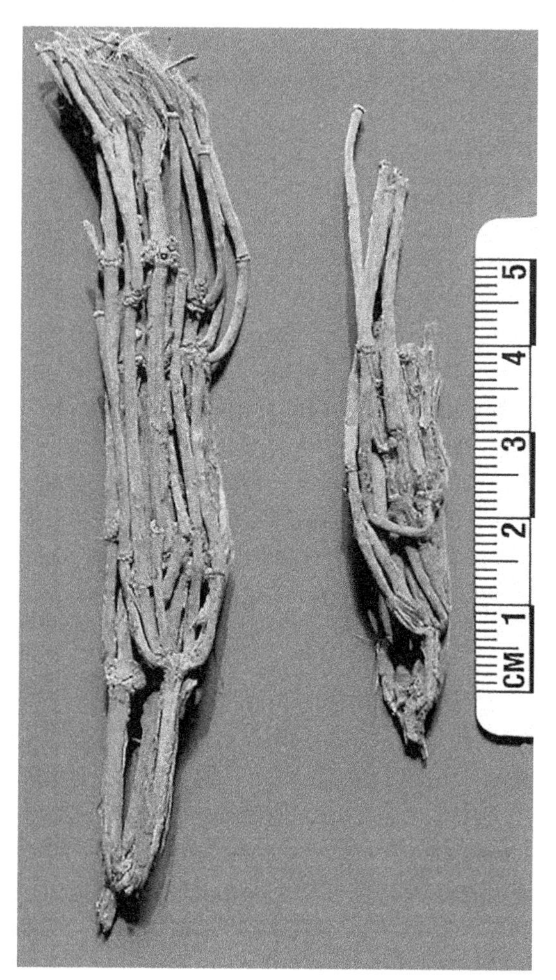

Figure 3.7. Ancient *Ephedra* twigs from the ancient cemetery at Gumugou, located in the Lop Nur region of northwestern China, dated circa 3800 BP (see Xie et al. 2013; Wang 1993). (Photograph courtesy of Hongen Jiang, Department of Archaeology and Anthropology, University of Chinese Academy of Sciences, Beijing.)

330). Recent archaeobotanical research indicates that these and other uses of *E. sinica* (or other species of *Ephedra*) may well have had ancient significance, especially early on in the arid native regions of western and northwestern China, such as in Xinjiang province, as well as in nearby regions beyond China in Central Asia.

Archaeological evidence of human presence and activity in Xinjiang traces back many thousands of years (Jiang et al. 2013); for example, stone artifacts have been recovered from the ancient site of Astana, Xinjiang, that date back about five thousand years (Wang 1993). For many centuries, if not millennia, Xinjiang served as an important area of passage linking the cultures of eastern and western Eurasia. Eventually it became well-known as the ancient "Silk Road" connecting Europe via Central Asia all the way to China. As a result, archaeological and archaeobotanical

Figure 3.8. Ancient *Ephedra* twig from the Yuergou site in Xinjiang province, dated circa 2300 BP (see Jiang et al. 2013). (Photograph courtesy of Hongen Jiang, Department of Archaeology and Anthropology, University of Chinese Academy of Sciences, Beijing.)

discoveries of ancient *Ephedra* associated with funeral ceremonies in Xinjiang, such as at Loulan City in the Lop Nor area and in the Yanghai Tombs in the Turpan basin dated circa 2800 BP (Jiang et al. 2007), are studied today with significant interest (Xia 1997; see also Li et al. 2013).

Over the past forty years or so, many cemeteries have been discovered in Xinjiang, in some cases with large numbers of tombs. In addition to the prehistoric graveyard in Lop Nur where Stein found ancient *Ephedra* remains, other early burial grounds relevant for this study include the Xiaohe cemetery, dated circa 3980–3540 BP (Li et al. 2013), the Gumugou cemetery (figure 3.7), dated circa 3800 BP (Wang 1993), and the Yuergou site (figure 3.8), dated circa 2400–2300 BP (Jiang et al. 2013). These archaeological sites, as well as many much-younger sites, provide great insight into the lives and beliefs of people living in ancient Xinjiang.

The mound-shaped cemetery at the extensive Central Asian oasis of Xiaohe forms a distinct landmark on the flat desert. This archaeological site is located near the downstream branch of the Kongque River in the Lop Nor desert about 175 kilometers east of the ancient Loulan City in Xinjiang. It was initially exposed in 1911 and was excavated to some degree at that time but was then forgotten until the past decade or so (Bergman 1939; Li et al. 2013). Approximately 170 tombs have now been excavated, although many of these were devastated by "treasure hunters." Palynological and other archaeobotanical evidence from the archaeological site of the Xiaohe cemetery dating back to circa 4000–3500 BP indicates that *Ephedra* was among the dominant native plants in the area and probably had relatively important uses, including ritualistic and spiritual significance. According to Li and colleagues (2013),

> *Ephedra* was considered as a magic plant by the Lop people. Also, it is very common to find *Ephedra* branches in most of the graves of the ancient Lop people in the Lop Nur area, such as LF, LS and LD graveyards, Cemetery 36, Gumugou cemetery, and graveyards around the ancient Loulan City [see Hedin and Bergman 1944; Wang 1983; Xia 1997]. Some Chinese archaeologists suggest that this phenomenon is a kind of plant worship and call it *Ephedra* worship [see Wang 1983; Xia 1997]. The medical use of *Ephedra* has been known for several thousand years in China. As a central nervous excitant, *Ephedra* was also used in ceremonies to produce feelings of exhilaration by various religious groups including Hindus [see Lee 2011; Xie et al. 2013]. As an ingredient of *Haoma* or *Soma*, *Ephedra* has been used for millennia in both Iran and India as a beverage to achieve longevity and immortality. (See also Mahdihassan 1987a, 1987b, 1987c, 1989, 1990; Eduljee 2014)

At the Gumugou archaeological site and ancient community graveyard, also located in the Lop Nor region of northwestern China, remarkable ancient macrofossil archaeobotanical evidence of *Ephedra*, in the form of twigs and dated to circa 3800 BP, has recently been recovered. This evidence is supported by the study of twig macro-remains that were examined by scanning electron microscope and gas chromatography–mass spectrometry for residual traits of biomarkers comparable to modern samples of *Ephedra*. Morphological similarities and the results of the chemical analysis, which identified *Ephedra*-type compounds such as benzaldehyde, tetramethyl-pyrazine, and phenmetrazine, in the chromatographs of both the ancient and the modern samples, confirm the identity of the ancient twigs as belonging to the genus *Ephedra*. Even though there is no direct archaeological evidence of exact use, the unified burial deposit in which the many *Ephedra* twigs were found strongly suggests that the human inhabitants of Gumugou were aware of the religious and medicinal potential of this plant. This interpretation is supported by the ancient traditions of people living in dry temperate regions of the

Northern Hemisphere, such as in Central Asia, where a series of native shrub species of *Ephedra* occur (e.g., see Abdullaev 2010). This customary association with *Ephedra* species is "a cumulative application history reaching back well over 2,000 years for the treatment of asthma, cold, fever, as well as many respiratory system diseases, especially in China," and is further supported by "ethnological and philological evidence of *Ephedra* worship and utilization in many Eurasia Steppe cultures" (Xie et al. 2013: 663; also see Wang 1983).

In another ancient Xinjiang archaeological site, Yuergou in the Turpan basin, three species of cultivated cereal grasses and two twigs of *Ephedra* dated to circa 2400–2300 BP were recently recovered as micro- and macrofossils among the twenty-one taxa of plant species discovered at the Yuergou site; these archaeobotanical remains were also found in association with ancient human burials (Jiang et al. 2013). Although the archaeobotanists and paleoanthropologists who excavated at the site have suggested that *Ephedra* may have been used here more than two thousand years ago as a "medicine," it could also have been utilized for ritualistic psychoactive purposes.

As noted above, plants in the genus *Ephedra* are believed to have been used by humans for thousands of years in China for medicinal or ritualistic purposes. In some areas of Eurasia, the dry twigs or stems (haulms) of *Ephedra* species are traditionally harvested in the fall and dried; these twigs, as well as the whole plant, are used to prepare traditional medicines and are commonly known in China as *ma huang*. Officially listed in the Chinese Pharmacopoeia, *ma huang*, as indicated previously, is among the oldest and most widely known traditional Chinese herbal medicines and has been used for many therapeutic purposes, including as an analeptic, an antiasthmatic, an antiallergenic, a diaphoretic, an antipyretic, and a diuretic (Chen 1974; Tang and Eisenbrand 1992). Although the *Ephedra* species most associated with this ancient healing relationship is *E. sinica*, other species, especially *E. intermedia* Schrenk & C. A. Mey and *E. equisetina* Burge (syn. *E. shennungiana* T. H. Tang), are also rather closely connected with *ma huang*. All three of these *Ephedra* species are found in the northern and western parts of China:

> *Mahuang* is a crude drug that has been utilized for perspiratory, antitussive, antipyretic and anti-inflammatory purposes in traditional Chinese medicine for centuries. The herbal origin of *Mahuang* is confined to the aerial part of *Ephedra sinica, E. intermedia* and *E. equisetina* in the Pharmacopoeia of China. The habitat of these 3 species is mainly

the northern and northwestern parts of China, such as Inner Mongolia, Gansu and Qinghai Provinces. Although other *Ephedra* species such as *E. gerardiana, E. likiangensis, E. przewalskii, E. minuta,* are also used as *Mahuang,* their reputation is not as good as the *Ephedra* species listed in the Pharmacopoeia of China, and their ephedrine content is reportedly lower. It is therefore inappropriate to use these species because their therapy effect has not been confirmed scientifically. (Long et al. 2004: 1080)

Although *E. sinica,* the most famous and commercially valuable of the *Ephedra* species, has been used predominantly in East Asia through the ages as a source of effective medication, the suggestion has been made that *E. sinica* and other species of *Ephedra* may also have been utilized in a variety of areas in Eurasia as mind-altering stimulating substances that have allowed people to transcend normal consciousness, often to facilitate cognitive communication with their ancestors or deities (e.g., see Mahdihassan 1978, 1981, 1982, 1983a, 1983b, 1987a, 1987b, 1987c, 1990; Mahdihassan and Mehdi 1989; Merlin 2003; Abdullaev 2010; Lee 2011; Dannaway 2010; Eduljee 2014; also see Zhang et al. 1989). This spiritual aspect of *Ephedra* use, in at least some areas of Eurasia, may be explained by the presence of the potent ephedrine alkaloids in some Old World *Ephedra* species.

When we look more closely at their natural distribution and customary usage, in both the Old and the New World during the present and the past, *Ephedra* species are indeed among the most widely used traditional medicinal plants in the ecosystems in which they are found. Although the alkaloid production of each *Ephedra* species differs, *Ephedra* plants generally have long served as a stimulant and therapeutic medicine for people, producing many tonic benefits because of their ability to serve as bronchodilator and decongestant in addition to other significant effects on the central nervous system. However, in some regions of Eurasia, when combined with other substances in the past, as perhaps in the case of haoma or even soma, *Ephedra* can have potent psychoactive as well as physiological effects: "Various religious groups, including Hindus and Parsees, used [*Ephedra* spp.] in their ceremonies to produce feelings of exhilaration. [*Ephedra*] acts as a central nervous excitant as a result of the rapid passage of ephedrine through the blood-brain barrier. This stimulates neurons in the limbic system, which also control part of the hypothalamus (supporting a variety of functions, including emotion)" (Lee 2011: 78).

ANCIENT *EPHEDRA* IN SOUTHERN CENTRAL ASIA AND THE INDIAN SUBCONTINENT

Throughout its wide biogeographical distribution, *Ephedra* species have been used by native cultures for a variety of medicinal purposes, which are discussed in some detail below. However, the ancient use of *Ephedra* species in important religious contexts has also been attributed to its psychoactive stimulant potential, especially in reference to its putative connection to the ancient soma plant/drug of the Indo-Iranian religion (e.g., see Stein 1931; Nyberg 1995). According to the ancient religious argument suggested by Mahdihassan and Mehdi (1989: 1),

> *Ephedra* juice is used as the drink of longevity given even to the new born. This is an Aryan custom mentioned in Rigveda and followed even by the Romans. To trace the history of this custom would lead to identifying Soma = *Ephedra*. The original species of *Ephedra* or Soma proper would be *Ephedra sinica*, the Chinese plant. It is the one species with yellow stalks. This has been illustrated so that it confirms the Rigveda speaking of Soma as "golden yellow." The name *Soma* is also a loan word from Chinese [*ma huang*] meaning "fire-yellow fibers of hemp."

Perhaps the most common scholarly associations that *Ephedra* has in East and South Asia are with its putative cultural connection to the famous psychoactive soma (plant/drink/god), as referred to above. However, along with ongoing debates regarding the alleged identification with such an important historic ethnobotanical relationship, *Ephedra* species occurring in the arid regions of southern Eurasia presumably have had long-standing customary use for therapeutic and other purposes. One early published example of direct observation comes from James E. T. Aitchison (1835–98), a medical doctor who collected plants for many years in northern India, Pakistan, and Afghanistan during the latter part of the nineteenth century. Aitchison (1888) reported in his treatise *The Botany of the Afghan Delimitation Commission* that *E. pachyclada* Boiss. (or another closely related *Ephedra* species) was a very common plant along his travels from "northern Baluchistan, through the Hari-rud valley, the Dadghis district, and Persia," where this plant was called "*hum, huma, yehma*" and was used in "tanning the skins of goats and water-bottles, and their ashes, when burnt, mixed with, or employed in lieu of snuff" (Aitchison 1888: 111–12).

Medicinally, *Ephedra* species are used to varying degrees by native cultures for an assortment of medicinal purposes in some but not all regions of their native biogeographic distribution within China as well as far beyond in other parts of Eurasia. These therapeutic applications include use as a cough medicine, an antipyretic, an antisyphilitic, a stimulant for poor circulation, and an antihistamine; the medicinal efficacy of these Old World *Ephedra* species for such uses is generally based on the presence of tannins and alkaloids, particularly ephedrine (e.g., Stevenson 1993).

In India, nine species of *Ephedra* distributed in the hot desert area of Arawali as well the cold deserts of western Himalaya have been identified. According to Sharma and colleagues (2010: 730), these include "*E. foliata* Boiss, *E. gerardiana* Wall. ex Stapf, *E. intermedia* Schr. & Meyer, *E. nebrodensis* Tineo, *E. pachyclada* Boiss, *E. saxatilis* (Stapf) Royle ex Florin, *E. regeliana* Florin, *E. przewalskii* Stapf, and *E. sumlingensis* Sharma & Uniyal."

Although Chopra (1982: 145) pointed out that the rhizomes of *E. gerardiana* produce large knobs "the size of footballs and are used as fuel by the Tibetans," he indicated that *Ephedra* was not used traditionally as a form of indigenous medicine throughout almost all of India even when species of this genus occurred within the local area (figure 3.9). Chopra (1982: 145–46) referred to *E. major* (syn. *E. nebrodensis*) as "the richest source of ephedrine" among the Indian species of *Ephedra* and stated that the nineteenth-century botanical collector Aitchison reported the medicinal use of *E. vulgaris* in "Lahoul" but went on to tell us that "the drug [*Ephedra*] is not mentioned in the Ayurvedic (Hindu) or Tibbi (Mohammedan) medicine." Chopra (1982: 145) did refer to the belief that "one variety of *Ephedra*, probably *E. intermedia*, is the famous 'soma' plant from which the favourite drink of the Rishis (ascetics) of the vedic period was prepared," but he contended that "there is little evidence to support this statement." The putative mystic associations of *Ephedra* species with the famous soma of the Indians and haoma of the Iranians are discussed in more detail below (also see Shah 2015).

South of the Xinjiang province of China lies Ladakh, one of the most sparsely populated regions of India (in the state of Jammu and Kashmir), between the Kunlun Mountain range in the north and the main Great Himalayas to the south; Ladakh, like some other areas of Eurasia, is inhabited by people of Indo-Aryan and Tibetan descent. In this Ladakh area, Angmo and colleagues (2012: 623) reported that a species of *Ephedra* along with other plants "are ground crushed and boiled together in a big pot of water to make medicinal water" and that in Ladakh this

Figure 3.9. Herbarium specimen of *Ephedra gerardiana* Wall. ex Stapf, a species that produces large woody knobs that are used as fuel by Tibetans. *E. gerardiana* occurs in various areas of the Himalayan Mountains from Bhutan to Afghanistan and is adapted to subalpine, arid uplands and high mountain deserts; indeed, *E. gerardiana* is the gymnosperm species that grows at the highest elevation in the world. During the winter, in its high mountain habitat, *E. gerardiana* plants reportedly serve as a significant source of sustenance for yaks and goats, which are apparently attracted to these plants because of their stimulating effects. In addition, during cremation ceremonies in Nepal, dried bundles of *E. gerardiana* are reportedly burned as incense, which produces a pleasant and spicy smoke that can be compared to the aroma of a forest fire (the specimen shown here is no. 1151217 in the Chinese National Herbarium [PE], Beijing; it was collected in 1978 at an elevation of 4,750 m). (Photograph by Mark Merlin.)

"medicinal hydrotherapy" is used to treat "people suffering from paralysis, rheumatoid arthritis, acid peptic disease or movement disorders" (for similar medicinal preparations associated with *Ephedra* spp., see Eduljee 2014). Angmo and colleagues (2012: 628) also reported that the "medicinal properties" of *E. gerardiana* (a low-growing *Ephedra* species) are used in Ladakh to treat "asthma, rheumatism and heart stimulant."

Manandhar (1980) referred to the use of a medicinal tea or incense in Nepal that included *E. gerardiana* and was recommended for treating colds, coughs, bronchitis, asthma, and other bronchial troubles, as well as arthritis and hay fever; according to Manandhar, in Tibetan medicine, a stimulating preparation including *E. gerardiana* also has been utilized for rejuvenation. According to Rätsch (1998: 226–27), *E. gerardiana* occurs in various areas of the Himalayan Mountains from Bhutan to Afghanistan and is adapted to subalpine, arid uplands and high mountain deserts. Rätsch tells that during the winter in these high mountain regions, the *E. gerardiana* plants serve as a significant source of sustenance for yaks and goats, which also delight in the stimulating effects of these plants. In addition, according to Rätsch, during cremation ceremonies in Nepal, dried bundles of *E. gerardiana* are burned as incense, which produces a pleasant and spicy smoke that can be compared to the aroma of a forest fire. Interestingly, Rätsch indicated that the remaining incense ashes may be used as a snuff, but only powerful shamans and high lamas consume parts of *E. gerardiana*, a plant that is treated with much respect and reverence.

In the Bhutan areas of Lingshi, Bumthang, and Dagala, Wangchuk and colleagues (2008: 54–57) carried out a field study of about 125 high-altitude plants, which they identified as being used "for day to day formulations in Bhutanese traditional medicine known as *gSo-ba-rig-pa*." These researchers listed *E. gerardiana* ("*Mtshe-idum*" in Bhutanese) as a plant whose aerial parts are "used for wounds, injury, fever, liver inflammation, stopping bleeding and as a rejuvenator." Given these reports concerning the variety and extent of human use of *Ephedra* species present in the remote Himalayan uplands, it seems obvious that more ethnobotanical research needs to be undertaken in these relatively remote mountainous, arid areas to determine more fully the past and present traditional uses of these plants.

Ephedra as the Putative Source of Soma and Haoma

The early use of *Ephedra* species in important religious contexts continues to be debated because of their psychoactive potential, especially in reference to their putative connection to the ancient soma/haoma plant/drug of Indo-Iranian religions (e.g., see Stevenson 1842; Stein 1931; Wasson 1968; Mahdihassan 1978, 1982, 1983a, 1983b, 1987a, 1987b, 1987c, 1990; Mahdihassan and Medhi 1989; Nyberg 1995; Abdullaev 2010; Dannaway 2010; Shah 2015). Although the focus here is on the evidence supporting one or more species of *Ephedra* as the ancient or original source, or later as a substitute for the religiously significant soma and haoma brews formerly used over a wide region of Eurasia, the true identity of the original, sacred, mind-altering species has remained a mystery for at least two centuries.

Bowman (1970: 12) has argued that "most modern scholars assume that *Ephedra* was the ancient haoma plant" (also see Merlin 2013). However, during the nineteenth and twentieth centuries, a large number of other taxa, both plants and fungi, have been "identified" as the soma and haoma plants. Some of the other contenders for the source of the active ingredient in the ancient ritualistic soma and haoma beverages include a species of wild rhubarb in the genus *Rheum* L. (e.g., Stein 1931; Hummel 1959), the fungus *Amanita muscaria* (L.) Lam. (e.g., Wasson 1968; Shah 2015), *Perganum harmala* L. (e.g., Flattery and Schwartz 1989), and a species of *Cannabis* L. (e.g., Mukerjee 1922; Merlin 1972, 2003; Bennett 2010; Clarke and Merlin 2013).

Whatever species or combination of species was used to produce the famous soma/haoma beverage (including perhaps *Ephedra*), this sacred drink has been closely identified with the ancient Indo-Iranians, people whose homeland was apparently located somewhere in Central Asia. According to most archaeological interpretations, these ancient people divided into two separate groups approximately four thousand years ago. One group became the ancient Iranian peoples, and the other developed into the Indo-Aryans who migrated south into what is now Afghanistan and the Indus Valley and eventually influenced much of South Asia (e.g., see Eduljee 2014; Shah 2015). These two groups of people preserved extensive, religious oral traditions that were subsequently rendered in written form as the Avesta of the Iranians and the Rig Veda of the Indians. Central rituals in both of these ancient cultural traditions involved consumption of a sacred psychoactive plant or fungus. This mind-altering species (or mixture of species) became known as haoma among the Iranians and soma among the Indians (for relevant discussions of Indo-Iranian linguistic and archaeological origins, see Bryant 2001; Witzel 2005; Lubotsky 2001).

Similar rituals are performed by some of the descendants of these people, who now use substitutes for soma or haoma that are not mind altering or different species within the same genus. For example, Bowman (1970: 12) points out that "in India the Brahmans now use the stalks of the *Pitica* [or *Putika*] plant [*Sarcostemma brevistigma* W. & A., Asclepiadaceae] to produce their *soma* and the Parsis in India, who believe that they are importing the original plant from Persia, now use the *Ephedra gerardiana* [Ephedraceae], which is found in Baluchistan, Afghanistan, Kashmir, and western Tibet." Bowman argues that "this plant" is very similar to the Avestan description of the ancient haoma plant; when it is in bloom, "the bush appears golden and it often bears the name zairi-gaona, 'golden color,'" and the pressed juice from its twigs "has a golden color, and it has an intoxicating and narcotic effect on the drinker." Bowman (1970: 14) further suggests, "People have been reluctant to surrender the precious substance which has long been believed to promote health and promise immortality."

Mahdihassan, a strong and persistent advocate for recognizing *Ephedra* as a source of soma/haoma, referred to *E. gerardiana* as very likely having been used in India since the Vedic period as a substitute for soma:

> There came a time when the Aryans were no longer able to find the original psychoactive plant known as soma, perhaps because the identity of that plant was kept so secret or perhaps because it had been lost, and so it was that many people took to preparing the sacred soma beverage with substitute plants, one of which was *E. gerardiana*. This is how the plant received the name *somalata*, "plant of the moon." The effects of *E. gerardiana* are more stimulating than visionary, however, suggesting that this plant is likely not the original soma of the Vedas. (Mahdihassan 1963: 370–71)

Mahdihassan (1990: 207) also referred to what he considered to be the importance of etymology "which guides us to the original species of soma," which comes from Boyce (1975), a scholar of the Avesta and therefore also a very competent student of Sanskrit: "She [Boyce] transliterates *soma* as *Sauma* which as sound comes close enough to *Haoma*. The original Chinese term appears to be *Hau-Ma, Ma* = Hemp [fiber] and *Hau* = Fire coloured or yellow, with [a] trace of [a] brown tinge. The stems of *Ephedra* are thus described [as] long and thin like fibres of hemp and also approaching the latter in colour. Thus that plant has been named in Chinese according to its main appearance discussed in [Mahdihassan's 1978 paper]."

After many decades of debate about the identity of the psychoactive substance in the soma/haoma drink, R. Gordon Wasson's (1968) publication of *Soma: Divine Mushroom of Immortality* contended persuasively for many readers that the fly-agaric mushroom, *Amanita muscaria* (L.) Lam., is the species in question. Wasson's argument is based mainly on ancient Indian sources. Many scholars accepted his thesis at the time. However, a couple of decades later, Flattery and Schwartz (1989) argued strongly for a perennial dicot species, Syrian rue or harmal rue (*Peganum harmala* L., Zygophyllaceae), which was originally identified as the source of soma by Sir William Jones in 1794. Flattery and Schwartz relied primarily upon Iranian evidence to support their assertion that soma should be identified with *P. harmala* because this species, with its psychoactive harmala alkaloidal content, is still well-known for its mind-altering effects in the homeland of the Indo-Iranians. Evidence that humans used *P. harmala* in the fifth millennium BC has been recovered from the Caucasus region (Lisitsyna and Prishcepenko 1977); according to Naomi Miller (pers. comm., 2003), *P. harmala* "becomes more common in the third millennium [BC] archaeobotanical samples in the Near East, and is therefore likely to be associated with overgrazing." However, Miller indicated that it may have been used for religious purposes or, as it is employed today in some areas of this region, simply to ward off evil spirits or as a "good luck charm."

As noted above, however, numerous scholars in modern times have identified *Ephedra* as the source of soma/haoma, including, for example, Mahdihassan (1963, 1978, 1981, 1982, 1983a, 1983b, 1984, 1987a, 1987b, 1987c, 1989, 1990; Mahdihassan and Mehdi 1989). More recently, remarkable archaeological evidence recovered from Russian excavations at Gonur Depe suggested once again that perhaps *Ephedra* was the source (or part) of the soma drug. The Gonur Depe site complex, centered in the Kara Kum desert of Turkmenistan, has been interpreted as the approximately four-thousand-year-old "Zoroastrian capital," known in ancient times as Margiana. These Central Asian archaeological remains, formerly recognized as part of the ancient Oxus civilization but now referred to as the Bactria-Margiana Archaeological Complex (BMAC), is part of the previously unknown Bronze Age civilization in Bactria (northern Afghanistan) and Margiana (Turkmenistan), which had two distinct cultural periods, the first approximately 1900–1700 BC and the second from 1700 to 1500 BC (Parpola 1994; these dates have been challenged by further archaeological dating, but the new dates are nevertheless very old [ca. 2300–1700 BC?], especially in terms of the microfossil and macrofossil evidence for *Ephedra* in the ancient BMAC complex [e.g., see Houben 2003]).

At Gonur Depe, archaeologists found monumental sites originally dated to the first half of the second millennium BC (Sarianidi 1994). The Gonur South area of this site comprises a fortified compound of buildings. One large structure, interpreted as being associated with holy fire, was situated within this compound and had two parts; one appears to have been used for public worship, while the other appears to have consisted of private rooms reserved for the priests (also see Rudgley 1998). Analysis of the contents in ceramic bowls found in at least one of these private rooms by Meier-Melikyan (1990) revealed traces of both *Cannabis* and *Ephedra*. The suggestion has been made that these psychoactive substances had been combined in the making of psychoactive drinks. Bennett (2010) published a very lengthy discussion and thought-provoking argument suggesting *Cannabis* as the true source of soma and haoma, which is also discussed by Clarke and Merlin (2013) in a comprehensive study of the evolution and ethnobotany of *Cannabis*.

Vessels found in a shrine at a third settlement of the BMAC, Togolok 21 (late second millennium BC), contained remains of mind-altering *Ephedra* and the opium poppy (*P. somniferum*); moreover, an engraved bone tube containing "poppy pollen" was also recovered from this same shrine (Sarianidi 1994; also see Sarianidi 1998, 2003). According to some, these ritual vessels, dated to circa 2000–1000 BC, "show that *soma* in its Iranian form *haoma* may be considered as a composite psychoactive substance comprising of [*sic*] *Ephedra* and *Cannabis* in one instance and *Ephedra* and opium (*Papaver somniferum* L.) in another" (Rudgley 1998; for additional perspectives see Parpola 1994; McGovern 2008).

According to Miller (pers. comm., 2003), photographs of the *Ephedra*, *Cannabis*, *Papaver*, and archaeological specimens presented in the Togolok 21 report by Meier-Melikyan (1990) appear to be consistent with the respective species; however, the determination of the *Papaver* species needs further study to confirm that it is *P. somniferum*. Indeed, Miller suggested that the poppy seeds could have come from field weeds or that poppy may have been used as a food plant rather than as an opiate source for medicine or ritual (also see Merlin 1984). In addition, Miller pointed out that in an arid climate, the woody parts of *Ephedra* could have been burned for fuel rather than having been used as medicine or in ritual; as noted earlier, Chopra (1982) referred to the use of large rhizomes of *E. gerardiana* for fuel among Tibetans.

In any case, the remarkable discoveries at the BMAC continue to focus on a psychoactive beverage, which theoretically can be identified as haoma or haoma-like drinks, the use of which in cult ceremonies and rituals appears to have been relatively common in ancient Central Asia. Pertinent associated evidence are the ancient microscopic twigs of *Ephedra* found in large vats in the Gonur Depe complex of the BMAC. Taillieu and Boyce (2003) have argued that the linguistic and ritualistic evidence weigh strongly in favor of a strong connection between these cult beverages and *Ephedra* and perhaps the opium poppy in ancient Central Asia, as well as having an important prehistoric association with ancient India and Iran:

> As for the plant yielding the extract in modern times, the Brahmans regularly used one of the Sarcostemmas (Asclepiads), which are evidently a substitute for ancient **sauma*, since they are plants of warm climates. From the late 19th century it has been known . . . that the Zoroastrians of Yazd use a variety of *Ephedra* which they call *huma, hum* and which they supply to their coreligionists in India, where *Ephedra*s do not grow. The plants flourish, however, in Inner Asia, the Indo-Iranian borderlands and Persia. Gradually it was discovered that in a number of living Iranian languages and dialects *Ephedra*s are known as *hōm* or some similar term, and that in the Indic languages of Gilgit and Kāferestān (Nurestān) they are called *som, soma*. Together linguistic and ritual evidence seemed decisive. (Taillieu and Boyce 2003; also see Taillieu 1998)

Dannaway (2010: 488) pointed out that *Ephedra* plants have religious, psychoactive, and/or medicinal traditional uses, varying from region to region; Dannaway cited Falk (1989), another Avestan scholar, for consideration of a particular *Ephedra* species: "The 'fragrant fuel' of the Avestan texts mentions various aromatics in combination with fragrant *hom* or *homa*, a name for the *Ephedra distachya*, yet another *haoma*/*soma* candidate." Dannaway (2010: 488–89) also referred to ongoing ritualistic *Ephedra* use: "The burning of magical and psychoactive plants continues with the heirs of these entheogenic traditions, as with the surviving Mandeans, and the Shia of Iran, who burn *Ephedra* and *Peganum harmala* for apotropaic purposes [i.e., to avoid evil influences or misfortune]. . . . The Indo-European complex of holy plants as means of communicating with the gods is found throughout Persian and Indian religious texts that group the plants together in prayers."

Mahdihassan (1987a: 105) describes *Ephedra* as an early source of an "anti-fatigue drink" that later "became a drink of immortality and longevity." As such, soma was used ritually as "the first drink of a newly born child," and this use "is mentioned in Rigveda," by which Mahdihassan (1987a: 106) clearly identifies the soma of the "Rigveda" (Rig Veda) with *Ephedra* species as well as describing its long and continuous use among Zoroastrians: "Now the Parsis of Bombay, as Orthodox Zoroastrians, have kept up this custom of administering a few drops of Haoma juice to the new born. Since Haoma, which is *Ephedra*, does not grow in the plains of India the Parsis of Bombay used to import *Ephedra* all the way from Persia where it grows profusely. No mother would tolerate using a substitute of genuine Haoma for that would not assure the longevity of her child."

Thus, Mahdihassan (1987a: 105) argues that *Ephedra* evolved culturally from its early use as an antifatigue beverage into "a panacea and drink of rejuvenation, finally of longevity, immortality and resurrection" (also see Eduljee 2014): "Gods were not born mortals. A drink of immortality made them immortal. This was given as the first drink of a newly born child. This use is mentioned in Rigveda: 3.48.2 and 3.32.9–10. Indra was such a drug made immortal god. West [1901] translates a Zoroastrian Holy scripture which also maintains pouring a few drops of *Ephedra* in the mouth of a new born. To expedite resurrection, it was also given to the dead. This custom has survived up-to-date so that to follow it is to realize Soma = Ephedra" (Mahdihassan 1987a: 109).

Shah (2015: 30) conjectured about the stimulating spiritual aspects of *Ephedra* use as a soma beverage in relationship to Buddhism and perhaps earlier religious traditions: "Like an amphetamine, *ephedra* increases both blood pressure and heart rate, decreases appetite, and makes the user feel energetic and enhances concentration[;] it is why it was used by the Buddhist monks. Possibly, the herb was used, in preparation of '*Soma* drink' as a general stimulant for alertness and energy and as an appetite suppressant, and to give concentration, at the times, when the Buddhist monks and preachers were required to travel far and long distances to promulgate Buddhism."

In sum, Mahdihassan's many articles, as well as other scholarly publications and extensive online discussions (e.g., Eduljee 2014), support traditional, long-lasting cultural associations in some areas of Eurasia with stimulating, ephedrine-rich plants belonging one or more species of *Ephedra*. However, further investigations involving experts from the disciplines of archaeology, archaeobotany, botany, ethnobotany, and pharmacology are needed to determine definitively the complex nature of the composition of the BMAC "cult beverage" and, more generally, the level of the plant knowledge of Central Asian priests involved with the relevant rituals and their putative botanical and alkaloidal sources of psychoactive inspiration.

Summary

Ephedra species have an ancient history of use in Eurasia and the Western Hemisphere, especially but not entirely in the arid areas of these extensive regions. More recently, archaeological and archaeobotanical evidence, along with deeper understanding of relevant written records, has provided us additional insight into the traditional utilization of this genus of unusual plants with very special alkaloids. *Ephedra* plants have long served as a stimulant and therapeutic medicine for people, producing many tonic benefits because of their ability to serve as a bronchodilator and a decongestant in addition to having other significant effects on the central nervous system. Furthermore, given the appropriate setting, *Ephedra* combined with other substances in the past, as perhaps in the case of haoma and/or soma, can have potent physiological and psychoactive effects. Some of the more challenging hypotheses relating to the ancient uses of *Ephedra* species in Eurasia have been described and analyzed in this chapter.

References Cited

Abdullaev, K. 2010. Sacred Plants and the Cultic Beverage Haoma. *Comparative Studies of South Asia, Africa and the Middle East* 30 (3): 329–40.

Adams, J. D., Jr., and C. Garcia. 2006. Women's Health among the Chumash. *Evidence-Based Complementary and Alternative Medicine* 3: 125–31.

Aitchison, J.E.T. 1888. *The Botany of the Afghan Delimitation Commission.* The Transactions of the Linnean Society of London: Second Series, Botany, vol. 3, pt. 1. London: Linnean Society of London.

Angmo, K., S. A. Bhupendra, and S. R. Gopal. 2012. Changing Aspects of Traditional Healthcare System in Western Ladakh, India. *Journal of Ethnopharmacology* 143: 621–30.

Bárcena, J. R. 2001. *Prehistoria del centro-oeste Argentino: La historia Argentina prehispánica.* Córdoba, Argentina: Brujas.

Bastien, J. W. 1987. *Healers of the Andes: Kallawaya Herbalists and Their Medicinal Plants.* Salt Lake City: University of Utah Press.

Bean, L. J., and K. S. Saubel. 1987. *Temalpakh: Cahuilla Indian Knowledge and Usage of Plants.* Morongo Indian Reservation, Calif.: Malki Museum Press.

Bennett, C. 2010. *Cannabis and the Soma Solution.* Walterville, Ore.: Trine Day.

Bensky, D., and A. Gamble. 1993. *Chinese Herbal Medicine: Materia Medica.* Seattle: Eastland Press.

Bergman, F. 1939. *Archaeological Researches in Sinkiang, Especially the Lop Nor Region.* Stockholm: Bokförlags Aktiebolaget Thule.

Blumenthal, M. 2003. *The ABC Clinical Guide to Herbs.* Austin, Tex.: American Botanical Council.

Blumenthal, M., and P. King. 1995. *Ma Huang*: Ancient Herb, Modern Medicine, Regulatory Dilemma. *HerbalGram* 34: 22–27, 42–43, 56–57.

Bowman, R. A. 1970. *Aramaic Ritual Texts from Persepolis.* Chicago Oriental Institute Publications, vol. 91. Chicago: University of Chicago Press.

Boyce, M. 1975. *A History of Zoroastrianism.* 2 vols. Leiden: Brill.

Bryant, E. F. 2001. *The Quest for the Origins of Vedic Culture: The Indo-Aryan Migration Debate.* New York: Oxford University Press.

Bussmann, R. W., D. Sharon, and J. Ly. 2008. From Garden to Market? The Cultivation of Native and Introduced Medicinal Plant Species in Cajamarca, Peru, and Implications for Habitat Conservation. *Ethnobotany Research and Applications* 6: 351–61.

Callahan, M. 2011. Signs of the Time: Kallawaya Medical Expertise and Social Reproduction in 21st Century Bolivia. PhD diss., University of Michigan, Ann Arbor.

Callaway, E. 2015. Teeth from China Reveal Early Human Trek Out of Africa. *Nature.* doi:10.1038/nature.2015.18566.

Callaway, E. 2017. Neanderthal Tooth Plaque Hints at Meals—and Kisses: Analysis Paints Picture of Diets, Medicine and Possible Intimacy with Humans. *Nature* 543, 163. doi:10.1038/543163a.

Caveney, S., D. A. Charlet, H. Freitag, M. Maier-Stolte, and A. N. Starratt. 2001. New Observations on the Secondary Chemistry of World *Ephedra* (Ephedraceae). *American Journal of Botany* 88 (7): 1199–1208.

Chang, C. 1962. *Chinese History of Fifty Centuries.* Vol. 1. Taipei: Institute for Advanced Chinese Studies.

Chen, K. K. 1974. Half a Century of *Ephedra*. *American Journal of Chinese Medicine* 2 (4): 359–65.

Chopra, R. N. 1982. *Ephedra gerardiana* Wall. (Gnetacae) and Allied Species. In *Indigenous Drugs of India: Their Medical and Economic Aspects,* 144–61. 2nd ed. Calcutta: Academic Press.

Clarke, R. C., and M. Merlin. 2013. *Cannabis: Evolution and Ethnobotany.* Berkeley: University of California Press.

Cooley, T. G., and L. J. Barrie. 2004. Archaeological Excavation at the Village of Pa'mu, Ramona Valley, California. *Proceedings of the Society for California Archaeology* 17: 43–46.

Cortés Rodríguez, E. 1988. *Estudio etnobotánico comparativo de los grupos indígenas Kumiai y Paipai del norte de Baja California.* Ensenada, Baja California: Universidad Autónoma de Baja California.

Dannaway, F. R. 2010. Strange Fires, Weird Smokes, and Psychoactive Combustibles: Entheogens and Incense Traditions. *Journal of Psychoactive Drugs* 42 (4): 485–97.

Duke, J. A. 1985. *Handbook of Medicinal Herbs.* Boca Raton, Fla.: CRC Press.

Dunk, C.L.W. 2006. An Archaeobotanical Investigation of Shields Pueblo's Pueblo II Period. MA thesis, Department of Archaeology, Simon Fraser University.

Eduljee, K. E. 2014. *Zoroastrian Heritage*. www.heritageinstitute.com/zoroastrianism/.
EFSA (European Food Safety Authority). 2013. Scientific Opinion on Safety Evaluation of *Ephedra* Species for Use in Food. *EFSA Journal* 11 (11): 3467.
Falk, H. 1989. Soma I and II. *Bulletin of the School of Oriental and African Studies* 52 (1): 77–90.
Flattery, D. S., and M. Schwartz. 1989. *Haoma and Harmaline: The Botanical Identity of the Indo-Iranian Sacred Hallucinogen "Soma" and Its Legacy in Religion, Language, and Middle-Eastern Folklore*. Berkeley: University of California Press.
Flaws, B., ed. 1998. *The Divine Farmer's Materia Medica: A Translation of the* Shen Nong Ben Cao Jing. Trans. Yang Shou-Zhong. Boulder, Colo.: Blue Poppy Press.
Freitag, H., and M. Maier-Stolte. 1989. The Ephedra-Species of P. Forsskal: Identity and Typification. *Taxon* 38: 545–56.
Freitag, H., and M. Maier-Stolte. 1993. Ephedraceae. In *Flora Europaea*, vol. 1, ed. T. G. Tutin, 49. 2nd ed. London: Cambridge University Press.
Freitag, H., and M. Maier-Stolte. 1994. Ephedraceae. In *Chorology of Trees and Shrubs in South-West Asia and Adjacent Regions*, ed. K. Browicz, 5–16, 39–52. Poznan, Poland: Bogucki Publishers.
Fu, L. K., Y. F. Yu, and H. Riedl. 1999. Ephedraceae. In *Flora of China*, vol. 4, *Cycadaceae through Fagaceae*, ed. C. Y. Wu and P. Raven, 97–101. Beijing: Science Press.
Goleniowski, M. E., G. A. Bongiovanni, L. Palacio, C. O. Nuñez, and J. J. Cantero. 2006. Medicinal Plants from the "Sierra de Comechingones," Argentina. *Journal of Ethnopharmacology* 107: 324–41.
Guerra-Doce, E. 2014. The Origins of Inebriation: Archaeological Evidence of the Consumption of Fermented Beverages and Drugs in Prehistoric Eurasia. *Journal of Archaeological Method and Theory* 22 (3): 751–82. doi:10.1007/s10816-014-9205-z.
Hardy, K., S. Buckley, M. J. Collins, A. Estalrrich, D. Brothwell, L. Copeland, A. García-Tabernero, et al. 2012. Neanderthal Medics? Evidence for Food, Cooking, and Medicinal Plants Entrapped in Dental Calculus. *Naturwissenschaften* 9(8): 617–26.
Hardy, K., S. Buckley, and M. Huffman. 2013. Neanderthal Self-Medication in Context. *Antiquity* 87 (337): 873–78. doi:10.1017/S0003598 × 00049528.
Harrington, T. 1968. *Toponimia del indio günuna Kúne*. Vol. 5. Buenos Aires: Academia Nacional de la Historia Investigaciones y Ensayos.
Hedin, S. A., and F. Bergman. 1944. *History of the Expedition in Asia, 1927–1935*. Gothenburg, Sweden: Elanders Boktryckeri Aktiebolag.
Hodgson, W. C. 2001. *Food Plants of the Sonoran Desert*. Tucson: University of Arizona Press.
Hollander, J. L., and S. B. Vander Wall. 2009. Dispersal Syndromes in North American *Ephedra*. *International Journal of Plant Sciences* 170 (3): 323–30.
Holloway, R. G. 1983. Diet and Medicinal Plant Usage of a Late Archaic Population from Culberson County, Texas. *Bulletin of the Texas Archaeological Society* 54: 319–29.
Houben, J.E.M. 2003. The Soma-Haoma Problem: Introductory Overview and Observations on the Discussion. *Electronic Journal for Vedic Studies (EJVS)*. www.ejvs.laurasianacademy.com/ejvs0901/ejvs0901a.txt.

Huang, J., and R. Price. 2003. Estimation of the Age of Extant *Ephedra* Using Chloroplast RBCL Sequence Data. *Molecular Biological Evolution* 20 (3): 435–40.
Huang, J., D. E. Giannasi, and R. A. Price. 2005. Phylogenetic Relationships in *Ephedra* (Ephedraceae) Inferred from Chloroplast and Nuclear DNA Sequences. *Molecular Phylogenetics and Evolution* 35: 48–59.
Hummel, K. 1959. Aus welcher Pflanzen stellen die arischen Inder den Somatrank her? *Mitteilungen der Deutschenpharmazeutischen Gesellschaft und der pharmazeutischen Gesellschaft der DDR* 4: 57–61.
Hunziker, J. H. 1949. Sinopsis de las species argentinas del genero *Ephedra. Lilloa* 17: 147–74.
Ibragic, S., and E. Sofić. 2015. Chemical Composition of Various *Ephedra* Species. *Bosnian Journal of Basic Medical Sciences* 15 (3): 21–27.
Ickert-Bond, S. M., C. Rydin, and S. S. Renner. 2009. A Fossil-Calibrated Relaxed Clock for *Ephedra* Indicates an Oligocene Age for the Divergence of Asian and New World Clades and Miocene Dispersal into South America. *Journal of Systematics and Evolution* 47 (5): 444–56.
Janni, K. D., and J. W. Bastien. 2004. Exotic Botanicals in the Kallawaya Pharmacopoeia. *Economic Botany* 58 (supp. 1): S274–79.
Jardín Botánico de la Patagonia Extra-Andina. 2002. *Usos tradicionales de las plantas en la meseta patagónica.* Puerto Madryn, Argentina: Centro Nacional Patagónico.
Jiang, H. E., X. Li, D. K. Ferguson, Y. F. Wang, and C. J. Liu. 2007. The Discovery of *Capparis spinosa* L. (Capparidaceae) in the Yanghai Tombs (2500 Years BP), NW China, and Its Medicinal Implications. *Journal of Ethnopharmacology* 113: 409–20.
Jiang, H. E., Y. Wu, H. H. Wang, D. K. Ferguson, and C. S. Li. 2013. Ancient Plant Use at the Site of Yuergou, Xinjiang, China: Implications from Desiccated and Charred Plant Remains. *Vegetation History and Archaeobotany* 22: 129–40.
Kakiuchi, N., M. Mikage, S. M. Ickert-Bond, M. Maier-Stolte, and H. Freitag. 2011. A Molecular Phylogenetic Study of the *Ephedra distachya/E. sinica* Complex in Eurasia. *Willdenowia* 41 (2): 203–15.
Kashikar, C. G. 1980. Antecedents of the Vedic Soma. *Hamdard-Medicus* 23 (1–2): 62.
Kiple, K. F., and K. C. Ornelas. 2000. *The Cambridge World History of Food.* Cambridge: Cambridge University Press.
Krippner, S., and E. S. Glenney. 1997. The Kallawaya Healers of the Andes. *Humanistic Psychologist* 25 (2): 212–29.
Kubitzki, K. 1990. Gnetatae. In *The Families and Genera of Vascular Plants*, vol. 1, *Pteridophytes and Gymnosperms*, ed. K. U. Kramer and P. S. Green, 378–91. Berlin: Springer-Verlag.
Ladio, A. H., and M. Lozada. 2009. Human Ecology, Ethnobotany and Traditional Practices in Rural Populations Inhabiting the Monte Region: Resilience and Ecological Knowledge. *Journal of Arid Environments* 73: 222–27.
Langley, M. C., C. Clarkson, and S. Ulm. 2008. Behavioural Complexity in Eurasian Neanderthal Populations: A Chronological Examination of the Archaeological Evidence. *Cambridge Archaeological Journal* 18: 289–307.

Lee, M. R. 2011. The History of *Ephedra* (*Ma-Huang*). *Journal of the Royal College of Physicians* 41: 78–84.
Leroi-Gourhan, A. 1975. The Flowers Found with Shanidar IV, a Neanderthal Burial in Iraq. *Science* 190 (4214): 562–64.
Li, J., I. Abuduresule, F. M. Hueber, W. Li, X. Hu, Y. Li, and C. Li. 2013. Buried in Sands: Environmental Analysis at the Archaeological Site of Xiaohe Cemetery, Xinjiang, China. *PLoS ONE* 8 (7): e68957. doi:10.1371/journal.pone.0068957.
Lietava, J. 1992. Medicinal Plants in a Middle Paleolithic Grave Shanidar IV? *Journal of Ethnopharmacology* 35 (3): 263–66.
Lisitsyna, G. N., and L. V. Prishcepenko. 1977. *Paleoethnobotanischeskie.* Nakhodki Kavkaza I Blizhnego Vostoka. Moscow: Nauka.
Long, D., N. Kakiuchi, A. Takahashi, K. Komatsu, S. Cai, and M. Mikage. 2004. Phylogenetic Analysis of the DNA Sequence of the Non-coding Region of Nuclear Ribosomal DNA and Chloroplast of *Ephedra* Plants in China. *Planta Medica* 70 (11): 1080–84.
Lubotsky, A. 2001. The Indo-Iranian Substratum. In *Early Contacts between Uralic and Indo-European: Linguistic and Archaeological Considerations*, ed. C. Carpelan, A. Parpola, and P. Koskikallio, 301–17. Helsinki: Suomalais-Ugrilainen Seura.
Macía, M. J., E. García, and P. J. Vidaurreb. 2005. An Ethnobotanical Survey of Medicinal Plants Commercialized in the Markets of La Paz and El Alto, Bolivia. *Journal of Ethnopharmacology* 97: 337–50.
Mahdihassan, S. 1963. Identifying *Ephedra* as Soma. *Pakistan Journal of Forestry* 13 (4): 370–72.
Mahdihassan, S. 1978. The Vedic Words *Soma* and *Sura* Traced to Chinese. *Hamdard-Medicus* 21 (7–12): 75–79.
Mahdihassan, S. 1981. Haoma of Irano Aryans, as the Medicinal Plant *Ephedra*. *Hamdard-Medicus* 24 (3–4): 3–28.
Mahdihassan, S. 1982. Evolution of *Ephedra* as the Soma of Rigveda. *Ancient Science of Life* 2 (2): 93–97.
Mahdihassan S. 1983a. Soma Juice as Administered to a Newly Born Child Being Mentioned in Rigveda. *American Journal of Chinese Medicine* 11 (1–4): 14–15.
Mahdihassan, S. 1983b. Identifying the Soma Plant as *Ephedra* from Rigveda and Avesta. *Hamdard-Medicus* 26 (3): 51–65.
Mahdihassan S. 1984. Soma as Energizer-cum-Euphoriant, versus Sura, an Intoxicant. *Ancient Science of Life* 3 (3): 161–68.
Mahdihassan, S. 1987a. *Ephedra*, the Oldest Medicinal Plant with the History of an Uninterrupted Use. *Ancient Science of Life* 7 (2): 105–9.
Mahdihassan, S. 1987b. Soma of the Aryans and Ash of the Romans. *Annals of the Bhandarkar Oriental Research Institute* 68 (1–4): 639–44.
Mahdihassan, S. 1987c. *The History and Natural History of* Ephedra *as Soma*. Islamabad: Pakistan Science Foundation.
Mahdihassan, S. 1989. The Seven Theories Identifying the Soma Plant. *Ancient Science of Life* 9 (2): 86–89.
Mahdihassan, S. 1990. A Brief Account of the Fractions of Soma. *Ancient Science of Life* 9 (4): 207–8.

Mahdihassan, S., and S. F. Mehdi. 1989. Soma and the Rigveda and an Attempt to Identify It. *American Journal of Chinese Medicine* 17 (1–2): 1–8.

Manandhar, N. P. 1980. *Medicinal Plants of Nepali Himalaya*. Katmandu, Nepal: Rama Pustak Bhandar.

McGovern, P. E. 2008. *Uncorking the Past: The Quest for Wine, Beer, and Other Alcoholic Beverages*. Berkeley: University of California Press.

Meier-Melikyan, N. R. 1990. Opredelenie Rastitel'nix Ostatkov iz Togolok-21 (Analysis of plant remains from Togolok-21). In *Drevnosti Strani Margush*, ed. V. I. Sarianidi, 203–5 and figs. 55–58. Ashgabat, Turkmenistan: Ilim.

Merlin, M. D. 1972. *Man and Marijuana: Some Aspects of Their Ancient Relationship*. Rutherford, N.J.: Farleigh Dickinson University Press.

Merlin, M. 1984. *On the Trail of the Ancient Opium Poppy: Natural and Early Cultural History of* Papaver somniferum. East Brunswick, N.J.: Associated University Presses.

Merlin, M. 2003. Archaeological Evidence for the Tradition of Psychoactive Plant Use in the Old World. *Economic Botany* 57 (3): 295–323.

Merlin, M. 2013. Some Aspects of the Traditional Use of *Ephedra* Species in Eastern Eurasia. *Ethnobotany* 25 (1–2): 1–17.

Miranda Chaves, S. A. de, and K. J. Reinhard. 2006. *Palaeogeography, Palaeoclimatology, Palaeoecology* 237: 110–18.

Monnier, G. 2012. Neanderthal Behavior. *Nature Education Knowledge* 3 (10): 11.

Mukerjee, B. L. 1922. The Soma Plant. *Journal of the Royal Asiatic Society* 53 (2): 241–44.

Nadel, D., A. Danin, R. C. Power, A. M. Rosen, F. Bocquetin, A. Tsatskin, D. Rosenberg, et al. 2013. Earliest Floral Grave Lining from 13,700–11,700-Y-Old Natufian Burials at Raqefet Cave, Mt. Carmel, Israel. *Proceedings of the National Academy of Sciences of the United States of America* 110 (29): 11774–78.

Nyberg, H. 1995. The Problem of the Aryans and the Soma: The Botanical Evidence. In *The Indo-Aryans of Ancient South-Asia: Language, Material Culture and Ethnicity*, ed. G. Erdosy, 382–406. Berlin: De Gruyter.

Parpola, A. 1994. *Deciphering the Indus Script*. New York: Cambridge University Press.

Price, R. A. 1996. Systematics of the Gnetales: A Review of Morphological and Molecular Evidence. *International Journal of Plant Science* 157 (suppl.): 40–49.

Radini, A., S. Buckley, A. Rosas, A. Estalrrich, M. de la Rasilla, and K. Hardy. 2016. Neanderthals, Trees and Dental Calculus: New Evidence from El Sidrón. *Antiquity* 90: 290–301. doi:10.15184/aqy.2016.21.

Rapoport, E. H., A. Ladio, and E. H. Sanz. 2003. *Plantas nativas comestibles de la Patagonia Andina argentino/chilena*. Bariloche, Argentina: Ediciones de Imaginaria.

Rätsch, C. 1998. *The Encyclopedia of Psychoactive Plants: Ethnopharmacology and Its Applications*. Rochester, N.Y.: Park Street Press.

Reinhard, K. J., D. L. Hamilton, and R. H. Hevly. 1991. Use of Pollen Concentration in Paleopharmacology: Coprolite Evidence of Medicinal Plants. *Journal of Ethnobiology* 11 (1): 117–32.

Reinhard, K. J., M. Daniels, D. R. Danielson, and S. Miranda Chaves. 2002. Multidisciplinary Coprolite Analysis. In *Bighorn Cave: Test Excavation of a Stratified Dry Shelter, Mojave County, Arizona*, ed. P. R. Geib and D. R. Keller, 135–52. Bilby Research Center Occasional Papers 1. Flagstaff: Northern Arizona University.

Roberts, N. C. 1989. *Baja California Plant Field Guide*. La Jolla, Calif.: Natural History Publishing.

Rudgley, R. 1998. *The Encyclopedia of Psychoactive Substances*. London: Little, Brown.

Rydin, C., and P. Korall. 2009. Evolutionary Relationships in *Ephedra* (Gnetales), with Implications for Seed Plant Phylogeny. *International Journal of Plant Science* 170 (8): 1031–43.

Sarianidi, V. 1994. Temples of Bronze Age Margiana: Traditions of Ritual Architecture. *Antiquity* 68: 388–97.

Sarianidi, V. 1998. *Margiana and Protozoroastrianism*. Athens, Greece: Kapon.

Sarianidi, V. 2003. Margiana and Soma-Haoma. *Electronic Journal of Vedic Studies* 9 (1).

Shah, N. C. 2015. Soma, an Enigmatic, Mysterious Plant of the Vedic Aryas: An Appraisal. *Indian Journal of History of Science* 50 (1): 26–41.

Sharma, P., P. L. Uniyal, and O. Hammer. 2010. Two New Species of *Ephedra* (Ephedraceae) from the Western Himalayas. *Systematic Biology* 35 (4): 730–35.

Shipley, G. P., and K. Kindscher. 2016. Evidence for the Paleoethnobotany of the Neanderthal: A Review of the Literature. *Scientifica* 2016. http://dx.doi.org/10.1155/2016/8927654.

Sobolik, K. D. 1988. The Importance of Pollen Concentration Values from Coprolites: An Analysis of Southwest Texas Samples. *Palynology* 12: 201–14.

Sobolik, K. D., and D. J. Gerick. 1992. Prehistoric Medicinal Plant Usage: A Case Study from Coprolites. *Journal of Ethnobiology* 12 (2): 203–11.

Solecki, R. S. 1975. Shanidar IV, a Neanderthal Flower Burial in Northern Iraq. *Science* 190 (4217): 880–81.

Sommer, J. D. 1999. The Shanidar IV "Flower Burial": A Re-evaluation of Neanderthal Burial Ritual. *Cambridge Archaeological Journal* 9 (1): 127–37.

Stapf, O. 1889. *Die Arten der Gattung* Ephedra. Denkschriften der Kaiserlichen Akademie der Wissenschaften, Mathematisch-Naturwissenschaftliche Klasse, vol. 56, pt. 2. Vienna: Kaiserlich-Königlichen Hof-und Staatsdruckerei.

Steibel, P. E. 1997. Nombres y usos de las plantas aplicados por los indios Ranqueles de la Pampa (Argentina). *Revista Facultad de Agronomía, Universidad Nacional de la Pampa* 9 (2): 1–38.

Stein, A. 1931. On the *Ephedra*, the Hum Plant, and the Soma. *Bulletin of the School of Oriental Studies* 4: 501–14.

Stevenson, D. W. 1993. Ephedraceae. In *Flora of North America*, ed. Flora of North America Editorial Committee, 428–34. New York: Oxford University Press.

Stevenson, J. 1842. *Translation of the Samhitá of the Sáma Veda*. 8 vols. London.

Story, D. A., and V. M. Bryant. 1966. A Preliminary Study of the Paleoecology of the Amistad Reservoir Area. Final report submitted to the National Science Foundation by University of Texas at Austin.

Taillieu, D. 1998. *Haoma Plant*. The Circle of Ancient Iranian Studies. http://cais-soas.com/CAIS/Religions/iranian/Zarathushtrian/haoma_plant.htm.

Taillieu, D., and M. Boyce. 2003. Haoma. In *Encyclopaedia Iranica* [electronic resource], ed. E. Yarshater. New York: Columbia University Center for Iranian Studies. This article is available in print: Vol. XI, Fasc. 6, pp. 659–67.

Tang, W., and G. Eisenbrand. 1992. *Chinese Drugs of Plant Origin*. Berlin: Springer-Verlag.

Teuscher, E. 1979. *Pharmakognosie*. Berlin: Akademie-Verlag.

Thomas, E. 2008. Quantitative Ethnobotanical Research on Knowledge and Use of Plants for Livelihood among Quechua, Yuracaré and Trinitario Communities in the Andes and Amazon Regions of Bolivia. PhD diss., Ghent University, Belgium.

Thomé, O. W. 1885. *Flora von Deutschland, Österreich und der Schweiz*. Gera-Untermhaus: F. E. Köhler.

Timbrook, J. 2007. *Chumash Ethnobotany: Plant Knowledge among the Chumash People of Southern California*. Santa Barbara Museum of Natural History Monographs no. 5, Publications in Anthropology no. 1. Berkeley, Calif.: Heyday Books.

Tosto, A.C.M., L. S. Burry, M. O. Arriage, and M. T. Cavalero. 2016. Archaeobotanical Study of Patagonian Holocene Coprolites, Indicators of Diet, Cultural Practices and Space Use. *Journal of Archaeological Science: Reports* 10: 204–11.

Trujillo, W. A., and W. R. Sorenson. 2003. Determination of Ephedrine Alkaloids in Dietary Supplements and Botanicals by Liquid Chromatography/Tandem Mass Spectrometry: Collaborative Study. *Journal of AOAC International* 86: 657–68.

Vandebroek, I., P. Van Damme, L. Van Puyvelde, S. Arrazole, and N. De Kimpe. 2004. A Comparison of Traditional Healers' Medicinal Plant Knowledge in the Bolivian Andes and Amazon. *Social Science* and *Medicine* 59 (4): 837–49.

Wang, B. 1983. Agricultural Archaeology in Xinjiang. *Nongye Kaogu* (Agricultural archaeology) 1: 102–21.

Wang, B. H. 1993. Archaeological Excavations at Gumugou Site, Kongque River, and a Preliminary Study on the Discoveries. In *Archaeobiological Survey of the Ancient Silk Road*, ed. B. Wang. Urumchi, China: Xinjiang People's Publishing House.

Wangchuk, P., U. Samten, J. Thinley, and S. H. Afaq. 2008. High Altitude Medicinal Plants Used in Bhutanese Traditional Medicine (gSo-ba-rig-pa). *Ethnobotany* 20: 54–64.

Wasson, R. G. 1968. *Soma: Divine Mushroom of Immortality*. New York: Harcourt, Brace, Jovanovich.

Wenke, M., ed. 1986. *Farmakologie*. Prague: Avicenum.

West, E. W., trans. 1901. *Sacred Books of the East*, vol. 5, *Pahlavi Texts*. Oxford: Oxford University Press.

Weyrich, L. S., K. Dobney, and A. Cooper. 2015. Ancient DNA Analysis of Dental Calculus. *Journal of Human Evolution* 79: 119–24.

Wilken, M. A. 2012. *An Ethnobotany of Baja California's Kumeyaay Indians*. MA thesis in anthropology, San Diego State University.

Witzel, M. 2005. Central Asian Roots and Acculturation in South Asia: Linguistic and Archaeological Evidence from Western Central Asia, the Hindukush and Northwestern South Asia for Early Indo-Aryan Language and Religion. In *Linguistics, Archaeology and the Human Past: Indus Project*, ed. T. Osada, 87–211. Kyoto: Research Institute for Humanity and Nature.

Xia, L. 1997. The Ancient Loulan People's Adaption to the Environment—A Cultural Interpretation of the Funeral *Ephedra* in Lop Nur Area. *Social Sciences in China* 3: 115–29 (in Chinese).

Xie, M., Y. Yang, B. Wang, and C. Wang. 2013. Interdisciplinary Investigation on Ancient *Ephedra* Twigs from Gumugou Cemetery (3800 BP) in Xinjiang Region, Northwest China. *Microscopy Research Technique* 76: 663–72.

Yang, Y. 2010. A Review on Gnetalean Megafossils: Problems and Perspectives. *Taiwania* 55 (4): 346–54.

Yang, Y., F. Dezhi, and Z. Guanghua. 2003. A New Species of *Ephedra* (Ephedraceae) from China. *Novon* 13: 153–55.

Yang, Y., B. Geng, D. L. Dilcher, Z. Chen, and T. A. Lott. 2005. Morphology and Affinities of an Early Cretaceous *Ephedra* (Ephedraceae) from China. *American Journal of Botany* 92: 231–41.

Zhang, J. S., Z. Tian, and Z. C. Lou. 1989. Quality Evaluation of Twelve Species of Chinese *Ephedra* (Ma Huang). *Yao Xue Bao* 24 (11): 865–71 (in Chinese).

Zhao, Z., and P. Xiao. 2009. Ma Huang (*Ephedra*). In *Encyclopedia of Medicinal Plants*, 342–45. Shanghai: Shanghai World Publishing.

4

Prehistoric Intoxicants of North America

SEAN M. RAFFERTY

Decades of research in the social sciences have made it clear that beyond the biological imperatives of subsistence, shelter, and reproduction, very few human behaviors are universal. Once one moves beyond these basic requirements, the idiosyncrasies of human action and thought are nearly infinite. One universal in human experience is the desire to experience altered states of consciousness (ASC), usually through the ingestion of various forms of intoxicant substances.

In this chapter I synthesize the available evidence about the prehistoric distribution of four prominent North American intoxicants, *Ilex*, *Datura*, peyote, and tobacco. These four plants contain powerful intoxicant alkaloids: caffeine, scopolamine, mescaline, and nicotine, respectively. These are all powerful intoxicant "drug" compounds, with diverse effects on human physiology and cognition. All four are endemic to the Americas in general or North America specifically. Each substance has been of great importance in the lives of modern or historically documented Native American societies, and each has significant evidence of use in prehistory. I conclude with speculations on the relative lack of the use of ethyl alcohol in North American aboriginal cultures, which is in marked contrast to most other world cultures, past and present.

Alkaloids in Ancient Society

Because the majority of intoxicant compounds used in the Americas are alkaloids, it is informative to discuss that category in general before turning to specific examples. Alkaloids are defined based on the following characteristics: they are organic molecules, generally containing at least one nitrogen atom, which is contained in a heterocyclic ring structure

(Roberts and Wink 1998: 2; Waterman 1998: 87–88). Additional groups, such as methyl radicals, give each alkaloid its unique chemical properties. Alkaloids are always basic in pH, and the resulting bitter taste is likely a primary evolutionary factor as a defense mechanism in the variety of vascular plants and fungi that contain them. Alkaloids are comparatively small for organic compounds, and atomic weights range typically between 100 and 300. These molecules are significant to archaeology because they occur widely in wild plants as natural toxins, so any prehistoric population is likely to have had a variety of alkaloid-bearing plants in the local environment. Of the available alkaloids, many are known to have a variety of biological effects on the human body and mind when ingested, and they can act as narcotics, stimulants, hypnotics, or hallucinogens to create altered states of consciousness. Cross-cultural surveys have shown that a majority of modern or historically documented cultures incorporate altered states of consciousness into fundamental belief systems (Bourguignon 1973; Merlin 2003). Therefore, alkaloid-bearing plants are likely to have been widely exploited as medicinal and/or psychoactive agents by prehistoric cultures worldwide. Many of these compounds, such as caffeine, nicotine, and morphine, are still utilized by modern societies (Rudgley 1993); many more were used in prehistory (Wink 1998).

Types and Standards of Evidence

A variety of types of evidence have been used to draw conclusions about the prehistory of various intoxicating compounds. Of course the strongest evidence for any substance would be direct, in the form of botanical remains or organic residues, ideally from a secure and dateable context. This standard of evidence is relatively rarely met, however, because of the vagaries of organic preservation, exacerbated by a lack of scholarly interest throughout much of the history of archaeology. Less direct, but more durable, types of evidence are artifacts associated with the ingestion of intoxicants: smoking pipes, enema tubes, and snuff trays are examples. Such artifacts can provide a wealth of information when recovered from dateable contexts. However, the specific substances that a given artifact was used to ingest are often unclear. A variety of substances can be smoked in a pipe, for example, limiting inferences in the absence of corroborating macrobotanical or residue evidence. The situation is more confusing for ceramic vessels used in the containment, processing, or ingestion of intoxicants, which may be similar or identical to "utilitarian" ceramics used for subsistence.

Less objective, but often utilized, types of evidence include analogies drawn from ethnographic observations or the interpretation of ethnohistoric sources. The ethnographic observation of living cultures using intoxicants can inform on the practices of ancient cultures using the same substances, especially if there is a historic connection between past and present. Likewise, recorded observations from historic documents can illuminate the behavior of prehistoric actors. However, the meanings and social roles of any practice, intoxicant use included, can change dramatically over time and across space, so the greater the geographic and chronological distance between an ethnographic source and a prehistoric subject, the more skepticism a researcher must maintain.

The least objective type of evidence for intoxicant use, and therefore the hardest to interpret, is iconographic in nature. Images or other depictions of the actual plants used as intoxicants can be relatively straightforward to interpret, such as representations of *Anadenanthera* or other hallucinogens in the art of prehistoric Andean cultures (Knobloch 2000). However, the degree of abstraction and subjectivity in many iconographic structures can make interpretation difficult and speculative. At the most subjective end of this interpretive continuum are supposed representations not of the intoxicants themselves but of phosphines or more elaborate hallucinations they may induce in the user (Lewis-Williams and Dowson 1988). Below, I describe the archaeological evidence for the prehistoric use of the four primary North American intoxicants.

ILEX

One alkaloid known to have been used in prehistoric Native America is caffeine. Probably the most ubiquitous of alkaloids used by both modern and ancient human cultures, caffeine (formally termed trimethylxanthine) works by binding to receptor sites for the neurotransmitter adenosine, increasing neuronal activity and stimulating the secretion of epinephrine. Caffeine also increases dopamine production, stimulating the brain's pleasure center. Caffeine is soluble in water, as well as ethanol, acetone, and chloroform. Caffeine is found in several well-known plants, such as *Coffea arabica*, or coffee, and *Theobroma cacao*, or cacao, the basic ingredient in chocolate. Cacao is native to South America and was a cultivated garden crop in prehistoric Mesoamerica. Linguistic analyses indicate the use of cacao by the Pre-Classic Olmec as early as 1500 BC (Coe and Coe 2007). The earliest physical evidence of cacao use in Mesoamerica dates to the Middle Pre-Classic period Maya. Hurst and colleagues (1989, 2002) conducted high-performance liquid chromatography (HPLC) analysis of a sample of ceramic vessels dating between 600 BC and AD 250 from the Mayan site of Colha. This analysis identified both caffeine and the related alkaloid theobromine. These vessels were likely used in the preparation of a cacao-based beverage. Such vessels are found primarily in elite burials, raising the possibility that the practice of drinking cacao beverages was socially restricted within Mayan society.

While the presence of caffeine in chocolate is well-known, that the alkaloid is also found in a variety of plants of the holly family, genus *Ilex* (figure 4.1), is less well-known. There are numerous *Ilex* species, three of which are known to contain caffeine (Hu 1979). For example, *Ilex guayusa* was identified in a shaman's burial from Bolivia dating to approximately AD 375, and significant levels of caffeine were detected in that sample (Holmstedt and Lindgren 1972; Wassén 1972). However, the species most often associated with Native American use is *Ilex vomitoria*, a shrub that is native to the American Southeast (Merrill 1979: 40). *Ilex* species were used in historic periods by Native American cultures in the Southeast such as the Cherokees and Creeks to brew a beverage generically referred to as "Black Drink" or "yaupon" (Hudson 1976). This was drunk under a variety of circumstances. In most cases, its use was confined to ritual occasions requiring spiritual purification. In some societies it was used by male warriors; in others it was restricted to individuals of high rank. Some accounts show the beverage used to facilitate social interaction between potentially hostile tribes, in much the same way as tobacco. In all cases, its use was a highly formalized affair; Black Drink was not a primarily secular beverage like coffee or tea (Merrill 1979). As with the Mayan use of cacao, there are characteristic material correlates for the use of *Ilex* infusions. Historic observations of cultures using Black Drink state that this was often done using shell cups. Similar cups were traded in the Mississippi Valley during late prehistoric times, often adorned with ritually significant decoration, and were found in the burials of high-ranked individuals, such as those in the Great Mortuary at the Spiro site in Oklahoma (Phillips and Brown 1975) and at the Belcher Mound in Louisiana (Webb 1959: 204).

Drinking the infusion of *Ilex vomitoria* had a profound physiological effect. Aside from the potent dosage of caffeine, and all its associated stimulatory and diuretic effects, the beverage has been described as having a powerful emetic effect, causing vomiting, as well as a diaphoretic effect, causing profuse sweating, both of which were believed to have a

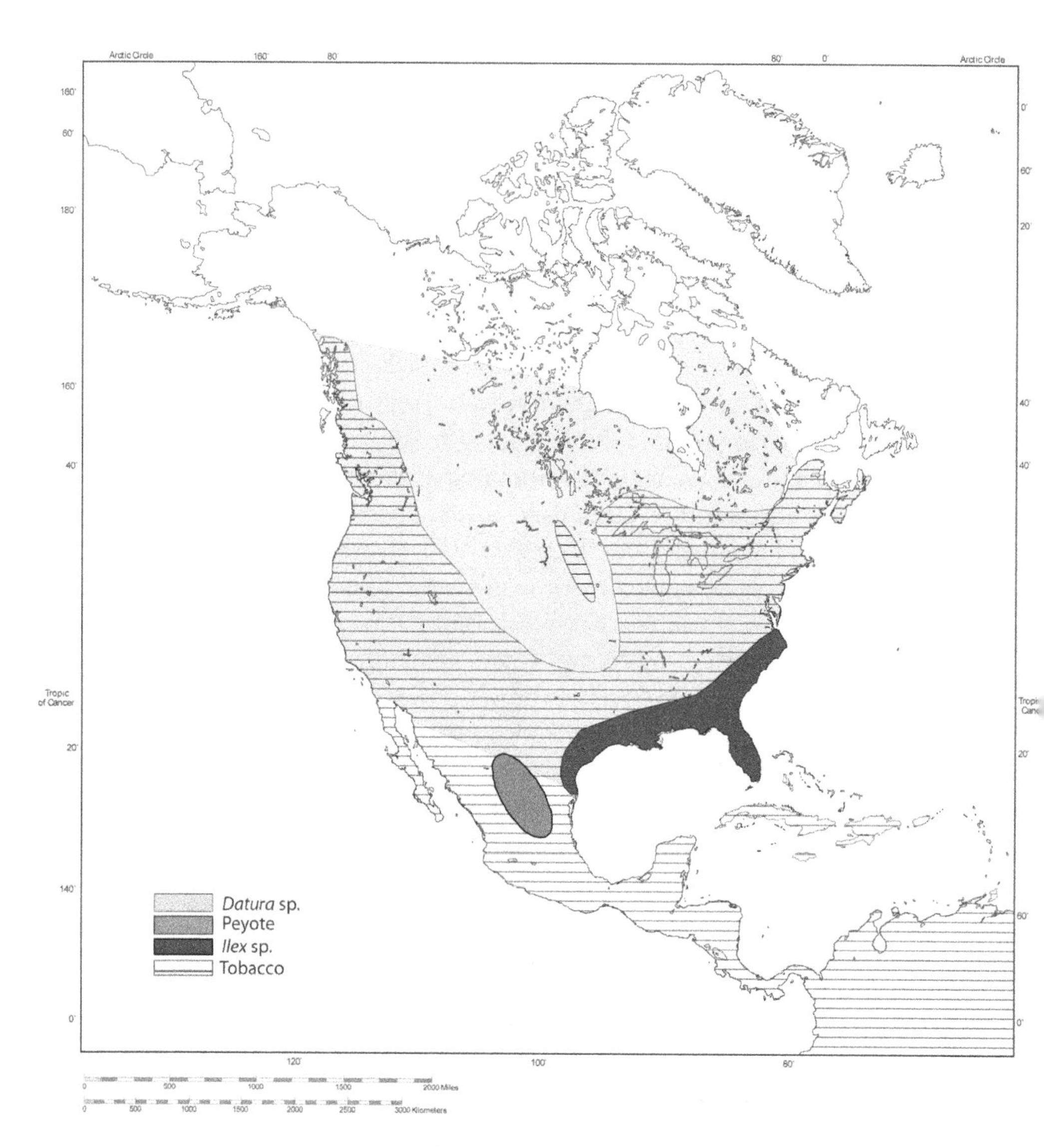

Figure 4.1. Approximate natural ranges of *Ilex* sp., *Datura* sp., peyote cactus, and tobacco. (Map by Matthew Napolitano.)

purifying effect on the body and spirit. However, whether these more extreme effects are due to the *Ilex* plants or to other additives at present are unknown.

Despite historical sources on the use of *Ilex* infusions in ritual settings by native societies, there is much we do not know. The effects of caffeine on the nervous system are well-known but do not explain all the documented effects of *Ilex* infusions, such as vomiting. Anecdotal evidence indicates that other plants were added, such as *Eryngium aquaticum* (button snakeroot); other accounts have indicated that some of these physiological effects were due to mixing seawater with the infusion or to drinking a large volume of the liquid (Swanton 1946). The emetic effect of *Ilex vomitoria* is further called into question by historic accounts of the Seminoles brewing an infusion that caused vomiting but did not include *I. vomitoria* (Sturtevant 1954).

Further research questions pertaining to *Ilex* relate to the types of material culture involved in processing and consuming the plant, as well as the context in which this occurred. The chemical identification of prehistoric instances of the use of *Ilex* would be straightforward; the identification of caffeine in organic residues would be a clear indicator. Analysis of shell cups and pottery for caffeine residues would provide confirming evidence that these artifacts were used to process *Ilex* infusions. Was the use of *Ilex* widespread in prehistoric societies, or was it limited to ritual contexts, as ethnohistoric accounts of the Black Drink ritual indicate? Were numerous types of ceramics used to process and consume *Ilex*, or was it limited to more elaborate pottery or shell vessels? Whether the more highly symbolically decorated cups of the Mississippian period were functional vessels for Black Drink consumption or were more-symbolic representations, like a modern church chalice, remains unproven. Analysis of shell vessels for caffeine residues would address this question. Comparisons of shell cup residues to residues from more-utilitarian vessels could also provide evidence for whether the Black Drink practice was truly a socially restricted practice in prehistory. If caffeine residues are common, and come from numerous contexts, then Black Drink may have not have conformed to the socially restricted contexts observed historically. If the opposite proves to be the case, with limited occurrences of caffeine residues on material culture found in ritual contexts, then the historically observed aspects of the Black Drink ritual may have had deep historical roots.

There have been some finds of *Ilex* macroremains from Native American sites, such as from the Mississippian period Moundville site in Alabama (Jackson and Scott 2003: 559). Residue analysis directed at answering these questions has been undertaken by Tushingham and colleagues (2011), and results of the analysis of experimentally produced *Ilex* residues are promising for the detection of archaeological samples (Reber and Kerr 2012). Direct analysis of the content of likely Black Drink vessels will greatly enhance our understanding of the prehistory of the practice, adding to the existing ethnographic, ethnohistoric, and analogic evidence.

DATURA

Another plant with significant cultural implications for Native American cultures is *Datura*, or jimsonweed (see figure 4.1). *Datura* is a member of the family Solanaceae, which includes other psychoactive plants such as nightshade, belladonna, and tobacco. *Datura* contains several potent alkaloids, including scopolamine, which is a powerful deleriant. Scopolamine can induce powerful hallucinations, disorientation, paranoia, and the sensation of falling. *Datura* is dangerous even beyond these extreme effects, as the lethal toxic dose is only slightly more than the minimum effective dose. *Datura* species such as *D. stramonium* and *D. meteloides* grow wild throughout much of North America, and other species are common throughout the Old World (Emboden 1979: 65). *Datura* was used in a number of Native American cultures and was ingested in a variety of ways, but infusions and smoking were the most common. *Datura* use was especially prevalent among Southwestern, Californian, and Great Basin Native American tribes, usually used during vision quests (Emboden 1979: 80; Winter 2000b) or by shamans (Gamble et al. 2001: 192). Use of *Datura* for these purposes extended into Mexico and was observed historically among the Huichols (Winter 2000c: 281) and the Aztecs (Winter 2000c: 298). *Datura* had other uses as well. Southwestern tribes such as the Hopis, Zunis, and Navajos used *Datura meteloides* as a ceremonial hallucinogen for healers to achieve a trancelike state in order to make diagnoses of illness, as a poison, or as a narcotic (Keur 1941: 12; Stevenson 1915; Vestal 1952; Whiting 1939). Eastern tribes such as the Iroquois and Algonquians also made use of *Datura* (Emboden 1979: 97; Herrick 1995: 200), though the use of *Datura* is poorly understood in eastern North America in comparison to the Southwest, Pacific Coast, and Mesoamerica.

The prehistoric roots of the use of *Datura* are poorly understood throughout the Americas, and archaeobotanical evidence is scant. Inferential evidence has been proposed based on certain stylistic attributes of vessels with spiked exteriors that are evocative of the fruit of the *Datura* plant (Litzinger 1981). There has been some archaeobotanical identification of *Datura* among prehistoric farmers in the American Southwest (Yarnell 1959). The remains of a ceremonial structure at the Mississippian period BBB Motor site in Illinois contained pottery with charred *Datura* residues (Emerson 1989: 48–49; Wagner 2000: 196), indicating that the plant was used in ritual practices in late prehistoric chiefdom societies in eastern North America. These roughly contemporary prehistoric occurrences of *Datura* use, widely separated by geography, attest to what was likely a widespread practice but one about which to date we have very little empirical data.

A variety of research questions are evident for the study of *Datura*. Is the ceramic stylistic evidence for *Datura* use in North America supported by empirical data? Comparisons of archaeological contexts of *Datura* residues could determine whether the ceremonial context of use documented historically had prehistoric roots. Are only high-status vessels associated with *Datura*, as was the case at the BBB Motor site, or was the use of *Datura* more widespread during and before the Mississippian period? This research question relates to the accessibility of altered states in prehistoric societies. Were they available to all members of a given culture, or were they monopolized by social elites or ritual specialists, such as priests and shamans? How was *Datura* ingested in prehistory: by infusion or by smoking or by both? Evidence of *Datura* on ceramic vessels, as was the case for Mississippian sites, is evidence of an infusion, but the possible smoking of *Datura* cannot be ruled out without empirical evidence to the contrary. Currently, the earliest smoking pipes in North America predate the earliest chemical evidence of tobacco—could the possible pretobacco pipes have been used for *Datura* instead of tobacco? There is ethnohistoric evidence that *Datura* and tobacco were used in conjunction in some instances, possibly mixed together in an infusion (Winter 2000a: 3). Attention to direct analysis of ceramic residues or macrobotanical samples for *Datura* remains or alkaloids would help answer these questions, but I am not aware of any such ongoing research.

PEYOTE

Peyote (*Lophophora williamsii*) is a spineless cactus native to desert regions of northern Mexico and southern Texas (see figure 4.1). Peyote flesh contains substantial concentrations of phenethylamine alkaloids, most notably mescaline. Mescaline is a serotonergic hallucinogen (in that its effect comes from binding to specific serotonin receptors in the brain) similar in effect to LSD or psilocybin. Mescaline-induced hallucinations tend to be less extreme than true delusions (seeing or hearing something that is not real), featuring the perception of geometric or fractal imagery, the exaggeration of illumination or colors, or synesthetic combinations of sight and sound (Diaz 1996; Giannini and Slaby 1989).

Much of what has been written about Native American peyote use has focused on its historic role in the Native American Church and its resulting ambiguous legal status. Leaving modern concerns aside, ethnohistoric sources attest to the cultural significance of peyote to numerous native societies in the Texas/northern Mexico region as early as the mid-1500s (Anderson 1996: 5). Seminal ethnographic research of peyote-using cultures, notably the Huichol, was conducted by Carl Lumholtz (1900) at the turn of the twentieth century and Peter Furst, the great scholar of Native American intoxicants, in the 1960s (Furst 1972). Space prevents a detailed description of the nuances of Huichol peyote rituals, but they can generally be described as guided (as opposed to individual) vision quests.

The archaeological challenges of recovering evidence of peyote use are substantial. Fleshy plants such as cacti are in general notorious for not preserving in archaeological contexts. The processing and ingestion of peyote do not intrinsically require specialized material culture. It is therefore hardly surprising that most of our evidence for prehistoric peyote use is indirect, in the form of ethnographic analogy or the interpretation of rock art iconography. For example, various geometric forms featured in northern Mexican rock art have been interpreted in terms of similar motifs drawn on the faces of participants in Huichol peyote rituals (Mountjoy 1982: 118). That said, what direct evidence there is for prehistoric peyote marks it as among the earliest known intoxicants used by Native Americans. A dried preserved piece of peyote recovered from northern Mexico was dated to between AD 810 and 1070 (Bruhn et al. 1978). Several cave or rock-shelter sites from Texas have yielded preserved peyote, with radiocarbon dates falling between 5000 and 5700 BP, well prior to the advent of any horticultural practices in the region, or indeed, for most of North America. Analysis of the sample detected mescaline. This remarkable discovery is currently one of the oldest examples of preserved intoxicant plants in North America (Bruhn et al. 2002; De Smet and Bruhn 2003; El-Seedi et al. 2005; Terry et al. 2006).

TOBACCO

Tobacco is the generic name for several species of the genus *Nicotiana* (figure 4.1). Many of these species grow within North America, though the species most commonly used in North America, *Nicotiana rustica*, is of South American origin (Pearsall 1992). *Nicotiana* species are defined by their high concentration of the alkaloid nicotine, and *N. rustica* has one of the highest nicotine contents of any species. Nicotine functions by binding to nicotinic acetylcholine receptors, causing increased heart rate, vasoconstriction, and increased alertness. In sufficient doses, nicotine can have hallucinogenic effects equivalent to indole alkaloids such as ibogaine and harmaline (Joniger and Dobkin de Rios 1973, 1976). Overdose can lead to convulsions and death. Early archaeobotanical evidence for tobacco is scanty. The oldest known dates for tobacco are from the northern coast of Peru, with dates ranging between 2500 and 1800 BC (Pearsall 1992: 178).

Tobacco seeds from the American Southwest have been recovered from contexts as early as 1000 BC (Bohrer 2004; Winter 2004). The earliest known *Nicotiana* species tobacco seeds recovered from eastern North America come from the central Mississippi Valley between AD 100 and 200 (Asch 1994: 45; Haberman 1984: 271; Wagner 2000; Winter 2000a). Early dates for the rest of Eastern North America fall between AD 400 and 800 (Asch and Asch 1985: 196; Haberman 1984: 272–73; Wagner 1998: 840). These data leave a sizeable temporal gap between the archaeobotanical evidence for tobacco and the archaeological evidence of smoking pipes in eastern North America. The earliest known tobacco pipes in eastern North America date to the Late Archaic period, more than a thousand years prior to the earliest known archaeobotanical evidence.

My past research has demonstrated that nicotine can be extracted from organic residues and detected using gas chromatography/mass spectroscopy. This research builds upon foundational research conducted on a range of tobacco discoveries using chemical analysis. Bruhn and colleagues (1976) identified nicotine using mass fragmentography in a collection of Bolivian material believed to be associated with a shaman's burial dating to approximately AD 400. Also, Basketmaker III associated pipes (ca. AD 700) were found to contain nicotine and nicotinic acid using chromatography (Johnson et al. 1959; Jones and Morris 1960).

In my own research, five pipes, including specimens from Adena sites in the Ohio Valley in Ohio and Pennsylvania, and a Middlesex cemetery site in Vermont, all dating to between 500 and 300 BC, were tested. These are some of the oldest smoking pipes in eastern North America (though they do postdate the oldest pipes of the Late Archaic period). Nicotine or characteristic nicotine degradation products—principally anabasine—were successfully detected in three pipes, indicating that they were used to smoke a species of tobacco, most likely *Nicotiana rustica* (Rafferty 2002, 2006; Rafferty et al. 2012). The chemical results from two pipes from Pennsylvania were suggestive of nicotine but not conclusive. These results extended the known chronology of tobacco by several centuries, though clearly more work is required. Other researchers are investigating the prehistory of tobacco smoking through direct analysis of residues (Tushingham et al. 2010).

Native American Alcohol?

Based on the examples of *Ilex*, *Datura*, peyote, and tobacco, we can say with confidence that the Native American prehistoric use of intoxicants is extensive geographically and has significant temporal depth. We can also see that we are barely scraping the surface of the phenomenon based on research conducted so far. The four plants I have discussed are prominent in Native American lifeways, but the list is not exhaustive. Other plants, such as the mescal bean (*Calia secundiflora*), need to be considered as well in any comprehensive analysis. *C. secundiflora* may have been used as an intoxicant, but its principal alkaloid, cytosine, causes only mild intoxication and is highly poisonous and unpleasant to ingest, if not fatal. Conventional wisdom is that mescal beans were eventually supplanted by peyote, but given the significant confusion of common names of plants in the region, native use of this species is poorly documented and requires additional confirmation.

There is much to learn about the substances discussed here. My suspicion is that as archaeologists look more actively for evidence of intoxicants, the data will become more geographically extensive and radiocarbon dates for intoxicant species will be pushed back to the earliest days of human presence in the Americas. This does not approach the issue that is, to me at least, the most intriguing question of all—the lack of North American evidence of the most common intoxicant in the rest of the world: alcohol.

The lack of North American evidence for fermentation has been summarized in a recent article: "The greatest mystery to an archaeologist is the absence of any prehistoric native alcoholic drink . . . north of Mexico" (White and Weinstein 2008: 254). This is a slight overstatement, as in fact there is evidence of the use of fermented corn beverages in the American Southwest (Borek et al. 2008) and wines of various berries along the Pacific Northwest coast (McGovern 2009: 227). These are isolated examples, and the southwestern cases are more appropriately viewed as the northernmost extension of a Mesoamerican tradition than as an indigenous North American practice. North and east of Arizona, evidence of fermentation is absent. This is indeed a puzzling phenomenon with no clear explanation.

Explanations that have been proposed for the absence of fermented beverages in North America lack plausibility. A possible absence of suitable environmental microorganisms for fermentation would not likely be continental in scale. I have heard anecdotes of northeastern Native American populations ingesting fermented maple sap, indicating both the chemical possibility of alcohol and native awareness of the process, but my literature reviews have not found any corroboration. The predominance of tobacco as the "intoxicant of choice" is a possible factor (McGovern 2009: 228), yet the use of numerous types of alcoholic drinks in Mesoamerica and South America (fermented corn primarily, as well as other beverages such as fermented agave) alongside tobacco undermines this explanation. The relatively late date of the adoption of maize agriculture in much of North America also lacks sufficient explanatory power, as evidence from Mesoamerica points to fermentation being one of the first practices associated with maize domestication, if not the original cause of domestication in the first place (Smalley and Blake 2003). The most plausible explanation I have come across was proposed by McGovern (2009: 229), who noted that northwestern Asia, the predominant source area of native North Americans, is itself lacking in fermentable substances. Thus, Native American ancestral populations had lost the tradition of fermentation (resorting instead to hallucinogens such as the fly-agaric mushroom) and only rediscovered the practice in Mexico and South America millennia later. Shedding additional light on this uniquely North American trend in intoxicant use would be a significant contribution to the field.

In conclusion, it is clear that prehistoric North Americans were no different from any other human population in terms of innate desires for intoxication. A variety of direct and indirect evidence supports this claim. There is, however, a fascinating regional twist, with a range of indigenous plants having local significance, a foreign cultigen (tobacco) achieving a pancontinental dominance, and the most popular intoxicant in the rest of the world, alcohol, having almost no presence at all. Scholarly attention has only relatively recently been directed to the issue in any meaningful way, much data is left to uncover, and many questions still need to be answered. Future prospects are bright, however. Residue analysis research is a rapidly expanding field. More and more artifacts are being investigated every year. The accuracy and precision of instruments are improving. Biomarker and lipid profiles for numerous plants—edible, medicinal, and intoxicant—are being isolated and published. As the chapters in this volume attest, the study of prehistoric intoxicants is a field finally coming into its own.

References Cited

Anderson, E. 1996. *Peyote: The Divine Cactus.* Tucson: University of Arizona Press.

Asch, D. L. 1994. Aboriginal Specialty-Plant Cultivation in Eastern North America: Illinois Prehistory and a Post-Contact Perspective. In *Agricultural Origins and Development in the Midcontinent,* ed. W. Green, 25–86. Iowa City: University of Iowa Press.

Asch, D. L., and N. B. Asch. 1985. Prehistoric Plant Cultivation in West-Central Illinois. In *Prehistoric Food Production in North America,* ed. R. I. Ford, 149–203. Ann Arbor: University of Michigan.

Bohrer, V. 2004. *Flotation Analysis from High Rolls Cave (LA 114103), Otero County, New Mexico.* Southwest Ethnobotanical Enterprises Report 39. Portales, N.Mex.

Borek, T., C. Mowry, and G. Dean. 2008. Analysis of Modern and Ancient Artifacts for the Presence of Corn Beer: Dynamic Headspace Testing of Pottery Sherds from Mexico and New Mexico. *MRS Proceedings* 1047: 185–94.

Bourguignon, E. 1973. *Religion, Altered States of Consciousness, and Social Change.* Columbus: Ohio University Press.

Bruhn, J. G., B. Holmstedt, J.-E. Lindgren, and S. H. Wassén. 1976. The Tobacco from Niño Korin: Identification of Nicotine in a Bolivian Archaeological Collection. In *Göteborgs Etnografiska Museum Årstryck 1976,* 45–48. Gothenburg, Sweden.

Bruhn, J. G., J.-E. Lindgren, B. Holmstedt, and J. M. Adovasio. 1978. Peyote Alkaloids: Identification in a Prehistoric Specimen of *Lophophora* from Coahuila, Mexico. *Science* 199: 1437–38.

Bruhn, J. G., P. De Smet, H. El-Seedi, and O. Beck. 2002. Mescaline Use for 5700 Years. *Lancet* 359: 1866.

Coe, S. D., and M. D. Coe. 2007. *The True History of Chocolate.* London: Thames and Hudson.

De Smet, P., and J. G. Bruhn. 2003. Ceremonial Peyote Use and Its Antiquity in the Southern United States. *HerbalGram* 58 (2003): 30–33.

Diaz, J. 1996. *How Drugs Influence Behavior.* Upper Saddle River, N.J.: Prentice Hall.

El-Seedi, H., P. De Smet, O. Beck, G. Possnert, and J. Bruhn. 2005. Prehistoric Peyote Use: Alkaloid Analysis and Radiocarbon Dating of Archaeological Specimens of *Lophophora* from Texas. *Journal of Ethnopharmacology* 101 (1–3): 238–42.

Emboden, W. 1979. *Narcotic Plants.* New York: Macmillan.

Emerson, T. E. 1989. Water, Serpents and the Underworld: An Exploration into Cahokia Symbolism. In *The Southeastern Ceremonial Complex: Artifacts and Analysis,* ed. P. Galloway, 45–92. Lincoln: University of Nebraska Press.

Furst, P. 1972. To Find Our Life: Peyote among the Huichol Indians of Mexico. In *Flesh of the Gods,* ed. P. Furst, 136–84. New York: Praeger.

Gamble, L., P. Walker, and G. Russell. 2001. An Integrative Approach to Mortuary Analysis: Social and Symbolic Dimensions of Chumash Burial Practices. *American Antiquity* 66 (2): 185–212.

Giannini, A. J., and A. E. Slaby. 1989. *Drugs of Abuse*. Oradell, N.J.: Medical Economics Books.

Haberman, T. W. 1984. Evidence of Aboriginal Tobaccos in Eastern North America. *American Antiquity* 49 (2): 268–87.

Herrick, J. W. 1995. *Iroquois Medical Botany*. Syracuse: Syracuse University Press.

Holmstedt, B., and J.-E. Lindgren. 1972. Alkaloid Analyses of Botanical Material More than a Thousand Years Old. *Etnologiska Studier* 32: 139–44.

Hu, S. Y. 1979. The Botany of Yaupon. In *The Black Drink: A Native American Tea*, ed. C. Hudson, 10–39. Athens: University of Georgia Press.

Hudson, C. 1976. *The Southern Indians*. Knoxville: University of Tennessee Press.

Hurst, J., R. A. Martin, S. M. Tarka Jr., and G. D. Hall. 1989. Authentication of Cocoa in Maya Vessels Using High-Performance Liquid Chromatographic Techniques. *Journal of Chromatography* 466: 279–89.

Hurst, J., S. M. Tarka Jr., T. G. Powis, F. Valdez Jr., and T. Hesterm. 2002. Cacao Usage by the Earliest Maya Civilization. *Nature* 418 (6895): 289.

Jackson, H. E., and S. L. Scott. 2003. Patterns of Elite Faunal Utilization at Moundville, Alabama. *American Antiquity* 68 (3): 552–72.

Johnson, V. C., F. L. Gager, and J. C. Holmes. 1959. A Study of the History of the Use of Tobacco. Paper presented on October 30 at the 13th Tobacco Chemists' Research Conference, Lexington, Kentucky.

Jones, V. H., and E. A. Morris. 1960. A Seventh-Century Record of Tobacco Utilization in Arizona. *El Palacio, Journal of the Museum of New Mexico* 67: 115–17.

Joniger, O., and M. Dobkin de Rios. 1973. Suggestive Hallucinogenic Properties of Tobacco. *Medical Anthropology Newsletter* 4 (4): 6–11.

Joniger, O., and M. Dobkin de Rios. 1976. *Nicotiana* an Hallucinogen? *Economic Botany* 30: 149–51.

Keur, D. L. 1941. *Big Bead Mesa: An Archaeological Study of Navaho Acculturation, 1745–1812.* Memoirs of the Society for American Archaeology no. 1. Menasha, Wis.

Knobloch, P. J. 2000. Wari Ritual Power at Conchopata: An Interpretation of *Anadenanthera colubrina* Iconography. *Latin American Antiquity* 11 (4): 387–402.

Lewis-Williams, J. D., and T. A. Dowson. 1988. The Sign of All Times: Entoptic Phenomena and Upper Paleolithic Art. *Current Anthropology* 29: 201–45.

Litzinger, W. J. 1981. Ceramic Evidence for Prehistoric *Datura* Use in North America. *Journal of Ethnopharmacology* 4 (1): 57–74.

Lumholtz, C. 1900. *Symbolism of the Huichol Indians*. Memoirs of the American Museum of Natural History no. 3. New York.

McGovern, P. 2009. *Uncorking the Past: The Quest for Wine, Beer, and Other Alcoholic Beverages.* Berkeley: University of California Press.

Merlin, M. D. 2003. Archaeological Evidence for the Tradition of Psychoactive Plant Use in the Old World. *Economic Botany* 57 (3): 295–323.

Merrill, W. L. 1979. The Beloved Tree: *Ilex vomitoria* among the Indians of the Southeast and Adjacent Regions. In *The Black Drink: A Native American Tea*, ed. C. Hudson, 40–82. Athens: University of Georgia Press.

Mountjoy, J. B. 1982. An Interpretation of the Pictographs at La Peña Pintada, Jalisco, Mexico. *American Antiquity* 47 (1): 110–26.

Pearsall, D. M. 1992. The Origins of Plant Cultivation in South America. In *The Origins of Agriculture: An International Perspective*, ed. C. W. Cowan and P. J. Watson, 173–205. Washington, D.C.: Smithsonian Institution Press.

Phillips, P. A., and J. A. Brown. 1975. *Pre-Columbian Shell Engravings from the Craig Mound at Spiro, Oklahoma*. Cambridge, Mass.: Peabody Museum Press.

Rafferty, S. M. 2002. Chemical Analysis of Early Woodland Period Smoking Pipe Residue. *Journal of Archaeological Science* 29 (8): 897–907.

Rafferty, S. M. 2006. Evidence of Early Tobacco in Northeastern North America? *Journal of Archaeological Science* 33 (4): 453–58.

Rafferty, S. M., I. Lednev, K. Virkler, and Z. Chovanec. 2012. Current Research on Smoking Pipe Residues. *Journal of Archaeological Science* 39 (7): 1951–59.

Reber, E. A., and M. T. Kerr. 2012. The Persistence of Caffeine in Experimentally Produced Black Drink Residues. *Journal of Archaeological Science* 39 (7): 2312–19.

Roberts, M. F., and M. Wink. 1998. Introduction. In *Alkaloids: Biochemistry, Ecology and Medicinal Applications*, ed. M. F. Roberts, 1–7. New York: Plenum Press.

Rudgley, R. 1993. *The Alchemy of Culture: Intoxicants in Society*. London: British Museum Press.

Smalley, J., and M. Blake. 2003. Sweet Beginnings: Stalk Sugar and the Domestication of Maize. *Current Anthropology* 44 (5): 675–703.

Stevenson, M. C. 1915. *Ethnobotany of the Zuni Indians*. Bureau of American Ethnology Annual Report 30. Washington, D.C.: Smithsonian Institution.

Sturtevant, W. C. 1954. The Medicine Bundles and Busks of the Florida Seminole. *Florida Anthropologist* 7: 52–55.

Swanton, J. R. 1946. *The Indians of the Southeastern United States*. Bureau of American Ethnology Bulletin 137. Washington, D.C.: Smithsonian Institution.

Terry, M., K. L. Steelman, T. Guilderson, P. Dering, and M. W. Rowe. 2006. Lower Pecos and Coahuila Peyote: New Radiocarbon Dates. *Journal of Archaeological Science* 33: 1017–21.

Tushingham, S., D. Ardura, M. Palazoglu, J. Eerkens, S. Shahbaz, and O. Fiehn. 2010. Gas Chromatography–Mass Spectrometry Analysis of Alkaloid Residues in Ancient and Experimental Pipes. Paper presented at the 75th annual meeting of the Society for American Archaeology, St. Louis, Missouri.

Tushingham, S., M. Palumbo, C. H. McNutt, and U. Anderson. 2011. The Biomolecular Archaeology of the Black Drink: Alkaloid Residue Analysis of *Ilex vomitoria* on Experimental Vessels and Applications for Prehistoric Specimens. Paper presented at the 68th annual meeting of the Southeastern Archaeology Conference, Jacksonville, Florida.

Vestal, P. 1952. *Ethnobotany of the Ramah Navajo*. Peabody Museum of American Archaeology and Ethnology, vol. 40, no. 1. Cambridge, Mass.: Harvard University.

Wagner, G. E. 1998. Tobacco. In *Archaeology of Prehistoric North America: An Encyclopedia*, ed. G. Gibbon, 840–41. New York: Garland Publishing.

Wagner, G. E. 2000. Tobacco in Prehistoric Eastern North America. In *Tobacco Use by Native Americans: Sacred Smoke and Silent Killer*, ed. J. C. Winter, 185–201. Norman: University of Oklahoma Press.

Wassén, S. H. 1972. A Medicine-Man's Implements and Plants in a Tiahuanacoid Tomb in Highland Bolivia. *Etnologiska Studier* 32: 7–114.

Waterman, P. G. 1998. Chemical Taxonomy of Alkaloids. In *Alkaloids: Biochemistry, Ecology and Medicinal Applications*, ed. M. F. Roberts and M. Wink, 87–107. New York: Plenum Press.
Webb, C. H. 1959. *The Belcher Mound: A Stratified Caddoan Site in Caddo Parish, Louisiana*. Memoirs of the Society for American Archaeology no. 16. Salt Lake City: University of Utah Press.
White, N. M., and R. A. Weinstein. 2008. The Mexican Connection and the Far West of the U.S. Southeast. *American Antiquity* 73 (2): 227–77.
Whiting, A. F. 1939. *Ethnobotany of the Hopi*. Museum of Northern Arizona Bulletin 15. Flagstaff.
Wink, M. 1998. A Short History of Alkaloids. In *Alkaloids: Biochemistry, Ecology and Medicinal Applications*. New York: Plenum Press.
Winter, J. C. 2000a. Introduction to the North American Tobacco Species. In *Tobacco Use by Native North Americans: Sacred Smoke and Silent Killer*, ed. J. C. Winter, 3–8. Norman: University of Oklahoma Press.
Winter, J. C. 2000b. Traditional Uses of Tobacco by Native North Americans. In *Tobacco Use by Native North Americans: Sacred Smoke and Silent Killer*, ed. J. C. Winter, 9–58. Norman: University of Oklahoma Press.
Winter, J. C. 2000c. From Earth Mother to Snake Woman: The Role of Tobacco in the Evolution of Native American Religious. In *Tobacco Use by Native North Americans: Sacred Smoke and Silent Killer*, ed. J. C. Winter, 265–304. Norman: University of Oklahoma Press.
Winter, J. C. 2004. Creating Tobacco: Native American Origins, Beliefs and Uses. Paper presented at Beloit College, Wisconsin.
Yarnell, R. A. 1959. Prehistoric Pueblo Use of Datura. *Palacio* 66: 176–78.

5

Pipes, Cups, Platform Mounds, and Mortuary Ritual in the Lake Okeechobee Basin of South Florida

VICTOR D. THOMPSON AND THOMAS J. PLUCKHAHN

Archaeologists have explored the role of psychoactive substances and other stimulants throughout the ancient world using a host of theoretical perspectives and analytical techniques. These studies range from the identification of plant or animal remains (e.g., Davis and Weil 1992; Merlin 2003) to the documentation of specific uses (e.g., Glass-Coffin 2010) and the discussion of the role that such activities played in the lives of individuals (e.g., shamans [see VanPool 2009]) and within larger social contexts. In this chapter, we consider the intersections between community, individual, place, and animate material culture in the production of altered states of consciousness. Specifically, we propose that to understand the role that such ritually related activities have for a given community, they must be contextualized and understood from a perspective that accounts for both the materiality and the history of such actions (see Howey and O'Shea 2006 for a similar approach).

In order to take the holistic approach that we advocate, we adopt a theoretical perspective that is at its base a form of historical processualism (Pauketat 2001a, 2001b). The specific aspect of this perspective that we find the most compelling is that the focus of archaeological questions centers on "what people did and how they negotiated their views of others and of their own pasts" (Pauketat 2001a: 73). We consider this in the context of not just the relationships such people have with other individuals but also how histories and traditions are made and remade though interactions with and beliefs regarding the animate nature of material culture (i.e., an animic ontology; for a discussion see Skousen and Buchanan 2015). We argue that such a perspective is essential if we are to consider the role that psychoactive substances played in ancient societies. Methodologically, this requires that we not only document the use of such substances but also consider how altered states were materialized through practices and created alternative identities, as well as how such actions contributed to history-making in communities.

Here, we apply our approach to the archaeological site of Fort Center in the Lake Okeechobee basin of south Florida. The site is a large earthwork complex located on the western edge of the lake along Fisheating Creek; it contains over twenty-four earthworks covering an area 1.5 kilometer long by 1 kilometer wide (Thompson and Pluckhahn 2012) (figure 5.1). The occupation of the site spans a considerable amount of time, from circa 800 BC, when people constructed the first earthworks at the site, to the sixteenth century, when the resident community was likely a tributary of the Calusa polity. Early research suggested that the occupants of Fort Center practiced intensive maize agriculture (Sears and Sears 1976; Sears 1982). The early view of the occupants of Fort Center as maize-based agriculturalists biased the interpretation of some of the features at the site, resulting in the assertion that many of the earthworks were a form of water-management technology, based on similarities with South American sites (Sears 1982). New research now indicates that the subsistence base was primarily fishing, hunting, and gathering of the productive wetland environments that surround the site (Hale 1984; Johnson 1990, 1991; Morris 2012; Thompson and Pluckhahn 2014; Thompson et al. 2013). Interpretations of these features, in light of new information on Fort Center subsistence practices, now describe these features as intimately intertwined with the construction of long-term ritualized landscapes that referenced the local ecology of the region (Thompson and Pluckhahn 2012).

Fort Center's Mound-Pond Complex

As Fort Center is a large and complicated archaeological landscape, we focus primarily on one part of the site, the mound-pond complex. Later in the discussion, we consider this suite of features within the larger context and overall history of Fort Center. The mound-pond complex is perhaps the most famous section of the site. Excavated in the 1960s and

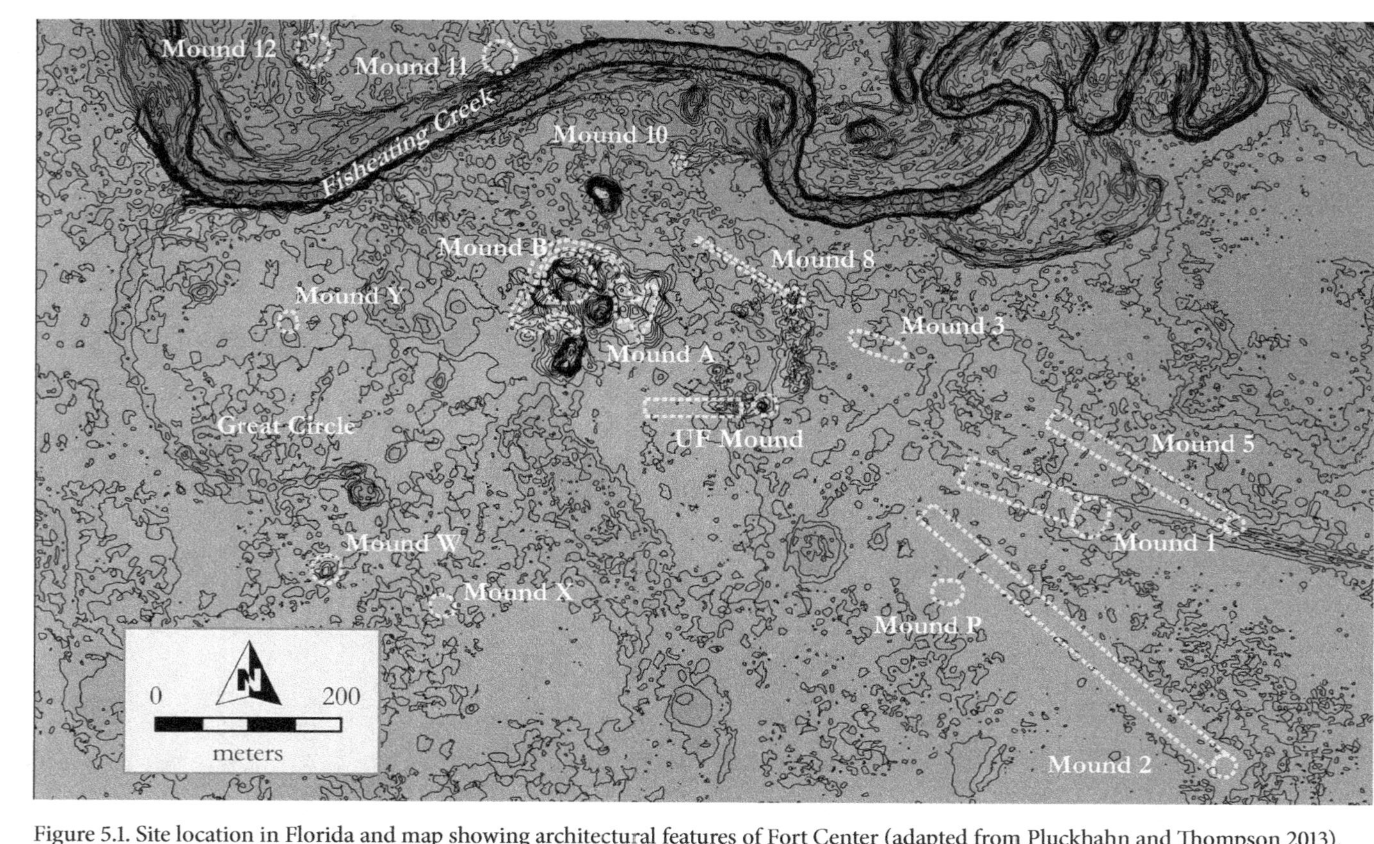

Figure 5.1. Site location in Florida and map showing architectural features of Fort Center (adapted from Pluckhahn and Thompson 2013).

early 1970s, two platform mounds (Mound A and Mound B), an artificially constructed pond, and a low earthen berm partially encircling the mounds constitute the complex (Sears 1982: 145) (figure 5.2).

The earliest date from the complex, 800–540 cal BC (2σ), comes from Mound B. While there are semi-fiber-tempered ceramics from the complex that corroborate early use during this time, the vast majority of the occupation, based on both ceramics and radiocarbon dates, suggests intensive use of the complex during later time periods (Thompson and Pluckhahn 2012: 59). In this chapter, we focus on the time frame up to cal AD 650, as this appears to be the point at which all the features in the complex were functioning as a whole (i.e., Early Woodland and Middle Woodland).

The two mounds are juxtaposed across the pond, with the irregularly shaped Mound A at 1 meter tall and the conical, truncated, flat-topped Mound B standing over 5.5 meters tall (Pluckhahn and Thompson 2012; Thompson and Pluckhahn 2012: 57). Sears's (1982: 174–75) excavation of large sections of both of these mounds identified posts associated with structures and the presumed domestic midden.

The pond is perhaps the most fascinating feature at the site. It is roughly circular and around 30 meters in diameter. Sears's (1982) excavations in the pond produced hundreds of wooden artifacts and burial remains. He hypothesized that at one point some type of wooden platform or structure stood over the pond where burials were placed. This structure then eventually burned and fell into the pond, preserving many of the wood carvings that he speculates were attached to this structure (Sears 1982). There is some debate as to whether this interpretation is correct. Wheeler (1996: 95–97) suggests that, based on the amount of wood and where it was recovered, there was no mortuary platform, but rather the effigy carvings were placed in other areas of the site before being interred with burials. In either case, people living in the mound-pond complex were interacting with the dead as well as a variety of other ceremonial artifacts.

In total, Sears recovered over 300 individuals from his excavations in the mound-pond complex. The pond contained around 150 individuals, which are the best-preserved skeletal remains from the site. Skeletal remains included both sexes. Most were adults aged twenty-one to fifty-five, with few subadults and elderly individuals (Miller-Shaivitz and Iscan 1991: 143). Relevant to our study is the finding of pseudopathological conditions on some (n = 8) of the long bones (i.e., humerus, radius, femur, and two tibiae), which Miller-Shaivitz and Iscan (1991: 143) attributed to maceration.

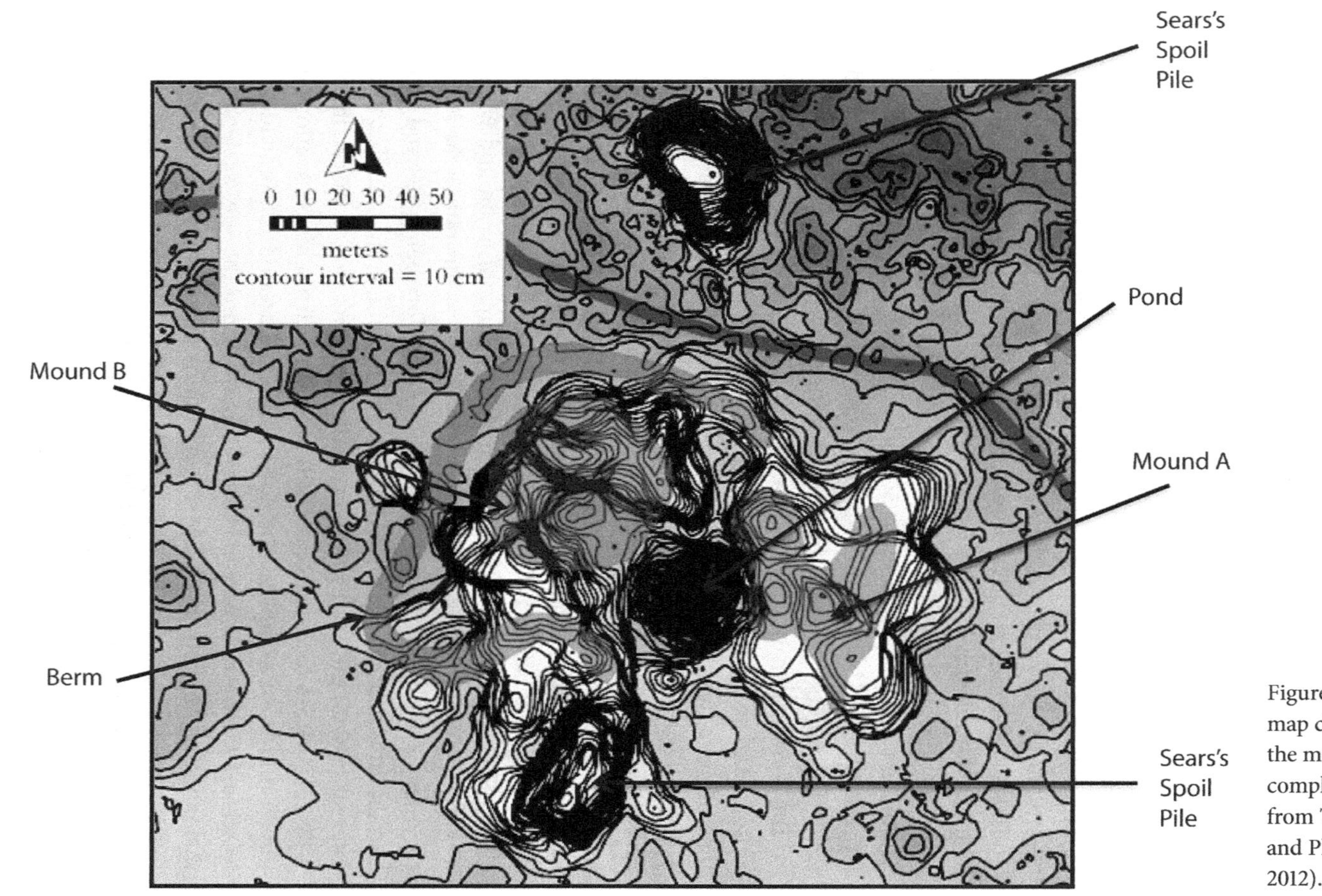

Figure 5.2. Site map close-up of the mound-pond complex (adapted from Thompson and Pluckhahn 2012).

The occupational midden on the mounds and possible evidence of maceration of individuals is consistent with Sears's (1982: 175) interpretation that the mound-pond complex served as the living area for ceremonial specialists involved in mortuary rituals. He likens the individuals participating in such activities to the Buzzard Men of the historic Choctaws (Sears 1982: 175). In addition, many other historic groups of the American Southeast customarily placed bodies on wooden platforms (Hudson 1976: 334–35), which is similar to Sears's interpretations. However, it is still possible that there was not a platform as Wheeler suggests, which would be consistent with Woodland period mound-top posts (Knight 2001; Pluckhahn 2003). We essentially agree with Sears in general that the mound-pond complex served not only as a place of the dead but also as the living space of those who handled and directed mortuary rituals, and as such they may have been accorded higher or special status within the greater community (Sears 1982; Thompson and Pluckhahn 2012). We are, of course, uncertain of exactly who these people were or what role they played in the larger society. And it may be impossible to know whether these individuals were full- or part-time specialists, a group of initiated males (e.g., men's house [see Milanich 1998]), or something akin to the Buzzard Men as Sears proposed. Regardless, the interpretation that certain people enacted activities associated with both spiritual and everyday life leads us to our central question of this chapter: how did these individuals perform and negotiate their roles in the community, and to what extent did they create history? To address this question, we must explore what activities were engaged in and how these people's material entanglements set them apart from the rest of community. In other words, how was difference enacted or performed in terms of their relationships with other agents (e.g., material culture) in their lived world?

Evidence for Altered States

One of the key activities that separate ritual specialists or other select individuals primarily engaged in ritual (e.g., shamans, priests, initiated males or females) from other members of society is their ingestion and use of substances that produce altered states of consciousness (e.g., VanPool 2003: 700). For Native American societies of the American Southeast, the two substances that could be included in this category are the Black Drink, known as yaupon (*Ilex vomitoria*), and tobacco (*Nicotiana rustica*) smoking, the latter being a mild hallucinogen (Siegel et al. 1977). Ethnohistoric accounts indicate that these substances were not limited to priests and other ritual specialists during the historic period in the American Southeast.

Tobacco seeds dating to as early as AD 160 ± 80 have been recovered (Haberman 1984: 271; Rafferty 2008: 279); however, recent chemical analysis of pipes in the Eastern Woodlands by Rafferty (2006: 453) suggests that the substance may have been in use as early as circa 300 BC. While there is no direct evidence in the paleobotanical record of tobacco, the mound-pond complex has a high frequency of pipes and pipe fragments (figure 5.3). In fact, the distribution of smoking pipes seems to be restricted to this area of the site, suggesting that this activity was primarily associated with either the ceremonial specialists or mortuary rituals conducted by initiated males (Milanich 1998; Sears 1982). Tobacco is the most likely substance used in these pipes, as all of these date primarily to Sears's Period II for the site, which coincides with the Middle Woodland period, the point at which tobacco use became widespread (Riley et al. 1990: 529).

The recovery of lime processing residue in the mound-pond complex is also perhaps related to the smoking of tobacco. The addition of lime to tobacco increases the hallucinogenic effects of the plant (VanPool 2003: 700; Wilbert 1987: 18). Sears (1982: 187–88) suggested that the lime was used to process maize; however, because our new research shows that maize played little to no role at the site (Thompson et al. 2013), this interpretation seems no longer valid. An alternative function of lime production could be for its use in the packing of tobacco pipes. Using ethnohistoric evidence, Marcus and Flannery (1996: 87) have suggested that lime was used in this way at Formative period sites in Mexico. Similarly, Pluckhahn and colleagues (2006: 277) have suggested a comparable use for limestone found in association with small-scale feasting at Kolomoki, a large Middle Woodland site contemporary with Fort Center.

Black Drink is the other key ceremonial substance for which evidence has been found at Fort Center. Recent microbotanical analysis of deposits dating to the Belle Glade I period (ca. 900 BC to AD 200) identified holly (*Ilex* sp.) pollen (Thompson et al. 2013). While not identifiable to species, this pollen may be *Ilex vomitoria*, commonly called yaupon holly, which is indigenous to Florida and was used by the Calusas in ceremonies (Austin 2006: 412). Future research will use residue analysis to examine this in more detail (see Reber and Kerr 2012 for a method to identify Black Drink). This plant was the key ingredient in making the Black Drink, a highly caffeinated tea used in ceremonies throughout the American Southeast (Hudson 1976, 1979). The physiological effects of ingesting

Figure 5.3. Some of the pipes recovered from the mound-pond complex. (Photograph courtesy of the Florida Museum of Natural History.)

massive quantities of this stimulant included clearer thought and sharpening of reaction time, among others (Hudson 1976: 228). On occasion, the Black Drink would be used as an emetic, and individuals would vomit or purge after ingesting large quantities of the liquid (Hudson 1976: 228). Often, consumption of the Black Drink would be accompanied by the smoking of tobacco (Fairbanks 1979; Hudson 1976: 228).

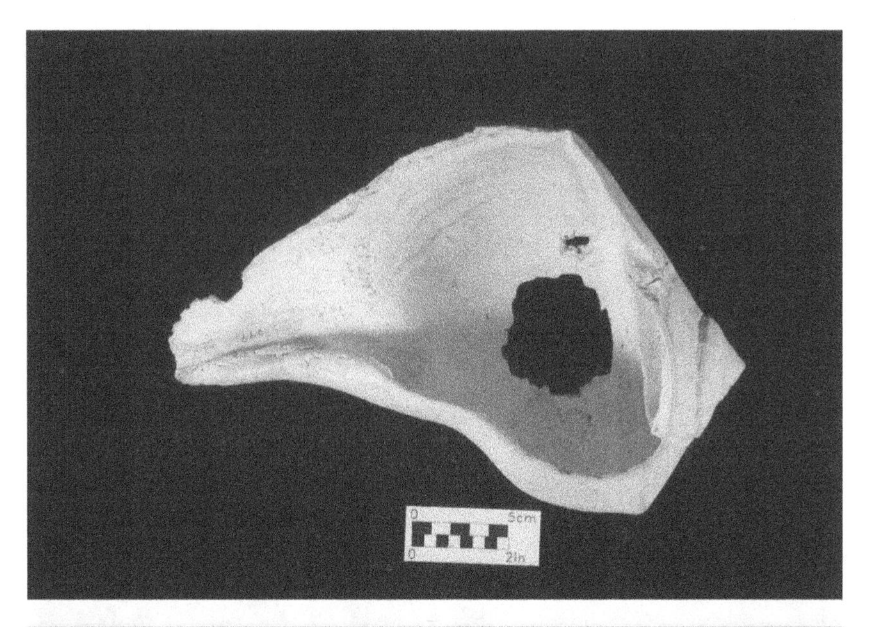

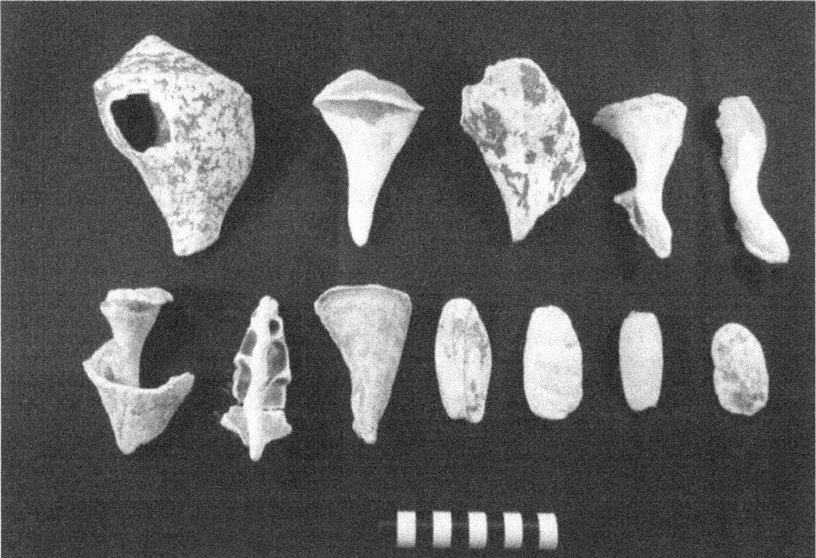

Figure 5.4. Some of the shell tools recovered from the mound-pond complex. (Photograph courtesy of the Florida Museum of Natural History.)

In coastal areas, Native Americans prepared the Black Drink in large pots and often drank the liquid from gastropod marine shell cups/dippers/vessels (e.g., *Busycon carica, Sinistrofulgur perversum* [formerly known as *Busycon sinistrum*], *Triplofusus giganteus* [formerly known as *Pleuroploca gigantea*]), which were often traded to interior groups for the same use (Fairbanks 1979; Marquardt and Kozuch 2016; Milanich 1979, 1994; Thompson and Worth 2011). Production of these cups involves removal of the columella and possible smoothing of the lip areas (for an explanation of production, see Marquardt 1992: 216).

Most of the shell vessels at Fort Center were produced from *Sinistrofulgur perversum* (lightning whelk), and the vast majority of shell artifacts/fragments in general ($n = 441$) come from the mound-pond complex (figure 5.4). Many of the vessels appear throughout the mounds; some are associated with specific individuals. One adult burial contained a fragment of an infant's cranium, seven lighting whelk dippers, and Venus clam shells, among other burial artifacts (Sears 1982: 157). We argue that these shells would have been used in rituals, including those associated with mortuary rites. Some of these shells exhibit "kill holes," indicating their ritual transformation before being interred in the mounds. We expand on this point later in our discussion. Finally, it is worth noting that Fort Center is around 100 kilometers from the coast, and any shell found at the site is the product of either trade or direct procurement and thus can be considered exotic.

The combined consumption of the Black Drink and tobacco, as well as the cultural practices we describe below, likely produced significant altered states of consciousness. Physical activities were often associated with the consumption of these substances among the Calusas. In one historic account, the men ate only berries, drank cassina (the Black Drink), and ran races for days, to the point of fatigue, at which point they were said to experience "death and rebirth" (Marquardt 1988: 172). As Marquardt (1988: 172) states, "Such exhaustion and ingestion of stimulants would quite likely cause hallucinations and out of body experiences." While we do not know whether such activities accompanied rituals at Fort Center, it is useful to consider what other activities might have enhanced the effects of these two substances.

Place and Materiality in Altered States

Beyond the mere ingestion of stimulants, as we outline above for Fort Center, we argue that place and everyday action and interaction with various aspects of material culture also play a part in the creation of identity for ritual specialists (see Jordan 2001). In such cases, material culture, ranging from sacred bundles to artifacts used in daily life, is important regarding the construction and reproduction of social relations from an agent-center perspective (see Dornan 2002; Giddens 1984; Hodder 1982).

As Inomata and Coben explain (2006: 13), there is a spectrum of performances that range from highly formalized behaviors (e.g., mortuary rituals) to everyday actions, which also work as "forms of human interactions and self-presentations." Thus, to understand how these ritual specialists performed identities and created histories, we must consider them within a broader social context that includes daily life (e.g., Jordan 2001; see also the discussion in Skousen and Buchanan 2015), as well as how such actions articulate within larger community histories. For Fort Center, this means considering the suite of artifacts and the structure of the architecture of the mound complex itself relative to the rest of the site.

As we have already pointed out, one of the characteristics that set the mound-pond complex apart from the rest of the site is its high frequency of smoking pipe fragments and shell vessels/cups/dippers. We argue that ritual specialists and perhaps some other members of the community consumed substances from these artifacts during ceremonies. Further, we suggest that, given the restricted distribution of these over the site, most of these types of activities took place within the mound-pond complex itself. If this interpretation is correct, then this would literally offset the individuals who resided on the mounds from the rest of the community during such times. The spatial separation of the mound-pond complex from the middens would have augmented the isolation of the residents of this feature, as would the circular embankment that defines the complex (Sears 1982: 145–48). Also highlighting the distinctive character of the mound-pond complex was the setting; Sears (1982: 163) characterized the pond itself as "scummy, green, evil-smelling." While this characterization may not be entirely applicable to the pond as it existed during the period under discussion, there can be little doubt that the decomposing bodies would have lent this area—and perhaps by extension its residents—a distinctive aura. However, beyond this we argue that such persons would have been viewed as "special" or "different" by the community at large because of their proximity to the dead and other mortuary-related artifacts (e.g., wood carvings) as they moved about their daily lives. Thus, every action in the lives of such people was in part a performance of difference, some consciously enacted and others unconsciously performed.

In addition to possible macerating of the dead and other mortuary-related activities, the individuals who occupied the mound-pond complex also may have been responsible for many of the effigy carvings associated with the pond burials. Steinen (1982: 90–91) suggests that shark teeth, a large number of which were recovered from the mound-pond complex, were used in a specialized tool kit related to wood carving—specifically, the numerous effigy carvings recovered from the pond. New microwear analysis by Keller and Thompson (2013) corroborates the idea that shark teeth were indeed used in this fashion. However, they argue that woodworking with shark teeth was not restricted to ritual carvings and likely occurred beyond the boundaries of the mound-pond complex, possibly for the production of utilitarian objects such as wooden bowls (Keller and Thompson 2013). Regardless of whether or not the individuals were the carvers of the effigies, they most likely handled them at some point. They also resided near the effigies, whether Sears's interpretation regarding their attachment to a platform is correct or they were inset in the pond and remained above the water level, later to be interred.

Sears (1982: 42–58) divides the wooden effigies into three categories: "large birds and beasts, two legged animals, and tenoned birds" (figure 5.5). Some of these carvings are of considerable size, standing over 3 meters tall, and could have been used as structural supports or freestanding effigies in the pond. Other effigies are much smaller, measuring up to 0.5 meters long. Some of these more diminutive effigies had tenons for sockets and were designed to be removed on occasion, possibly for certain ceremonies or rituals (Sears 1982; Purdy 1991: 91). It is also quite possible that some of these effigies were painted. Wooden artifacts recovered from other south Florida sites have traces of pigments on them (Purdy 1991). The recovery of pigment from the complex suggests that the occupants may have been involved in this process (Sears 1982: 48).

Many of the effigies are naturalistic representations of animals that were present in south Florida at the time Native Americans occupied Fort Center. Some of the more obvious animals include raptorial birds of prey (e.g., falcon, eagle, osprey, owl), otters, bears, and large cats (e.g., Florida panther, bobcat), as well as other birds (Sears 1982). These animal representations are interpreted by Widmer (1989: 173) to represent an "emphasis on rituals or ceremonies either derived from or pertaining to supernatural relationships with animals composing or found in the subsistence base." While this certainly could be the case for some of the animals portrayed in wood at Fort Center, we are less certain of this for the ones that represent apex predators, such as the large cats (i.e., panthers) (figure 5.6).

Recently, Wheeler (2011) examined the role of panthers (*Puma concolor couguar*) among the peoples of Florida. He states that panthers were probably rarely eaten and had little correlation with social rank (Wheeler 2011: 151). In contrast, he suggests that there is some evidence connecting panthers with shamanic practices (Wheeler 2011: 151). In at least two

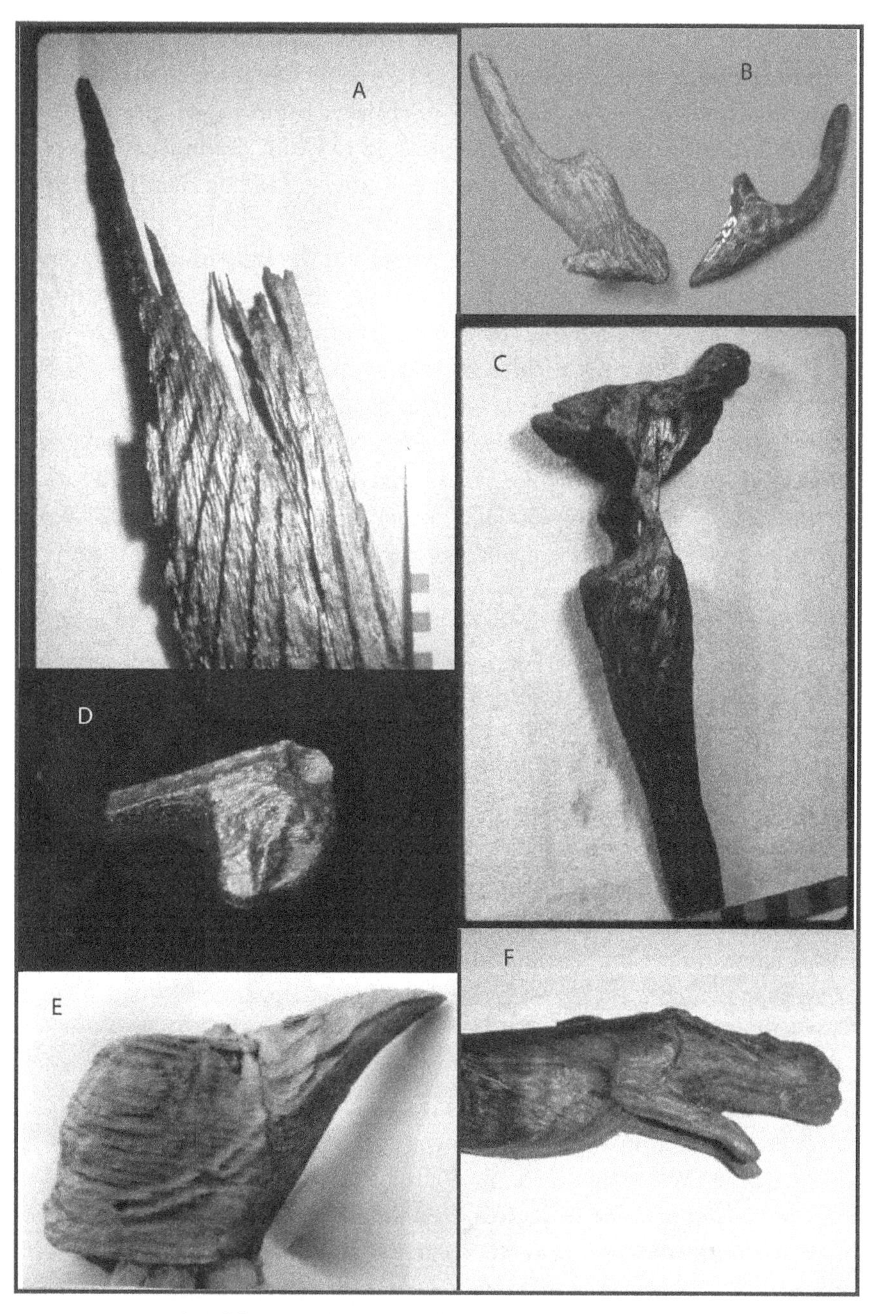

Figure 5.5. Examples of the carved wooden effigies recovered from the mortuary pond. (Photograph courtesy of the Florida Museum of Natural History.)

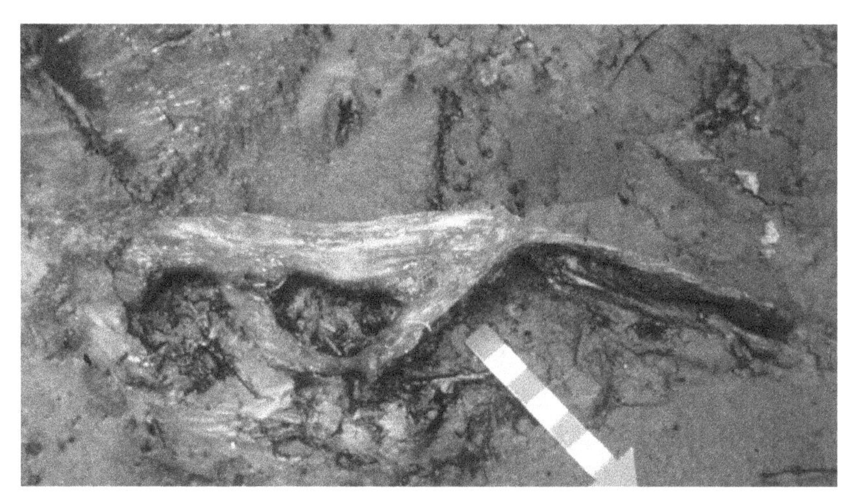

Figure 5.6. Example of one of the carved feline effigies from the mortuary pond. (Photograph courtesy of the Florida Museum of Natural History.)

cases, there are wooden effigies at other contemporaneous sites in Florida that represent the transformation of human to cat or vice versa (i.e., the Key Marco cat and the Padgett figure from Palm Hammock) (Wheeler 2011). While none of the large cat figures from Fort Center represents such transformations, we nevertheless argue that their presence most likely parallels beliefs held about the animal that south Florida peoples held in common, such as an association with the supernatural world.

Our final points regarding the production of difference of individuals who occupied the mound-pond complex is directly related to the place itself. At the height of its use, the mound-pond complex would have been near or at the center of the site, thus serving as a possible axis mundi. Certainly, the juxtaposition of architectural features of mounds (possibly representing the upper world), the pond (possibly representing the underworld), and evidence of domestic occupation (representing the world of people) has not been lost on researchers (Pluckhahn and Thompson 2013; Steinen 2007). The inhabitants of Fort Center also might have viewed the mound-pond complex and the people who inhabited the location as potentially dangerous. Hall (1976) argues that the platform over the pond and many other circular berms and ditches at Fort Center were constructed as barriers for the dead. If this is the case, then those who resided with the dead would have been viewed similarly. While we might never know exactly how the occupants viewed this complex, we argue that the key attributes of these features and their position together would have been meaningfully constituted and intentional in terms of insiders and outsiders.

Performing Histories of Difference

The example from Fort Center provides us with a case study suggesting, for at least some societies, that altered states require more than simply the ingestion of stimulants and other substances. In this chapter, we document a suite of material culture that ranges from the artifacts necessary to ingest such substances (e.g., pipes, cups) to those that were instrumental in the context of such activities (e.g., wood carvings, mounded architecture, burial pond). We argue that to understand the role of the individuals who took part in such activities, we must contextualize them within a large social and material realm that includes not only actions and material culture as active agents related to rituals but also how these aspects related to the daily life of the people who took part in such activities.

In this chapter, we focus on the individuals who occupied the mound-pond complex and recognize that this part of Fort Center had a long history. We argue that part of the tradition of occupying this particular space was enacting difference, not only for the individuals but also for the place itself (i.e., the mound-pond complex). Thus, the enactment of difference included reference to the past in the present (Pauketat 2001b: 2). We suggest that part of the way in which individuals did this was by dwelling within mortuary spaces, which included a suite of relationships—not only with other people but also with animals, ancestors, places, objects, and so forth. Such relationships were likely informed by a kind of animic ontology, which views identity as webs of various pathways rather than a single bounded individual (e.g., Bird-David 1999; Ingold 2006; for a discussion of this for the Green River, see Moore and Thompson 2012).

We also suggest that individuals within the mound-pond complex referenced these various relational pathways in terms of actions associated with rituals as well as in their day-to-day lives. The consumption of psychoactive substances not only created a means for individuals to interact with supernatural entities but also reinforced relationships with people who could not partake in such journeys. Relationships were also performed through their interaction with ritual-related material culture, not only during such times but also during daily activities. Further, the use of nonlocal materials in both mortuary rituals (i.e., shell cup/vessel/dipper) and everyday tools (i.e., shell hammers, shark teeth) would have also reinforced aspects of difference and cited the larger geographic and spiritual pathways and webs that defined the occupants of the mound-pond complex in the community, in history, and in the universe.

We view the relationships that people had with such objects not simply as people reacting to material culture or using material culture to assert identity. Instead, we argue that the material culture associated with mortuary ritual and the daily life of the people who occupied the mound-pond complex functioned as active agents within the network of interaction webs that were part of ritual practices at Fort Center. Thus, the shell cup with a "kill hole" (see figure 5.4) present was just as much an actor, possessing a kind of personhood (sensu VanPool and Newsome 2012), in mortuary rituals as were human actors. Like humans, such artifacts required transformation (i.e., puncturing the bottom) before they could travel to the world of the dead (see VanPool and Newsome 2012 for a comparable example regarding pots in the American Southwest).

Similarly, the effigy carvings could also be considered through the lens of animism. Given the ubiquity of wood carvings found throughout south Florida and their documented role in rituals and in ceremonial architecture, it is likely that these materials played more than a passive role in these societies. And any consideration of the role of ritual must include the notion that such items were also active participants in such rituals. As VanPool and Newsome (2012: 259) state, we cannot model such worldviews if "the spiritual essence of a significant number of social entities framed within it is denied or ignored." We take this statement to be an imperative part of our analysis. We suggest that part of the way in which humans interacted with the sprits that inhabited the effigies, cups, and pipes was through entering altered states. By entering such states, individuals were able to access not only the spirits but also the histories that they have to tell or were a part of. Thus, by engaging with such beings, individuals are able to reinforce tradition (sensu Pauketat 2001a, 2001b) within society.

In conclusion, a perspective that incorporates material culture as active agents, place, self, and society aids us in considering the histories that such individuals constructed for themselves, as well as how they may have been viewed by the community at large. The constant enactment of difference and the citation of such individuals' larger web of relationships with both the dead and the spirits that inhabited the material world would have been something that not only occupied the minds of the people performing such actions and interacting with such beings but also was considered by the community at large. Thus, even when such individuals were not engaging in the ingestion of stimulants and contacting the ancestors, spirits, or the like, their daily lives—by virtue of dwelling in such spaces surrounded by the dead and ritualized animate material culture—would have been a constant reminder of the fact that such people were always between worlds in a state of permanent liminality.

Acknowledgments

We thank Scott Fitzpatrick for his invitation to participate in the Society for American Archaeology session "Psychoactive Substances in Ancient Societies," as well as this volume. The research at Fort Center was supported by funds from a National Geographic Society (Grant #8772-10), the Ohio State University, and the University of South Florida. We thank Amanda Roberts-Thompson, Hannah Morris, Margaret Spivey, and the OSU 2010 archaeological field school students for their help. Our research also would not have been possible without the support of the Fisheating Creek WMA and the Florida Bureau of Archaeological Research, particularly Beth Morford, Ryan Wheeler, and Louis Tesar. We also thank William Marquardt, Karen Walker, Jerald Milanich, Ann Cordell, Mellissa Ayvaz, Elise LeCompte, Donna Ruhl, and Ellen Burlingame Turck for their assistance. Jerald Milanich commented on an earlier draft of this chapter, which improved its overall quality.

References Cited

Austin, D. F. 2006. *Florida Ethnobotany*. Boca Raton, Fla.: CRC Press.

Bird-David, N. 1999. Animism Revisited: Personhood, Environment, and Relational Epistemology. *Current Anthropology* 40: S67–91.

Cummings, L. S., and C. Yost. 2011. Pollen and Phytolith Analysis of Circular Earthwork Samples from the Fort Center Site, 8GL13, Glades County, Florida. Paleo-Research Institute Technical Report 10-133. Submitted to the Department of Anthropology, Ohio State University, Columbus.

Davis, W., and A. T. Weil. 1992. Identity of a New World Psychoactive Toad. *Ancient Mesoamerican* 3: 51–159.

Dornan, J. 2002. Agency and Archaeology: Past, Present, and Future Directions. *Journal of Archaeological Method and Theory* 9: 303–29.

Fairbanks, C. H. 1979. The Function of Black Drink among the Creeks. In *Black Drink: A Native American Tea*, ed. C. M. Hudson, 120–49. Athens: University of Georgia Press.

Giddens, A. 1984. *The Constitution of Society*. Cambridge, U.K.: Polity Press.

Glass-Coffin, B. 2010. Shamanism and San Pedro through Time: Some Notes on the

Archaeology, History, and Continued Use of an Entheogen in Northern Peru. *Anthropology of Consciousness* 21: 58–82.
Haberman, T. W. 1984. Evidence of Aboriginal Tobaccos in Eastern North America. *American Antiquity* 49 (2): 268–87.
Hale, H. S. 1984. Prehistoric Environmental Exploitation around Lake Okeechobee. *Southeastern Archaeology* 3 (2): 173–87.
Hall, R. T. 1976. Ghosts, Water Barriers, Corn, and Sacred Enclosures in the Eastern Woodlands. *American Antiquity* 41 (3): 360–64.
Hann, J. H. 1991. *Missions to the Calusa*. Gainesville: University Press of Florida.
Hodder, I. 1982. Theoretical Archaeology: A Reactionary View. In *Symbolic and Structural Archaeology*, ed. I. Hodder, 1–16. Cambridge: Cambridge University Press.
Howey, M.C.L., and J. M. O'Shea. 2006. Bear's Journey and the Study of Ritual in Archaeology. *American Antiquity* 71 (2): 261–82.
Hudson, C. 1976. *The Southeastern Indians*. Knoxville: University of Tennessee Press.
Hudson, C. M. 1979. Introduction. In *Black Drink: A Native American Tea*, ed. C. M. Hudson, 1–9. Athens: University of Georgia Press.
Ingold, T. 2006. Rethinking the Animate, Re-animating Thought. *Ethnos* 71 (1): 9–20.
Inomata, T., and L. S. Coben. 2006. Overture: An Invitation to the Archaeological Theater. In *Archaeology of Performance: Theaters of Power, Community, and Politics*, ed. T. Inomata and L. S. Coben, 11–46. Oxford, U.K.: AltaMira Press.
Johnson, W. G. 1990. The Role of Maize in South Florida Aboriginal Societies: An Overview. *Florida Anthropologist* 43 (3): 209–14.
Johnson, W. G. 1991. Remote Sensing and Soil Science Applications to Understanding Belle Glade Cultural Adaptations in the Okeechobee Basin. PhD diss., University of Florida, Gainesville.
Jordan, P. 2001. The Materiality of Shamanism as a "World View": Praxis, Artefacts and Landscape. In *The Archaeology of Shamanism*, ed. N. S. Price, 87–104. London: Routledge.
Keller, B., and V. D. Thompson. 2013. A Preliminary Report on the Role of Shark Teeth at Fort Center (8GL13). *Florida Anthropologist* 66 (1–2): 23–30.
Knight, V. J. 2001. Feasting and the Emergence of Platform Mound Ceremonialism in Eastern North America. In *Feasts: Archaeological and Ethnographic Perspectives of Food, Politics, and Power*, ed. M. Dietler and B. Hayden, 11–33. Washington, D.C.: Smithsonian Institution Press.
Marcus, J., and K. Flannery. 1996. *Zapotec Civilization: How Urban Society Evolved in Mexico's Oaxaca*. London: Thames and Hudson.
Marquardt, W. 1988. Politics and Production among the Calusa of South Florida. In *Hunters and Gatherers: History, Evolution, and Social Change*, vol. 1, ed. T. Ingold, D. Riches, and J. Woodburn, 161–88. Oxford, U.K.: Berg.
Marquardt, W. 1992. Shell Artifacts from the Caloosahatchee Area. In *Culture and Environment in the Domain of the Calusa*, ed. W. H. Marquardt, 191–227. Institute of Archaeology and Paleoenvironmental Studies, Monograph 1. University of Florida, Gainesville.
Marquardt, W., and L. Kozuch. 2016. The Lightning Whelk: An Enduring Icon of Southeastern North American Spirituality. *Journal of Anthropological Archaeology* 42: 1–26.

Merlin, M. D. 2003. Archaeological Evidence for the Tradition of Psychoactive Plant Use in the Old World. *Economic Botany* 57 (3): 295–323.

Milanich, J. T. 1979. Origins and Prehistoric Distributions of Black Drink and the Ceremonial Shell Drinking Cup. In *Black Drink: A Native American Tea*, ed. C. M. Hudson, 83–119. Athens: University of Georgia Press.

Milanich, J. T. 1994. *Archaeology of Precolumbian Florida*. Gainesville: University Press of Florida.

Milanich, J. T. 1998. *Florida's Indians from Ancient Times to the Present*. Gainesville: University Press of Florida.

Miller-Shaivitz, P., and M. Y. Iscan. 1991. The Prehistoric People of Fort Center: Physical and Health Characteristics. In *What Mean These Bones: Studies in Southeastern Bioarchaeology*, ed. M. L. Powell, P. S. Bridges, and A. M. Wagner Mires, 131–47. Tuscaloosa: University of Alabama Press.

Moore, C., and V. D. Thompson. 2012. Animism and Green River Persistent Places: A Dwelling Perspective of the Shell Mound Archaic. *Journal of Social Archaeology* 12 (2): 264–84.

Morris, H. R. 2012. Paleoethnobotanic Investigations at Fort Center (8GL13), Florida. Master's thesis, Ohio State University.

Pauketat, T. R. 2001a. Practice and History in Archaeology. *Anthropological Theory* 1 (1): 73–98.

Pauketat, T. R. 2001b. A New Tradition in Archaeology. In *The Archaeology of Traditions: Agency and History Before and After Columbus*, ed. T. R. Pauketat, 1–16. Gainesville: University Press of Florida.

Pluckhahn, T. J. 2003. *Kolomoki: Settlement, Ceremony, and Status in the Deep South, A.D. 350–750*. Tuscaloosa: University of Alabama Press.

Pluckhahn, T. J., and V. D. Thompson. 2012. Integrating LiDAR and Conventional Mapping Data: Methodological Insights and Appraisal of Results from Mapping of the Fort Center Site in South-Central Florida (8GL13). *Journal of Field Archaeology* 37 (4): 289–301.

Pluckhahn, T. J., and V. D. Thompson. 2013. Constituting Similarity and Difference in the Deep South: The Ritual and Domestic Landscapes of Kolomoki, Crystal River, and Fort Center. In *The Ritual and Domestic Landscapes of Early and Middle Woodland Peoples in the Southeast*, ed. A. Wright and E. Henry, 181–95. Gainesville: University Press of Florida.

Pluckhahn, T. J., J. M. Compton, and M. T. Bonhage-Freund. 2006. Evidence of Small Scale Feasting from the Woodland Period Site of Kolomoki, Georgia. *Journal of Field Archaeology* 31 (3): 263–84.

Purdy, B. A. 1991. *The Art and Archaeology of Florida's Wetlands*. Boca Raton, Fla.: CRC Press.

Rafferty, S. M. 2006. Evidence of Early Tobacco in Northeastern North America? *Journal of Archaeological Science* 33 (4): 453–58.

Rafferty, S. M. 2008. Smoking Pipes and Early Woodland Mortuary Ritual: Tubular Pipes in Relation to Adena. In *Transitions: Archaic and Early Woodland Research in the Ohio Country*, ed. M. Otto and B. G. Redmond, 271–83. Athens: Ohio University Press.

Reber, E., and M. T. Kerr. 2012. The Persistence of Caffeine in Experimentally Produced Black Drink Residues. *Journal of Archaeological Science* 39 (7): 2312–19.
Riley, T., R. Edging, and J. Rossen. 1990. Cultigens in Prehistoric Eastern North America: Changing Paradigms. *Current Anthropology* 31: 525–41.
Sears, E., and W. H. Sears. 1976. Preliminary Report on Prehistoric Corn Pollen from Fort Center, Florida. In *Proceedings of the Thirty-Second Southeastern Archaeological Conference, Gainesville, Florida, November 6–8, 1975*, ed. D. A. Peterson Jr., 53–56. Southeastern Archaeological Conference Bulletin 19. Memphis, Tenn.
Sears, W. H. 1982. *Fort Center: An Archaeological Site in the Lake Okeechobee Basin.* Gainesville: University Press of Florida.
Siegel, R. K., P. R. Collings, and J. L. Diaz. 1977. On the Use of *Tagetes lucida* and *Nicotiana rustica* as a Huichol Smoking Mixture: The Aztec "Yahutli" with Suggestive Hallucinogenic Effects. *Economic Botany* 31 (1): 16–23.
Skousen, B. J., and M. E. Buchanan. 2015. Advancing an Archaeology of Movement and Relationships. In *Tracing the Relational: The Archaeology of Worlds, Spirits, and Temporalities*, ed. M. Buchanan and J. Skousen, 1–19. Salt Lake City: University of Utah Press.
Steinen, K. T. 1982. Other Nonceramic Artifacts. In *Fort Center: An Archaeological Site in the Lake Okeechobee Basin*, ed. W. H. Sears, 68–110. Gainesville: University Press of Florida.
Steinen, K. T. 2007. Fort Center Revisited: Stratigraphy, Ethnographic Analogy and Middle Woodland Ceremonialism in Florida. Poster presented at the 64th Annual Meeting of the Southeastern Archaeological Conference, Knoxville.
Thompson, V. D., and T. J. Pluckhahn. 2012. Monumentalization and Ritual Landscapes at Fort Center in the Lake Okeechobee Basin of South Florida. *Journal of Anthropological Archaeology* 31 (1): 49–65.
Thompson, V. D., and T. J. Pluckhahn. 2014. The Modification and Manipulation of Landscape at Fort Center. In *Precolumbian Archaeology in Florida: New Approaches to the Appendicular Southeast*, ed. N. Wallis and A. Randall, 163–82. Gainesville: University Press of Florida.
Thompson, V. D., and J. E. Worth. 2011. Dwellers by the Sea: Native American Coastal Adaptations along the Southern Coasts of Eastern North America. *Journal of Archaeological Research* 19 (1): 51–101.
Thompson, V. D., K. Gremillion, and T. J. Pluckhahn. 2013. Challenging the Evidence for Prehistoric Wetland Maize Agriculture at Fort Center, Florida. *American Antiquity* 78 (1): 181–93.
VanPool, C. S. 2003. The Shaman-Priests of the Casas Grandes Region, Chihuahua, Mexico. *American Antiquity* 68 (4): 696–717.
VanPool, C. S. 2009. The Signs of the Sacred: Identifying Shamans Using Archaeological Evidence. *Journal of Anthropological Archaeology* 28 (2): 177–90.
VanPool, C. S., and E. Newsome. 2012. The Spirit in the Material: A Case Study of Animism in the American Southwest. *American Antiquity* 77 (2): 243–62.
Wheeler, R. 1996. Ancient Art of the Florida Peninsula: 500 B.C. to A.D. 1763. PhD diss., University of Florida, Gainesville.

Wheeler, R. 2011. On the Trail of the Panther in Ancient Florida. *Florida Anthropologist* 64 (3–4): 139–62.

Widmer, R. 1989. Ceremonial Artifacts from South Florida. In *The Southeastern Ceremonial Complex: Artifacts and Analysis*, ed. P. Galloway, 166–82. Lincoln: University of Nebraska Press.

Wilbert, J. 1987. *Tobacco and Shamanism in South America*. New Haven, Conn.: Yale University Press.

6

Power From, Power To, Power Over?

Ritual Drug-Taking and the Social Context of Power among the Indigenous People of the Caribbean

QUETTA KAYE

Could control of drugs (psychoactive substances) used in ritual contexts in the pre-Columbian Caribbean have led to the acquisition of power? And, if so, by whom, what kinds of power were involved, and for what purposes? In this chapter, I examine ritual drug use as part of the dynamics of power and power relations using archaeology and ethnohistory to contextualize the deployment of drugs and the material culture of drug use.

By utilizing different bodies of evidence, I address empowerment as manifested in material culture and look at how representational objects and ritual drug-taking were used to elicit meaning. This relationship between material objects and ritual is explored as the possible basis of empowerment of the political-religious leadership of the prehistoric and protohistoric people of the Caribbean.

The idea of power to provide a way in which an examination of drug-related artifacts, mainly collected over the centuries as "art," could be viewed in a social context also allows for the question to be asked—if not answered yet—whether the acquired knowledge or power accrued to an individual, as part of society, or to his/her social role. Power can be generally conceived either as the intentional capacity of individuals to realize their objectives or as a structural feature of social systems in which definitions of power are associated with either forceful control or structurally determined class relations (Hodder 1984; Miller and Tilley 1984). And did the artifact itself—through style or form, or material or size, or decoration or distribution, or by any other perspective—provide part of the answer, in which case it could also tell us about social complexity in the Caribbean? There are three ways in which to study the ritual process to consider how trends in artifactual use and distribution could reflect the dynamics of power and empowerment. These include agency and personal empowerment, group or communal power, and social power. Given the ritual process as a state of transition, the use of psychoactive substances to induce altered states, and thereby provide access to the supernatural (and the fact that the person engaging with the supernatural is often playing a role), suggests that these are the three kinds of power at stake: (1) empowerment as a device for accruing *personal power,* in which a human uses drugs to access the supernatural or to see things that widens his or her understanding and knowledge; (2) *group power* or *communal power,* in which the individual experience is similar but knowledge gets harnessed by the community; and (3) *social power,* in which certain individuals, either aspiring to leadership or already in leadership positions, aspire to accrue power to legitimize their position or even to increase the power wielded with respect to the rest of the social group. This latter might be especially significant at times of conflict or instability (Flannery 1976; Parsons 1991: 423–25).

As ethnographic research has shown (Helms 1979: 119), power was gained *from* the use of psychoactive substances by contact with the spirit world and the subsequent acquisition of knowledge. But two other distinctions are revealed in the analysis of power: "power *to,*" as a positive concept of empowerment to do things that need not involve other people; and "power *over,*" which, linked to social control, at a general level indicates the concept of power as a modifying or transforming agent that enables people to alter the conditions of their existence or outcomes of specific situations (Barfield 1997: 373–75; Bowie 2000: 57; Miller and Tilley 1984: 5). Generally, but not solely, viewed as a function of the economic, "power over" implicitly requires a relationship with other people, implying power differentials. In technologically simple and small-scale societies, this power could be a factor in, for example, access to rituals. But in more complex societies, it could include access to food and other resources such as materials for tools as well as threats of violence and exclusion whereby certain classes of people are restricted owing to their lack of power (Miller and Tilley 1984: 5).

The following sections focus on the background of the indigenous peoples of the Caribbean islands, followed by an examination of the ritual use of psychoactive substances, the related material culture, and the social context of power.

The Caribbean

The Caribbean area (figure 6.1) is generally divided between the smaller, largely volcanic islands in the south, the Lesser Antilles, and the larger islands in the north, those "discovered" by Columbus in 1492, the Greater Antilles, a geographical rather than a political or ethnic division.

The origins and migration of Early Ceramic Age Amerindian populations to the Caribbean, defined as circa 500 BC–AD 650 (Rouse 1992), and the order in which the islands were settled are subjects of much debate at the present time. But archaeological evidence indicates that circa 500 BC peoples known as the Saladoid (named from the type site of Saladero on the Orinoco River in Venezuela) migrated to the islands, bringing various cultural behaviors with them. These early groups functioned at the level of a complex tribe (Versteeg and Schinkel 1992: 201): that is, "cultures which conduct communal activities have status variation, but no centralised authority" (Siegel 1989: 202).

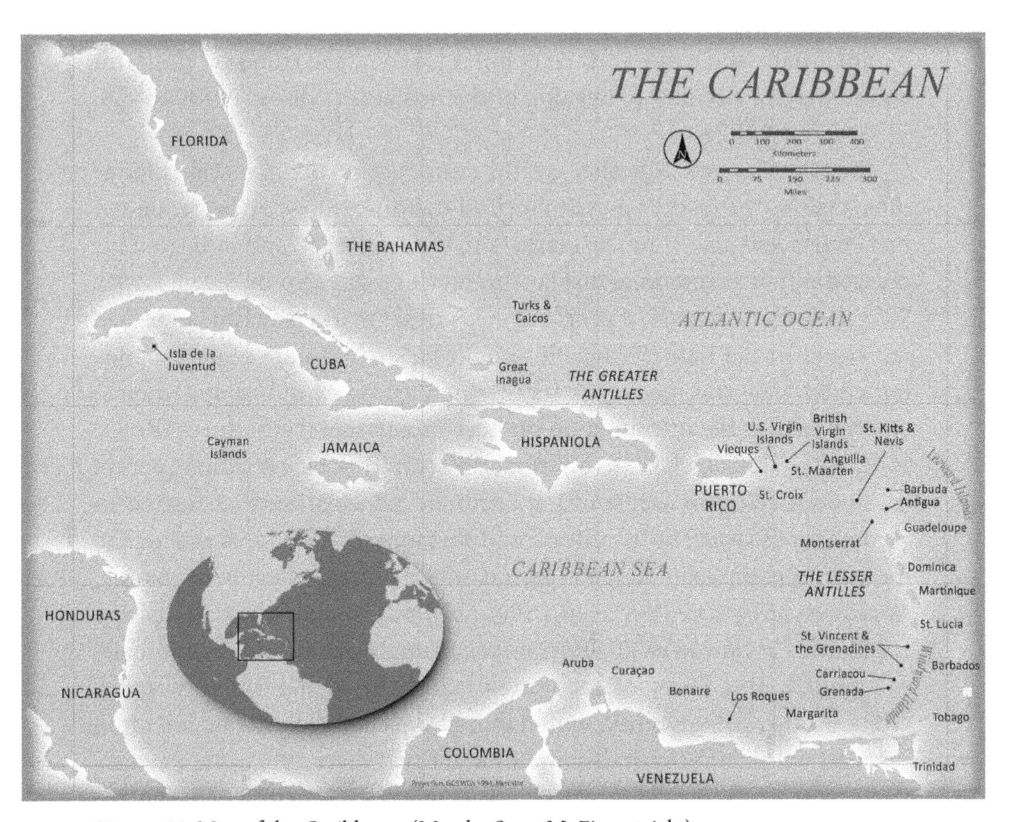

Figure 6.1. Map of the Caribbean. (Map by Scott M. Fitzpatrick.)

In contrast with this designation for the Early Ceramic Age, many archaeologists suggest that the society of the Late period Taino of the Greater Antilles (ca. AD 1000–1492—the people whom Columbus encountered) was hierarchically organized, with paramount and local chiefs, or caciques, at the apex of political-religious power, although it has been suggested that the Spaniards used the term *cacique* ("chief") quite loosely, referring to anyone they saw as in a position of authority (Keegan and Maclachan 1989: 626). But recent research acknowledges that levels of sociopolitical development were not the same on all islands. If chiefs existed, none had achieved political control, direct or indirect, over an entire island, let alone additional islands (Cassa 1990; Keegan 1992; Rouse 1992; Veloz Maggiolo 1997; Wilson 1997a, 1997b).

However, processes associated with social complexity have been identified in the archaeological record in the Caribbean which would indicate that there had been a move from egalitarian to ranked societies. For example, the Late period saw a change of emphasis in material culture with such markers including increased ceremonialism with greater emphasis on the ritual use of hallucinogens; greater emphasis on impressive ritual paraphernalia and a move from ceramics to wood and stone carving with an increase in size and patterning of the artifacts (Wilson 1990: 46–56, 1993; Curet 2002).

The Late Ceramic Age also saw the construction of large-scale monuments taking the form of massive incised standing stones that surrounded ball courts and also stood as markers in the landscape and indicated increased public ceremonial display—a development said by Siegel (1999: 232) to mark a "change of gear." As these ritual markers in the landscape increased in the Late period, this could be seen as part of an expanding ritual view that conveyed increasingly complex public statements, emphasized by the introduction of these monumental structures (Rouse 1992: 105–37; Siegel 1999; Wilson 1999: 6). This bigger ritual picture created a device for transmitting symbolic information that related to ownership of space, both cultural and metaphysical. Did this mirror the increasing complexity of Late period sociopolitical systems over time, as suggested by Roe (1991: 326)? Possibly, but a wider ritual landscape could also be viewed as an effort to keep rituals public and communally sanctioned. This flurry of decoration could also signal societies under stress. Anthropologists have noted that groups that feel threatened often respond with flamboyant displays of identity (Oliver 1997: 141; Reichel-Dolmatoff 1976). But integral to increasingly complex ritual was the use of psychoactive substances known as cohoba.

Cohoba

The early Spanish chroniclers reported their view of the important role that rituals and ceremonies played in the islanders' lives, with detailed descriptions of the rituals involved with the inhalation of a hallucinogenic powder—cohoba. Among the descriptions of the use of cohoba in ritual is that of the early Spanish chronicler Fernández de Oviedo (1975: 92), who noted that "without the opinion of the Devil they undertook nothing of importance." Ramón Pané (1999: 15) reported that cohoba was "a certain powder that they take at times to purge themselves and for other effects." In addition to the powdered psychoactive plant material itself, cohoba was also the name used to describe the ceremony during which the hallucinogenic snuff was imbibed: "Those powders and these acts were called cohoba . . . [which they took, among other things,] in order to hold their councils or to decide difficult matters" (Las Casas 1999: 60).

Pané's (1999: 26) description of the cohoba ceremony climaxed with "You may judge in what state his brain may be, for they say they think they see the houses turn upside down, with their foundations in the air, and the men walk on foot toward the heavens." Peter Martyr Anghiera (Anghiera 1999: 52) described what was said of cohoba: "Such is the efficacy of that ground powder of the cohoba that it immediately takes the sense away from him who takes it."

Interpretations of the descriptions of the early chroniclers and observed use on the South American mainland suggest that cohoba was obtained from either the highly hallucinogenic plant *Anadenanthera peregrina* or a species of *Virola*—both of which have the same tryptamine derivatives and β-carbolines. *A. peregrina*, in addition, however, contains 5-hydroxy-N,N-dimethyltryptamine (5-OH-DMT). 5-OH-DMT is known as bufotenin because it was first isolated in the skin of toads (*Bufo* spp.) and is thought to have the effect of altering serotonin levels (Schultes and Hofmann 1980, 1992). Toads of the species *Bufo marinus* are known to have a place in Central American, South American, and Mesoamerican mythology, particularly among the Olmecs and Mayas, with toad imagery occurring in archaeological stonework (Kennedy 1982; Morgan 1986).

Many artifacts, including paraphernalia for ingesting psychoactive substances, show similarities in form and decorative imagery across the islands, indicating cultural contact over long distances and/or the trade and exchange of prestige goods, with implications for control over long-distance trade. The increase in artifact size and elaboration, including the

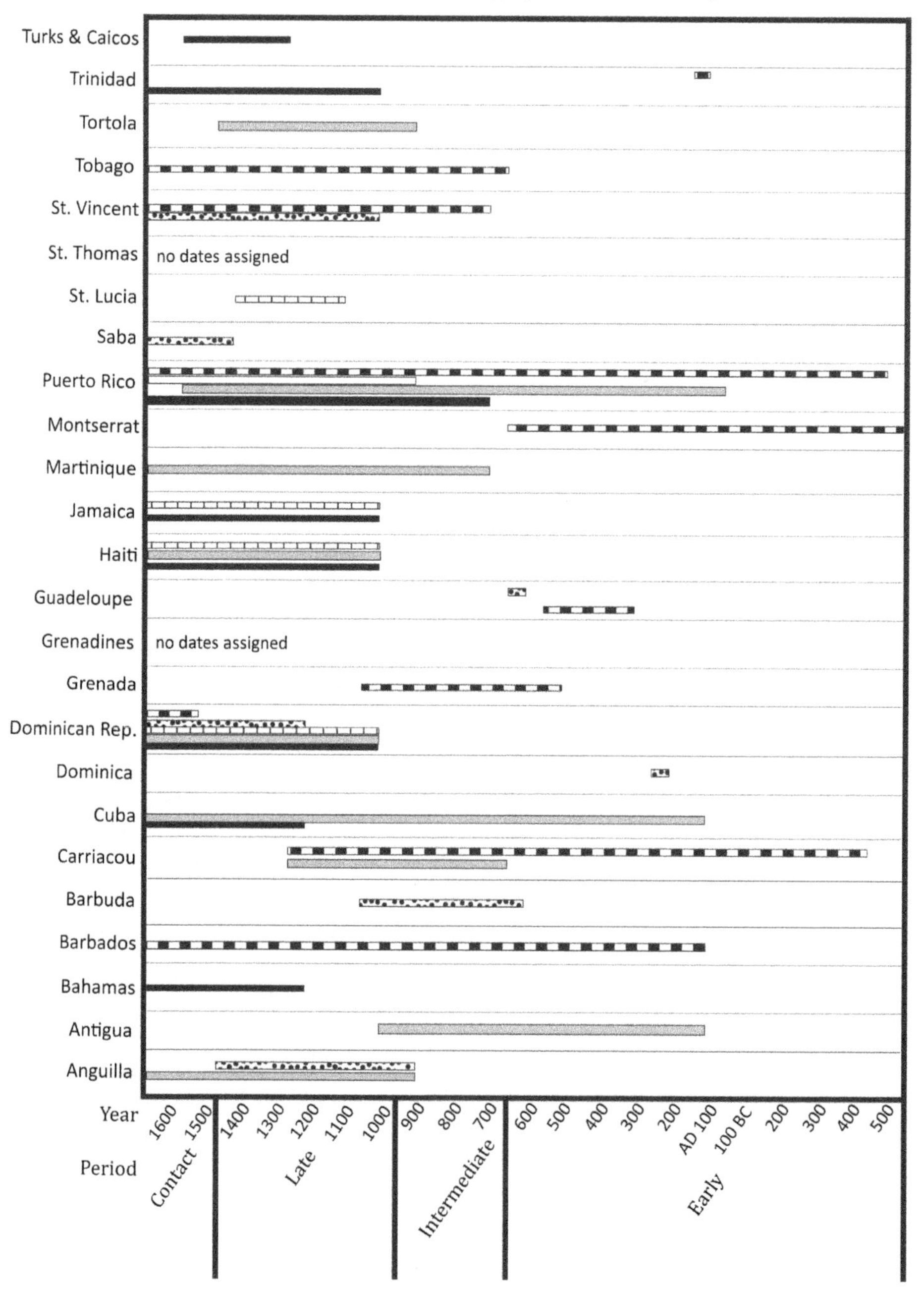

Figure 6.2. The distribution of paraphernalia for ingesting psychoactive substances indicates cultural contact and exchange over long distances. (Figure by Matthew Napolitano.)

drug-related artifacts (which can be seen from figure 6.2 as occurring at a later date than the less complex ones), would indicate that these evolved for *public* ceremonies.

A study of the rituals involving drug-taking shows that these can be seen to crosscut religious, social, and political spheres. Ritual activities included those found cross-culturally, such as births, marriages, and deaths, those rituals of transference from one state to another (Turner 1967; Renfrew 1994), as well as those that include the celebration of harvests, the welcoming of dignitaries, dances, and ball games. The islanders' rituals were also noted to be performed in the hope of achieving a desired outcome or favorably influencing events in an attempt to create an order in the world—a world that reflected human dependency on, or vulnerability to, among other things, the volatile natural environment of the islands (Oliver 1997; Viveiros de Castro 2002: 307).

The rituals could also serve as a potential mechanism of developing social hierarchy. Knowledge as power could have been appropriated by developing elites under some conditions but perhaps not others. The approach of this chapter assumes that the material culture of drug-taking can act as a window on the ways in which either social equality was maintained or inequality was generated by the appropriation of power.

Material Culture

The paraphernalia associated with drug-taking rituals include those that are functional, like tubes and spouted bowls, and others—the *duhos*, effigy figures, and spatulas—that are associated in different ways with the drug-taking experience.

Inhaling tubes (figure 6.3) are described as used to sniff a powder from the trays of effigy figures, or *cemis*—the spiritual "essence," which could be given various physical forms and reflected the islanders' overarching belief in an active spirit world—a world that had to be negotiated with through the ingestion of cohoba in order to attempt to effect a positive outcome.

The role of the *cemi* (sometimes spelled "zemi") given material form was to become a vehicle or conduit by which the individual negotiated with the supernatural. This is described in detail by Pané (1999: 25–26) when he noted that an individual was authorized by the taking of cohoba to create a cemi from a tree. Some cohoba ceremonies reported by the chroniclers have as an agenda precisely this sort of negotiation with spiritual forces, such as taking the drug before the council meetings called to

Figure 6.3. Bifurcated inhaling tube holder. Note that the tubes are missing; the object's authenticity is unconfirmed, though it is very similar to others that have been documented in the Greater Antilles. (Photograph courtesy of Walters Art Museum.)

decide difficult matters, for example, "if they ought to make war or undertake important matters," as cited by Las Casas (1999: 60). The implication here is that in certain circumstances all individuals took cohoba and their experiences helped to decide the community's outcome.

Effigy figures (figure 6.4), always male and with a prominent erect phallus, generally take a crouched form with a dish or bowl emerging from the spine (central nervous system?) or the top of the head—the active material therefore being absorbed literally directly through the body of the cemi (taking human form, the form of a symbolic bird or animal, or a bimorphic form) directly into the system of the participant in the ritual.

Figure 6.4. Wooden cohoba plate effigy figure. Museo del Hombre Dominicano, on permanent loan from the Smithsonian Institution. (Photograph courtesy of José Oliver.)

Figure 6.5. Vomit spatula made of bone (human?), from the Hacienda Grande site, Puerto Rico. Private collection. (Photograph courtesy of José Oliver.)

Cohoba effigy figures are found mainly in the Greater Antilles and rarely found in the Lesser Antilles, but a crude ceramic effigy figure was recovered from Tobago in the southern Caribbean, an indication that the ideas, and therefore perhaps the ritual, had permeated to the far southerly islands, if not the technological expertise of manufacture. The practice of taking drugs from head-plated effigy figures is not known elsewhere in the Americas—where flat dishes or plates are used.

An essential cleansing precursor to the ritual process incorporated the use of spatulas to induce vomiting (figure 6.5). These could be small

Figure 6.6. Red marble duho from Los Colégicos, Arecibo, Puerto Rico, with the head placed before the legs. Instituto de Cultura Puertorriqueña collection, San Juan. (Photograph courtesy of José Oliver.)

curved spatulate items made from bone, shell, or stone or, more rarely, large curved wooden objects, as in an example from the Dominican Republic, which measures 46 centimeters in length. A spatula of this length is presumed to be for ceremonial use, as it would obviously be too large to be easily inserted into the throat. Spatulas have been recovered in large numbers from the Greater Antilles but also from the Lesser Antilles, including an example made from turtle shell excavated on the small island of Carriacou in the southern Grenadines (Kaye et al. 2007).

Described as integral to the ritual snuffing were small seats, or duhos, upon which the main participant leading the ritual sat. Duhos could be high or low backed and were intricately carved from extremely hard woods or even stone (figure 6.6). Duhos have been recovered almost exclusively from the Greater Antilles, but a crude example was also found in the pitch lakes of Trinidad (Yale University Accession notes ANT.145145).

As reported by Las Casas (1999: 60–63), "They took it [the cohoba] seated on some low but very well-carved benches that they called duhos. . . . He would stay awhile with his head turned to one side and his arms placed on his knees, and afterwards he would lift his face towards heaven and speak his certain words . . . then everyone would respond . . . with a great clamour of voices . . . and he would give an account of his vision." Another account (Anghiera 1999: 52) repeated a similar description of the ceremony, adding that the cacique, or leader, "puts his

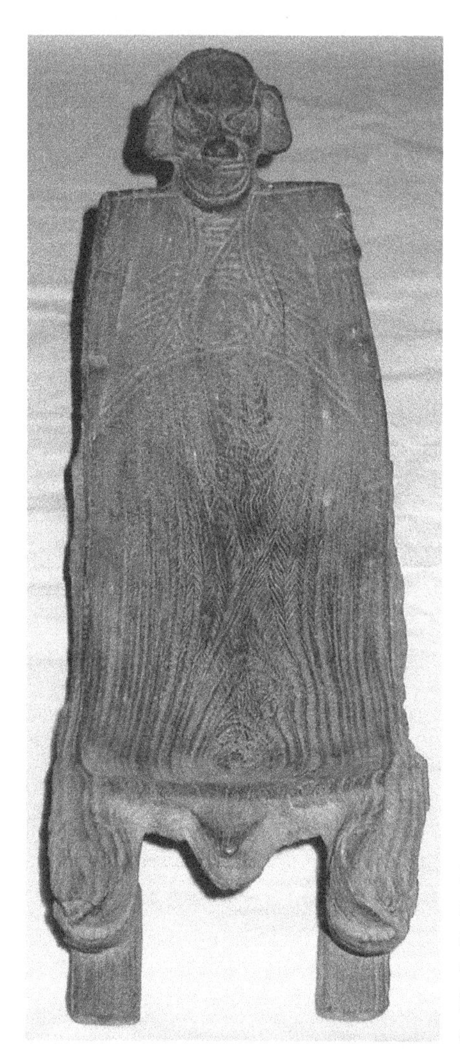

Figure 6.7. Wooden duho from Dominican Republic, with the head at the rear of the seat (height, 49 cm; length, 30 cm; width, 18 cm). Royal Kew Gardens collection, England. (Photograph courtesy of José Oliver.)

head down, grasping his legs with his arms, and staying stupefied awhile in this state, he lifts his head like a somnambulant."

The incorporation of a figure either between the legs at the front of the seat of a duho (as in figure 6.6) (either as an extension of the seat or emerging from underneath the front of it) or at the back on the rear of the "tail" (figure 6.7) conforms to a reference to "a beast" in an early description of duho design written by the historian of the Indies, Antonio de Herrera (1565–1625) quoted in Fewkes (1907: 203–4). Herrera, in referring to the first mention of the seats in Columbus's diary note of November 6, 1492, described the Spaniards as sitting on "seats made of a solid piece of wood in the shape of a beast with very short legs and the tail held up, the head before with eyes and ears of gold."

Where a carved phallus is prominently displayed at the front of the seat, this would then protrude between the legs of the seated person, enhancing perceptions of virility, potency, or power. But when seated on the duho with the carving of the head at the *front* of the seat, it would be the head of the form, often a fierce, glaring face with eyes and teeth enhanced with shining inlay, which would be thrusting forward between the legs of the seated person, taking the place of the phallus, transforming and personifying his genitalia and potency with the strength of the image, or in the case of a woman, it would perhaps appear as a head emerging, as though she were giving birth.

Numerous examples exist from across the Americas of artifactual imagery that resonate with the altered states of consciousness experience and feature complicated figures, sometimes of mythical creatures or figures in transition, which commonly combine with complex patterning (Schultes and Hofmann 1980, 1992; McEwan 2001). In the Americas, the work of Reichel-Dolmatoff (1972, 1978: 7–152) supports that of Lewis-Williams (1991, 1997, 2002a, 2002b) in suggesting that inspiration for many elaborate decorative motifs emanated from the entoptic visual distortions derived from hallucinogenic experiences. McGinnis (2001: 100) and Oliver (2005) are among a number of researchers working in the Caribbean who suggest that the detailed and intricate patterning with which so many of the Antillean drug-related artifacts are incised was in fact entoptically derived. Parallels in the form and decoration of this range of paraphernalia, and other artifacts, which can be seen in the symbolic motifs and mythological references duplicated in the different paraphernalia, would indicate a degree of either intensive communication or cultural cohesion across the islands.

A fifth category of drug-taking artifact has also been recovered in the Caribbean. The use of spouted bowls is not specified by the chroniclers, but various researchers have connected the use of spouted bowls to the nasal absorption of a liquid—rather than powdered—material (Wilbert 1987; Durand and Petitjean-Roget 1991: 60) (figure 6.8). The nasal drinking of tobacco liquid has been reported by Wilbert (1987) of the Wapishana shamans in the Guyana savannas, who pour tobacco juice down their noses through single-spouted gourd vessels. Archaeological examples of both single-spouted and bifurcated ceramic bowls dating to the second century BC are known from Costa Rica (Stone 1966; Snarksis 1981: 200, 1982: 94–100) and western Mexico (Furst 1974: 9, 1998;

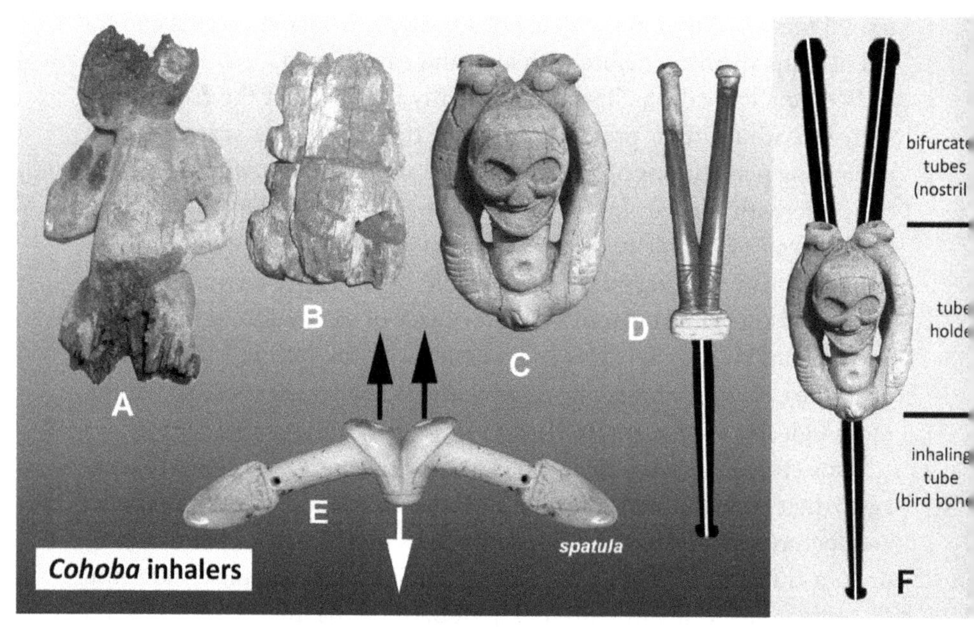

Figure 6.8. Inhalers from Puerto Rico and the Dominican Republic. Specimens A, B, and D are from the Cueva de El Faro and Coto sites, Puerto Rico, presently at the Museo de Historia, Arte y Antropología at the University of Puerto Rico; specimen C is from the La Cucama site and is currently held at the Museo de la Fundación García in Arevalo in Santo Domingo, Dominican Republic; specimen E is from Cueva de la Cohoba (Ciales, Puerto Rico) and is in a private collection. The reconstruction shown on the far right is the same as specimen C. Note that specimen E has been modified; the original is broken through the center. This reconstruction assumed bilateral (mirror) imagery to show how the specimen would have looked when complete. (Photographs courtesy of José Oliver.)

Winning 1974: 16). Ceramic effigy figures from Mexico demonstrate the nasal use of spouted bowls (Furst 1974: 9, plate 11). But other than this, no information from which to draw hypotheses about use in different contexts is available, but the spouted bowl is the artifact type with the widest geographical spread across the Caribbean islands.

Although known from Puerto Rico as early as the second century BC, most spouted bowls across the Antilles have been dated only stylistically. However, the partial remains of a spouted bowl excavated from Carriacou in 2007, together with two specimens from the local museum with no known provenance, were dated using thermoluminescence and optical-stimulating luminescence, which revealed dates averaging 400 ± 189 BC. Because the excavated sample was recovered from midden deposits that were radiocarbon dated much later in time (between circa AD 1000 and

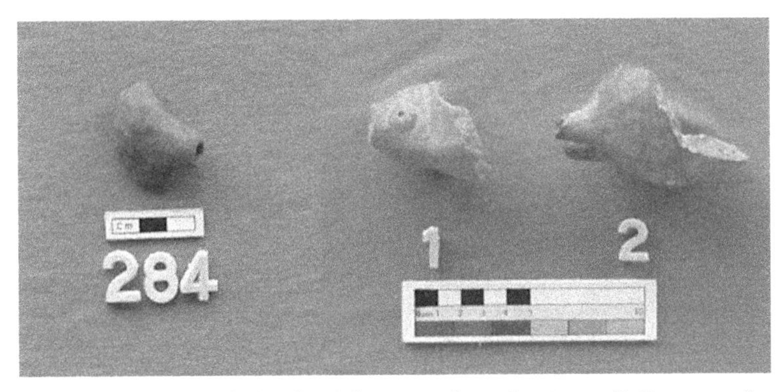

Figure 6.9. Ceramic inhaling bowl fragments from Carriacou: (*left*) excavated fragment and (*right*) two unprovenanced museum examples. (Photographs by Quetta Kaye.)

1200), as were several stylistically distinct ceramic sherds from the same context, and the fact that all samples appeared to be made with nonlocal materials suggested that these spouted bowls were kept and passed down as heirlooms over a period of centuries (figure 6.9) (see Fitzpatrick et al. 2008). Given the known spread of spouted bowls, it would therefore suggest possible cultural contact or ideological links deriving from Central America at a very early date in the prehistory of the Caribbean.

It could be said, therefore, that symbolism that is expressed in the material culture of drug use has a history that might reflect either the actual movement of peoples with their ideas, and subsequent exchange of those ideas, or the diffusion of ideas from one or multiple sources (Rouse 1992; Fernández Méndez 1993; Johnson 1999: 18, 19, 27; Wilson et al. 1998).

As can be seen in figure 6.10, with the exception of spouted bowls, the majority of the artifacts related to ingesting cohoba have been recovered from islands in the Greater Antilles, and isolated finds of psychoactive-related material recovered elsewhere could be evidence of cohoba-related rituals. Alternatively, their presence could be as a result of trade, whereby items were imported with the implication that their value or ritual significance was recognized.

In terms of chronological distribution, figure 6.2 shows that the artifacts clustering toward the Late period are those that could be used in public displays. This is in contrast to the smaller individual use of the spouted bowls, which have much earlier dates, as shown by the Carriacou examples, which were dated through direct luminescence dating to centuries earlier than the context in which they were found—prior to known colonization of the island by humans.

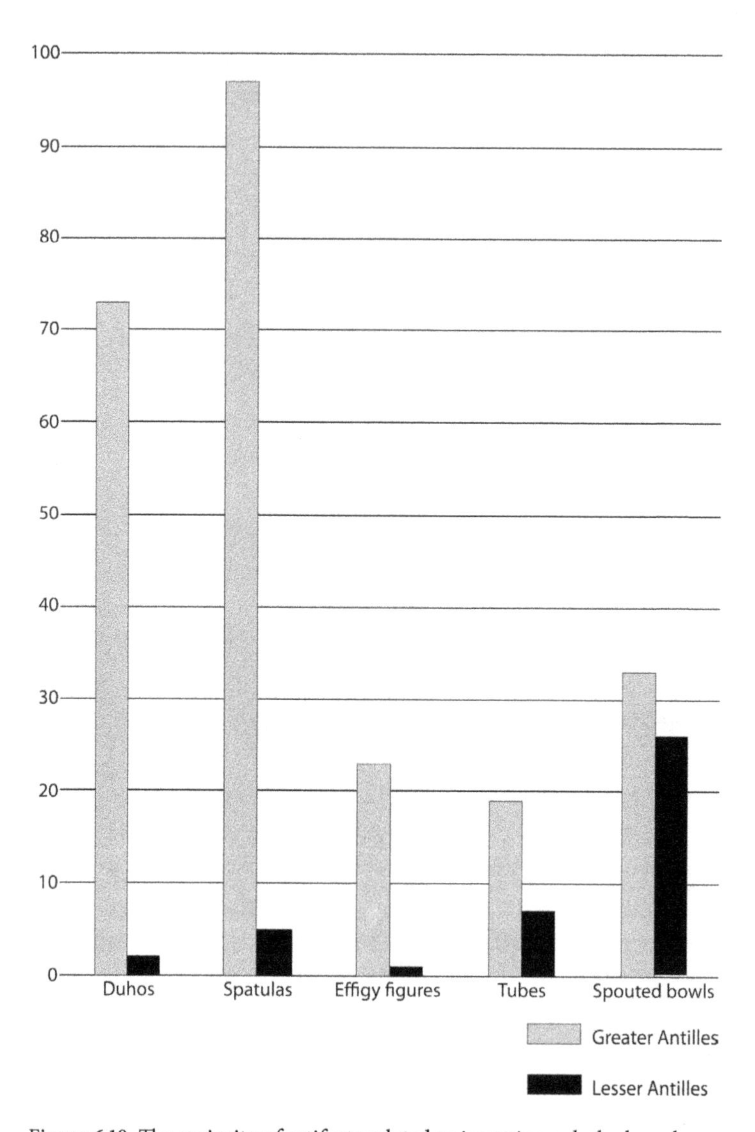

Figure 6.10. The majority of artifacts related to ingesting cohoba have been recovered from islands in the Greater Antilles.

The absence of spouted bowls (so far) in Puerto Rico during the period circa AD 600–1200 (as revealed by figure 6.2) could also be a result of organizational changes in Puerto Rican society that affected, and are reflected in, the way in which ritual drug-taking was practiced, or it could have a cultural basis suggesting, perhaps, that the people who used spouted bowls no longer occupied this area.

Conclusions

The study of material culture used to ingest psychoactive substances—in this case cohoba—suggests that the artifacts in question are not just material objects but are also, by virtue of their form and use, "embodiments of meaning" that helped to construct, maintain, or alter social relationships. Interest in part, therefore, also lies in exploring ways in which meaning can be derived from artifacts that are abundant but without good context. The aim in this regard is to enhance understanding of the ways the precontact islanders' rituals, and the artifacts used in them, figure in social change or stasis in the Caribbean, although it must be emphasized that the proposals presented here are hypotheses only, to be negated or supported by future research.

It is the nature of power associated with access to, and use of, ritual that is relevant to the Caribbean context. Did use of cohoba, or control of cohoba (and other) rituals, provide access to power? Study of the reports of early chroniclers has permitted examination of the active or reactive role of the participants within the ritual; the contexts or ritual zone in which the activity occurred, and whether it was a public or private locus of performance; the sequence of ritual events if, in fact, a sequence existed or was required to achieve the desired effect; and the perceived effect of the rituals. Analysis of these behaviors has the potential to imbue the associated material culture with life and meaning (Kaye 2010).

Given that the ritual process was a state of transition, the use of psychoactive substances used to induce altered states provided access to the supernatural. The fact that the person engaging with the supernatural was often playing a role suggests that three kinds of power are at stake (discussed at the beginning of the chapter): individual power, community or communal power, and social power (Miller and Tilley 1984; Mann 1986: 10, 22).

Because the majority of artifacts in this collection have no provenance information, any conclusions about context are highly speculative. However, there are some interesting tendencies, including that the small or fragmented items (such as spouts disconnected from spouted bowls) overlooked by collectors but recovered from excavations have the potential to alter what we know about artifact distributions and types.

For example, the fact that the majority of spouted bowls have come from midden (occupation) deposits (see figure 6.11), whereas none have been found in caches, suggests that their use was associated more with the user and his movements or residence than with a particular or fixed

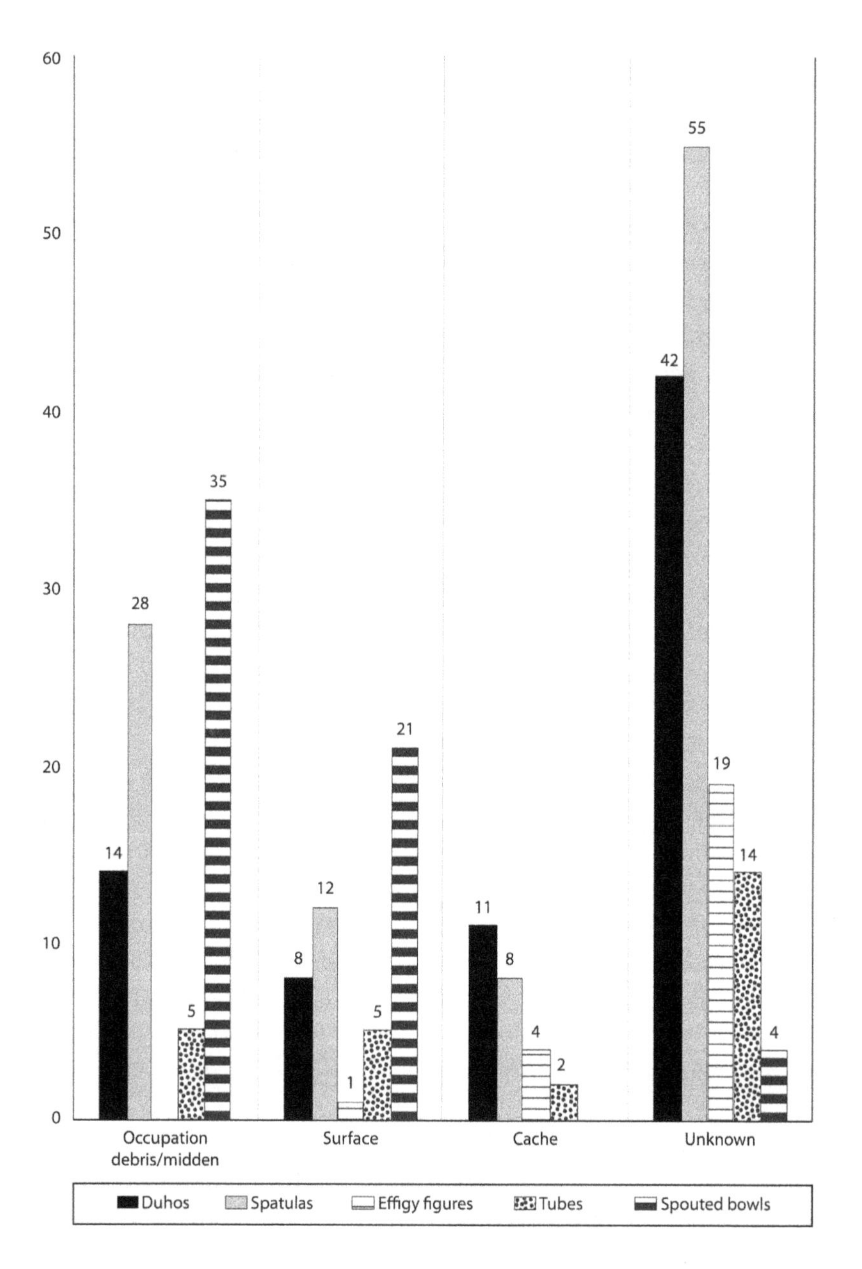

Figure 6.11. The locations where paraphernalia for ingesting psychoactive substances have been found indicate that some items may be reserved for more-elaborate and strictly ritual settings, while others may have been used in more-residential settings.

ritual setting. This also indicates a more flexible context of use and perhaps even a less elaborate or formal ritual. This reinforces the hypothesis that spouted bowls were not likely artifacts to be used as expressions of social power.

In contrast, spatulas, duhos, effigy figures, and inhaling tubes have been found in caves, with duhos being the most numerous type of artifact found in caves, followed by spatulas, effigy figures, and tubes. The cave locus is important in studies of ritual power and power relations over time because caves are liminal places where access to the supernatural is possible, as related in islanders' mythologies (Arrom 1997: 73; Oliver 1997; Pané 1999: 6). Other important loci (such as those that are water related) are open, public, and therefore more likely to be associated with rituals that confirm community coherence.

Additionally, caches—a term that implies intentionality—of artifacts recovered from caves may have particular significance. For example, if one looks at the categories of artifacts recovered from caches within caves (spatulas, duhos, effigy figures, and tubes), one can assume that these artifacts had been deliberately selected to be secreted away, possibly to be placed as offerings and protected or preserved, and that led to their ultimate survival (given that the artifacts recovered from the caches are all made from wood). The context of their recovery, therefore, suggests that ritual significance or special status can be attributed to these objects and, by extension, to those who were empowered to select and secrete them. Their deposition, given the cave locations, also reinforces association with psychoactive substances and liminality. If caches (that include drug-taking paraphernalia) can be seen as offerings or efforts to remove valuable objects from circulation for some purpose related to spiritual or otherworldly power, then they may reflect a context of changing power relations in this world.

It is important to note that no artifacts in this sample were found with burials. But while certain artifacts (such as bowls and dishes, animal remains, and work tools) are found to have been placed in direct association with skeletons, confirming the practice of burial with offerings described at the time of the Spanish conquest, other artifacts have not been chosen to be deposited in this way. Overall, it would seem that the material culture of drug-taking falls into this latter category, because certain of the cohoba-related artifacts have never been recovered from burials. As Bradley (1990: 94) suggests, where certain artifacts are not linked to an individual, they are not likely to be included in the final rites of passage (i.e., the individual's burial). The absence of cohoba-related paraphernalia in burials, therefore, suggests that the power of these elements of material culture was not generally associated with the power or status of an individual, such that it would accompany him or her in death, but instead, any ascribed power lay through the mediation of the living: the dead person had already entered the other world.

The implications from the foregoing trends in context and locus suggest that ritual objects functioned in multiple contexts. Certain artifacts can be said to owe their preservation to deposition in the favorable microenvironment of caves or to preservation under wetland or anaerobic conditions. This explains the relatively high proportion of surviving artifacts made from wood and could imply that deposition of cohoba-related artifacts in wetland or water-related sites had a special significance if the artifacts appeared to have been deliberately placed in the locus from which they were recovered and were not the result of secondary deposition. Water, too, based on the mythological references to turtles, frogs, and other wetland creatures (Oliver 1997; Pané 1999; Moravetz 2003, 2005), represents liminality in their ability to travel from one world to another (van Gennep 1960; Turner 1967, 1969, 1986).

Caves, mainly found in the limestone of the Greater Antilles, may have been the setting for rituals in which duhos and effigy figures were used and in which inhaling tubes and spatulas were used to varying extents. Only spouted bowls seem not to have been used in cave rituals. Controlled access, via rank or status, may therefore have been important to the rituals in which duhos and effigy figures were used.

The rituals in which spatulas and spouted bowls were used most of the time, in contrast, seem not to have been cave rituals. Controlled access based on rank or status, therefore, may not have been important to the rituals in which they were used at all; or access to the rituals may have been regulated in a different way. Spouted bowls could also have been used for less prestigious or less important drugs.

As discussed previously, some drug-related artifacts have been found in archaeological contexts that reflect ritual settings, such as caches, caves, and water-related loci. Although many of the artifacts have no known provenance information, where this is known the sites of recovery for the majority of the artifacts have been from coastal areas. Many of these find sites are coastal areas that are also in close proximity to rivers or other freshwater sources.

Do any of the hypotheses, based on artifact descriptions, reflect agency and personal empowerment in drug-related ritual? On the whole, the overall paucity in numbers suggests that drug-related artifacts were not generally in the hands of everyone. If caches (that include drug-related artifacts) can be seen as offerings or efforts to remove valuable objects from circulation for some purpose related to spiritual or otherworldly power, then they may reflect a context of changing power relations in this world.

Yet the spread of spouted bowls in both space and time, and their midden contexts (see figure 6.11), suggests that this type of artifact may well have continued to serve individuals, despite increases in social complexity through time, in their quest for guidance about their own lives or in feasting ceremonies. If so—and the hypothesis would need further support from the archaeological record by way of continued recovery from household or midden contexts and a wide range in dates and locales—then this would say something very interesting about Caribbean society.

Still within the realm of agency and empowerment (although at a level at which a particular individual takes on a role in which he serves the community but, by serving, would be personally empowered), Pané (1999: 21–24) gave the specific example of the *behique* (medicine man) taking the cohoba and conducting curing rituals in the privacy of the house of someone who was ill. In this case, a specific individual was empowered with curing. This suggests that the partaking of cohoba was communal in the sense that the power was related to sharing and/or using knowledge.

Individual insights are important to the group, however, and power can be limited by social controls. Amazonian societies reflect ways in which the rituals enable the individuals involved to gain insights that are important to the group at the same time that this power is highly controllable socially, which guards against an increase in status (Clastres 1989: 27–47).

In contrast to personal empowerment, in considering group or communal power, the shaman is a good example of how power can accrue to an individual. The role of that individual is to act as an intermediary who undertakes trance-inspired journeys to make personal contact with the spirit world and spirit ancestors. The resultant individual insights are important to the group, and power can be limited by the group. Harner (1973), Lewis (1971), Roe (1997), and Siegel (1999) demonstrate the pivotal role held by the shaman in this respect. The ritual process itself is a critical transformational social process whereby individuals gain insights related to decision making, but in which the decisions have an impact at the level of the community.

Social significance, or significance to the group, is generally manifested on the level of effectiveness of communication with the supernatural. In this context, rather than assuming that effigies on artifacts are idols or gods (as in the case of the effigy figures or anthropomorphic representations on spatula handles, for example) (Kaye 2010), one can view these elements as emblematic of the ways in which the individual (using the artifact) has his or her effectiveness as a communicator maximized. The design elements can also be seen and interpreted as setting the boundaries, or marking the pathway, for the ways in which the individual's communication with the supernatural (the spirit world) facilitated group welfare, rather than enabling the individual to use the acquired power for personal aggrandizement or family or status increase. This can be seen as the "power" in the artifact that is tapped by the individual, but it is nonetheless a transient power and part of the ritual process: the artifact alone is powerless or passive.

In considering the development of social complexity in the Caribbean, that is, a move from egalitarian to ranked societies, we need to develop hypotheses on possible ways in which power could have been appropriated to engender hierarchy, that is, social power. One such hypothesis is that duhos and effigy figures have a cultural significance that may indicate, along with other features yet to be confirmed, efforts to appropriate a role in a drug-related ritual for elite legitimization. This remains conjectural, but as discussed earlier, in looking at the chroniclers' accounts of indigenous rituals, legitimization of elite status could have been acquired by the user of the duho when operating in various political arenas (greeting dignitaries, dances, ball games, and other festivals), many of which have been shown to incorporate use of cohoba.

Siegel (1999: 232) has written of the shaman's power over the supernatural being as a possible "front" for his power over the political landscape. Having shown how fundamental various manifestations of cemis were to every aspect of the lives of the islands, the early Spanish chroniclers attested to the fact that acquisition of a cemi, and the theft of one, was a demonstration of the power with which the cemis were imbued. Thus, in this case, given the power invested in a cemi effigy, the theft of one could be seen as a literal and direct attempt for an individual to acquire additional strength and to diminish the power of a rival community or possibly an individual leader or shaman. In this way, the attempt by an individual to gain a competitive advantage could be translated into political (or social) power.

Times of instability, such as environmental stress (climate change) or a catastrophic event (e.g., tsunamis, hurricanes, volcanic eruptions), might also provoke a situation in which a chief, shaman, or someone similar could accrue individual power that becomes socially sanctioned. There is empirical evidence indicating that the situations in which the shaman comes into his/her own are those in which social and environmental pressures recur with sufficient frequency (Lewis 1971: 29; Flannery 1972).

This last point, of the pivotal role that ritualized behavior plays in societies in times of stress of one form or another, was investigated by Laughlin and colleagues (1979: 280–318). Their research indicates that where environmental stress is high, they would expect to find heavy reliance on what they term "collective action alternatives" (1979: 282). This would particularly include ceremonial ritual because of its effectiveness in modelling social and cosmological organization. Stressful times, or times of instability, mean that if an individual chooses to, he/she has a better chance of manipulating power.

If cohoba diversified through the centuries from being a personalized, individual experience to being part of a public ceremony with control of the ritual passing to an elite—but requiring, nevertheless, the participation of the community to be effective, that is, evolving from a social function (cohesion and so forth) to a political one (coercion conformation)—then the use of cohoba could be seen as a long-lasting tradition that was co-opted by emerging ranked groups (elites) to exercise control, perhaps even monopoly, of political power.

References Cited

Anghiera, P. Martire d'. 1999. Appendix B. In *An Account of the Antiquities of the Indians*, ed. and trans. S. C. Griswold, 46–53. Durham, N.C.: Duke University Press.

Arrom, J. J. 1997. The Creation Myth of the Taino. In *Taino: Pre-Columbian Art and Culture from the Caribbean*, ed. F. Bercht, E. Brodsky, J. A. Farmer, and D. Taylor, 68–79. New York: Monacelli Press.

Barfield, T., ed. 1997. *The Dictionary of Anthropology*. Oxford, U.K.: Blackwell.

Bowie, F. 2000. *The Anthropology of Religion*. Oxford, U.K.: Blackwell.

Bradley, R. 1990. *The Passage of Arms*. Cambridge: Cambridge University Press.

Cassa, R. 1990. *Los Tainos de la Española*. Santo Domingo, Dominican Republic: Editora Búho.

Clastres, P. 1989. *Society against the State*. New York: Zone Books.

Curet, L. A. 2002. The Chief Is Dead, Long Live . . . Who? Descent and Succession in the Protohistoric Chiefdoms of the Greater Antilles. *Ethnohistory* 49 (2): 259–80.

Durand, J. F., and H. Petitjean-Roget. 1991. A propos d'un collier funeraire a Morel, Guadeloupe: Les Huecoides sont-ils un mythe? In *Proceedings of the 12th International Congress for Caribbean Archaeology, Cayenne, French Guiana*, ed. L. S. Robinson, 53–72. Martinique, Lesser Antilles: International Association for Caribbean Archaeology.

Fernández Méndez, E. 1993. *Art and Mythology of the Taino Indians of the Greater Antilles.* San Juan, Puerto Rico: Ediciones El Cemi.
Fewkes, J. W. 1907. The Aborigines of Porto Rico and Neighbouring Islands. In *Twenty-Fifth Annual Report of the U.S. Bureau of Ethnology to the Secretary of the Smithsonian Institution, 1903–04,* 203–4. Reprint, 1970, New York: Johnson Reprint.
Fitzpatrick, S. M., Q. P. Kaye, J. Feathers, J. A. Pavia, and K. M. Marsaglia. 2008. Evidence for Inter-island Transport of Heirlooms: Luminescence Dating and Petrographic Analysis of Ceramic Inhaling Bowls from Carriacou, West Indies. *Journal of Archaeological Science* 36: 596–606.
Flannery, K. V. 1972. The Cultural Evolution of Civilizations. *Annual Review of Ecology and Systematics* 3: 399–426.
Flannery, K. V. 1976. *The Early Mesoamerican Village.* New York: Academic Press.
Furst, P. T. 1974. *Archaeological Evidence for Snuffing in Prehispanic Mexico.* Botanical Museum Leaflets, vol. 24, no. 1. Cambridge, Mass.: Harvard University.
Furst, P. T. 1998. Shamanic Symbolism, Transformation and Deities in West Mexican Funerary Art. In *Ancient West Mexico: Art and Archaeology of the Unknown Past,* ed. R. F. Townsend, 169–89. Chicago: Art Institute of Chicago.
Harner, M. J., ed. 1973. *Hallucinogens and Shamanism.* Oxford: Oxford University Press.
Helms, M. W. 1979. *Ancient Panama: Chiefs in Search of Power.* Austin: University of Texas Press.
Hodder, I. 1984. Post-processual Archaeology. In *Advances in Archaeological Method and Theory,* vol. 8, ed. M. B. Schiffer, 1–26. New York: Academic Press.
Johnson, M. 1999. *Archaeological Theory: An Introduction.* Oxford, U.K.: Blackwell.
Kaye, Q. P. 2010. Ritual Drug Use, Material Culture and the Social Context of Power among the Indigenous Peoples of the Caribbean Using Ethnographic, Ethnohistoric and Archaeological Data. PhD diss., University College London.
Kaye, Q. P., S. Burnett, S. M. Fitzpatrick, and M. Kappers. 2007. Ongoing Archaeological Investigations on Carriacou, West Indies: 2nd July–3rd August 2007. *Papers from the Institute for Archaeology* (University College London) 18: 167–76.
Keegan, W. F. 1992. *The People Who Discovered Columbus.* Gainesville: University Press of Florida.
Keegan, W. F., and M. D. Maclachan. 1989. The Evolution of Avunculocal Chiefdoms: A Reconstruction of Taino Kinship and Politics. *American Anthropologist* 91 (3): 613–30.
Kennedy, A. 1982. *Ecco Bufo*: The Toad and Olmec Iconography. *Current Anthropology* 23: 273–90.
Las Casas, B. de. 1999. Appendix C. In *An Account of the Antiquities of the Indians,* ed. and trans. S. C. Griswold, 54–67. Durham, N.C.: Duke University Press.
Laughlin, C. D., E. d'Aquili, and J. McManus. 1979. *The Spectrum of Ritual: A Biogenetic Structural Analysis.* New York: Columbia University Press.
Lewis, I. M. 1971. *Ecstatic Religion: A Study of Shamanism and Spirit Possession.* London: Routledge.
Lewis-Williams, J. D. 1991. Wrestling with Analogy: A Methodological Dilemma

in Upper Palaeolithic Art Research. *Proceedings of the Prehistoric Society* 57 (1): 149–62.

Lewis-Williams, J. D. 1997. Agency, Art and Altered Consciousness: A Motif in French (Quercy) Upper Palaeolithic Parietal Art. *Antiquity* 71 (274): 810–30.

Lewis-Williams, J. D. 2002a. Consciousness and the Origins of Art. Seminar, University College London, October 17, 2002.

Lewis-Williams, J. D. 2002b. *The Mind in the Cave*. London: Thames and Hudson.

Mann, M. 1986. *The Sources of Social Power*. Vol. 1. Cambridge: Cambridge University Press.

McEwan, C. 2001. Seats of Power: Axiality and Access to Invisible Worlds. In *Unknown Amazon*, ed. C. McEwan, C. Barreto, and E. Neves, 176–97. London: British Museum Press.

McGinnis, S. 2001. Patterns, Variations, and Anomalies in Ideographic Expression in the Pre-Columbian Caribbean. In *Proceedings of the 18th Congress of the International Association for Caribbean Archaeology, St. George, Grenada, West Indies*, 99–114.

Miller, D., and C. Tilley. 1984. Ideology, Power and Prehistory: An Introduction. In *Ideology, Power and Prehistory*, ed. D. Miller and C. Tilley, 1–15. New Direction in Archaeology 5. Cambridge: Cambridge University Press.

Moravetz, I. 2003. Identification and Significance of Sea Turtles in Saladoid Art. In *Proceedings of the 19th Congress of the International Association for Caribbean Archaeology, Aruba, July 2001*, vol. 2, 158–70.

Moravetz, I. 2005. *Imaging Adornos: Classification and Iconography of Saladoid Adornos from St Vincent, West Indies*. BAR International Series 1445. Oxford, U.K.: Archaeopress.

Morgan, A. 1986. Who Put the Toad in Toadstool? *New Scientist* (London): 44–47.

Oliver, J. R. 1997. The Taino Cosmos. In *The Indigenous People of the Caribbean*, ed. S. M. Wilson, 140–53. Gainesville: University of Florida Press.

Oliver, J. R. 2005. The Proto-Taino Monumental Cemis of Caguana: A Political-Religious "Manifesto." In *Ancient Borinquen: Archaeology and Ethnohistory of Native Puerto Rico*, ed. P. E. Siegel, 230–84. Tuscaloosa: University of Alabama Press.

Oviedo, F. de. 1975. *The Conquest and Settlement of the Island of Boriquen or Puerto Rico*. Trans. D. Turner. Avon, Conn.: Limited Editions Club.

Pané, R. 1999. *An Account of the Antiquities of the Indians*, ed. and trans. S. C. Griswold, 3–38. Durham, N.C.: Duke University Press.

Parsons, T. 1991. *The Social System*. London: Routledge.

Reichel-Dolmatoff, G. 1972. The Cultural Context of an Aboriginal Hallucinogen: *Banisteriopsis caapi*. In *Flesh of the Gods*, ed. P. D. Furst, 84–113. Long Grove, Ill.: Waveland Press.

Reichel-Dolmatoff, G. 1976. Cosmology as Ecological Analysis: A View from the Tropical Rainforest. *Man: Royal Anthropological Institute of Great Britain and Ireland* 2: 207–18.

Reichel-Dolmatoff, G. 1978. *Beyond the Milky Way: Hallucinatory Imagery of the Tukano Indians*. Latin American Studies 42. Los Angeles: UCLA Latin American Center Publications.

Renfrew, C. 1994. The Archaeology of Religion. In *The Ancient Mind: Elements of Cognitive Archaeology*, ed. C. Renfrew and E.B.W. Zubrow, 55–74. Cambridge: Cambridge University Press.

Roe, P. G. 1991. Petroglyphs of Maisabel: A Study in Methodology. In *Proceedings of the 12th Congress of the International Association for Caribbean Archaeology, Cayenne, French Guiana*, ed. L. S. Robinson, 317–70. Martinique, Lesser Antilles: International Association for Caribbean Archaeology.

Roe, P. G. 1997. Just Wasting Away: Taino Shamanism and Concepts of Fertility. In *Taino Pre-Columbian Art and Culture from the Caribbean*, ed. F. Bercht, E. Brodsky, J. A. Farmer, and D. Taylor, 124–57. New York: Monacelli Press.

Rouse, I. 1992. *The Tainos: Rise and Decline of the People Who Greeted Columbus.* New Haven, Conn.: Yale University Press.

Schultes, R. E., and A. Hofmann. 1980. *The Botany and Chemistry of Hallucinogens.* Springfield, Ill.: Charles C. Thomas.

Schultes, R. E., and A. Hofmann. 1992. *Plants of the Gods: Their Sacred, Healing and Hallucinogenic Powers.* Rochester, N.Y.: Healing Arts Press.

Siegel, P. E. 1989. *Early Ceramic Population Lifeways and Adaptive Strategies in the Caribbean.* BAR International Series 506. Oxford, U.K.: British Archaeological Reports.

Siegel, P. E. 1999. Contested Places and Places of Contest: The Evolution of Social Power and Ceremonial Space in Prehistoric Puerto Rico. *Latin American Antiquity* 10 (3): 209–38.

Snarksis, M. J. 1981. *Precolumbian Art of Costa Rica: Between Continents/Between Seas.* New York: Harry N. Abrams.

Snarksis, M. J. 1982. *La ceramica precolumbina eon Costa Rica.* San Jose, Costa Rica: Instituto Nacional de Seguros.

Stone, D. 1966. Synthesis of Lower Central American Ethnohistory. In *Handbook of Middle American Indians*, vol. 4, *Archaeological Frontiers and External Connections*, ed. G. F. Ekholm and G. R. Willey, 209–33. Austin: University of Texas Press.

Turner, V. W. 1967. Betwixt and Between: The Liminal Period in *Rites de Passage.* In *The Forest of Symbols*, 93–111. Ithaca, N.Y.: Cornell University Press.

Turner, V. W. 1969. *The Ritual Process: Structure and Anti-structure.* London: Routledge and Kegan Paul.

Turner, V. W. 1986. Dewey, Dilthey and Drama: An Essay in the Anthropology of Experience. In *The Anthropology of Experience*, ed. V. W. Turner and E. M. Bruner, 33–44. Urbana: University of Illinois Press.

Van Gennep, A. 1960. *The Rites of Passage.* London: Routledge and Kegan Paul. Originally published as *Rites de passage* (Paris, 1909).

Veloz Maggiolo, M. 1997. The Daily Life of the Taino People. In *Taino Pre-Columbian Art* and *Culture from the Caribbean*, ed. F. Bercht, E. Brodsky, J. A. Farmer, and D. Taylor, 34–45. New York: Monacelli Press.

Versteeg, A. H., and K. Schinkel. 1992. *The Archaeology of St. Eustatius: The Golden Rock Site.* Publication of the St. Eustatius Historical Foundation 2, Publication of the Foundation for Scientific Research in the Caribbean Region 131. St. Eustatius and Amsterdam.

Viveiros de Castro, E. 2002. Cosmological Deixis and Amerindian Perspectivism. In *A Reader in the Anthropology of Religion*, ed. M. Lambeck, 306–26. Oxford, U.K.: Blackwell.
Wilbert, J. 1987. *Tobacco and Shamanism in South America*. New Haven, Conn.: Yale University Press.
Wilson, S. M. 1990. *Hispaniola: Caribbean Chiefdoms in the Age of Columbus*. Tuscaloosa: University of Alabama Press.
Wilson, S. M. 1993. The Cultural Mosaic of the Indigenous Caribbean. In *The Meeting of Two Worlds: Europe and the Americas, 1492–1650*, ed. W. Bray, 37–66. Proceedings of the British Academy 81. Oxford: Oxford University Press.
Wilson, S. M. 1997a. The Caribbean before European Contact. In *Taino Pre-Columbian Art* and *Culture from the Caribbean*, ed. F. Bercht, E. Brodsky, J. A. Farmer, and D. Taylor, 15–17. New York: Monacelli Press.
Wilson, S. M. 1997b. The Taino Social and Political Order. In *Taino Pre-Columbian Art* and *Culture from the Caribbean*, ed. F. Bercht, E. Brodsky, J. A. Farmer, and D. Taylor, 46–56. New York: Monacelli Press.
Wilson, S. M. 1999. *The Indigenous People of the Caribbean*. Gainesville: University Press of Florida.
Wilson, S. M., H. B. Iceland, and T. R. Hester. 1998. Preceramic Connections between Yucatan and the Caribbean. *Latin American Antiquity* 9 (4): 342–52.
Winning, H. Von. 1974. *The Shaft Tomb Figures of West Mexico*. Southwest Museum Papers no 24. Los Angeles, Calif.

7

Intoxication Rituals and Gender among the Ancient Maya

DANIEL M. SEINFELD

Scenes of drinking and enema use on Late Classic period (ca. AD 600–900) Maya vase paintings provide a window into the social aspects of intoxicant use. These paintings offer a unique perspective on gender ideology among the ancient Maya. Gender ideologies are notions of what is considered proper behavior for individuals based on their culture's gender categories (Conkey and Spector 1984; Stockett 2005: 567). In this chapter, I argue that analyses of Maya vase paintings depicting intoxicant use further our understandings of the nature of gender relations among the ancient Maya. I explore the sociocultural aspects of intoxication events and highlight the male and female behaviors associated with drinking and enemas. This work underscores the importance of considering social identities, including gender, when examining intoxication in the ancient world (Dietler 2001, 2006). As this example from the ancient Maya demonstrates, customs and prohibitions surrounding intoxicants may have reflected wider norms surrounding gender and other social identities.

The Late Classic Period Maya

The ancient Maya lived in the present-day states of southern Mexico, Guatemala, Belize, and parts of Honduras and El Salvador. The Maya are known for their hieroglyphic writing system, monumental architecture, and distinctive artistic tradition. The Classic period (AD 300–900) is marked by the proliferation of writing, recorded calendrical dates, and the expansion of many cities, especially in the southern Maya lowlands.

The Classic period is divided into two subperiods: the Early Classic (AD 300–600) and the Late Classic (AD 600–900). The Late Classic period witnessed increased political competition and the eventual depopulation of many major population centers in the southern lowlands (Demarest 2004).

The Classic period Maya political system was largely stratified, with a distinct class of nobles who ruled over polities with shifting political alliances. Elites used public ritual and monumental artwork to tout their connection to the supernatural in order to secure political power (Demarest 1992, 2004; Freidel and Schele 1988; Freidel et al. 1993; Inomata 2006). Warfare and exchange also played vital roles in the political life of the Classic period Maya elites (Demarest 2004). Aspects of this history and elite life are illustrated on the decorated monuments and ceramic wares used by the elites. The vessels examined in the present study come from a tradition of painted wares that were used in feasting and may have been presented as gifts among the nobility (Houston et al. 2006: 129; Loughmiller-Newman 2008). Images on these polychrome vases depicting individuals engaging in intoxication events provide evidence for the structuring of gender roles among the ancient Maya elites.

Gender among the Ancient Maya

Male and female gender roles were often complementary among the Classic period Maya (Josserand 2002; Joyce 1996, 2001). Gender complementarity refers to how the ideologies and roles of the different genders were distinct and fundamentally interconnected within the cultural system. Females are typically depicted in artwork performing complementary roles during rituals, often assisting males in ritual actions (Josserand 2002; Joyce 1996: 169, 2001). Examples include depictions on monumental artwork of female kin helping during accession rituals, such as in the Oval Palace Tablet from Palenque, where Lady Zak K'uk hands a headdress, symbolizing rulership, to her son Pakal (Josserand 2002: fig. 8.1). These rituals were properly completed with the complementary participation of both genders.

Gender complementarity is not gender equality. Although male and female roles in a ritual may be complementary, they may have unequal status (Stockett 2005). There was often simultaneous expression of gender complementarity and hierarchy in artwork among the Classic period Maya (Josserand 2002; Stockett 2005). Images of females assisting males in rituals (Josserand 2002), such as the accession ritual discussed above, communicate complementarity through males and females working together in prescribed, gender-specific ritual roles. Such images also express gender hierarchy in that the males are the primary ritual actors. Despite this inequity, complementarity remained a key concept in these rituals because of the work females contributed (Josserand 2002).

Males and females are often distinguished in iconography through their costume and physiology. Classic period Maya women are generally shown wearing *huipiles*—traditional, elaborately woven dresses that cover their entire body. These huipiles largely obscure their physiology and make the garment the primary focus of the individual (Joyce 2001: 60, 65). Males are generally shown shirtless and wearing loincloths.

Despite these conventions, gendered costume was at times flexible among the Classic period Maya. In depictions of rituals, men are sometimes shown wearing a net skirt that is often seen on females (Joyce 2001). Females are also sometimes shown topless, in which case their sex is marked by the presence of exposed breasts. The Moon Goddess is often shown with a nude torso, in contrast to most other Maya females, who are almost always clothed (Ayala Falcón 2002: 108). Looper (2002) suggested that these men and women, including the Maize God and Moon Goddess, might represent distinct gender categories among the Classic period Maya. These categories may have included manly women, biological women who assumed male gender identities, and womanly men, biological men who assumed more typically female gender identities. Alternatively, these types of depictions could reflect a flexibility in gender roles that was dependent on specific events rather than distinct gender categories.

Intoxication Rituals

For the current analysis, I examined scenes of enema use and of groups of individuals drinking and becoming intoxicated. These vessels vividly depict scenes of elite life and ritual as well as mythological events (Jackson 2009). Vessels may have been used to hold festive beverages, such as alcohol and cacao (Miller 2004: 24). Polychrome vessels were frequently given as gifts among elites, and they often depict festive occasions (Houston et al. 2006: 129; Jackson 2009). Participants in intoxication event scenes are shown dancing, staggering, and falling over (de Smet and Hellmuth 1986; Grube 2000b; Stross and Kerr 1990). Most drinking and enema scenes are exclusively male, showing groups of young noblemen drinking to the point of intoxication, such as in vase number K1092.[1] Images of individuals simply drinking were not considered intoxication scenes, because they could be drinking other, nonintoxicating beverages, such as cacao. Enema use co-occurs with drinking in some scenes, suggesting that drinking and enemas were related activities (de Smet 1985: 59–60; de Smet and Hellmuth 1986: 219; Stross and Kerr 1990). Evidence of visible intoxication includes individuals falling over, vomiting, and looking into the distance with a glazed look in their eyes. Drinking scenes generally include depictions of material culture used in drinking, such as ollas (large ceramic containers) from which drinks were served, drinking cups, and enema bags (de Smet 1985: 57; de Smet and Hellmuth 1986: 216–20). Ollas in intoxication scenes often have a restricted neck, and the drinking cups are generally small enough to be held in one hand. Other iconographic cues, such as the *a-chi* glyph, are sometimes shown on vessels to indicate that they contain intoxicating beverages (de Smet 1985: 62–65; de Smet and Hellmuth 1986: 221–22, 245–47; Houston et al. 2006: 116; Kerr 1989: 58, 77; Stross and Kerr 1990: 354).

Previous studies of intoxication in prehistory have tended to focus on the role of festive intoxication in manipulating political economies (Dietler 1990, 1996, 2001, 2006; Joffe 1998). These authors have discussed how ritualized festive intoxication events were a setting for leaders to attract followers through reciprocal obligations to the host. Dietler (2001) and Joffe (1998) also noted the importance of drinking festivities for publicly performing social identities, such as political power and gender. Dietler (2001: 90–93) described multiple ways in which gender is marked at feasts, including permission to consume or prohibition of consuming certain items, such as alcoholic beverages and other intoxicants. Distinctions in the types of behaviors that are permissible, such as visible drunkenness, are also used to define gender roles (Dietler 2001: 91). The performance of gender roles through such distinctions at festive events reifies gender identities for participants (Dietler 2001: 90, 2006: 234). Cross-culturally, drinking is generally considered a masculine activity. Females often are expected to abstain or drink less and manifest different behaviors when intoxicated (Dietler 2006: 236).

The ancient Maya had access to a wide variety of intoxicants including alcohol, tobacco, hallucinogenic plants, and stimulants (de Smet 1985;

1 Vase images are presented with "K-numbers," which correspond to numbers from Justin Kerr's catalogue of rollout photographs of vase paintings. Full images of the rollout photographs can be seen at http://research.Mayavase.com/kerrportfolio.html by entering the corresponding K-number.

de Smet and Hellmuth 1986; Schultes et al. 1998: 26; Zagorevski and Loughmiller-Newman 2012). Traditionally, people in the Maya region brewed alcoholic beverages from several materials including maize, various fruits, and honey (Bruman 2000; Smalley and Blake 2003). *Balché*, a honey-wine flavored with the bark of the *jab'in* tree (*Lonchocarpus longistylus*), is an integral part of present-day Lacandón Maya rituals (McGee 1990, 2002).

In addition to fermented beverages, Mesoamerica is home to the greatest diversity of psychoactive plants in the world (Schultes et al. 1998: 26). Tobacco often contributed to intoxicated experiences and was often smoked while other inebriants were being ingested (de Smet 1985: 61; Grube 2000b: 295). Chemical analysis of a Late Classic period Maya vessel demonstrated that it had residues of nicotine and therefore had held tobacco leaves (Zagorevski and Loughmiller-Newman 2012). Alcoholic beverages were sometimes combined with other psychoactive plants to produce potent brews. These mixtures may have been used in enemas because of their harsh taste or tendency to induce vomiting (Bruman 2000: 106; de Smet and Hellmuth 1986: 252; Gage [1648] 1958; Grube 2000b; Stross and Kerr 1990). The Maya also used enemas for the ingestion of alcohol because they allowed for faster and more intense intoxication than one could achieve through drinking the relatively low alcohol beers that were available (de Smet 1985; de Smet and Hellmuth 1986: 255; Grube 2000b: 295; Houston et al. 2006: 120).

Many researchers (de Smet 1985; de Smet and Hellmuth 1986; Dobkin de Rios 1974; Furst and Coe 1977; Grube 2000b; Stross and Kerr 1990) have noted the likely use of alcohol and hallucinogenic substances in enemas during ancient Maya rituals. Intoxication was of such great significance to the Maya that they had a god of intoxication, drinking, and enema use named Akan, also known as God A (Grube 2000a, 2000b). Akan is typically depicted wearing black face paint and drinking, vomiting, and carrying an enema bag (Grube 2000a). Akan also had more foreboding connotations as a god associated with death, disease, and the underworld (Grube 2000a).

Houston and colleagues (2006) explored intoxicant use, especially drinking and enemas, as corporeal phenomena, considering alcohol as an ingestible, in the same category as food and tobacco. They discussed the erotic nature of enema scenes, in which younger females pampered older males (Houston et al. 2006: 117). Houston and colleagues (2006: 117–18) focused on the physical experiences of enema rituals, which may have taken place in sweat baths and often included vomiting and contact with the supernatural. The overall physicality of enema rituals—involving sexuality, sweating, vomiting, enema ingestion, and intoxication—served a cleansing function that restored physical and spiritual order to participants.

Gender and Drinking in Late Classic Period Maya Vase Paintings

In addition to these supernatural and corporeal aspects, analysis of images of intoxicant use containing both males and females demonstrates clear patterns in gender roles during these events. Before discussing these themes, I review the corpus of eight vase paintings that show men and women in intoxication events.

K3027 (figure 7.1) depicts seated pairs of males and females participating in an intoxication event. The men wear loincloths and body paint. The women wear long huipiles, the typical attire of Classic period noblewoman (Joyce 2001). The woman of the left pair (individual B) helps a male (individual A) drink out of the large ceramic vessel. This pot presumably holds an alcoholic beverage, given the presence of drinking cups and enema bags elsewhere in the scene. The two males of the center pair gesture to each other; one (individual C) holds a drinking cup with an enema bag in his loincloth, and the other (individual D) holds an enema bag. This painting reinforces the link between drinking and enema use. The rightmost pair consists of a woman (individual E) helping a man (individual F) drink. This scene illustrates a primary theme concerning gender roles and intoxication rituals depicted in the vase paintings: males are shown becoming intoxicated while the women assist without imbibing.

Figure 7.1. Festive scene of male drinkers being assisted by females (K3027). (Photograph by Justin Kerr.)

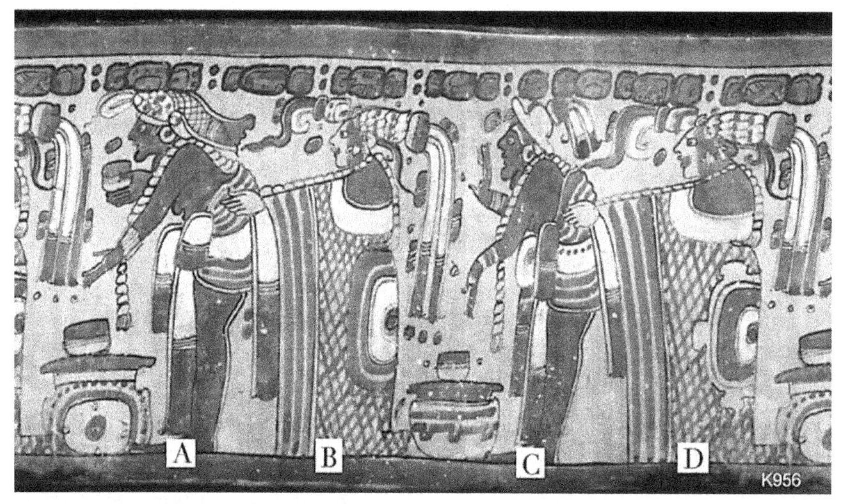

Figure 7.2. Scene of two males preparing to drink and being assisted by females (K956). (Photograph by Justin Kerr.)

K956 (figure 7.2) shows two female-male pairs in which the women help the men drink. The men (individuals A and C) are shown wearing loincloths and elaborate headdresses, suggesting high status. They have chubby, sagging torsos, suggesting a prosperous lifestyle and perhaps advanced age. The women (individuals B and D) are shown wearing elaborate huipiles and headdresses, suggesting that they, like the men, are of a high status. The men are hunched and standing over serving containers with cups. One male is holding a cup as if about to drink, and the other is performing a hand gesture. The women are shown standing behind the men, holding them by the torso as if to support them. This scene follows the wider theme of paired groups of females assisting males who are imbibing.

K530 (figure 7.3) shows four pairs of older men and young women (labeled as pairs A, B, C, and D) facing a supernatural being sitting in a cave with several supernatural beings behind them. The men are wearing loincloths and appear elderly with their flabby skin and edentulous mouths. These males may be associated with a supernatural figure called God N (Houston et al. 2006: 117). The females appear younger; two are dressed in full-length huipiles (in pairs A and C), and the other two are in long dresses (in pairs B and D). The women in the huipiles are paired with the more elaborately dressed males (labeled A and C) and are sitting closer to the cave with the supernatural being. The males are sitting in front of pots with enema bags resting on top. The men have a dazed

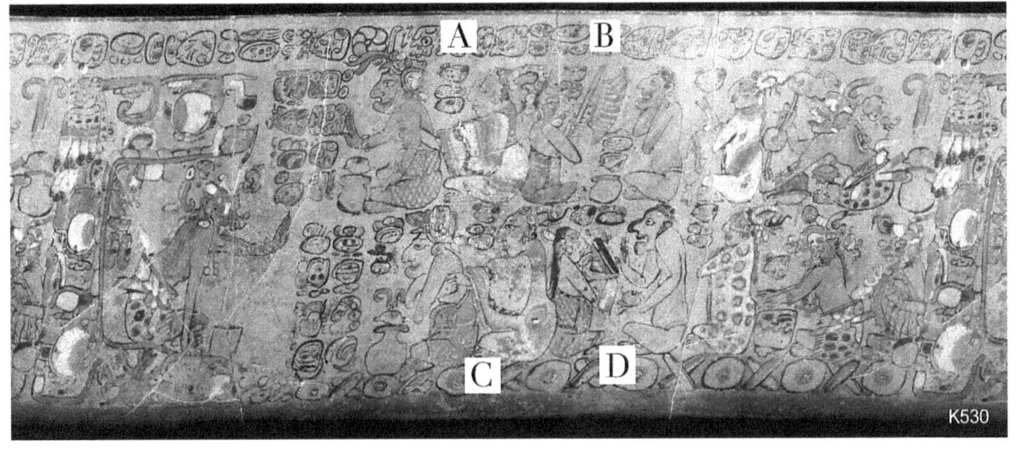

Figure 7.3. Scene of pairs of elderly male drinkers and enema users being assisted by female attendants while facing a supernatural being in a cave (K530). (Photograph by Justin Kerr.)

look in their faces with half-shut eyes and smiles, suggesting that they are intoxicated. These huipil-attired women (in pairs A and C) are sitting behind the males, holding their torsos in a similar pose to those in K956 (figure 7.2). The other women are facing their partners (in pairs B and D) and are positioned back to back with the huipil-wearing ones. These women are smaller than their huipil-clad counterparts, perhaps reflecting a difference in age or status (Loughmiller-Newman 2008). The men facing the dress-wearing women have a dazed, intoxicated look similar to that of the other males in the scene. One woman is fanning the male (in pair B), and the other holds a mirror (in pair D).

K7898 (figure 7.4) shows a variation on the theme of females assisting males during intoxication rituals. This scene shows two males (individuals B and C) bending over and holding drinking cups. The men are standing over vessels with enema bags sitting on top of them. A woman (individual A) is shown facing the two men with a stern facial expression and an outstretched, gesturing hand. This woman seems to be guiding the men in the ritual.

K5005 (figure 7.5) depicts a narrative scene of a male-female pair performing an enema ritual. Enema scenes often show females administering the enemas (Stross and Kerr 1990). In the first part of the scene, a man (individual B) is bent over with a woman (individual A) standing behind him holding a drinking cup. The second part of the scene shows the woman putting the cup into his backside. The man opens his eyes wide in an expression of pain, surprise, or ecstasy. This scene shows the

Figure 7.4. Scene of a female directing two males who are about to partake in drinking and enemas (K7898). (Photograph by Justin Kerr.)

woman directly facilitating intoxication by administering the enema. This scene is unique because it shows a drinking cup rather than an enema bag as a delivery device.

K1550 (figure 7.6) depicts a woman (individual C) administering an enema to a reclining male (individual B). A speech scroll emanates from his mouth while a bird flies overhead. A seminude male (individual A) to the left of the reclining figure is putting something into a large vessel, perhaps preparing an enema. The speech and the bird suggest that the reclining individual is becoming intoxicated as a way to communicate with

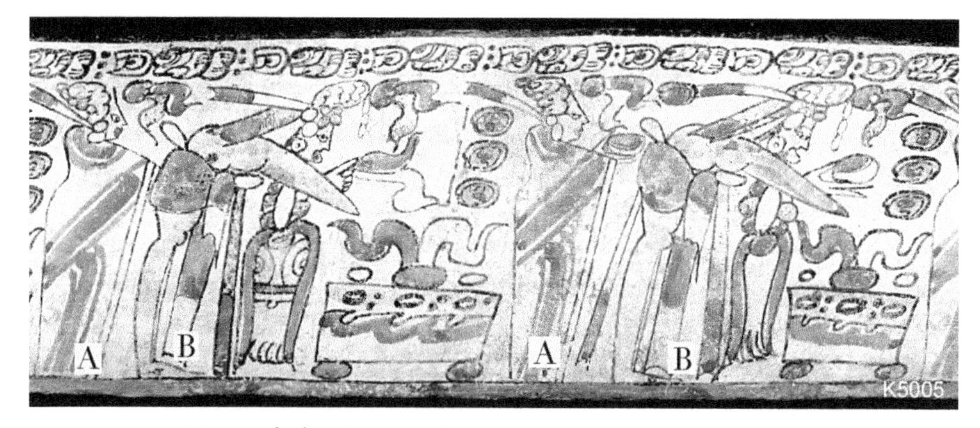

Figure 7.5. Scene of a female administering an enema in a cup to a male (K5005). (Photograph by Justin Kerr.)

Figure 7.6. Scene of a reclining male receiving an enema from a female while a bird flies overhead, perhaps acting as a supernatural messenger (K1550). (Photograph by Justin Kerr.)

the supernatural. Birds often act as supernatural messengers in Maya mythology (Rice 2007: 72; Tedlock 1996), and this scene may show a single bird in a narrative sequence grabbing the reclining individual's words to deliver them to supernatural forces. The Lacandón believe that intoxication helps their words be heard by the gods (McGee 1990: 73), and this image suggests that the Classic period Maya may have had a similar belief system.

K1890 (figure 7.7) shows females preparing and administering enemas to different males and consulting with a supernatural figure over an enema pot. The presence of the supernatural serpentine being in the lower portion of the vessel (scene D) suggests a link between enema use and supernatural powers.

K114 (figure 7.8) offers an exception to the rule of females acting as assistants to male intoxication. This image shows a bare-chested woman (individual B) sitting in a temple and drinking from a cup in a scene with numerous supernatural figures. She sits behind a male (individual A) who is facing a supernatural being (individual C), with a large pot between the two. The supernatural individual holds a cup while the male makes a hand gesture similar to the one made by the female in K7898 (individual A in figure 7.4), which may indicate offering a beverage. The pairing of smaller cups with the larger, urn-like vessels looks similar to other examples of paraphernalia associated with alcoholic beverage consumption as seen in K956 and K7898 (figures 7.2 and 7.4). The lack of enemas or clear drunken behavior is distinct from other drinking scenes. The female drinker in K114 (individual B in figure 7.8) wears clothing that differs

Figure 7.7. Painting of various males and a serpentine supernatural figure visiting female ritual specialists who prepare and administer enemas (K1890). The painting depicts seven scenes, with the female to the right of the male in all of them. The females and males in each scene are distinct, as suggested by the different clothing. In scene A, the female holds a baby while a male consults her with an enema pot sitting between them. In scene B, a woman adds a substance to a drinking cup while consulting a man. In scene C, a female consults a male while the male administers an enema to himself. In scene D, a female consults a serpentine supernatural with an enema pot between the two. In scene E, a woman administers an enema to a man. In scene F, a woman consults a man with an enema pot between the two. In scene G, a female consults a male wearing a serpentine headdress. (Photograph by Justin Kerr.)

from that of females in other scenes: the drinking female is bare chested and wears only a skirt, suggesting that she is of a different status than the other women. K114 lacks much of the paraphernalia and actions associated with male drinkers in other scenes. First, the scene lacks enema gear, which is common in other depictions of intoxication rituals, such as in K3027, K530, K7898, and K5005 (figures 7.1, 7.3–7.5). Second, the female drinker does not exhibit the openly drunken behavior, such as a drunken glazed look on her face, that is seen in male drinkers in other intoxication ritual scenes, such as K3027, K956, and K530 (figures 7.1–7.3). These features suggest a special status for this female drinker and indicate that she was not simply acting as a male.

Vase paintings that depict men and women participating in intoxication rituals contribute to understanding gender among the Classic period Maya and the significance of gender in cultural norms regarding intoxication. Several themes are evident in analyzing the paintings described above. Women are not shown drinking, with one possible exception in K114 (figure 7.8). Only men are shown receiving enemas. This pattern of illustrating males becoming intoxicated while females abstain served

Figure 7.8. Scene of a male and a female drinking in a structure while hosting four supernatural beings on the left half of the scene (K114). (Photograph by Justin Kerr.)

to reinforce the dominant gender roles and hierarchy during intoxication events. Despite being prohibited from imbibing, females played a key role in intoxication events through performing their gender-specific roles alongside their male counterparts. This key role of women in some intoxication events supports the idea of concurrent gender complementarity, in which females and males served distinct and complementary roles (Josserand 2002; Joyce 2001; Stockett 2005). The types of poses and actions found in the vase paintings suggest prescribed gender roles during intoxication events. Women's role as assistants to men becoming intoxicated took several forms:

- Women standing behind men holding their sides (K956 and K530 [figures 7.2 and 7.3]).
- Women serving men out of drinking vessels (K3027 [figure 7.1]).
- Women administering enemas (K5005, K1550, and K1890 [figures 7.5–7.7]).
- One instance of a female directing males in a ritual (K7898 [figure 7.4]).
- Women performing other assisting actions including fanning or holding a mirror (K530 [figure 7.3]).

Male behaviors during intoxication events also fall into a handful of categories:

- Men in the scenes are visibly intoxicated (K3027, K956, K530, K7898 [figures 7.1–7.3, 7.5]).

- Men are shown receiving enemas or drinking (K3027, K5005, K1550, K1890, and K114 [figures 7.1, 7.5–7.8])
- Men are shown preparing to receive enemas or drink (K956, K530, K7898, K1890, and K114 [figures 7.2–7.4, 7.7–7.8]).

The poses and actions in the vase paintings mirror those described by the seventeenth-century Spanish clergyman Diego de Landa (Tozzer 1941) among the early colonial period Yucatecan Maya. Landa's description of people seated in "couples or by fours" (Tozzer 1941: 92) is similar to the scenes of females positioned beside males seen in K3027, K956, K530, and K114 (figures 7.1–7.3 and 7.8). The vase paintings of females serving males drinks or enemas, such as K3027, K5005, K1550, and K1890 (figures 7.1, 7.5–7.7), are reminiscent of Landa's (Tozzer 1941: 92–93) description of females serving males drinks. Landa's accounts indicate that there was a pattern of males imbibing and females assisting them. One passage in particular highlights this role of women as helpers and men as the intoxicated: "And they ate with dances and rejoicings, seated in couples or by fours. And after the repast the cup-bearers, who were not accustomed to get drunk, poured out drink from great tubs, until they (those celebrating) had become as drunk as scimitars, and the women took it upon themselves to get their drunken husbands home" (Tozzer 1941: 92).

The depictions of males becoming intoxicated in the vase paintings mirror Landa's (Tozzer 1941: 92) description of how men became "as drunk as scimitars" during early colonial period drinking festivities. The images of females assisting males during intoxication rituals, especially those of females standing behind males holding their sides, such as in K956 and K530 (figures 7.2 and 7.3), are reminiscent of Landa's (Tozzer 1941: 92) account of women helping bring their drunken husbands home after feasts.

Through performing their defined gender roles during intoxication events, individuals may have publicly reaffirmed their identities to others in attendance, including supernatural beings depicted in some scenes (figures 7.3, 7.6–7.8). Generally, males reinforced their masculinity through imbibing, and females reinforced their femininity through assisting men. This juxtaposition between sober females and intoxicated males would have highlighted differences in gender identities and the special nature of the intoxicated experience.

Gender roles varied somewhat depending on the setting of the intoxication ritual. This variability supports the idea that ancient Maya gender roles were flexible (Ardren 2002; Stockett 2005) and changed in different situations. Some scenes, including K956, K7898, and K5005 (figures 7.2, 7.4, and 7.5), involve between three and four individuals. These scenes feature pairings between males and females, possibly husbands and wives. K7898 (figure 7.4) is distinct in that it shows a female leading the two males in a ritual rather than the more common female-male pairings. These scenes (K956, K7898, and K5005 [figures 7.2, 7.4, and 7.5]) lack overtly supernatural figures and represent smaller-scale intoxication rituals conducted by nobles, possibly in domestic settings. K1550 (figure 7.6) also shows a small group of nobles conducting an intoxication ritual; however, this image has supernatural themes with the avian imagery and more explicit erotic themes. The scene depicted on this vase highlights the more spiritual and transcendental aspects of intoxication rituals among the ancient Maya nobility.

Intoxication rituals could also be more rowdy, as seen in K3027 (figure 7.1). This image has several participants and may feature more obviously drunken behavior, such as the individual drinking out of the large vessel. More formalized behaviors, such as the way the women help the men drink and the individuals making hand gestures in the center of the image, demonstrate that these larger drinking events remained ritualized despite potentially raucous elements.

Some drinking scenes involved supernatural beings in ritual settings. K530 (figure 7.3) depicts a group of supernatural beings or elites participating in an intoxication ritual in front of a structure or in its courtyard. The male imbibers and their female attendants face a supernatural being seated in a structure. In K114 (figure 7.8) a female and male are shown performing a drinking ritual in their house while facing a group of four supernatural beings, one of whom is drinking. This scene may show the woman and man offering an alcoholic beverage to the supernatural beings. In K1890 (figure 7.7), female ritual specialists are depicted preparing and administering enemas for different men and interacting with a serpentine supernatural being. A woman is shown caring for an infant in the top left portion of the image (figure 7.7, section A), which suggests that this event may take place in a domestic setting. The scene may represent a type of intoxication ritual in which individuals visited specialists to perform intoxication rituals that may have been aimed at summoning or communicating with supernatural beings. These paintings highlight the ancient Maya belief that they could commune with the supernatural during intoxication rituals.

Vase paintings of intoxication rituals reflect a dominant gender ideology in which women could have considerable power but remained auxiliary figures in the overall male-dominated power structure. My analysis of these images supports Stockett's (2005: 573) assertion that gender hierarchy existed simultaneously with gender complementarity among the ancient Maya. Although women and men serve complementary roles in these rituals, there is an implicit hierarchical distinction in their relationship.

A further expression of gender hierarchy is evident in the general exclusion of females from becoming intoxicated. The one image of a drinking female in K114 (figure 7.8) does not show her to be visibly intoxicated. Additionally, I have seen no images of females receiving enemas, which likely delivered more-potent intoxicants (de Smet 1985; de Smet and Hellmuth 1986; Grube 2000b). Transcendental communication with supernatural powers through intoxication was likely a prized mental state among ancient Mesoamericans (Grube 2000a, 2000b; Mitchell 2004; Stross and Kerr 1990). Although women played a key role in ancient Maya intoxication rituals, their exclusion from experiencing intoxicated states of mind suggests that these rituals expressed a hierarchical gender ideology.

This treatment mirrors the exclusion of women from aspects of the Lacandón balché ritual, during which intoxication was seen as a means for achieving transcendental experiences (McGee 1990). Communal events involving balché consumption are an integral part of traditional Lacandón social and ritual life (McGee 1990, 2002). Formal participation in the balché ritual is exclusively for men (McGee 1990). All men who are old enough to drink participate. Women are forbidden from entering the "god house" during the ritual and do not directly participate in it. Nevertheless, women are integral, albeit informal, participants: females sit in the clearing outside the god house during the ritual and talk with their husbands and male kin, who occasionally leave the god house to bring women balché to drink (McGee 1990: 80).

Classic period Maya vase paintings of intoxication rituals may also illustrate idealized behaviors of noble husband-wife pairings as a way to reinforce dominant gender ideologies. Female-male pairings in most of the illustrations analyzed in this study show individuals who are wearing similarly high-status clothing, suggesting that they are both of elite social status (figures 7.1, 7.2, 7.4–7.6, and 7.8). Ethnohistoric accounts describe married couples working together during intoxication rituals and also describe wives assisting their husbands during early colonial period drinking festivities (Tozzer 1941: 92). As idealized images of intoxication rituals, these vase paintings would have reflected how married couples should properly behave during such events. Through showing nonimbibing wives assisting their husbands during these rituals, the vase paintings reinforced a domestic gender hierarchy that gave unequal power to males. Wives were expected to assist their husbands while being prohibited from the central ritual action of intoxication except on relatively rare occasions, as seen in K114 (figure 7.8).

Intoxication events conform to a wider pattern of denying women equal access to political and ritual power among the Classic period Maya elites. Despite some notable exceptions, such as Lady Xoc's bloodletting in Yaxchilán lintels 24 and 25 (Josserand 2002: 129–33, figs. 8.10 and 8.11), women were rarely depicted as the primary ritual actors in monumental artwork. Women were usually shown as assistants to their husbands or male kin (Josserand 2002; Joyce 2001). Much of women's formal political power came from being dynastic links between powerful elite families (Josserand 2002). Women's roles as dynastic links were especially significant given the frequency at which elite males were killed or captured during warfare (Josserand 2002).

Western culture similarly uses intoxication as a setting for pursuing identity enactment and perpetuating gender inequality. Joffe (1998: 298) noted that in Western cultures, drinking is traditionally seen as a male bonding activity in which women are relegated to being servers and objects of desire. Western culture's idealized gender roles of males as bonding alcohol consumers and females as servers and objects of sexual desire are illustrated in beer advertisements, which often show "regular guys" enjoying themselves with beer while being served by attractive women. Such advertisements depict an idealized notion of drinking and sexual and gender identities that serve to sell products through reflecting and reinforcing the culture's dominant gender ideology.

COMPLEMENTARITY

The male as receiver and the female as provider of intoxicants may have been a metaphorical action for the wider complementary, although unequal, relationship between the genders in which women assisted males in rituals such as accession rites (Josserand 2002). The role of women as complementary helpers during rituals has a long history among the ancient Maya. The San Bartolo murals, which date to approximately the third century BC (Saturno et al. 2005, 2006), feature scenes of females assisting in various rituals performed by male protagonists. We see a similar pattern of gender roles in monumental art, in which women are usually shown as attendants to males who are performing rituals (Josserand 2002; Joyce 2001: 90). Examples include stone monuments showing males being handed headdresses by female kin during rituals, such as in the Oval Palace Tablet from Palenque (Josserand 2002: fig. 8.1).

On a more practical level, as the only sober participants, females would have played a key role in managing intoxication events. Images of intoxicated males, coupled with the ethnohistoric accounts (Tozzer 1941: 92), suggest that men became highly intoxicated during these rituals. Sober female actors would have helped guide ritual actions of the intoxicated males. K956 and K530 (figures 7.2 and 7.3) depict women physically supporting and guiding intoxicated males through a ritual, and K7898 (figure 7.4) shows a female directing intoxicated, or soon to be intoxicated, males. These images suggest that sober females maintained order during intoxication events. These gatherings were also social affairs, and females would have played a key role in mediating relationships between intoxicated participants. The proclivity of drunken individuals toward antisocial behavior would have made sober females a valuable asset in avoiding and defusing confrontations between intoxicated males. De Landa gives some evidence for this aspect of female involvement in intoxication rituals among early colonial period Maya with his description of sober females assisting their drunken husbands (Tozzer 1941: 92).

GENDER ROLE REVERSALS IN INTOXICATION EVENTS

Vase paintings of intoxication events may depict instances of gender role reversals during certain rituals. Diversion from the cultural norms of gender roles during some rituals has been described in ethnographic accounts of other parts of the world (Bateson 1958; Turner 1969: 183–85). Breaking normal gender roles during rituals highlighted gendered behaviors and identities, thereby reinforcing the dominant gender ideology (Bateson 1958; Turner 1969: 183–85). Penetration of males by females, as seen in K5005, K1550, and K1890 (figures 7.5–7.7), represented an eroticized ritualized gender role reversal (Houston et al. 2006: 117). The sexual nature of enema scenes is reinforced by the presence of male genitals in K1550 (figure 7.6), which is generally unusual in Maya art (Houston et al. 2006; Joyce 2001; Meskell and Joyce 2003).

This eroticized male/female enema imagery is reminiscent of the Lacandón conception of balché as being a seductive female whom male drinkers hope to keep by avoiding vomiting (McGee 1990: 81). Although balché consumption is largely associated with males, the balché itself is personified in songs as a female. During the ritual, men sometimes sing a song that on the surface appears to be a love song to a woman. In fact, it is actually about a man begging his balché—called "little woman" in the song—not to leave him. McGee (1990: 81) suggests that the man's plea for balché to stay is allegorical of the singer's desire to avoid vomiting, which would cause him to sober up. Among both the modern Lacandón and the Classic period Maya, the intoxicated individual is generally male and the facilitator of intoxication female. This evidence suggests that the Maya conceived that during intoxication events, the male-gendered individuals submitted themselves to the female-gendered intoxicants. Despite this specific role reversal of females penetrating males, the wider gender role of females abstaining while assisting males in intoxication events holds true in these images.

A different type of deviation from normal gender roles may be depicted in the image with the possible female drinker in K114 (figure 7.8). The female in K114 (figure 7.8) drinks, thereby partaking in a normally male activity. She also wears a more male costume, going bare chested rather than wearing the more traditional body-length huipil typically seen on women in Classic period Maya art (Joyce 2001: 65). This individual may be of a manly woman gender category, such as those described by Looper (2002). Alternatively, this scene, as with those involving female-administered enemas, may represent a special ritual in which gender roles deviated, allowing women to wear different clothing and to drink.

Conclusions

Examination of Late Classic period Maya vase paintings demonstrates that intoxication events were settings for enacting and constructing gender identities. These images provide a previously unexplored line of evidence in the study of gender among the Classic period Maya. Patterns of behavior among males and females demonstrate that males became intoxicated during these events. Women acted primarily in serving men alcoholic beverages, administering enemas, or assisting with the ritual in other ways.

My analysis supports the notion that gender identities were simultaneously complementary and hierarchical among the ancient Maya (Stockett 2005). Intoxication rituals included aspects of a gender hierarchy such as the role of women as ritual assistants and the prohibition of women from becoming inebriated. Despite this hierarchy, complementary aspects of gender dynamics among the Classic period Maya are evident in the prominent portrayal of females in these scenes. In addition to assisting males in drinking and taking enemas, women played a key role in organizing and keeping order during these sometimes-raucous festivities.

The prominence and complexity of gendered behaviors in vase paintings of intoxication rituals support Dietler's (2001, 2006) assertion that feasts, especially those involving drinking and other forms of inebriation, were key settings for enacting gender identities and reflecting gender ideologies in the ancient world. This chapter highlights how scholars must consider the different ways that people participated in intoxication events according to their place in society. Intoxicant use, or prohibition thereof, often depended on one's wider social identities, including gender. Furthermore, this examination of gendered behaviors regarding intoxication can illuminate previously unexplored aspects of gender roles and identities in ancient cultures.

Acknowledgments

I thank Joshua Englehardt, Mary Pohl, Michael Carrasco, and Bridget McDonnell for their advice and for reading drafts of this chapter. I also thank the late Dr. Kathryn Josserand for her advice and encouragement in studying ancient Maya vase paintings of intoxication rituals. I am grateful for Justin Kerr's superb rollout photographs of Maya vase paintings and thank Mr. and Mrs. Kerr and the Foundation for the Advancement of Mesoamerican Studies Inc. (FAMSI) for making this image archive available online for study.

References Cited

Ardren, T. 2002. Women and Gender in the Ancient Maya World. In *Ancient Maya Women*, ed. T. Ardren, 1–11. Walnut Creek, Calif.: AltaMira Press.

Ayala Falcón, M. A. 2002. Lady K'awil, Goddess O, and Maya Warfare. In *Ancient Maya Women*, ed. T. Ardren, 105–13. Walnut Creek, Calif.: AltaMira Press.

Bateson, G. 1958. *Naven: A Survey of the Problems Suggested by a Composite Picture of the Culture of a New Guinea Tribe Drawn from Three Points of View*. Stanford: Stanford University Press.

Bruman, H. J. 2000. *Alcohol in Ancient Mexico*. Salt Lake City: University of Utah Press.

Conkey, M. W., and J. D. Spector. 1984. Archaeology and the Study of Gender. In

Advances in Archaeological Method and Theory, vol. 7, ed. M. B. Schiffer, 1–38. Orlando, Fla.: Academic Press.
Demarest, A. 1992. Ideology in Ancient Maya Cultural Evolution: The Dynamics of Galactic Politics. In *Ideology and Pre-Columbian Civilizations*, ed. A. Demarest and G. Conrad, 135–57. Santa Fe, N.Mex.: School of American Research.
Demarest, A. 2004. *Ancient Maya: The Rise and Fall of a Rainforest Civilization*. Cambridge: Cambridge University Press.
de Smet, P.A.G.M. 1985. *Ritual Enemas and Snuffs in the Americas*. Latin American Studies 33. Amsterdam, Netherlands: Centro de Estudios y Documentación Latinamericanos (CEDLA).
de Smet, P.A.G.M., and N. M. Hellmuth. 1986. A Multidisciplinary Approach to Ritual Enema Scenes on Ancient Maya Pottery. *Journal of Ethnopharmacology* 16: 213–62.
Dietler, M. 1990. Driven by Drink. *Anthropological Archaeology* 9 (4): 352–406.
Dietler, M. 1996. Feasts and Commensal Politics in the Political Economy. In *Food and the Status Quest: An Interdisciplinary Perspective*, ed. P. Wiessner and W. Schiefenhövel, 87–125. Providence, R.I.: Bergham Books.
Dietler, M. 2001. Theorizing the Feast: Rituals of Consumption, Commensal Politics, and Power in African Contexts. In *Feasts: Archaeological and Ethnographic Perspectives on Food, Politics, and Power*, ed. M. Dietler and B. Hayden, 65–114. Washington, D.C.: Smithsonian Institution Press.
Dietler, M. 2006. Alcohol: Anthropological/Archaeological Perspectives. *Annual Review of Anthropology* 35: 229–49.
Dobkin de Rios, M. 1974. The Influence of Psychotropic Flora and Fauna on Maya Religion. *Current Anthropology* 15 (2): 147–64.
Freidel, D. A., and L. Schele. 1988. Kingship in the Late Preclassic Maya Lowlands: The Instruments and Places of Ritual Power. *American Antiquity* 90 (3): 547–67.
Freidel, D. A., L. Schele, and J. Parker. 1993. *Maya Cosmos: Three Thousand Years on the Shaman's Path*. New York: William Morrow.
Furst, P. T., and M. D. Coe. 1977. Ritual Enemas. *Natural History* 86: 88–91.
Gage, T. (1648) 1958. *Thomas Gage's Travels in the New World*. Ed. J.E.S. Thompson. Norman: University of Oklahoma Press.
Grube, N. 2000a. Akan: The God of Drinking, Disease and Death. In *Continuity and Change: Maya Religious Practices in Temporal Perspective*, ed. D. G. Behrens, N. Grube, C. M. Prager, F. Sachse, and E. W. Teufel, 59–76. Acta Mesoamericana 14. Bonn: University of Bonn.
Grube, N. 2000b. Intoxication and Ecstasy. In *Maya: Divine Kings of the Rainforest*, ed. N. Grube, 294–95. Venice, Italy: Könemann Verlagsgesellschaft.
Houston, S., D. Stuart, and K. Taube. 2006. *The Memory of Bones: Body, Being, and Experience among the Classic Maya*. Austin: University of Texas Press.
Inomata, T. 2006. Plazas, Performers, and Spectators: Political Theaters of the Classic Maya. *Current Anthropology* 47 (5): 805–42.
Jackson, S. E. 2009. Imagining Courtly Communities: An Exploration of Classic Maya Experiences of Status and Identity through Painted Ceramic Vessels. *Ancient Mesoamerica* 20: 71–85.

Joffe, A. 1998. Alcohol and Social Complexity in Western Asia. *Current Anthropology* 29 (3): 297–322.
Josserand, J. K. 2002. Women in Classic Maya Hieroglyphic Texts. In *Ancient Maya Women*, ed. T. Ardren, 114–51. Walnut Creek, Calif.: AltaMira Press.
Joyce, R. A. 1996. The Construction of Gender in Classic Maya Monuments. In *Gender and Archaeology*, ed. R. P. Wright, 167–95. Philadelphia: University of Pennsylvania Press.
Joyce, R. A. 2001. *Gender and Power in Prehispanic Mesoamerica*. Austin: University of Texas Press.
Kerr, J. 1989. *The Maya Vase Book:* A *Corpus of Rollout Photographs of Maya Vases*. New York: Kerr Associates.
Looper, M. G. 2002. Ancient Maya Women-Men (and Men-Women): Classic Rulers and the Third Gender. In *Ancient Maya Women*, ed. T. Ardren, 171–202. Walnut Creek, Calif.: AltaMira Press.
Loughmiller-Newman, J. 2008. Canons of Painting: A Spatial Analysis of Classic Period Polychromes. *Latin American Antiquity* 19: 29–42.
McGee, R. J. 1990. *Life Ritual and Religion among the Lacandon Maya*. New York: Wadsworth Publishing.
McGee, R. J. 2002. *Watching Lacandon Lives*. Boston: Allyn and Bacon.
Meskell, L. M., and R. A. Joyce. 2003. *Embodied Lives: Figuring Ancient Maya and Egyptian Experience*. London: Routledge.
Miller, M. E. 2004. *Courtly Art of the Ancient Maya*. New York: Thames and Hudson.
Mitchell, T. 2004. *Intoxicated Identities: Alcohol's Power in Mexican History and Culture*. New York: Routledge.
Rice, P. M. 2007. *Maya Calendar Origins: Monuments, Mythistory, and the Materialization of Time*. Austin: University of Texas Press.
Saturno, W. A., K. Taube, and D. Stuart. 2005. *The Murals of San Bartolo, El Petén, Guatemala*. Part 1, *The North Wall*. Ancient America 7. Barnardsville, N.C.: Center for Ancient American Studies.
Saturno, W. A., D. Stuart, and B. Beltrán. 2006. Early Maya Writing at San Bartolo, Guatemala. *Science* 311 (5765): 1281–83.
Schultes, R. E., A. Hofmann, and C. Rätsch. 1998. *Plants of the Gods: Their Sacred, Healing, and Hallucinogenic Powers*. Rochester, N.Y.: Healing Arts Press.
Smalley, J., and M. Blake. 2003. Sweet Beginnings: Stalk Sugar and the Domestication of Maize. *Current Anthropology* 44 (5): 675–703.
Stockett, M. K. 2005. On the Importance of Difference: Re-envisioning Sex and Gender in Ancient Mesoamerica. *World Archaeology* 37 (4): 566–78.
Stross, B., and J. Kerr. 1990. Notes on the Mayan Vision Quest through Enema. In *The Maya Vase Book*, vol. 2, ed. J. Kerr, 349–61. New York: Kerr Associates.
Tedlock, D. 1996. *Popol Vuh: The Definitive Edition of the Mayan Book of the Dawn of Life and the Glories of the Gods and Kings*. New York: Simon and Schuster.
Tozzer, A. 1941. *Landa's* Relación de las Cosas de Yucatan*:* A *Translation*. Papers of the Peabody Museum of American Archaeology and Ethnology 18. Cambridge, Mass.: Harvard University. Reprint, Millwood, N.Y.: Kraus Reprint.

Turner, V. 1969. *The Ritual Process: Structure and Anti-structure.* Hawthorne, N.Y.: Aldine de Gruyter.
Zagorevski, D., and J. A. Loughmiller-Newman. 2012. The Detection of Nicotine in a Late Mayan Period Flask by Gas Chromatography and Liquid Chromatography Mass Spectrometry Methods. *Rapid Communications in Mass Spectrometry* 26: 403–11.

Mayan Ritual Beverage Production

Considering the Ceramics

JENNIFER LOUGHMILLER-CARDINAL

Drinking is an act loaded with significance. It is cultural fact on which thousands of years, millions of gestures have accumulated.

—Turmo 2001: 130

This chapter addresses areas where more attention could be focused toward the bridging of the material goods and behavior. The research presented here considers the artifact as both the outcome of a need and an artifact in and of a process. While vessels are easily identified in the material record, we must also examine the behavior that surrounds them in order to better interpret ancient practices of ritual consumption, the images that depict such events, and the texts that refer to them. One area of particular interest and well suited to thorough evaluation of these relationships is the production of fermented beverages, the containers from which they were consumed, and the contexts in which these vessels were used.

The various attributes of pottery vessels are frequently used to address complex questions about the behaviors of the ancient Mayans, both those specifically related to the vessel use and more-general aspects of function. Extra attention has been given to elite drinking containers, especially those vessels bearing texts and/or images. This scrutiny has led to epigraphic discovery that prominent text (typically around the rim, otherwise identified as the Primary Standard Sequence) often contains folk names potentially identifying the vessel type (Boot 2009; Houston 1989; Houston et al. 1989; Kettunen and Helmke 2010: 36; MacLeod 1990: 315;

Tedlock 2002: 174), the names of owners and patrons, and the names of foods consumed by the Mayans (see Stuart 1988, 2005; see esp. Stuart 2006; but also see Beliaev et al. 2010; Coe and Coe 1996; Hull 2010; Kaufman and Justeson 2003, 2006, 2007; McNeil 2006; McNeil et al. 2006; Mora-Marín 2004; Rain 2004: 167; Stross 2006).

Iconographic and image analyses have identified particular events, the participants of those events, and the context or location of certain depictions (Alcorn et al. 2006; Christenson 2004; Colop 1999; Sachse 2008; Sharer and Morley 1994; Stross 2006; Tedlock 1996; Townsend 2000).

The vessels themselves have been subjected to many kinds of evaluations to help answer archaeologically derived research questions. There are differences, however, between vessels that have been recovered archaeologically and vessels that are depicted in the art. Mesoamerican scholars, however, have had difficulty directly connecting material goods to graphic depictions of behavior. This is not to say that correspondences between archaeological and iconographic elements are not common, but linking specific behavior to material objects shown in the iconography has been problematic.

Events involving the consumption of drinks are among those most commonly captured in the art. Many of these scenes suggest consumption of what are presumed to have been alcoholic beverages (discussed further below). The portrayal of a wide range of vessel forms related to beverages and consumption supports this interpretation. These events are depicted not only in murals and monuments but also on the vessels associated with drinking.

Typically, Mayan illustrations (especially those featured on vessels) were not static representations of a moment but instead represented a view of an ongoing action (Loughmiller-Newman 2008). Such scenes typically depict political deliberations, noteworthy discussions, mythological events, war, hunting, or sacrificial processional or patrician rites. These scenes depict noteworthy segments of time but hint at a more protracted sequence of events surrounding that time frame. This can be identified through the depiction of regularly occurring objects and accoutrements associated with event type and actor status (such as kings, lords, and secondary nobles). These items were culturally identifiable elements and would have been immediately recognized for their intended purpose or use within that scene. Thus, an object depicted within such a scene necessarily performed an understood role within that sequence of action. Unfortunately for modern researchers, most of these cultural symbols are still poorly understood.

A depicted vessel (e.g., a cup, bowl, cylinder, or olla—a vessel meant for drinking will be generically called a *cup* throughout this chapter) will have an intended function associated with its form. This is true in our own lives: for example, a wine glass on a reception invitation. In general performance a cup is what will hold, is holding, or has held a beverage. This meaning is present when a vessel is depicted in a scene, regardless of whether it is depicted as actively being employed in consumption. Its presence in a scene simply represents the performance of some activity related to beverage consumption as well as a *pars pro toto* indication of the sequence of events that necessitated its presence. The depiction of a drinking vessel, therefore, represents some larger series of behaviors involving a beverage. The beverage itself had to be acquired or produced, possibly stored, provided or served, and finally consumed. Each of these activities would have had some set of associated actions related to material artifacts, and possibly some set of associated ritual or other socially recognizable behavior as well. Each such set of actions is indirectly implied by the depiction of a drinking vessel.

There are very few liquids, if any, that would have been immediately available for consumption to the Classic Mayans without some form of preparation. Water would have needed to be purified, fruit would have had to have been processed, and the fermented beverages would have undergone specific preparatory steps. Colonial documents and recent ethnographic work have highlighted the significance of the rituals involved in the preparation of certain beverages—ritual drinks were born out of ritualized acts (e.g., balché rituals [see Boremanse 1981; Hoil and Roys 1967; McGee 1984, 1988; Slotkin 1954; Tozzer 1907]). This underscores the fact that the act of drinking a beverage is not a self-contained event but instead one intrinsically linked to the preparation of the liquid. The act of preparation would conclude with consumption, but the consumption would not be the only aspect considered significant.

A cup directly symbolizes only the final act of consumption by an individual, but consumption itself further necessitates and symbolizes by implication all the prior events as well. An olla generally indicates a penultimate state of consumption during which a liquid is expected to be served in a cup. The presence of ollas also suggests either that numerous participants will be consuming the beverage or that the participants will be consuming a greater quantity than that held by a single cup.

The production of alcohol requires specific steps and care, as does the production of significant foodstuffs. Recipes and required steps or content can reasonably be assumed. Significant goods would not have

Figure 8.1. Example of an olla with elements shown above the vessel (K4113). (Photograph by Justin Kerr.)

been reasonably left to experimentation, especially those that are rare, difficult to procure, or require a great amount of effort to produce. This would likely be especially true if they were required for use in an imminent ritual. Ritualized production would function broadly as a recipe, thus ensuring a reasonable amount of success leading to a predictable and consistent final product.

The Mayans, in concert with the whole of ancient Mesoamerica, celebrated many calendars tied to planting, growth, and harvest (Stuart 2011). The act of planting, harvesting, or collecting the ingredients must also be included in the consideration of the cup. Clearly, archaeologists cannot attain a full material record of the expression of these behaviors, but it should nevertheless be possible to assemble evidence of their practice by reasonable interferences.

It can be ascertained from the drinking scenes that not all events depicted are of equivalent importance, and the drinks present in the scenes play highly variable roles. The variation in which vessel forms are illustrated may indicate more about the event than we have yet considered. One means of evaluating the event depicted is to consider the contents of large ollas and basins, which are commonly shown with single glyphic labels or denoted by associated icons (such as elements protruding from the top) (figure 8.1). If potential contents can be broadly identified, then archaeologists have the opportunity to study the behavior represented as a sequence of events. The images typically show one of the following libations: maize/beer, honey/mead, or agave/pulque. Broadly, we know that each of these beverages has material goods associated with its production, ethnographically known expressions, and ethnohistorical documentation.

Social Contexts of Mayan Drinking

Alcoholic beverages are among the very first processed foods. The process of fermentation is naturally occurring, and it enables longer storage and usage of food items by inhibiting bacterial growth (Steinkraus 1983; Ulloa 1987; Vargas 2001). The term *drinking*, or *to have a drink*, typically refers to imbibing alcoholic or exotic liquids (Chatwin 2001; de Garine 2001; Douglas 1987). Drinking or to share a drink, as Mandelbaum (1965) argues, symbolizes social solidarity (see Washburne 1961). "Ceremonial drinking [among the Japanese] took place also—as it still does—at weddings, funerals, banquets, and 'congratulatory occasions' such as New Year" (Sargent 1983: 279). In some cultures, drinking is only a social activity. For instance, "All drinking [among the Meo of Laos] occurs as a social activity. Alcohol usage is closely integrated with other elements of Meo culture: rites of passage, important extra-kin relationships, unpredictable crises, annual celebrations" (Westermeyer 1983: 290).

The physiological effect of consuming alcoholic drinks is well established. The general effects include relaxation and reduced inhibitions. The pharmacological properties of alcohol create a bodily reaction, which to the brain seems strikingly different from that of daily experience. Drinks, especially alcoholic beverages, have traditionally been included in ritual activities to exploit this psychoactive effect (Dietler 1990, 1996; Heath 1976; Mandelbaum 1965; Marshall 1983b). Many Mesoamerican cultures used potent drinks for ceremonial purposes. The extent to which they combined intoxicants to achieve an altered state is still under investigation, but archaeological evidence and depictions of ceremonial paraphernalia indicate frequent ritual usage (de Smet 1985; Reents-Budet et al. 1994; Schele and Miller 1983). Given their antiquity and geographical distribution, alcoholic beverages remain the best known and most widely used means of altering human consciousness (see, e.g., Steinkraus 1983).

Fellowship among community members is encouraged by social drinking events (Healy et al. 1983). According to Jesuit scholar Bernabe Cobo ([1599] 1943: 254), "The public banquets in Peru lasted a long time and participants would drink heavily at these feasts until they became inebriated. . . . They would take turns offering each other chicha in the following way: the one who was offering would get up and go over to a member of the other group carrying two glasses of chicha in his hands, giving one glass to his counterpart and keeping the other himself, they would drink together."

The relationships established and reinforced by drinking are as individualistic as they are communal. According to Madsen and Madsen (1983), in the village of Tecospa, Mexico, social pulque consumption creates a contract between participants similar to that of a potlatch. To accept pulque from the host is to acknowledge his land and his family, while to refuse the pulque is to reject the host (Madsen and Madsen 1983: 44). "Alcohol is not socially disruptive among them, but a mechanism of social integration" (Bunzel 1940: 372). Intoxication is believed to intensify group cohesion and express the sense of community.

BEVERAGES AS PERFORMATIVE MEDIUM

> Rituals are episodes of repeated and simplified cultural communication in which the direct partners to a social interaction, and those observing it, share a mutual belief in the descriptive and prescriptive validity of the communication's symbolic contents and accept the authenticity of one another's intentions. It is because of this shared understanding of intention and content, and in the intrinsic validity of the interaction, that rituals have their effect and affect. Ritual effectiveness energizes the participants and attaches them to each other, increases their identification with the symbolic objects of communication, and intensifies the connection of the participants and the symbolic objects with the observing audience, the relevant "community" at large. (Alexander 2004: 527)

Participation in ritualized or otherwise formal social events often relies on the participants' thorough knowledge and enactment of the etiquettes and paraphernalia of the event. In this context, the consumption of a beverage is part of the formal performances of the participant or participants, and therefore the beverage becomes part of that performance—both as paraphernalia and as a necessary part of the etiquette. Depending on that context, the production, preparation, and service of the beverage (and all material paraphernalia and actions associated with that sequence) equally become part of that performance. The proper conduct of those actions and possession of those accoutrements establish the validity and success of the participants in the view of a cultural observer.

In the performance of ceremony and ritual, the settings and accoutrements utilized are intrinsically tied to the legitimacy of the actions and performers, the delineation of performer and observer, and the evaluation of the success of the performance. Social actions are strategically constituted to communicate each of these roles to all participants—both actors and audience. Although consisting of broadly prescribed and proscribed sequences of actions and events, the success of ritual performance depends on the adequate and strategic utilization of all available semiotic referents. This is in order to satisfy not only the intentions of the performer but also the expectations of the observers. In this sense, socially legitimated actors and the social body of legitimating observers are equal participants.

Prestigious goods used in formal affairs are easily distinguished from mundane utilitarian wares. They are distinguished as elite artifacts by their quality of craftsmanship, use of exotic forms that limit pragmatic usability, ornate surface embellishment, and unique occurrences of image and text. Examples of such high-quality items are presented in Justin Kerr's database of Mayan vessels. Such ornate vessels are recovered most often in ritual contexts, and drinking vessels are the most frequent forms found in the elite ritual contexts. *Ritual* is used here to refer to an event that requires specific behaviors and paraphernalia to enact. These contexts result in cultural activities that fall outside routine or daily behaviors. The archaeological identification of highly ornate service ware suggests that some events required exotic service to satisfy ritual or other prescribed actions. "There were contexts in which both the consumables and the vessels and other equipment used in their consumption were designed to set the rituals and their participants apart from others" (Pollock 1983: 25).

DRINKING AS SOCIAL PERFORMANCE

What and how one consumes is intrinsically related to who one is (Bourdieu 1984). When consumption is set within specific communal circumstances (e.g., that act generally known as feasting), it becomes a socially charged event in which participants engage in a range of significant activities that directly influence social formation, maintenance, and operation. With its focus on the company, context, service, and consumables, the act of feasting creates a situation unlike daily consumption and interaction. Therefore, socially consuming foodstuffs in the context of a feast fixes the consumer to a class of behavior by both the context and the content of the actions. That class is defined by the host and event and is further made manifest by the service and foodstuffs (see Douglas and Isherwood 1979: 62).

The symbolic elements present in any such event refine the participation by a series of signals weighted against other lesser and greater signals, each of which is designed to convey particular information to the other participants and observers (Brumfiel 1987, 1994; Brumfiel and Earle 1987; LeCount 1999; Sabloff 1986). Those who participate in affairs of this magnitude express their position by seamlessly performing expected acts and etiquettes, which are further supported and accompanied by the appropriate paraphernalia.

These expectations, such as consuming expected goods or possessing the required tools, can express and detect the distinction of those items against all others. These inalienable possessions are described by Weiner (1992: 33) as "symbolic repositories of genealogies and historical events[;] their unique, subjective identity gives them absolute value placing them above the exchangeability of one thing for another." Legitimate members of the associated social stratum readily identify a fraud, a fake, or an error in decorum. In this way, restriction through specialized knowledge and performance of status-affiliated events keeps nonparticipant observers from attempting infiltration into this exclusive arena.

PRODUCTION AND SERVICE AS SOCIAL PERFORMANCES

Although much attention regarding Mayan vessels has been focused on the subsequent acts of consumption and feasting, the formal etiquettes and rituals involved in the preparation, presentation, and service for the event may equally be considered performative acts. Such preparatory behaviors and material paraphernalia are bound within the same cultural perceptions and conventions and may equally contribute to the same forms of social currency or sanction as a result. Formal preparations for ritualized events and the manner of presentation may be highly visible indicators of the host's adherence to and success in the conventions of ritual performances, regardless of the success of the culminating acts of the event.

Despite the pragmatic and functional nature of the preparations and service for an event, Mayan art is not known to depict the mundane in any aspect. It is reasonable to conclude, then, that the depiction of these acts is indicative of their particular significance to the overall sequence of ritual preparations and behavior. As such, their presence in the iconography makes them prominent and necessary contributors meant to communicate some pertinent information regarding the nature or significance of the events being portrayed. They are, in some manner, qualifying or specifying some particular nature of the event that is not otherwise germane to all similar events (i.e., indicating the particular manner or intent of the feast or ritual). If that is the case, then the specific implements and materials depicted as the preparatory rituals for an event serve a significant functional role and warrant closer scrutiny.

Significance of Drinking to the Classic Mayans

Outside of the codices (Post-Classic, AD 900–1500), I am aware of only one known depiction of anyone in the act of eating.[1] There are, however, numerous depictions of figures in some state of a drinking event (only six depictions where a cup or bowl is raised to their lips: K3027, K3264, K4377, K4907, and K5513 [Kerr numbers], as well as one in the Calakmul murals) throughout the Classic and Post-Classic periods. Additionally, a far greater number of drinking vessels bear hieroglyphic texts and decoration compared to bowls or plates. Inasmuch as drinking is more commonly depicted in elite art than is eating, drinking seems to have been a more significant semiotic referent. This suggests that drinking rather than eating had the greater normative salience and performative consequence to the Mayans.

Feasting and drinking events of the Classic period apparently involved copious amounts of alcoholic beverages and probably other naturally occurring intoxicants. In several scenes, the participants are shown to have consumed enough to vomit (e.g., K6020). The gods are also depicted partaking in these events, as often and as much as do the humans. The archaeologically known vessel forms that are depicted in these scenes include handheld cups or bowls, cylinders of various sizes, multiple sizes of ollas, and clysters (enema bags). The Mayans frequently consumed alcohol by enema as well as by drinking. The primary distinction between feasting and drinking scenes and scenes of other events is that there is little difference between the main figure (if there is one), the vessels he has, and the ones used by everyone else. Scenes of other events, by contrast, hold to certain canonical conventions that indicate the evident social roles of the scene's participants.

---

1 Las Pinturas murals at Calakmul portray an individual who has food clearly raised to the mouth. Although there are numerous scenes in which food is present or is being proffered, this is the only example thus far known that unambiguously depicts an individual in the act of eating.

Ritual Libations

Drinking as a medium through which humans interact with the supernatural realm is a common thread among many ancient and modern cultures (Carstairs 1954; Leacock 1983; Sargent 1983; Underhill 2000; Westermeyer 1983). The altered state leads one to experience things that cannot otherwise be seen. Underhill (2000: 116) suggests that the psychoactive properties of alcohol are responsible for such things as "making mourners feel that they could communicate with deceased loved ones." Reduced inhibition, increased sensitivity, and impaired focus are among the conditions created through inebriation. Such an inebriated state can be easily exploited, thus allowing ritual events to be more potent in the perceptions experienced by the participants. The interaction and reaction, individually and collectively, is made distinct from other common events by the intoxicants.

The ancient Mayans employed other means to alter their perceptions, such as their use of costumes (see K533) in the guise of a specific god (see K764) (Houston and Stuart 1998; Stone 1991). These costumes and disguises are depicted in association with drink containers, suggesting that intoxication was likely part of the event as well. The gods themselves are often associated with specific intoxicants, such as the association of God A with honey/mead (see K2286) and God L with tobacco.

Images that suggest tribute or transfer of goods (see K1728) frequently include images of drinking vessels. Similarly, drink vessels are usually present in the depictions of political interactions where all key figures are seated. There are multiple reasons for drinks being served in these venues. It is possible that intoxication, leading to impaired judgment, could have been used strategically in socioeconomic affairs or exploited for its relaxing qualities for ameliorating tense or tenuous social situations. In other words, the reason for the presence of drinks may not have been a ritual act or initially a ritual act. In addition to rituals, drinking may well have been indulged in for very basic somatic responses of aiding comfort or furthering another agenda.

Commensal Drinking at Feasts

Feasting as a communal activity generally consists of both food and drink. The primacy of drink, however, tends to outweigh the presence of the food in many circumstances. Evaluating the relative focus on food or drink suggests that a different framework is in place for events where drinks are primary. In some cases, the presence of alcohol would seem to be meant as entertainment, such as at the feasts held in medieval Europe. In other cases, alcohol is consumed in reverence to the gods, such as to Mayahul, the Aztec goddess of pulque. Drinking specific libations can also be considered a mark of ethnicity or status: the Greeks, for example, focused on the consumption of wine for the *symposion* as evidence of elevated status.

Mesoamerican evidence of feasting has been described at length by many scholars, such as Danien (2002), Hendon (2003), Houston and colleagues (1992), Hurst and colleagues (2002), Martin (1996, 2005), Masson (2002), McNeil (2006), Reents-Budet and colleagues (1994), and West (2002), among many others. "Feasting among the Maya is well documented ethnohistorically and ethnographically in the Maya region, and it was probably common in the Classic period" (McAnany 1995: 31). After the conquest, both Diego de Landa and Bernardino de Sahagún (Durán 1971; Sahagún 1953; also see Tozzer 1941) noted that at the conclusion of an elite feast, both the Mayans and the Aztecs would give lavish gifts to their guest for participating. "To each guest they [the Maya] give a roasted fowl, bread and drink of cacao in abundance; and at the end of the repast, they were accustomed to give a manta to each to wear, and a little stand and vessel, as beautiful as possible" (Tozzer 1941: 92).

The primary motivation of a feast is to satisfy some socially recognized intention or purpose through the specific gathering of people and goods thought to address that need. The goals of a feast are in large part dependent on the event and the participants, but any number of secondary intentions may be interlaced with these goals (Arnold 1993; Dietler 1990, 1996; Potter 2000). The arrangement of a feast and festivities must be culturally permissible (i.e., broadly recognized as legitimate within society), with every actor aware of his or her role (see Baumann et al. 1988; Bourdieu 1984). The consequences of the event are legitimized by social witnessing and recognition. For the Mayans, the pottery is a lasting symbol of these events and one's participation, which is given as an enduring signifier of affiliation and participation.

Drink feasts, like meal-central feasts, required special venues, service wares, and unique and rare consumables. Guests were as constrained by social interactions as those observed during meal-central feasts. In essence, the drink-central feasts follow most of the constraints of the meal-central feast. So why, then, are there differences, and what do they suggest about these formal gatherings? I suspect that drinking alcohol was of far greater importance to the Mayans than is yet fully realized. Even though fermented beverages were consumed daily, overindulgence was sanctioned only for select days and in select places.

The social dangers of overindulgence in drinking were more immediate than those of food consumption. Only when a food-central feast became too lavish, thus affecting the status quo, were sumptuary laws enacted to curtail overindulgence. In addition, drinking with the intention of getting drunk means that the guests must also adopt a second set of behavioral constraints (or etiquette) governing drunken behavior. This includes not only public behavior but also potential behavior in the presence of deities.

MAYAN BEVERAGES AND THEIR PRODUCTION

The Mayan elites of the Classic period had the wealth, influence, and trade networks to acquire nearly any substance available throughout Mesoamerica. With their knowledge of fermentation and the availability of a vast array of natural intoxicants, the Mayans had numerous recipes for beverages of which we still know very little. Decoding and interpretation of food-related text is still an ongoing area of study. However, there appear to have been a relatively limited number of beverage bases to which additional ingredients were added, often in the form of intoxicants or other culturally significant substances such as *kakaw* (Loughmiller-Newman 2012). Drink bases of honey, maize, and agave are widely known from the ethnohistorical and ethnographic documentation, and their use by the ancient Mayans is supported by current understanding of the food texts available.

Honey Beverages

Honey was a known sweetener (see K681) and was used to create mead (figure 8.2). Mead was the primary base of balché (discussed below), but the sweet liquid created from honey (fermented or otherwise) would also likely have been a sweetening additive to cacao (see Houston et al. 2006: 116–17; Hull 2010: 241; Reents-Budet et al. 1994: 75). Both Landa (1975) and Díaz del Castillo (1953) noted that honey was added to maize and cacao drinks. The Mayans were beekeepers and collected honey from stingless bees. One of the most productive species has been *Melipona beecheii*, or in Yukatec Maya, *xunan kàab'. Myrmecocystus* ants (related to carpenter ants) also produce large quantities of honey, perhaps even more than the melipona bees. Presently, nothing in the glyphs is known to distinguish between the two types of honey.

In the Classic images, God A' is frequently associated with bees, honey,

Figure 8.2. Example of beehive and honey collection (K1254). (Photograph by Justin Kerr.)

and mead. He is commonly shown holding an olla marked with the glyph *'ak'ab'* (night or darkness). There are other related depictions of this god severing his own head with an axe. Among the images showing ollas marked with bees or *'ak'ab',* there are others that are not graphically labeled but have a severed head on top (possibly harkening back to the decapitation of God A'). All of these ollas are probably indicating that the contents are mead.

Balché (*Lonchocarpus violaceus*) seems to have had an important but less visually and iconographically traceable place in Classic Mayan culture, and it is likely one of the most common of the honey-based beverages. Balché is typically a form of mead created from fermented honey mixed with the bark of the balché tree. The fermentation is rapid, but it does not produce a highly alcoholic drink. Henderson and Joyce (2006: 152; see also Baer and Merrifield 1971; cf. Coe and Coe 1996) suggest that fermented cacao was sometimes mixed with balché.

Sources, such as the *Relación de Yucatan,* described that the Yucatec Maya were fond of the drink balché. The drink was easy to prepare, was frequently consumed, and had widespread use. Encomendero Giraldo Diaz Alpuche of Dzohot and Tizimin described it in this way:[2] "Before the Spanish entered the country . . . they [the Maya] made a wine of water and honey and in it placed the root which is called balche in their language, and pouring this into great vessels of wood like great troughs . . . and this cooked and boiled two days, all by itself, and they made something very strong which had a vile smell. During their dances, when they were dancing, they gave them some of this to drink in little cups and often, and in a short time they got drunk" (Blom 1956). The Motul dictionary (dating around 1590) also records the presence of such drinks, stating that "*balché* is wine made from the bark of the tree to get drunk on." This form

2 *Colección de documentos inéditos relativos al descubrimiento, conquista y organización de la antiguas posesiones españolas de ultramar,* 2d ser., vol. 2.

of production is described in several texts, all noting the frequency with which this beverage is consumed. "Of the bark mixed with the watered juice of sugar cane or honey the Lacadone Indians, like the ancient Mayas of Yucatan, make a fermented drink, giving it the same name as the tree with which they make themselves drunk during ceremonies . . . the drink, of white milky color and acid smell[,] contains only a small quantity of alcohol, for which reason a great amount has to be taken before drunkenness ensues" (Miranda 1952: 199). Miranda further states that the balché tree grows well along cornfields and is typically planted there by the Lacandón Mayas. Because of harvesting for the drink, this tree rarely reaches full maturity (Miranda 1952; see also Boremanse 1981).

Maize Beverages

Chicha has become a term used to describe native beers, but it has also been used to describe native fermented beverages in general (figure 8.3). The Nahuatl term *chicha* was taken by the Spaniards from the Mayan highland societies to different regions of the Americas in referring to fermented intoxicants in general (Staller 2006: 449–50). Chicha as a maize beer was, and still is, widely consumed in the Americas, especially in communal settings. It is a drink that can be created by the majority of the population, the nutritional properties are significant in supplementing a poor diet (Steinkraus 1983: 352–54), and it has a high caloric value and a low alcohol content of around 3 percent. This drink is the beverage most regularly consumed in communal settings. Ollas containing *sa'* (maize

Figure 8.3. Example of SA', "maize gruel," on olla (K5062). (Photograph by Justin Kerr.)

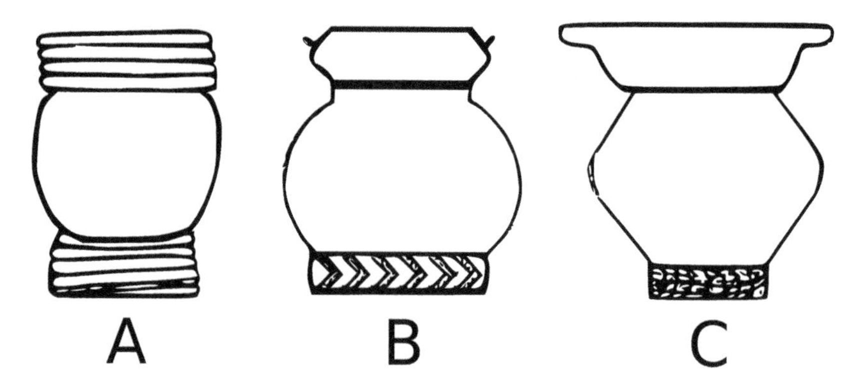

Figure 8.4. Example of ancient lauter tuns or sieves on large clay vessels. Example A, from ancient Egyptian beer making, is a basket over a large clay vessel seated on a thick reed mat (Art Museum of San Antonio). Example B, from Central Mexico, is a perforated vessel over a large olla seated on a thick woven mat (Museo Nacional de Antropología, Mexico City). Example C, from a Las Pinturas mural at Calakmul, is a wooden vessel or basket over a large olla seated on a thick woven mat.

gruel) are depicted in several drinking scenes. These vessels are decorated with a large crossband glyph thought to be the logogram SA'. These containers may have been the form used to hold fermented maize products.

Beer is produced through several steps of the fermentation of a grain. This involves the starch converting to a sugar during the malting process and the sugar to alcohol in the fermentation process. The general process for producing maize beer is to soak the kernels, lay them out on mats, and then cover them with leaves or mats until they sprout. Once the immature sprouts have formed diastases, the sprouted kernels are ground into a paste. This paste is added to water and boiled into slurry. Once broken down, the homogeneous syrup is poured into a sieve or lauter tun, which allows the sugary liquid to be separated from the mash (figure 8.4). This liquid is fermented (i.e., the sugar is converted to ethanol) in a large olla. This process has been documented for the making of *tesgüino* (the Spanish name), a particularly strong beer made from maize (Bruman 2000: 41).

Wine can also be made from the maize stalks, which contain a high proportion of sugar, especially when they are immature. Crushed maize stalks produce syrup that can be collected for a sweetener, and this same syrup easily ferments into a wine. Bruman (2000: 60) notes several drinks consumed by the K'iche' Mayas and Huastecos that are formed from fermented stalk wine and toasted maize.

Agave Beverages

Aguamiel is the sweet sap produced by the hulled maguey; it needs to be consumed within the first days of extraction because fermentation occurs naturally and rapidly to form pulque (figure 8.5). Aguamiel may also be boiled down to form a thick syrup or a solid sugar. As syrup or sugar, however, agave sap is much more durable, and surpluses can readily be stored over a period of months or longer.

Pulque is a thick, bitter drink with relatively low alcohol content. The word **kiih* 'agave/pulque' is widely attested in the Mayan languages. Every branch of the Mayan languages has cognates of the word *chiih* for pulque, indicating that this word existed in deep time going back to proto-Mayan. Ollas depicted on the polychrome vessels are often labeled with *chiih*, but there is only one known example of the word *chiih* in the PSS (see Stuart 2005: 145 [Tikal vessel MT219]). The depiction of fermentation ollas tagged with *chiih* gives us good reason to believe that this beverage or one very similar to it was used in high-profile consumption activities.

Pulque is a Central Mexican drink, and it is not known to be produced in the Mayan area. True pulque-producing maguey (i.e., *Agave salimiana* and *Agave atrovirens*) is viable only at elevations above 1,800 meters (Nobel 1994; Steinkraus 1983; Youman and Estep 2005). Pulque has often been considered to be the drink of the Aztec masses (Havard 1896: 1). The varieties known to produce pulque grow in Central Mexico, the homeland of the Aztecs and Otomi. "Nearly all documentary descriptions of Aztec feasts mention the consumption of pulque (or *octli*) and

Figure 8.5. Example of *chiih*, "agave/pulque," on an olla (K1092). (Photograph by Justin Kerr.)

cacao. . . . It seems clear from both pictorial and written sources that pulque was consumed quite often at Aztec rituals and feasts" (Smith et al. 2003: 257; see also Henderson 2008).

The ease of access and high nutritional content of the agave sap (*aguamiel* 'honey water') has made it an important staple for the vast populations of Central Mexico (Correa-Ascencio et al. 2014; Smith et al. 2003). The problematic connection of pulque with the Mayans, of course, is the otherwise unestablished possibility of growing pulque-producing agave in the humid Maya lowlands. Furthermore, pulque ferments within twenty-four hours of harvest and becomes highly fermented after forty-eight hours. At no point under normal conditions does pulque fully ferment, however, so the fermentation is continuous, as is the expansion of the gases released (Nobel 1994; Steinkraus 1983; Youman and Estep 2005). It is unlikely that any vessel in transport from Central Mexico could withstand the continuously increasing pressure of the expanding gases produced during fermentation on the long journey to the lowlands.[3]

I suspect that pulque was transported to the lowlands in the form of either sugar or syrup. When boiled down, pulque becomes a sweet black ooze. Perhaps this was the form of pulque that was familiar to the Mayans. Because honey was undoubtedly used for fermented drinks, the sugary sap of the agave likewise may have been used in such a manner, since it breaks down to produce alcohol. High-sap-yielding agaves may have once grown in the Mayan highland areas, but currently there is no evidence of this. It is also possible, although there have been no studies to confirm it, that the heart or thick leaves of smaller agaves could have been boiled to extract sugar. In several examples on the Mayan polychrome vases, there are depictions of large flared ollas labeled with the hieroglyphic *chi-(hi)* 'pulque' and many others with long leaves (similar to those of the agave) protruding from the top. Consumed in the same contexts as cacao, pulque was represented as being in the highest Mayan courts for special celebrations and feasts.

The Material Culture of Mayan Beverages

For the Classic period, numerous vessel forms are known to be associated with either the production or the consumption of beverages. The most widely recognized vessel form from this period is the elongated cylinder vessel. The heavily decorated cylinders (commonly called vases) are

3 From Mexico City to Tikal, Guatemala (where *chiih* is recorded on at least one olla) is over 1,400 kilometers. The average person can walk about 20 to 25 kilometers in twelve hours.

associated with the great kings, their kingdoms, and elite burials. These same vessels are frequently represented in the art, which indicates that some portion of their function was as the accoutrements of the kings and gods and as gifts from important figures (including spirits and gods).

Cups or small bowls are extremely well represented in the archaeological record, and their presence in the art is equally as well known. Their presentation in the art is less prestigiously demarked in placement and importance, and cups are represented as a more utilitarian item. They are commonly associated with a larger vessel and with larger groupings of figures.

Service vessels such as ollas and large vats are usually centrally placed within the scene and are clearly an item of importance to the scene. Interactions, conversations, and other activities are typically depicted occurring around the vessel. The large service vessels are also commonly associated with smaller containers such as cups or clysters, indicating that the contents are being drawn out for consumption by numerous participants.

VESSELS USED FOR CONSUMPTION

The goblet, flask, cup, or chalice has become an icon of feasting throughout the ancient world and often is associated with religious or ceremonial events (de Garine 2001; Strong 2002; Vargas 2001). In ancient times, much as now, social gatherings often focused on the imbibing of drinks as often as, or even more than, the eating of food. This would include gatherings for ritual purposes (see de Garine 2001; Goldstein 2003; Jennings et al. 2005; Joffe 1998; Leacock 1983; Madsen and Madsen 1983; Mandelbaum 1965, 1983; Marshall 1983b; Nelson 2003; Nobel 1994; Pollock 1983). "In most of the feasting scenes, the consumption of drink, rather than food, seems to predominate" (Pollock 1983: 24).

Although Pollock was specifically discussing the depiction of Early Dynastic Mesopotamian feasts, the same predominant theme is true for ancient Mayan depictions as well. The heightened sense of festivity or significance created by adding a decadent drink, in contrast to the more commonplace activity of eating, may be the precise reason why icons focused on drinking are more emblematic of commensality than are images of food. More simplistically, perhaps, a fancy cup is more recognizable as a symbol of commensality than is a plate.

The function of many of these vessels is unquestionably tied to such feasting events. As discussed previously, the act of communally consuming food can have major social ramifications for the participants. An elite vessel can be a token signifying one's participation in that event. The significance of feasts is prominent in the discussion here, since high-end vessels often derive their significance through their association with such significant social events. This holds true regardless of whether a specific vessel ever actually was used in such an affair. The form, type, and design of high-end vessels are inescapably associated with formal events in general and are frequently associated with feasting in particular.

More generally, formal dining and service wares are typically more ornate than are daily utilitarian wares, a trend that has carried into modern times. The delicate or refined nature of these goods makes them undesirable or impractical for daily use. Their nonutilitarian attributes, in such cases, relegate them to other uses in which their possession or display is more important than their practicality: for example, their purpose may be more to impress guests at communal engagements or to signify the status or role of the host. The vessels used in high-end feasts were not only more elegant but also larger and technically created to enhance the presentation of food or drink. "The appearance, and thus the experience, of food is affected by the wares on which it was served since pottery affects both the taste and [the] presentation of food" (Smith 2003: 54; see also Rice 1987: 456). The behavioral framework of feasting and its potential social outcomes have been the focus of much archaeological research (e.g., Blitz 1993; Clark and Blake 1994; Dietler 1990; Earle 2002; Friedman and Rowlands 1978; Hayden 2003; Jennings 2004; Jennings et al. 2005; LeCount 2001; Potter 2000; Smith et al. 2003; Smith 2003).

Cups

Vessels broadly categorized as "cups" are high-walled forms, which are specifically fashioned to hold liquid contents. Cups are considered direct consumption vessels—that is, a utensil is unlikely to have been necessary to obtain the contents from the vessel for consumption. The depth and narrow opening control the amount of liquid received by the consumer. The interior of a cup would be expected to be the most impervious of all surfaces, since the contents are most frequently liquid. This would suggest that the surfaces are highly burnished inside and out and the surfaces are slipped. Decoration of the interior would make little sense, as the liquid would cover it completely unless drained. It would also be difficult for anyone but the consumer to see such decoration. The exterior, in contrast, is an ideal location for decoration, because the high walls are never covered with food and can be highly decorated.

The cup is highly portable, has a straightforward function, and with surface decoration may send any number of messages to the viewer.

Pottery evidence from Mexico indicates that some of the earliest feasting assemblages included a high proportion of ornate drinking vessels (Clark and Blake 1994; Lesure 1998). Drinking vessels are an especially visible means of presenting graphic communication, as the typically high-walled shape of drinking utensils facilitates decoration. At the height of elaboration, the utensil itself is prominently decorated and associated with extreme wealth. Many of these ornate drinking vessels accompanied their owner into the grave (Justeson 1978; Samuel 1996).

Bowls

Bowls are low- to medium-walled vessel forms that allow both liquid and semiliquid foods to be efficiently held and reasonably accessible. A bowl would be considered a direct consumption vessel, because foods can be extracted without the use of a tool; simply tipping the bowl to the mouth would deliver the contents. The interior of bowls would be expected to be highly burnished and slipped in order to increase impermeability as much as possible. Creating such a surface would not be difficult, as the container remains rather open and accessible. Interior decoration would be easily worn down and damaged by frequent usage. Exterior decoration would not be covered with food, but the sloping walls would make the full image/surface difficult to see.

'Uk'ib' Folk Classifications

The Mayan verb *'uk,* "drink," and instrumental suffix *'iib',* "for drinking," is the typical construction found in the text and is often written with the third person possessive (*y*), leading to the common gloss of *yuk'ib',* "his/hers/its for drinking"[4] (Houston 1989; Houston et al. 1989; MacLeod 1990: 315). This class of vessel seems to be applied to a great number of sizes and shaped containers associated with an aspect of drinking or liquid containment, from small enough to fit in the human hand to larger than two hands can reasonably handle, and nearly all are approximately cylindrical or bowl shaped.

A variant of this vessel is the *jaay,* "thin" (Justeson, pers. comm., 2005), seemingly describing the *yuk'iib',* "his thin [thing] for drinking." This description likely has little to do with the actual thickness of the vessel, as there is no perceivable difference between vessels bearing *jaay* or

4 Aulie and Aulie (1978: 125) write this as *'uch'ibal* for Ch'olan; Wisdom (1950: 750), *'uch'p'ir* for Ch'orti'; Laughlin (Laughlin and Haviland 1988: 159), *'uch'obil* for Colonial Tzotzil. The word *'uch* is a cognate of *'uk'.* See also Kaufman and Justeson 2003: 982.

without. As noted by Kettunen and Helmke (2010: 36), rounded or bowl-like *'uk'iib'* are correlated with the presence of the word *jaay*. Tedlock (2002: 174) describes modern Mayan wedding ceremonies that require the consumption of cacao out of a calabash vessel, a tradition based on the Popol Vuh.[5] He suggests that the use of *jaay* is for vessels with "thin walls, thinner and stronger than those of gourds," which are among "the principal distinguishing features of calabashes" (Tedlock 2002: 174). As stated above, Kettunen and Helmke (2010) observed that the *jaay* occurs on bowl-like vessels that are in the shape of calabash drinking vessels.

Vessels Used for Production and Storage

Jars and ollas are designed for containment of food products that are accessed intermittently. In the case of a jar, the container is used not for direct consumption but for a measure of its contents to be extracted, and an olla, typically used for liquids, is used in much the same way: drink is extracted and poured into another vessel (a cup or bowl). The olla is not a vessel from which one would consume the contents directly. These forms of vessels are designed with large bodies and narrowing shoulders and neck. The curved shoulder and neck protect the contents from evaporation if liquid and from easy spillage.

The interior treatments of storage containers would be directly related to the intended contents held. For instance, the interior bases of ollas have highly burnished interiors. Technically, water ollas are designed with striated exteriors, allowing a minute amount of water to seep through the vessel and evaporate (Schiffer 1987); the evaporation allowed by this surface treatment keeps the contents of the vessel somewhat cooler than the ambient temperature.

Tecomate vessels have a curving wall with no neck and a restricted rim. This vessel form, one of the oldest known types to ancient Mesoamerica, is present from the Barra phase (1550–1400 BC) onward. It resembles the base of a bottle gourd with the top segment removed. Numerous archaeologists have speculated that this vessel was used for a variety of purposes, among them (and probably most commonly) liquid containment. The lack of any evidence of exposure to fire and the relatively small sizes of certain examples make them most comparable to ollas, interpreted elsewhere as serving vessels (Clark and Gosser 1995; Lesure 1998).

An olla is similar to the tecomate, with the addition of a constricted

5 The Popol Vuh presents a Mayan creation myth. See Tedlock 1996.

neck and flared rim. Two of these vessels are the largest in the sample, with one 0.5 meters in height and the other nearly a meter in height. These vessels were commonly used for water containment as well as fermentation of alcoholic beverages.

Depictions of Drinking and Drink Preparations

Mayan artwork depicts scenes that involve beverages and/or drinking in a number of behavioral contexts. Feasting scenes are typically identified and defined by the presence of foodstuffs and beverages highlighted in the depiction. In other scenes, however, no foodstuffs are present but drinks or drinking is indicated by the presence of one or more vessels or direct consumption. Thus the general thematic content of the scene emphasizes some other event or occurrence than what we traditionally understand to be a feast. While some of these scenes may, in fact, also represent another form of feasting or feast-like event, such a direct association is made ambiguous by the prevalence of other iconographic content.

As discussed previously, numerous social occasions (both formal and informal) would have included the presence of beverages, particularly alcoholic beverages. The contexts of Mayan feasting have received considerable archaeological and ethnohistorical attention, although these beverage-centered events are somewhat less well understood. In addition, the depictions of beverage production and preparation have largely been overshadowed by the focus on their associated events; specifically, the correlations between the depicted vessel forms and archaeological vessel forms may provide a relatively untapped resource for the archaeological and ethno-archaeological understanding of Mayan practices.

There is much variation in the types of events portrayed in nonfeasting scenes, which makes strict delineation of categorical types difficult. Whereas feasting events are made distinct by the presence of foods, other events that include depictions of drinks or drinking are more generally in the context of palace scenes or mythical scenes. These may be depicting formal political affairs, religious rituals, mythological events, or (as is typical of Mayan art) some combination of these. As such, any concrete categorical distinctions become to some degree moot.

Mythic and Ritual Scenes

Nonhuman actors are depicted as often as or more often than figures that are clearly human. In some instances, we may be looking at humans in costume, but in the absence of identifying texts or a clear indication that these are human actors, the interpretations are limited. Many of the images that involve ritual events contain god, spirit, or animal figures consuming beverages. Among these are birdmen heavily indulging in drink (see K1900).

There are many images of way or spirit companions, which are typically depicted in a series of three figures. In the majority of these scenes, the figures are shown holding vessels filled with severed hands and feet. In other images where more way figures are depicted, they are shown in tiers in which some appear to have overindulged in some intoxicant (see K927), leading to bloating, vomiting, or severe pain.

Another common theme involves old men with young women serving them enemas. Images of individuals self-administering enemas are also well-known (see K1897). In the images where women are assisting in the administration, the arrangement is very predictable (as described above). In scenes where women are not present, the event is less rigid. These scenes suggest a less formalized event, which typically involved the presence of nonhuman actors (see K1386).

PALACE SCENES

In the Late Classic, polychrome vessels are often painted with texts and images that feature historical sociopolitical events (Marcus 1992: 221–24; Schele and Miller 1986). The scenes commonly depicted on the polychrome vases show that lords were in frequent contact with foreign dignitaries. The typical scene is of the *'ajaaw*, "lord/king," seated on a dais or bench and facing left toward a figure seated on the ground. This figure is the highest-ranked individual of the visiting group. The entourage of either party is standing behind the primary characters (see Loughmiller-Newman 2008). Cylindrical vessels are placed on the ground next to the dais of the 'ajaaw; in some instances, the cylinder is placed on the dais in front of the 'ajaaw. The common arrangement for Mayan art is to place the two most important actors in the center (left-facing being the dominant actor), with lesser ranks lined up behind those primary actors. Not all of these arrangements suggest the interaction of visiting emissaries, however; in some cases, these scenes appear to be intrasite administrative events.

Vessels similar to those found in the burials and caches at Calakmul are depicted in the Las Pinturas murals (Carrasco Vargas and Bojalil 2005; Carrasco Vargas and Cordeiro Baqueiro 2006; Martin 2005), which are housed in a building to the northwest of the Grand Acropolis. Several of the scenes depict figures serving drinks and food to figures consuming these products. These illustrations are extraordinary for their detail regarding consumption behaviors. Along with the many depicted ollas, medium-sized cylinders, and bowls, there are depictions of basketry used in the production of foodstuffs and wooden implements such as ladles. These vessels and implements are depicted in use. With the brief texts that accompany these images, we have at least some idea what the vessels were being used to hold.

FEASTING SCENES

Mayan feasts are never depicted as an overabundant or gluttonous revelry. Instead, feasting scenes typically entail a small assemblage of plated food items such as balled maize foodstuffs. Along with the foods, there is often a selection of ollas, cylinders, and smaller cups. Oddly, the number of vessels rarely matches the number of figures present in the scene. Generally, there are far fewer vessels present than one would expect for a full dining service, though most of the foods could also have been consumed by hand. Drinking vessels also rarely match the number of figures, with fewer vessels than there are key figures (presumably the ranking lords). This suggests that at least some of these vessels are shared during consumption. It is also quite likely that not all the figures present at such events partook in the foods or drinks (see K1775).

DRINK PREPARATION

Preparation of a beverage may be shown on K511, in which a female figure is pouring a liquid from one vessel to another (presumably for the pregnant woman seated nearby). The act of frothing a beverage is well-known for Mayan drinks (see McNeil 2006; McNeil et al. 2006). Although the act of frothing a drink is typically associated with cacao drinks, other Mayan beverages would require considerable mixing as well in order to suspend spices, drugs, or other additives in thick alcoholic liquids.

In several scenes, an enema is being prepared by a female for a male recipient seated either directly across from her or directly in front of her (see K1890). These scenes suggest that liquid is extracted from an olla and poured into the clyster. Vessels depicted in transport are also a common theme. Ollas are frequently shown being carried by gods and way figures. God A' is frequently shown carrying a small olla associated with bees and presumably honey/mead. Way figures often carry similar vessels. In other images with human characters, vessels are denoted as being transported by a crossbanding around the midsection indicating that the vessel was lashed to a backrack or transported by a tumpline (see K1550). Vessel

K1254 depicts a mythological scene in which a woman is collecting honey from a beehive; she is carrying a small olla on her shoulder.

The Calakmul murals show several scenes in which beverages are being served from large ollas and service vessels (see figure 8.4). The consumers are named by what they are consuming (i.e., "He of the maize gruel"). In most of the scenes, the beverages are being served to male consumers by well-dressed females. These murals present aspects of consumption and production that are not otherwise known in the art found on vessels. The focus of the subject matter in the murals is unusually on consumption in a less formal atmosphere, and here we see some of the process of production rather than just the final products.

Another image in the same murals shows a female apparently in the process of making maize beer. In this image, she is shown using a sieve or basket that is resting on a large olla. The image is strikingly similar to images and related artifacts known from Egyptian beer making, which involved a large flat perforated pan over an olla-type vessel or a basket over a large olla. Another figurine held in the San Antonio Museum of Art shows an Egyptian male pressing mash through an ancient lauter tun. Similar vessels from Central Mexico are on exhibit in the National Museum of Anthropology in Mexico City. While perforated pans may have been uncommon for the Mayans, basketry could have served the same purpose as the perforated pans. With the discovery of the Calakmul murals, a Mayan correlate has been demonstrated iconographically for the use of such a sieve.

ASSESSMENT OF DRINKING SCENES

I conducted a preliminary examination of 110 images from the Kerr database, all of which contain a depiction of at least one vessel associated with drinking. In 3 of the images, figures are shown drinking from an olla. Two of these figures, however, are mythical dog creatures (see K505). In 2 other images, figures are clearly shown drinking out of cylinders/vases. In the remaining images of people in the act of drinking ($n = 6$), all are consuming from small cups or bowls that are approximately the size of one's hand. An equal number of images ($n = 15$) depict figures participating in consumption by enema. Only enema scenes that are also associated with drinking vessels were counted. In the majority of the scenes, drinking or storage vessels are present and the content of the scene suggests beverage production, service, and/or consumption—but the actual actions are not themselves depicted.

What these preliminary data reveal is that there is very little actual *drinking* portrayed in the images examined. As previously noted, an image of the direct consumption of food is extremely rare (i.e., only one known example). The majority of the scenes examined show vessels that are associated with a key figure (the main figure) by proximity within the scene or vessels being presented to such a figure. They also show that there are a limited number of scenes in which food is present—only 18 images out of the 110 examined.

Concluding Remarks

Scenes typically described as demonstrating drinking or feasting events have rarely been defined with respect to how they are distinct from any other image. The mere presence of food or drink is broadly interpreted as connoting consumption and thereby a "feast" (figure 8.6). A closer examination of the images, however, shows that the representation of food does not always indicate the act of a feast, nor does the presence of a cup necessitate a *symposion*. What the images do support is a more qualified interpretation that these vessels, and hence their contents, were appropriate to some aspect of a particular event. Actual scenes that would clearly indicate feasting or drinking by directly depicting consumption are, instead, the minority of the images that depict vessels. This disparity suggests that the common interpretation is in some way misidentifying the communicative intent of these images.

Figure 8.6. Example of a feast (or at least a scene in which food is present) where both food and vessels are shown in a relatively limited amount (K1775). (Photograph by Justin Kerr.)

The suspected contents of the vessels shown within the scenes are most likely idealized following the typical conventions of Mayan art (Proskouriakoff 1960). The Mayans were known to artistically represent figures and events following a prescribed scenario, rather than a reflection of the actual occurrence. Therefore, the linking of actual behavior to images and texts is fraught with difficulties. The actual contents of archaeologically recovered cups, cylinders, and ollas may not match what is depicted in the scenes for the same depicted forms and vessels. Granted, this is not the topic of this chapter, but the point is that what is being represented is a sequence of events that are an idealized depiction of real events.

A monumental stone image of a king may not be an accurate depiction of his stature, demeanor, visage, or even accomplishments—that is not necessarily the purpose of the image. Instead, the king is being represented because he is the king (see discussions in Gillespie 2001, 2010). The events of feasting and other contexts of food and beverage consumption depicted in Mayan art may similarly represent, through the presence of food-associated vessels, idealized renditions of actual rituals and events. Their presence within and supporting the scene stands as a culturally recognizable indication of practices, which would presumably be known to a Mayan viewer, by invoking semiotic referents related to specific practices, rituals, or substances.

The events the Classic Mayans chose to represent are considerably limited and difficult to fully parse, even when narrative and labels are present. The contexts are surprisingly limited, with only a few broad themes involved. Even more importantly, only elite figures, gods, and spirit figures are shown, and their accoutrements are limited. While this might appear to be a difficult data set to work with, there is still a surprising amount of information available to consider. Primarily, we must remain open to the idea that there is veracity to these depictions and the representations are not fully imaginary, fictional, or fantastical.

Names of real figures have been decoded, historical dates have been isolated, and real locations have been identified. Moreover, the vessel forms shown in the images are known in the archaeological record, as are many artifact equivalents. The Mayan conventions of artistic representation, however, do not allow for simple or literal interpretations of these scenes. Instead, the Mayan conventions appear to use symbolic indicators to imply actions and events by material or contextual proxies. By doing so, they require familiarity with specific references to ritualized actions or events for the viewer to fully decode the meaningful content of a scene.

To advance our understanding of the events and rituals depicted, the sequence of behavior that leads to the materials present within the scene needs to be determined. Ongoing analysis of beverage production and material correlates is currently being performed by myself as well as many other researchers in the Mayan area and greater Mesoamerica. This is supported archaeologically through identification and analysis of the vessel forms present within the scenes. It has been demonstrated in this chapter that the beverages shown in the images are real drinks and are still consumed today by modern Mayans. The process by which they are procured can be configured and identified. The material used in the process should be present in some form in the record. If those patterns are found and the actual contexts identified, then the rituals that are depicted are approachable. Rather than the cup being looked at as an artifact in isolation and expressive of behavior, the viewshed needs to be expanded to the contents and that container, and then out to the initial actions.

References Cited

Alcorn, J. B., B. Edmonson, and C. Hernandez Vidales. 2006. Thipaak and the Origins of Maize in Northern Mesoamerica. In *Histories of Maize: Multidisciplinary Approaches to the Prehistory, Linguistics, Biogeography, Domestication, and Evolution of Maize*, ed. J. E. Staller, R. H. Tykot, and B. F. Benz, 600–611. Amsterdam: Elsevier/Academic Press.

Alexander, J. C. 2004. Cultural Pragmatics: Social Performance between Ritual and Strategy. *Sociological Theory* 22 (4): 527–73.

Arnold, J. E. 1993. Labor and the Rise of Complex Hunter-Gatherers. *Journal of Anthropological Archaeology* 12 (1): 75–119.

Aulie, H. W., and E. W. de Aulie. 1978. *Diccionario ch'ol-español, español-ch'ol.* Vocabularios indígenas 21. 1st ed. Mexico City: Instituto Lingüístico de Verano.

Baer, P., and W. R. Merrifield. 1971. *Two Studies on the Lacandones of Mexico.* Norman: University of Oklahoma, Summer Institute of Linguistics.

Baumann, G., G. Elwert, B. Lindskog, and P. Stirling. 1988. On Ethnology and Development Policy. *Current Anthropology* 29 (2): 301–5.

Beliaev, D., A. Davletshin, and A. Tokovinine. 2010. Sweet Cacao and Sour Atole: Mixed Drinks on Classic Maya Ceramic Vases. In *Pre-Columbian Foodways: Interdisciplinary Approaches to Food, Culture, and Markets in Ancient Mesoamerica*, ed. J. E. Staller and M. D. Carrasco, 257–72. New York: Springer.

Blitz, J. H. 1993. Big Pots for Big Shots: Feasting and Storage in a Mississippian Community. *American Antiquity* 58 (1): 80–96.

Blom, F. 1956. On Slotkin's "Fermented Drinks in Mexico." *American Anthropologist* 58 (1): 185–86.

Boot, E. 2009. Otot as a Vessel Classification for a Footed Bowl: Short Epigraphic Note on a Bowl in the Collection of the Museum of Fine Arts, Boston. In *Mayavase.com Essays.* Electronic document, www.mayavase.com/otot.pdf.

Boremanse, D. 1981. Una forma de clasificación simbólica: Los encantamientos al balché entre los Lacandones. *Journal of Latin American Lore* 7 (2): 191–214.
Bourdieu, P. 1984. *Distinction: A Social Critique of the Judgement of Taste*. Cambridge, Mass.: Harvard University Press.
Bruman, H. J. 2000. *Alcohol in Ancient Mexico*. Salt Lake City: University of Utah Press.
Brumfiel, E. M. 1987. Consumption and Politics at Aztec Huexotla. *American Anthropologist* 89 (3): 676–86.
Brumfiel, E. M. 1994. *The Economic Anthropology of the State*. Monographs in Economic Anthropology. Lanham, Md.: University Press of America.
Brumfiel, E. M., and T. K. Earle. 1987. *Specialization, Exchange, and Complex Societies*. New Directions in Archaeology. Cambridge: Cambridge University Press.
Bunzel, R. L. 1940. The Role of Alcoholism in Two Central American Cultures. *Psychiatry* 3: 361–87.
Carrasco Vargas, R., and A. Bojalil. 2005. Nuevos datos para la historia del arte y la iconografia del Clásico temprano en el área Maya: El reino de Ka'an. *La Pintura Mural Prehispánica en México* 11 (23): 24–32.
Carrasco Vargas, R., and M. Cordeiro Baqueiro. 2006. *Pintura mural y arquitectura como medios de transmisión ideológica: La acrópolis Chiik Naab'.* Memorias del XV Encuentro Internacional: Los investigadores de la cultura Maya 14. Campeche, Mexico: Universidad Autónoma de Campeche.
Carstairs, G. M. 1954. Daru and Bhang: Cultural Factors in the Choice of Intoxicant. *Quarterly Journal of Studies on Alcohol* 15 (2): 220–37.
Chatwin, M. E. 2001. Tamadoba: Drinking Social Cohesion at the Georgian Table. In *Drinking: Anthropological Approaches*, ed. I. de Garine and V. de Garine, 181–90. New York: Berghahn Books.
Christenson, A. J. 2004. *Popol Vuh: Literal Poetic Version*. Norman: University of Oklahoma Press.
Clark, J. E., and M. Blake. 1994. The Power of Prestige: Competitive Generosity and the Emergence of Rank Societies in Lowland Mesoamerica. In *Factional Competition and Political Development in the New World*, ed. E. M. Brumfiel and J. W. Fox, 17–30. New Directions in Archaeology. Cambridge: Cambridge University Press.
Clark, J. E., and D. Gosser. 1995. Reinventing Mesoamerica's First Pottery. In *The Emergence of Pottery: Technology and Innovation in Ancient Societies*, ed. W. Barnett and J. W. Hoopes, 209–22. Smithsonian Series in Archaeological Inquiry. Washington, D.C.: Smithsonian Institution Press.
Cobo, B. (1599) 1943. *Historia del nuevo mundo*. Colección Cisneros. Madrid: Ediciones Atlas.
Coe, M. D. 1999. *Breaking the Maya Code*. Rev. ed. New York: Thames and Hudson.
Coe, S. D., and M. D. Coe. 1996. *The True History of Chocolate*. New York: Thames and Hudson.
Colop, L.E.S., trans. 1999. *Popol wuj*. Colecciacuteon Biblioteca Guatemala. Guatemala City: F&G Editores.
Correa-Ascencio, M., I. G. Robertson, O. Cabrera-Cortes, R. Cabrera-Castro, and R. P. Evershed. 2014. Pulque Production from Fermented Agave Sap as a Dietary

Supplement in Prehispanic Mesoamerica. *Proceedings of the National Academy of Science of the United States of America* 11 (39): 14223–28.

Danien, E. C. 2002. *Guide to the Mesoamerican Gallery at the University of Pennsylvania Museum of Archaeology and Anthropology.* Philadelphia: University of Pennsylvania Museum of Archaeology and Anthropology.

de Garine, I. 2001. For a Pluridisciplinary Approach to Drinking. In *Drinking: Anthropological Approaches,* ed. I. de Garine and V. de Garine, 1–11. New York: Berghahn Books.

de Smet, P.A.G.M. 1985. *Ritual Enemas and Snuffs in the Americas.* Latin American Studies 33. Amsterdam, Netherlands: Centro de Estudios y Documentación Latinamericanos (CEDLA).

Díaz del Castillo, B. 1953. *The Discovery and Conquest of Mexico, 1517–1521.* Trans. A. P. Maudslay from five-volume 1908 Hakluyt Society edition. Mexico City: Ediciones Tolteca.

Dietler, M. 1990. Driven by Drink: The Role of Drinking in the Political Economy and the Case of Early Iron Age France. *Journal of Anthropological Archaeology* 9 (4): 352–406.

Dietler, M. 1996. Feasts and Commensal Politics in the Political Economy: Food, Power, and Status in Prehistoric Europe. In *Food and the Status Quest: An Interdisciplinary Perspective,* ed. P. W. Wiessner and W. Schiefenhövel, 87–125. Providence, R.I.: Berghahn Books.

Douglas, M. 1987. *Constructive Drinking: Perspectives on Drink from Anthropology.* Cambridge: Cambridge University Press.

Douglas, M., and B. C. Isherwood. 1979. *The World of Goods.* New York: Basic Books.

Durán, F. D. 1971. *Book of the Gods and Rites and the Ancient Calendar.* Trans. F. Horcasitas and D. Heyden. Norman: University of Oklahoma Press.

Earle, T. 2002. Feasts: Archaeological and Ethnographic Perspectives on Food, Politics, and Power. In *Feasts: Archaeological and Ethnographic Perspectives on Food, Politics, and Power,* ed. M. Dietler and B. Hayden, 1236–38. Washington, D.C.: Smithsonian Institution Press.

Friedman, J., and M. J. Rowlands, eds. 1978. *The Evolution of Social Systems: Proceedings of a Meeting of the Research Seminar in Archaeology and Related Subjects, Held at the Institute of Archaeology, London University.* Pittsburgh: University of Pittsburgh Press.

Gillespie, S. D. 2001. Personhood, Agency, and Mortuary Ritual: A Case Study from the Ancient Maya. *Journal of Anthropological Archaeology* 20 (1): 73–112.

Gillespie, S. D. 2010. Maya Memory Work. *Ancient Mesoamerica* 21 (2): 401–4.

Goldstein, P. S. 2003. From Stew-Eaters to Maize-Drinkers: The Chicha Economy and the Tiwanaku Expansion. In *The Archaeology and Politics of Food and Feasting in Early States and Empires,* ed. T. L. Bray, 143–72. New York: Kluwer Academic/Plenum Publishers.

Havard, V. 1896. *Drink Plants of the North American Indians.* New York: Torrey Botanical Club.

Hayden, B. 2003. *Shamans, Sorcerers, and Saints: A Prehistory of Religion.* Washington, D.C.: Smithsonian Books.

Healy, P. F., J.D.H. Lambert, J. T. Arnason, and R. J. Hebda. 1983. Caracol, Belize: Evidence of Ancient Maya Agricultural Terraces. *Journal of Field Archaeology* 10 (4): 397–410.

Heath, D. B. 1976. Anthropological Perspective on Alcohol: An Historical Review. In *Cross-Cultural Approaches to the Study of Alcohol: An Interdisciplinary Perspective*, ed. M. W. Everett, J. O. Waddell, and D. B. Heath, 41–101. World Anthropology. The Hague: Mouton.

Henderson, J. S., and R. A. Joyce. 2006. Brewing Distinction: The Development of Cacao Beverages in Formative Mesoamerica. In *Chocolate in Mesoamerica: A Cultural History of Cacao*, ed. C. L. McNeil, 140–53. Maya Studies. Gainesville: University Press of Florida.

Henderson, L. 2008. Blood, Water, Vomit, and Wine: Pulque in Maya and Aztec Belief. In *Mesoamerican Voices: Art, Writing, and Archaeology of Middle America*, ed. J. Palka, 53–76. Chicago: Beaker Press for Chicago Maya Society.

Hendon, J. A. 2003. Feasting at Home: Community and House Solidarity among the Maya of Southeastern Mesoamerica. In *The Archaeology and Politics of Food and Feasting in Early States and Empires*, ed. T. L. Bray, 203–33. New York: Kluwer Academic/Plenum Publishers.

Hoil, J. J., and R. L. Roys. 1967. *The Book of Chilam Balam of Chumayel*. Civilization of the American Indian. Rev. ed. Norman: University of Oklahoma Press.

Houston, S. D. 1989. *Maya Glyphs: Reading the Past*. Berkeley: University of California Press; London: British Museum.

Houston, S. D., and D. Stuart. 1998. The Ancient Maya Self: Personhood and Portraiture in the Classic Period. *RES: Anthropology and Aesthetics* 33 (Spring): 73–101.

Houston, S. D., D. Stuart, and K. A. Taube. 1989. Folk Classification of Classic Maya Pottery. *American Anthropologist* 91 (3): 720–26.

Houston, S. D., D. Stuart, and K. Taube. 1992. Image and Text on the "Jauncy Vase." In *The Maya Vase Book*, vol. 3, *A Corpus of Rollout Photographs of Maya Vases*, ed. J. Kerr, 498–512. New York: Kerr Associates.

Houston, S. D., C. Mazariegos, O. Fernando, and D. Stuart. 2001. *The Decipherment of Ancient Maya Writing*. Norman: University of Oklahoma Press.

Houston, S. D., D. Stuart, and K. A. Taube. 2006. *The Memory of Bones: Body, Being, and Experience among the Classic Maya*. Joe R. and Teresa Lozano Long Series in Latin American and Latino Art and Culture. Austin: University of Texas Press.

Hull, K. M. 2010. An Epigraphic Analysis of Classic-Period Maya Foodstuffs. In *Pre-Columbian Foodways: Interdisciplinary Approaches to Food, Culture, and Markets in Ancient Mesoamerica*, ed. J. E. Staller and M. D. Carrasco, 235–56. New York: Springer.

Hurst, J. W., S. M. Tarka Jr., T. Powis, F. Valdez Jr., and T. R. Hester. 2002. Archaeology: Cacao Usage by the Earliest Maya Civilization. *Nature* 418 (6895): 289–90.

Jennings, J. 2004. La Chichera y El Patrón: Chicha and the Energetics of Feasting in the Prehistoric Andes. *Archeological Papers of the American Anthropological Association* 14 (1): 241–59.

Jennings, J., K. L. Antrobus, S. J. Atencio, E. Glavich, R. Johnson, G. Loffler, and C. Luu. 2005. "Drinking Beer in a Blissful Mood": Alcohol Production, Operational Chains, and Feasting in the Ancient World. *Current Anthropology* 46 (2): 275–303.

Joffe, A. H. 1998. Alcohol and Social Complexity in Ancient Western Asia. *Current Anthropology* 39 (3): 297–322.
Justeson, J. S. 1978. Mayan Scribal Practice in the Classic Period: A Test-Case of an Explanatory Approach to the study of writing systems. PhD diss., Stanford University.
Kaufman, T., and J. Justeson. 2003. *A Preliminary Mayan Etymological Dictionary.* Foundation for the Advancement of Mesoamerican Studies Inc. www.famsi.org/reports/01051/index.html.
Kaufman, T., and J. Justeson. 2006. The History of the Word for "Cacao" and Related Terms in Ancient Meso-America. In *Chocolate in Mesoamerica: A Cultural History of Cacao,* ed. C. L. McNeil, 117–39. Gainesville: University Press of Florida.
Kaufman, T., and J. Justeson. 2007. The History of the Word for *Cacao* in Ancient Mesoamerica. *Ancient Mesoamerica* 18 (2): 193–237.
Kerr, J., and M. D. Coe, eds. 1989. *The Maya Vase Book: A Corpus of Rollout Photographs of Maya Vases.* Vol. 1. New York: Kerr Associates.
Kerr, J., and M. D. Coe, eds. 1990. *The Maya Vase Book: A Corpus of Rollout Photographs of Maya Vases.* Vol. 2. New York: Kerr Associates.
Kerr, J., and M. D. Coe, eds. 1992. *The Maya Vase Book: A Corpus of Rollout Photographs of Maya Vases.* Vol. 3. New York: Kerr Associates.
Kerr, J., and M. D. Coe, eds. 1995. *The Maya Vase Book: A Corpus of Rollout Photographs of Maya Vases.* Vol. 4. New York: Kerr Associates.
Kerr, J., and M. D. Coe, eds. 1997. *The Maya Vase Book: A Corpus of Rollout Photographs of Maya Vases.* Vol. 5. New York: Kerr Associates.
Kerr, J., and M. D. Coe, eds. 2000. *The Maya Vase Book: A Corpus of Rollout Photographs of Maya Vases.* Vol. 6. New York: Kerr Associates.
Kettunen, H., and C. Helmke. 2010. *Introduction to Maya Hieroglyphs.* Available at www.wayeb.org.
Landa, D. de. 1975. *The Maya: Diego de Landa's Account of the Affairs of Yucatán.* Trans. and ed. A. R. Pagden. Chicago: Philip O'Hara.
Laughlin, R. M., and J. B. Haviland. 1988. *The Great Tzotzil Dictionary of Santo Domingo Zinacantán, with Grammatical Analysis and Historical Commentary.* Smithsonian Contributions to Anthropology. 3 vols. Washington, D.C.: Smithsonian Institution Press.
Leacock, S. 1983. Ceremonial Drinking in an Afro-Brazilian Cult. In *Beliefs, Behaviors, and Alcoholic Beverages: A Cross-Cultural Survey,* ed. M. Marshall, 81–93. Ann Arbor: University of Michigan Press.
LeCount, L. J. 1999. Polychrome Pottery and Political Strategies in Late and Terminal Classic Lowland Maya Society. *Latin American Antiquity* 10 (3): 239–58.
LeCount, L. J. 2001. Like Water for Chocolate: Feasting and Political Ritual among the Late Classic Maya at Xunantunich, Belize. *American Anthropologist* 103 (4): 935–53.
Lesure, R. G. 1998. Vessel Form and Function in an Early Formative Ceramic Assemblage from Coastal Mexico. *Journal of Field Archaeology* 25 (1): 19–36.
Loughmiller-Newman, J. A. 2008. Canons of Maya Painting. *Ancient Mesoamerica* 19 (1): 29–42.

Loughmiller-Newman, J. A. 2012. The Analytic Reconciliation of Classic Mayan Elite Pottery: Squaring Pottery Function with Form, Adornment, and Residual Contents. PhD diss., State University of New York, Albany.

MacLeod, B. 1990. *Deciphering the Primary Standard Sequence.* Austin: Department of Anthropology, University of Texas.

Madsen, W., and C. Madsen. 1983. The Cultural Structure of Mexican Drinking Behavior. In *Beliefs, Behaviors, and Alcoholic Beverages: A Cross-Cultural Survey,* ed. M. Marshall, 38–53. Ann Arbor: University of Michigan Press.

Mandelbaum, D. G. 1965. Alcohol and Culture. *Current Anthropology* 6 (3): 281–93.

Mandelbaum, D. G. 1983. Alcohol and Culture. In *Beliefs, Behaviors, and Alcoholic Beverages,* ed. M. Marshall, 14–35. Ann Arbor: University of Michigan Press.

Marcus, J. 1992. *Mesoamerican Writing Systems: Propaganda, Myth, and History in Four Ancient Civilizations.* Princeton: Princeton University Press.

Marshall, M. 1983a. Overview of Alcoholic Studies and Anthropology. In *Beliefs, Behaviors, and Alcoholic Beverages,* ed. M. Marshall, 13. Ann Arbor: University of Michigan Press.

Marshall, M. 1983b. *Beliefs, Behaviors, and Alcoholic Beverages: A Cross-Cultural Survey.* Ann Arbor: University of Michigan Press.

Martin, S. 1996. *Calakmul en el Registro Epigráfico.* Mexico City: Instituto Nacional de Antropología e Historia.

Martin, S. 2005. Of Snakes and Bats: Shifting Identities at Calakmul. *PARI Journal* 6 (2): 5–15.

Martin, S., and N. Grube. 2000. *Chronicle of the Maya Kings and Queens: Deciphering the Dynasties of the Ancient Maya.* London: Thames and Hudson.

Masson, M. A. 2002. Community Economy and the Mercantile Transformation in Postclassic Northeastern Belize. In *Ancient Maya Political Economies,* ed. M. A. Masson and D. A. Freidel, 335–64. Walnut Creek, Calif.: AltaMira Press.

McAnany, P. A. 1995. *Living with the Ancestors: Kinship and Kingship in Ancient Maya Society.* 1st ed. Austin: University of Texas Press.

McGee, R. J. 1984. The Influence of Pre-Hispanic Maya Religion in Contemporary Lacandon Maya Ritual. *Journal of Latin American Lore* 10 (2): 175–87.

McGee, R. J. 1988. *Lacandon Maya Balche Ritual.* Video, 40 min. Distributed by University of California Extension Center for Media and Independent Learning, Berkeley.

McNeil, C. L. 2006. Traditional Cacao Use in Modern Mesoamerica. In *Chocolate in Mesoamerica: A Cultural History of Cacao,* ed. C. L. McNeil, 341–66. Maya Studies. Gainesville: University Press of Florida.

McNeil, C. L., W. J. Hurst, and R. J. Sharer. 2006. The Use and Representation of Cacao during the Classic Period at Copan, Honduras. In *Chocolate in Mesoamerica: A Cultural History of Cacao,* ed. C. L. McNeil, 224–52. Maya Studies. Gainesville: University Press of Florida.

Miranda, F. 1952. *La vegetación de Chiapas.* Vol. 1. Tuxtla Gutiérrez, Mexico: Ediciones del Gobierno de Chiapas, Departamento de Prensa y Turismo.

Mora-Marín, D. F. 2004. The Preferred Argument Structure of Classic Lowland Mayan Texts. In *The Linguistics of Maya Writing,* ed. S. Wichmann, 339–60. Salt Lake City: University of Utah Press.

Nelson, S. M. 2003. Feasting the Ancestors in Early China. In *The Archaeology and Politics of Food and Feasting in Early States and Empires*, ed. T. L. Bray, 65–89. New York: Kluwer Academic/Plenum Publishers.

Nobel, P. S. 1994. *Remarkable Agaves and Cacti*. New York: Oxford University Press.

Pollock, S. 1983. Feasts, Funerals, and Fast Food. In *The Archaeology and Politics of Food and Feasting in Early States and Empires*, ed. T. L. Bray, 17–38. New York: Kluwer Academic/Plenum Publishers. Online resource published 2003.

Potter, J. 2000. Pots, Parties, and Politics: Communal Feasting in the American Southwest. *American Antiquity* 65 (3): 471–92.

Proskouriakoff, T. 1960. Historical Implications of a Pattern of Dates at Piedras Negras, Guatemala. *American Antiquity* 25 (4): 454–75.

Rain, P. 2004. *Vanilla: The Cultural History of the World's Most Popular Flavor and Fragrance*. New York: Jeremy P. Tarcher/Penguin Books.

Reents-Budet, D., with contributions by J. W. Ball, R. L. Bishop, V. M. Fields, and B. MacLeod and photographs by J. Kerr. 1994. *Painting the Maya Universe: Royal Ceramics of the Classic Period*. Durham, N.C.: Duke University Press in association with Duke University Museum of Art.

Reents-Budet, D., S. Boucher–Le Landais, R. Bishop, and M. J. Blackman. 2010. Codex-Style Ceramics: New Data Concerning Patterns of Production and Distribution. Paper presented at the 24th Symposium of Archaeological Investigations, Guatemala City, Guatemala.

Rice, P. M. 1987. *Pottery Analysis: A Sourcebook*. Chicago: University of Chicago Press.

Sabloff, J. A. 1986. Interaction among Maya Polities: A Preliminary Examination. In *Peer Polity Interaction and Socio-Political Change*, ed. C. Renfrew and C. F. Cherry, 109–16. Cambridge: Cambridge University Press.

Sachse, F. 2008. Over Distant Waters: Places of Origin and Creation in Colonial K'iche'an Sources. In *Pre-Columbian Landscapes of Creation and Origin*, ed. J. E. Staller, 123–60. New York: Springer.

Sahagún, B. de. 1953. *Florentine Codex: General History of the Things of New Spain*. Book 3, *The Origins of the Gods*. Trans. A.J.O. Anderson and C. E. Dibble. School of American Research Monographs 14 (4). Santa Fe, N.Mex.: School of American Research and University of Utah.

Samuel, D. 1996. Investigation of Ancient Egyptian Baking and Brewing Methods by Correlative Microscopy. *Science* 273: 488–90.

Sargent, M. J. 1983. Changes in Japanese Drinking. In *Beliefs, Behaviors, and Alcoholic Beverages*, ed. M. Marshall, 709–22. Ann Arbor: University of Michigan Press.

Schele, L., and J. H. Miller. 1983. *The Mirror, the Rabbit, and the Bundle: "Accession" Expressions from the Classic Maya Inscriptions*. Studies in Pre-Columbian Art and Archaeology 25. Washington, D.C.: Dumbarton Oaks.

Schele, L., and M. E. Miller. 1986. *The Blood of Kings: Dynasty and Ritual in Maya Art*. Photographs by J. Kerr. New York: G. Braziller; Fort Worth, Tex.: Kimbell Art Museum.

Schiffer, M. B. 1987. *Formation Processes of the Archaeological Record*. 1st ed. Albuquerque: University of New Mexico Press.

Sharer, R. J., and S. G. Morley. 1994. *The Ancient Maya*. Stanford: Stanford University Press.

Slotkin, J. S. 1954. Fermented Drinks in Mexico. *American Anthropologist* 56 (6): 1089–90.

Smith, M. E., J. B. Wharton, and J. M. Olson. 2003. Aztec Feasts, Rituals, and Markets: Political Uses of Ceramic Vessels in a Commercial Economy. In *The Archaeology and Politics of Food and Feasting in Early States and Empires*, ed. T. L. Bray, 235–68. New York: Kluwer Academic/Plenum Publishers.

Smith, S. T. 2003. Pharaohs, Feasts, and Foreigners: Cooking, Foodways, and Agency on Ancient Egypt's Southern Frontier. In *The Archaeology and Politics of Food and Feasting in Early States and Empires*, ed. T. L. Bray, 39–64. New York: Kluwer Academic/Plenum Publishers.

Staller, J. E. 2006. The Social, Symbolic, and Economic Significance of *Zea mays* L. in the Late Horizon Period. In *Histories of Maize: Multidisciplinary Approaches to the Prehistory, Linguistics, Biogeography, Domestication, and Evolution of Maize*, ed. J. E. Staller, R. H. Tykot, and B. F. Benz, 449–67. Amsterdam: Elsevier/Academic Press.

Steinkraus, R. H. 1983. *Handbook of Indigenous Fermented Foods*. Microbiological Series 9. New York: Marcel Dekker.

Stone, A. J. 1991. Aspects of Impersonation in Classic Maya Art. In *Sixth Palenque Round Table, 1986*, ed. M. G. Robertson and V. M. Fields, 194–202. Palenque Round Table Series 8. 1st ed. Norman: University of Oklahoma Press, Norman.

Strong, R. C. 2002. *Feast: A History of Grand Eating*. London: Jonathan Cape.

Stross, B. 2006. Maize in Word and Image in Southeastern Mesoamerica. In *Histories of Maize: Multidisciplinary Approaches to the Prehistory, Linguistics, Biogeography, Domestication, and Evolution of Maize*, ed. J. E. Staller, R. H. Tykot, and B. F. Benz, 577–98. Amsterdam: Elsevier/Academic Press.

Stuart, D. 1988. The Rio Azul Cacao Pot: Epigraphic Observations on the Function of a Maya Ceramic Vessel. *Antiquity* 62 (234): 153–57.

Stuart, D. 2005. *The Inscriptions from Temple XIX at Palenque: A Commentary*. San Francisco, Calif.: Pre-Columbian Art Research Institute.

Stuart, D. 2006. The Language of Chocolate: References to Cacao on Classic Maya Drinking Vessels. In *Chocolate in Mesoamerica: A Cultural History of Cacao*, ed. C. L. McNeil, 184–201. Maya Studies. Gainesville: University Press of Florida.

Stuart, D. 2011. *The Order of Days: The Maya World and the Truth about 2012*. New York: Harmony Books.

Tedlock, D. 1996. *Popol Vuh: The Definitive Edition of the Mayan Book of the Dawn of Life and the Glories of Gods and Kings*. New York: Simon and Schuster.

Tedlock, D. 2002. How to Drink Chocolate from a Skull at a Wedding Banquet. *RES: Anthropology and Aesthetics* 42 (Autumn): 166–79.

Townsend, R. F. 2000. *The Aztec*. Rev. ed. London: Thames and Hudson.

Tozzer, A. M. 1907. *A Comparative Study of the Mayas and the Lacandones*. Archaeological Institute of America Report of the Fellow in American Archaeology, 1902–1905. New York: MacMillan.

Tozzer, A. M., ed. and trans. 1941. *Landa's "Relacion de las Cosas de Yucatan."* Papers of the Peabody Museum of American Archaeology and Ethnology 18. Cambridge, Mass.: Harvard University.

Turmo, I. G. 2001. Drinking: An Almost Silent Language. In *Drinking: Anthropological Approaches*, ed. I. de Garine and V. de Garine, 130–41. New York: Berghahn Books.

Ulloa, M. H. 1987. *Fermentaciones tradicionales indigenas de México.* Mexico City: Instituto Nacional Indigenista.

Underhill, A. P. 2000. An Analysis of Mortuary Ritual at the Dawenkou Site, Shandong, China. *Journal of East Asian Archaeology* 2 (1–2): 93–127.

Vargas, L. A. 2001. Thirst and Drinking as a Biocultural Process. In *Drinking: Anthropological Approaches*, ed. I. de Garine and V. de Garine, 11–21. New York: Berghahn Books.

Washburne, C. 1961. *Primitive Drinking: A Study of the Uses and Functions of Alcohol in Preliterate Societies.* New York: College and University Press.

Weiner, A. B. 1992. *Inalienable Possessions: The Paradox of Keeping-while-Giving.* Berkeley: University of California Press.

West, G. 2002. Ceramic Exchange in the Late Classic and Postclassic Maya Lowlands: A Diachronic Approach. In *Ancient Maya Political Economies*, ed. M. A. Masson and D. A. Freidel, 140–96. Walnut Creek, Calif.: AltaMira Press.

Westermeyer, J. 1983. Use of Alcohol and Opium by the Meo in Laos. In *Beliefs, Behaviors, and Alcoholic Beverages*, ed. M. Marshall, 289–96. Ann Arbor: University of Michigan Press.

Wisdom, C. 1950. *Materials on the Chorti Language.* Chicago: University of Chicago Library.

Youman, B., and B. Estep. 2005. *Liquid Mexico: Festive Spirits, Tequila Culture, and the Infamous Worm.* Tempe, Ariz.: Bilingual Press.

9

The Origins of the Ayahuasca/Yagé Concept

An Inquiry into the Synergy between Dimethyltryptamine and Beta-Carbolines

CONSTANTINO MANUEL TORRES

Everything happened through the eye.
—Tukano creation tale (Reichel-Dolmatoff 1978: 4)

This chapter presents the results of an inquiry into the origins of the ayahuasca/yagé concept (América Indigena 1986; Beyer 2009, 2012; Labate and Cavnar 2014; Luna 1986; Ott 1994). Ayahuasca and yagé are analogous potions that exert their psychotropic action through the synergism of their basic component alkaloids: harmine, tetrahydroharmine, harmaline, and dimethyltryptamine (DMT). These potions have a long history of use throughout the Amazon basin. This investigation reveals, instead of a fixed recipe, a complex series of potions, each an attempt at synergy between the different component alkaloids, with an emphasis on beta-carbolines (β-carbolines) and tryptamines. The components of these potions vary according to regional plant availability and perhaps what could be seen as cultural predilections for specific methods of administration (e.g., smoking, snuffing, drinking, enemas). Ayahuasca and yagé are the potions most commonly used today but not necessarily the most ancient. The beginning stages of my inquiry focused on the origins of these two pharmacologically complex beverages. However, it soon became apparent that questions of origin were not restricted to sets of specific recipes, prescriptions, and localities. Instead, a construct related to plant interaction and modulation began to emerge from this research.

In addition to the ayahuasca and yagé recipes currently available, in an inquiry about origins, analogous potions and brews should be considered.

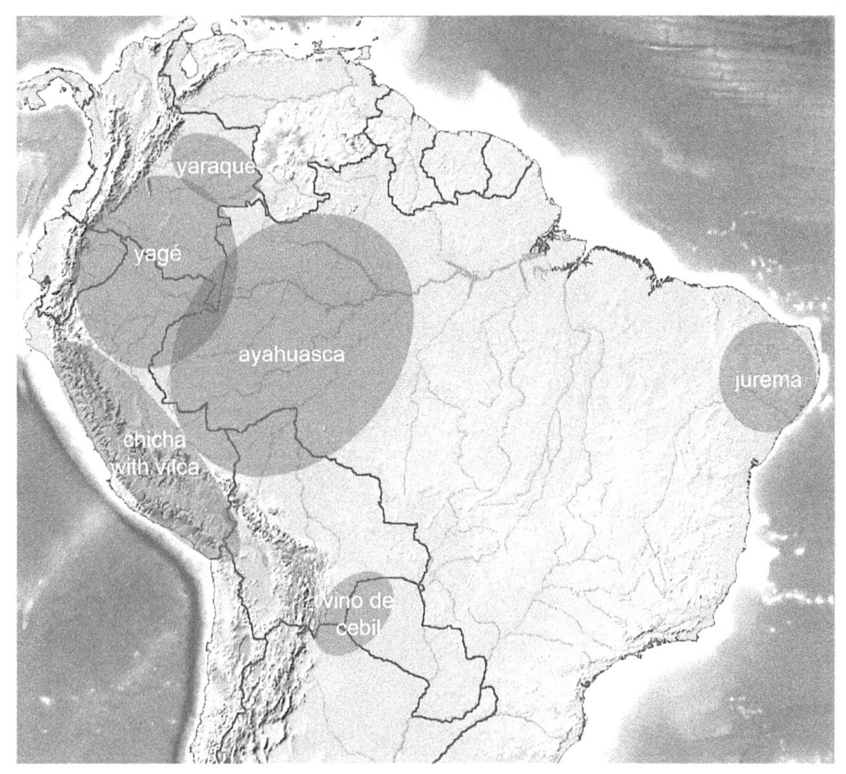

Figure 9.1. Map of South America indicating approximate distribution of potions mentioned in the text.

Significant among these are *vinho de jurema, yaraque, vino de cebil,* and *chicha* with an admixture of *Anadenanthera* seeds (figure 9.1). Each is discussed in detail below. These potions must be seen within the total context of tryptamine activation throughout South America (smoking, snuffing, enemas, unguents). The use of psychoactive plants and preparations on the South American continent is characterized by a predilection for visionary agents containing potent, short-acting tryptamines (N,N-DMT, 5-MeO-DMT, and 5-HO-DMT). The area of San Pedro cactus (*Trichocereus* sp.) use in northern Peru and southern Ecuador is an exception to the previous statement (figure 9.2).

In this chapter I first present a survey of potions and brews that attempt to activate tryptamines by the addition of these alkaloids to a β-carboline (e.g., harmine, tetrahydroharmine, harmaline) base. Second, the antiquity of these drinks is established by reference to early colonial documents as well as ethnographic information collected in the eighteenth through twentieth centuries. Third, after the temporal data for these potions are

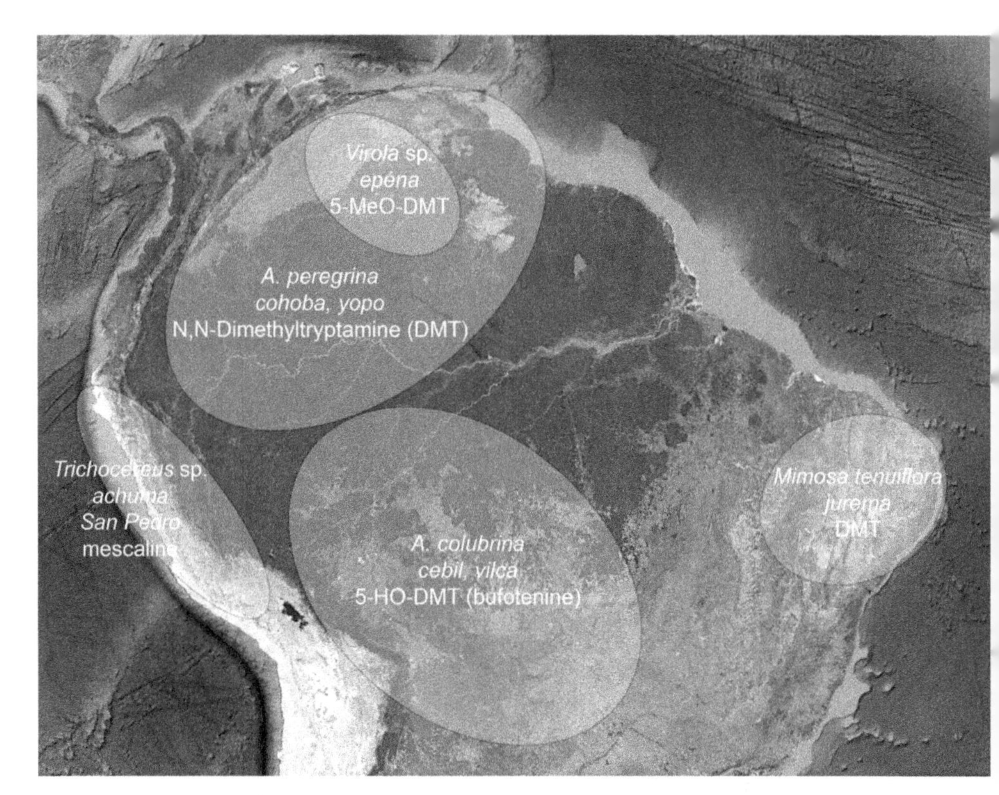

Figure 9.2. Map of South America with approximate distribution of tryptamine use.

presented, a review of pre-Columbian iconography follows in a discussion of possible use of ayahuasca-like potions in the preconquest period.

Survey of Potions

The vine *Banisteriopsis caapi* (Spruce ex Griseb) Morton (Malpighiaceae) forms the basis of modern (post-1750) ayahuasca and yagé potions. Sometimes the potion is prepared with only the stem or bark of *Banisteriopsis* species, without the addition of other ingredients. In some instances (e.g., among the Piaroa), a simple *Banisteriopsis* tea is drank to lengthen and enhance the effect of tryptamine-containing snuff powders (Rodd 2002: 276). Most often, the leaves or bark of various other plants is added to the *Banisteriopsis* potion to modify the effect. The species used most frequently are *Diplopterys cabrerana* (Cuatrecasas) Gates (previously known as *Banisteriopsis rusbyana*) and *Psychotria viridis* Ruiz & Pav. Solanaceous additives are also common, including *Nicotiana*, *Brugmansia*, and *Brunfelsia* species. For convenience, and to avoid confusion, in this chapter the term *ayahuasca* refers to the basic mixture of *Banisteriopsis caapi* and *Psychotria viridis* (*chacruna*), while yagé primarily consists of *Banisteriopsis caapi* and *Diplopterys cabrerana* (*ocoyagé*). Ayahuasca is generally manufactured in Brazil and Peru, and yagé in Colombia and Ecuador. Approximately a hundred species from forty plant families are reported as ayahuasca/yagé admixtures, many of them also psychoactive plants (Ott 1994: 27–31).

The problem of oral administration is a complex one. Psychoactive tryptamine alkaloids (e.g., N,N-DMT), such as those found in *D. cabrerana* and *P. viridis*, are deaminated by the enzyme monoamine oxidase (MAO); therefore, snuffing, smoking, enemas, and unguents are the most direct means of administration. Unlike DMT, bufotenine (5-HO-DMT) and 5-MeO-DMT maintain some oral activity, but the effect notably diminishes (Ott 2001: 279). The oral activity of these alkaloids can be activated or enhanced through the addition of plants that contain β-carbolines (such as harmine and harmaline), which have the effect of temporarily inhibiting the activity of MAO. Holmstedt and Lindgren (1967: 365) first proposed the notion of synergy between β-carbolines and tryptamines when they detected the presence of harmine and harmaline in tryptamine-rich Piaroa and Surará snuffs of the Orinoco basin: "The occurrence of both tryptamines and β-carbolines in the South American snuffs is pharmacologically interesting. The β-carbolines are monoamine-oxidase inhibitors, and could potentiate the action of the simple indoles. The combination of β-carbolines and tryptamines would thus be advantageous."

The predominant means of modifying states of consciousness in ancient and contemporary South American ritual practices is through the activation of visionary tryptamines. These are obtained from a variety of plants, largely determined by regional availability. The seeds of the leguminous *Anadenanthera peregrina* and *A. colubrina* are smoked, inhaled, administered as an enema, or applied as an unguent to activate bufotenine (5-HO-DMT), the predominant alkaloid in these plant species. The Yanomamo of the Orinoco basin snuff the resin of myristicaceous *Virola* species, which contain 5-MeO-DMT. Most notable, for the purpose of this study, are the repeated accounts (Gragson 1997: 380; Reichel-Dolmatoff 1944: 480; Rodd 2002, 2008; Spruce [1908] 1970, 2: 428) of chewing caapi stems in preparation for snuffing sessions to prolong and strengthen the effect of the short-acting tryptamine alkaloids present in the snuff powders (figure 9.3). Potions pursuing the synergy between β-carbolines and tryptamines should be seen within the wider

Figure 9.3. Map of South America with area of concomitant use of beta-carbolines and tryptamines.

South American context of the pursuit of tryptamine activation and not as isolated classes of potent psychoactive beverages.

Ayahuasca, yagé, vino de cebil, jurema, and chicha with visionary admixtures have been selected for consideration here because of their distribution throughout South America. An investigation into the origins of ayahuasca reveals numerous beverages distributed throughout South America, each distinct, varying according to plant availability, cultural predilections for ingestion, and ritual requirements. No fixed recipe exists, and the composition of the potion varies. Instead of pursuing the origins of a specific recipe, this inquiry attempts a search for the beginnings of a concept that addresses issues of synergy between plant components, such that an effect can be modulated, enhanced, and prolonged.

AYAHUASCA AND YAGÉ

Ayahuasca includes stems of *Banisteriopsis caapi* and leaves of *Psychotria viridis* (*chacruna*). In yagé, the basic mixture consists of *B. caapi* and leaves of *Diplopterys cabrerana* (*chagropanga, ocoyagé*). The leaves of *P. viridis* and *D. cabrerana* contain N,N-dimethyltryptamine (DMT), while the stems and bark of *B. caapi* include β-carboline alkaloids that act as MAO-A inhibitors. There are no fixed recipes; instead, the mixtures exhibit constant variation even within the practice of an individual shaman—it is a methodology marked by continuous change. Beyer (2009: 210), in his work on mestizo shamanism in the upper Amazon, notes that one of the shamans that shared information with him "for a period of time . . . made his ayahuasca drink with leaves of both *chacruna* and *ocoyagé*."

Numerous myths tell how the *Banisteriopsis* vine has been a companion to human beings since the moment of creation. Tukano origin myths, for example, describe the first inhabitants of the Earth descending from the Milky Way in a large anaconda canoe transporting a man and a woman with three plants: manioc, coca, and caapi. Other Tukano stories tell of a yagé-woman who gave birth to a luminous child born in a blinding flash of light. Yagé-woman walked to the "House of Waters," her place of origin. Once there, she asked, "Who is the father of this child?" The men replied, "We are all fathers of the child." Each man tore off a part of the child and kept it for himself. Ever since, each Tukano community has had its own visionary vine (Reichel-Dolmatoff 1978: 3–4).

Harmine has been detected in the hair of two mummies from archaeological sites (ca. AD 500–1000) in the Azapa Valley, Chile, although the results of the analyses are inconclusive (Ogalde et al. 2009; see also Trout 2008). Species of *Banisteriopsis, P. viridis*, and *D. cabrerana* have not been detected in archaeological sites. This is to be expected, since the habitat of these plants is not conducive to the preservation of organic remains. In addition, the great distance and climatic difference between the Atacama desert and the Amazon make the presence of *Banisteriopsis* in the Azapa Valley unlikely.

The earliest postcontact reports of ayahuasca appear to be those of José Chantre y Herrera (1901) and Pablo Maroni (1988). Chantre y Herrera compiled a history of Jesuit activity in the Marañon River area from 1637 to 1767. His compilation includes a brief description of an ayahuasca ritual and a clear reference to the mixing of a liana with other plants. He did not provide a specific date for the following observation: "The diviner hangs his bed in the middle or makes himself a seat or a small platform and next to it places a hellish brew called ayahuasca, remarkably effective in depriving [one] of the senses. He makes a tea of the vine or of bitter herbs, which after much boiling will become very thick. As it is so strong [as] to disrupt judgment in [a] small quantity[,] side effects are light, and the drink fits into two small cups" (Chantre y Herrera 1901: 80). Pablo Maroni (1988: 172), a Jesuit missionary to the Amazon River area circa 1738–40, attributed divinatory qualities to ayahuasca: "For divination . . . a beverage known vulgarly as ayahuasca is ingested. . . . [It is] very efficient in depriving the individual of his senses and sometimes of life. It is drunk by those who wish to prophesy[;] . . . the diviner, deprived of his senses, lays face down to avoid being suffocated by the power of the herb, and remains in this position for many hours and sometimes two or three days." Subsequently, travelers, explorers, and missionaries mentioned ayahuasca and yagé in their writings. These descriptions are brief but sometimes contain useful bits of information. Juan Magnin's (1988: 475) description of medicinal flora for the province of Quito, circa 1734–40, mentions several vines, including ayahuasca: "They have for that matter, roots, juices, vines, such as the hurupschi, ayahuasca, corahuana, Maviari or flowers of love, and others."

The first botanist to identify the liana that forms the basis of ayahuasca and yagé as belonging to the genus *Banisteriopsis* was Richard Spruce (1873: 184). Spruce encountered the use of *Banisteriopsis* vines several times during his travels, circa 1852–53. He states,

> Having had the good fortune to see the two most famous narcotics in use, and to obtain specimens of the plants that afford them sufficiently perfect to be determined botanically, I propose to record my observations on them, made on the spot.
>
> The first of these narcotics is afforded by a climbing plant called Caapi in North Brazil and Venezuela, but Aya-huasca, or Dead-man's Vine, about the eastern foot of the Andes of Peru and Ecuador. It belongs to the family of Malpighiaceae and I drew up the following brief description of it, from living specimens, in November, 1853 . . . Banisteria Caapi, Spruce . . .

The history of admixtures to a basic *Banisteriopsis* potion is unclear. Chantre y Herrera (1901) mentions plant additives but is not specific about their purpose. Spruce (1873: 184) also describes additives to the *Banisteriopsis* potion: "The lower part of the stem is the part used. A quantity of this is beaten in a mortar, with water, and sometimes with the addition of a small portion of the slender roots of the *Caapi-pinima.* When sufficiently triturated, it is passed through a sieve, which separates the woody fibre, and to the residue enough water is added to render it drinkable." Spruce (1873: 184) identified *Caapi-pinima* (painted caapi) "as an Apocyneous twiner of the genus Haemadictyon, of which [he] saw only young shoots, without any flowers."

Alfred Simson (1886: 196), during his exploration of the Putumayo River area in 1886, was the first to mention specific plant additives in preparing ayahuasca. He states, "Like the Zaparos, the Piojés also drink ayahuasca mixed with yajé, sámeruja leaves, and guanto wood, an indulgence which usually results in a broil between at least the partakers of the beverage."

Simson clearly differentiates between ayahuasca and yagé. It could be proposed that *yajé* in this instance, given the locality and preparation described, refers to *Diplopterys cabrerana.* Schultes (1957: 6) identified *guanto* as a "tree-species of *Datura*." Identification of *sámeruja* leaves remains elusive; I do not know of any other references in which this term has been used.

Theodore Koch-Grünberg (2005: 309), in 1904, during his travels among the Tukano, mentions two types of caapi: "The Tucano distinguish two species of *Kaapí*, one they call *kaapí* and the other *kúlikaxpiro*." He does not identify the second variety, likely another liana given the context of this documentation. Richard Evans Schultes proposed *Tetrapterys methystica* (see below) as the second caapi referred to by Koch-Grünberg (Schultes and Hofmann 1980: 183).

The rubiaceous shrub *Psychotria viridis* was correctly identified as to genus and species in 1967. That year, Schultes reported the discovery by Homer Pinkley, one of his students, of the use of *Psychotria viridis* among the Kofán. Pinkley collected botanical samples that were determined to be *Psychotria viridis*. The Kofán assert that they add the leaves as well as the fruits of this plant for the same reason that they add the leaves of *Diplopterys cabrerana*: to "increase their visions and to make them of longer duration" (Pinkley 1969a: 535).

Prior to Pinkley, Joaquin Rocha mentioned a probable *Psychotria* additive in a book about his 1904 travels in the Colombian Amazon. The term *chiripanga*, referred to as an ayahuasca admixture in the text quoted below, is infrequent and likely refers to *Diplopterys cabrerana*. "Yagé is a vine that Indians do not allow the whites to see, and consequently, I do not know [what it is]. They prepare the [ayahuasca] beverage by cooking it overnight, and when it gives the appearance of thick honey, it is ready to be tasted. They mitigate the effects [of this beverage] when it is administered only as a purgative, by mixing it with other vegetables, especially an herb they call *chiripanga* that I also do not know" (Rocha 1905: 45).

The renowned novelist William Burroughs, author of *The Yagé Letters* and *Naked Lunch*, during his search for yagé between 1952 and 1956 documented the addition of leaves to the *Banisteriopsis* potion (Burroughs et al. 2006: 95–97). While on a visit to Pucallpa, Burroughs met a young healer who shared a strong ayahuasca potion. The same healer later taught Burroughs how to prepare a potion combining *Banisteriopsis* and a bundle of leaves. Burroughs collected samples of the leaves and, with the help of an unnamed Peruvian botanist, identified the leaves as belonging to the Rubiaceae.

> The Doctor has showed me his method of preparing yagé—(Usually a trade secret)—He mashes pieces of the fresh cut vine and boils two hours with the leaves of another plant tentatively identified by a Peruvian botanist as *Palicourea* species Rubiaceae. The effect of yagé prepared in this manner is qualitatively different from cold water infusion of yagé alone, or yagé cooked alone. The other leaf is essential to realize the full effect of the drug. Whether it is itself active, or merely serves as a catalyzing agent, I do not know. This matter needs the attention of a chemist. (From Burroughs's March 1956 "Yagé Article" manuscript, quoted in Burroughs et al. 2006: 97)

Until the work of Burroughs and Pinkley, the identity of *Psychotria viridis* as an ingredient in *Banisteriopsis* potions was unknown. It is particularly relevant here that Burroughs and Pinkley emphasize how the addition of *Psychotria* leaves enhances and modifies the effect of a potion made of *Banisteriopsis* alone.

According to Pinkley (1969b: 307–8), the Kofán also added *Diplopterys cabrerana* (*chagropanga, ocoyagé*) leaves to the *Banisteriopsis* potion. Probable additions of *D. cabrerana* leaves to the ayahuasca potion have been reported since the early 1930s (Schultes 1957: 35). In 1953, Schultes (1957: 35) collected samples of *D. cabrerana* in Mocoa and reported its use, together with *B. caapi*, as an ingredient for yagé.

The information presented above suggests that underlying the numerous recipes that use stems of *B. caapi* as a basic potion exists an understanding of how to modulate plant interaction to obtain the desired effects. Ayahuasca and yagé could have points of origin located in northwestern Amazonia (figure 9.1; Brabec de Mori 2011: 42) perhaps not earlier than the initial period of contact with Europeans. The paucity of archaeological data and the apparent lack of information about ayahuasca in early colonial documents, as well as imprecise descriptions of its use prior to AD 1850, suggest this approximate date.

Subsequently, ayahuasca and yagé recipes multiplied and were adapted not only to regional demands but also to individual practitioners, in a continuous search for a variety of methods to enhance and modify the visionary state. In contrast, snuffing and smoking are present in the archaeological record since at least four thousand years ago (Fernández Distel 1980; Oyuela-Caycedo and Kawa 2015: 32) and were documented by Spanish chroniclers from the earliest moments of the conquest (e.g., Aguado 1956; Pané 1999). The use of tobacco is certainly of great antiquity: *Nicotiana* species have been recovered in Caral, Peru, circa BC 2000 and in Niño Korin, Bolivia, circa AD 375 and AD 1120 (Bondeson 1972: 181–83; Oyuela-Caycedo and Kawa 2015: 32: Wassén 1972: 28). Tobacco is a frequent additive to ayahuasca and yagé (Bruhn et al. 1995).

The relatively late date, post–AD 1900, for the identification of plant admixtures to ayahuasca and yagé suggests that during the eighteenth and nineteenth centuries, potions were still transforming into the formulas we know today. If this date is correct, it points to viable South American pharmaceutical practices surviving well after European contact and into the contemporary world.

TETRAPTERYS METHYSTICA

According to Schultes (1957: 40–41), *T. methystica* could be the second type of caapi referred to by Koch-Grünberg (see above). In 1948, Schultes witnessed among the Makú, of the Tikié River, Brazil, the preparation of a cold-water infusion of a flowering vine without the addition of any other plants. He identified the vine as *Tetrapterys methystica* (reclassified as *T. styloptera*; Ott 1996: 402), a malpighiaceous genus. Schultes described the potion as having "proven narcotic properties" and a yellowish hue, in contrast with ayahuasca and yagé, which have a darker brown color. Unfortunately, the material he collected was lost when his canoe overturned. Consequently, chemical components of the plant are unknown and further studies are needed.

JUREMA (*AJUCÁ, VINHO DE JUREMA*)

Roots and bark of *Mimosa hostilis*, *M. verrucosa,* and *M. ophthalmocentra* form the basis of an inebriating potion from northeastern Brazil known as *vinho de jurema* (Da Mota 1997; Samorini 2016: 91–92; Sampaio-Silva 1997: 63). DMT has been reported from *M. hostilis,* suggesting that the potion may also contain MAO inhibitors (Ott 1996: 400; see also Ott 1998).

The first mention of the inebriating qualities of vinho de jurema is found in documents relating to a meeting that took place on September 16, 1739, in Recife, Pernambuco (Medeiros 2006). One of the objectives was to discuss the use of jurema by natives of the missions of Paraíba, in northeastern Brazil: "The precise means have been investigated in order to remedy the errors that have been introduced among the Indians, such as consuming certain drinks which they call Jurema, by which they are deceived and victims of hallucinations" (Medeiros 2006: 8). There are also legal documents pertinent to the prohibition of the use of jurema carried out by the governor of Pernambuco in 1741 (Medeiros 2006: 8).

José Monteiro de Noronha (2006: 25) related that during his travels, circa 1768, in the arid *sertão* of northeastern Brazil, he learned of the consumption of jurema: "In their major festivities those who are skilled in warfare use a drink made from the root of a bush they call jurema whose virtue is excessively narcotic." In 1942, Osvaldo Gonçalves de Lima (1946) identified the source plant of jurema as *Mimosa tenuiflora* (also known as *M. hostilis*) and described its preparation:

> On our arrival we found that the chief was already at the place where the festival was to take place. He was just about to prepare the ajucá, the miraculous drink made from the jurema root. I witnessed the entire preparation. First the root is scraped, then washed in order to eliminate any dirt that might still cling to it. Then it is placed on a stone and beaten again and again with another stone in order to crush it. Afterwards the completely crushed mass is thrown into a vessel filled with water, and pressed out by hand by the person who prepares it. The water gradually turns into a reddish and frothy syrup, at which point it is ready to drink. The froth is quickly removed, thus leaving a clear liquid. Now old Serafim lighted a tubular pipe made from the jurema root and placed the lit end into his mouth. Then he blew on the liquid in the vessel, making the smoke form the figure of a cross. (Trans. from Schleiffer 1974: 94)

At this moment the antiquity of vinho de jurema cannot be ascertained beyond the eighteenth-century report by Monteiro de Noronha (2006). Use of jurema still survives among the Tuxá, indigenous people of northeastern Brazil (Sampaio-Silva 1997). Tuxá ceremonial life includes rituals in which the *pajé* (shaman) and assistants enter in contact with ancestors inhabiting an enchanted kingdom (*reino encantado*). The ancestor spirits are incorporated into ritual paraphernalia, assisted by the drinking and smoking of jurema root (Sampaio-Silva 1997: 56).

The concomitant use of *Banisteriopsis* stems and nasal inhalation of *Anadenanthera* seeds has been witnessed by Spruce and others since the mid-nineteenth century. Circa 1852, Spruce ([1908] 1970, 2: 428) described the chewing of *Banisteriopsis caapi* bark in conjunction with snuffing yopo (*A. peregrina*):

> The Guahibo had a bit of caapi hung from his neck, along with the snuff box, and as he ground his niopo he every now and then tore off a strip of caapi with his teeth and chewed it with evident satisfaction. "With a chew of caapi and a pinch of niopo," said he, in his broken Spanish, "one feels so good! No hunger—no thirst—no tired!" From the same man I learnt that caapi and niopo were used by all the nations on the upper tributaries of the Orinoco, i.e. on the Guaviare, Vichada, Meta, Sipapo, etc.

The chewing of *Banisteriopsis caapi* is also documented by Gerardo Reichel-Dolmatoff (1944: 480) in his description of a class of Guahibo protective ritual events in which the shaman serves as an intermediary between humans and the supernatural. In these rites, participants must snuff copious amounts and to chew caapi in order to be in an ecstatic state from the beginning of the performance. The practice of chewing caapi bark and snuffing yopo during the course of all-night ceremonies seems to be frequent in the region. The Guahibo of the Vichada River perform multinight ritual events that include, in addition to snuffing yopo and chewing caapi, the smoking of tobacco and the drinking of yagé (Wassén 1965: 104). The Pumé of the Arauca and Capanaparo Rivers conduct all-night shamanic events in which they chew the stems and the root of *Banisteriopsis caapi* in conjunction with a snuff powder made from the seeds of *A. peregrina* (Gragson 1997: 380).

Current investigations among the Piaroa of southern Venezuela have shed light on the relationship between *Anadenanthera peregrina* (yopo) and *Banisteriopsis caapi* (Rodd 2002, 2008). Piaroa shamans consume *B. caapi* prior to snuffing and include caapi cuttings in the preparation of the snuff powder.

> To the Piaroa shamans who use them, yopo and *B. caapí* are intimately tied. As one shaman said, "The force of yopo and the force of caapi work together." Beyond inclusion in the preparation of yopo, Piaroa shamans almost always consume *B. caapí* (*tuhuipe*) orally one to six hours prior to snuff inhalation. A small cutting of the inner bark of the *B. caapi*

plant, maintained in every shaman's garden, is sucked for one to three hours prior to consumption of snuff. When particularly strong visions are desired for the purposes of divination, initiatory training (*maripa reui*) or witchcraft battles, a beverage made from the grated cuttings of *B. caapí* is taken. José-Luis explained that "Capi extends yopo and makes it stronger. Without capi, yopo only lasts a short while. Visions are weak." (Rodd 2002: 276)

The ethnographic evidence and pharmacologic research on the MAO-inhibiting effects of the harmala alkaloids clearly suggest that sustained chewing of caapi bark could enhance the effects of the tryptamine-containing snuffs (see Holmstedt and Lindgren 1967; Ott 2001). This concomitant consumption utilizes the human body to provoke the synergy between the harmala alkaloids present in caapi and the tryptamines in yopo. The antiquity of this practice cannot be determined at this time.

ANADENANTHERA POTIONS

Oral ingestion of *Anadenanthera* seeds has been recorded among diverse cultures. The seeds of trees of this genus were so important in ancient South American ideologies that the Taíno brought the tree to the Greater Antilles during their migrations, approximately 2,000–2,500 years ago. The snuff prepared from *A. peregrina* seeds was of great importance in their ritual practices. "Taíno" is the appellative given to the Arawakan speakers who occupied the Bahamas, most of the Greater Antilles, and the Virgin Islands at the time of first contact with Europeans (1492). The Arawak language family is widespread in northern South America, and the ancestors of the Taíno are generally assumed to have originated in that area. They were probably responsible for the introduction of *Anadenanthera* into the Greater Antilles (Reis Altschul 1964: 42): the distribution of the tree coincides with the Taíno occupation of Hispaniola, Puerto Rico, and Jamaica. However, there is no mention in the early chronicles of potions containing *Anadenanthera* seeds. Ramón Pané (1999), a friar who resided on the island of Hispaniola from 1494 to 1498, documented the use of a potion called *güeyo* that included various plants. Pané's document makes clear that güeyo is dependent on an admixture of plants to cause its effect, although the information given by Pané (1999: 22–24) is not sufficient to identify the ingredients. Pane's description indicates that one of the purposes of drinking this potion was to interact with the supernatural realm. The *behique* (shaman) went through a restricted and prolonged diet before drinking the potion. Contemporary Amazonian healers likewise go through a rigorous ritual diet that might last two or three weeks. Bartolomé de Las Casas (cited in Pané 1999: 31) also mentions the drinking of a visionary potion among the Taíno: "They would fast for four months and more at one stretch, without eating anything except only a certain juice of an herb or herbs." The evidence presented above suggests the existence of a probable ayahuasca analogue among the Taíno (for an extensive discussion of ritual practices in the Caribbean, see Kaye, chapter 6, this volume).

The Guahibo prepared a drink called *yaraque*, which included yopo powder (Reis Altschul 1972: 31). Mario Califano (1976: 16–18, 46), in his study of shamanism among the Wichi (Mataco of the Gran Chaco, mentioned the drinking of vino de cebil, an *Anadenanthera*-based potion, in relation to shamanic initiation. Califano does not provide any details regarding the components of this beverage. Vino de cebil allowed the drinker, said to perceive her- or himself as purely of bone, to enter the spirit world (Califano 1976: 16). The addition of vilca (*A. colubrina*) to fermented drinks has also been amply documented in the Peruvian Andes during the early colonial period (Cobo 1964: 158, 272; Ondegardo 1916, 3: 29–30). Iconographic evidence suggests (as discussed below) that the Moche (ca. AD 300–800) of the northern Peruvian coast were drinking an *Anadenanthera*-based potion.

The earliest evidence for smoking in South America consists of *A. colubrina* var. *cebil* seeds found at the site of Inca Cueva (IC c7) in the Puna de Jujuy, in northwestern Argentina (Fernández Distel 1980). At this site, two smoking pipes made of puma bone (*Felis concolor*) were found. Chemical analysis of pipe residue indicated the presence of tryptamine alkaloids. Radiocarbon testing yielded dates of 4080 ± 80 BP and 4030 ± 80 BP (Aguerre et al. 1975: 213; Aschero and Yacobaccio 1994: 7). The oldest evidence for snuffing is provided by snuff trays and tubes excavated by Junius Bird at the site of Huaca Prieta, Chicama Valley. Bird (1948: 27) unearthed two whalebone snuff trays and a bird- and fox-bone tube, dated circa 1200 BC (Wassén 1967: 256). The minimal preparations required for smoking and snuffing most likely preceded the elaboration of complex potions such as ayahuasca and yagé.

Juan Polo de Ondegardo (1916, 3: 29–30) made the first known reference to vilca (*A. colubrina*) as a chicha additive in 1571:

> Those who wish to know an event of things past or of things that are to come . . . invoke the demon and inebriate themselves and for this practice in particular make use of an herb called *vilca*, pouring its juice

in *chicha* or drinking it by another way. Note that even though it is said that only old women practice the craft of divination and of telling what happens in remote places and to reveal loss and thievery, it is also used today by Indians not only by the old but also by the young.

Felipe Guamán Poma de Ayala (1980: 57), in his *El primer nueva corónica y buen gobierno,* written circa 1612–16, provided the following recipe for the preparation of a potion with vilca as one of its basic ingredients: "They had the custom of purging themselves each month with a purge known among them as *bilca tauri.* Three pairs of weighed grain are mixed with macay, ground and drunk by mouth and the other half is ingested below with a medicine [*melecina* in the original] and a clyster called *vilcachina.* This gave them much strength for battle and enhanced their health, and their lives lasted the time of two hundred years and they ate with much delight."

This particular oral preparation includes two other ingredients in addition to vilca seeds. The appellative *bilca tauri* suggests that *tauri,* or *tawri,* was used as an ingredient in the preparation of this purge. *Tawri* usually refers to the seeds of *Lupinus mutabiles,* a highland cultivar (Guamán Poma de Ayala 1980: 1102), with no psychoactive properties attributed to it. Cristóbal de Albornoz (in Duviols 1967: 36) described *macay,* the third ingredient, as a substance so powerful that a small amount added to a drink would cause a strong inebriation. Albornoz further stated that this plant was frequently used in ancient native rites and ceremonies.

Anadenanthera seeds are essential ingredients of *llampu,* a potent concoction used in ceremonial payments to mountain deities known as *wamanis;* it wards against illnesses caused by these deities. In addition to vilca seeds, *llampu* includes grains of corn (only large-grain white corn is used), *wayluru* (*Cytharexylon herrerae*) seeds, coca seeds, one pair of white carnation flowers, and lastly, pieces of two minerals. There must be pairs of all ingredients, which are ground to a powder and added to the ceremonial drink (Isbell 1978: 155–57).

Bernabé Cobo (1964: 272), writing circa 1653, identified vilca as a tree the size of an olive tree, which produced flat pods containing shiny brown seeds shaped like small coins. He noted that its seeds were added to chicha. Reports of visionary fermented drinks are included in early colonial reports but are not specific as to ingredients. Garcilaso de la Vega ([1609] 1970: 499) documented a particularly strong chicha, known as *uiñapu,* made from sprouted corn: "Some Indians, more passionate about inebriation than the rest of the community, steep the corn (*sara*) until it begins to sprout. They then grind it and boil it in the same water as other things. Once this is strained it is kept until it ferments. A very strong drink, which intoxicates immediately, is thus produced." The evocative name of *chicha con ojos* (*ñabiyoc*) is given to a drink that forms part of sacrificial rituals (Duviols 2003: 359). This sixteenth-century document briefly describes a drink made from a large quantity of corn that forms an oily skin suggestive of eyes. It is reasonable to assume that chicha sometimes served as a base beverage to which various plants were added to provoke effects appropriate to locality and situation.

The Archaeological Evidence

Archaeological evidence for psychoactive potions is difficult to identify. I am unaware of published chemical analysis of archaeological chicha residues. Unlike smoking and snuffing, which require distinctive paraphernalia specific to their respective tasks, the sole presence of elaborate drinking vessels should not be seen as evidence of visionary potions. In some instances, iconographic evidence could reveal probable use of psychoactive beverages. Moche and Wari iconography provide evidence to explore the possibility of such potions in pre-Columbian cultures.

Moche fine-line painting, perhaps the most descriptive of all Andean art forms, provides us with an iconographic sample large enough to allow a glimpse into the probability of an *Anadenanthera*-based potion consumed in pre-Columbian times. The Moche occupied the arid north coast of present-day Peru, near the modern city of Trujillo, between circa AD 100 and 800. Depiction of *Anadenanthera* trees in Moche ceramics was first proposed by Peter Furst (1974: 84), based on the design of a Moche IV pottery dipper painted with a deer-hunting scene (figure 9.4). The bipinnate compound leaves and the sinuate, irregularly contracted pods with cuspidate apices are all characteristic of *Anadenanthera* (see Donnan 1976: 104, fig. 88; Furst 1974: 84, fig. 18). In addition, in Moche ceramics, the tree is represented with its typical slightly arched branches. All these features clearly distinguish this genus from other leguminous trees abundant throughout the western slopes of the Andes and along the Pacific coast such as algarrobo (*Prosopis* sp.) and espino (*Acacia macracantha*). Usually the tree is represented in Moche pottery, but in some instances only pods or seeds are shown.

It could be argued that *Anadenanthera* is not the tree represented in Moche pottery, since it does not currently grow in Moche territory; instead, the depicted tree could be identified as algarrobo. However,

Figure 9.4. Deer hunting scene painted on a Moche pottery dipper from the north coast of Peru (after Furst 1974: fig. 18). Donna McClelland, PH.PC.001, Christopher B. Donnan and Donna McClelland Moche Archive, 1963–2011, Image Collections and Fieldwork Archives, Dumbarton Oaks, Trustees for Harvard University, Washington, D.C.

algarrobo is a generic term used in Spanish to refer to diverse American leguminous trees similar to the tree known in southern Spain as algarrobo (*Ceratonia siliqua* L., carob tree, St. John's bread). In Peru, Bolivia, and northern Chile, the term usually refers to species of *Prosopis*. Algarrobo notably differs from *Anadenanthera* species in generally being a contorted tree shaped by the winds (Arabic exonym *al-Gherīb*, "of the winds"), in contrast to *Anadenanthera*, with its slightly arched branches and bifurcated trunk (figure 9.5). *Anadenanthera* pods are constricted between the seeds, while *Prosopis* pods present a smoother profile. The tree represented in Moche pottery clearly resembles *Anadenanthera* in the form of its trunk, its branches, and the profile of its seedpods.

Figure 9.5. Ceramic vessel with representation of *Anadenanthera* trees and lizards (29.2 × 15 cm), Moche, circa AD 500–650, Peru. (By permission of Michael C. Carlos Museum, coll. number 1989.8.78, Emory University, Atlanta, Ga.; photograph by Michael McKelvey.)

Many native groups import visionary plants from areas far from their place of residence. The pre-Columbian inhabitants of the Atacama procured *Anadenanthera* seeds from neighboring northwestern Argentina (Angelo and Capriles 2000; Pérez Gollán and Gordillo 1994; Torres 1998). Among the Yanomamo, villages proximate to wild or feral populations of *Anadenanthera* trees may specialize in the trade of its seeds, which are peeled, then packed into foot-long cylinders and traded over an extensive range. The Maruiá Waiká make annual trips to collect *Anadenanthera* seeds from trees growing in open pastures (Prance 1972: 236, fig. 14). The Wixárika (Huichol) of the Sierra Madre Occidental, Mexico, extensively use peyote (*Lophophora williamsii*) and make a long pilgrimage to Wirikuta (approximately 300 miles), located in the desert north of San Luis Potosí. Therefore, the absence of *Anadenanthera* populations in the Peruvian north coast does not preclude its use by the ancient Moche.

Anadenanthera representations are restricted to painted stirrup-spout vessels and ladles, where it is usually associated with a deer, identified by Donnan (1982: 236) as the white-tailed deer (*Odocoileus* sp.) (figures 9.4, 9.6). Male and female animals are depicted, although male representations are twice as common as female (Donnan 1982: 238). *Anadenanthera* trees generally form part of deer-hunting scenes. These seem to be ritualistic in character, since elaborately dressed individuals, sometimes with supernatural attributes, conduct the hunt. Several other factors reinforce the ritualistic or symbolic connotations of the hunt. For example, Donnan (1982: 246) remarked that evidence for eating deer meat was totally absent from the Moche archaeological record. In addition, the deer on Moche pottery are usually spotted. This is a rare feature on white-tailed deer, and a white spot that is sometimes painted on the deer's neck does not seem to occur in nature. The ritualistic nature of these scenes is reinforced by the constant presence of fruiting *Anadenanthera* trees.

There is no evidence for snuffing among the Moche; however, several scenes involving deer depicted on three stirrup-spout vessels suggest the possibility that *Anadenanthera* preparations might have been administered orally (figures 9.6–9.8). The first represents a scene that takes place within a clearly delimited space (figure 9.6). Above the scene, a personage is seated on a litter. Attached to this individual's nose is an element reminiscent of *Anadenanthera* seeds on other Moche vessels. Two elaborately dressed individuals hunting deer are assisted by dogs in contorted poses. Spruce ([1908] 1970, 2: 429) reported that Catauixí hunters administered *Anadenanthera* seed enemas to themselves and their hunting dogs "to clear their vision and render them more alert!" The Piro of the upper

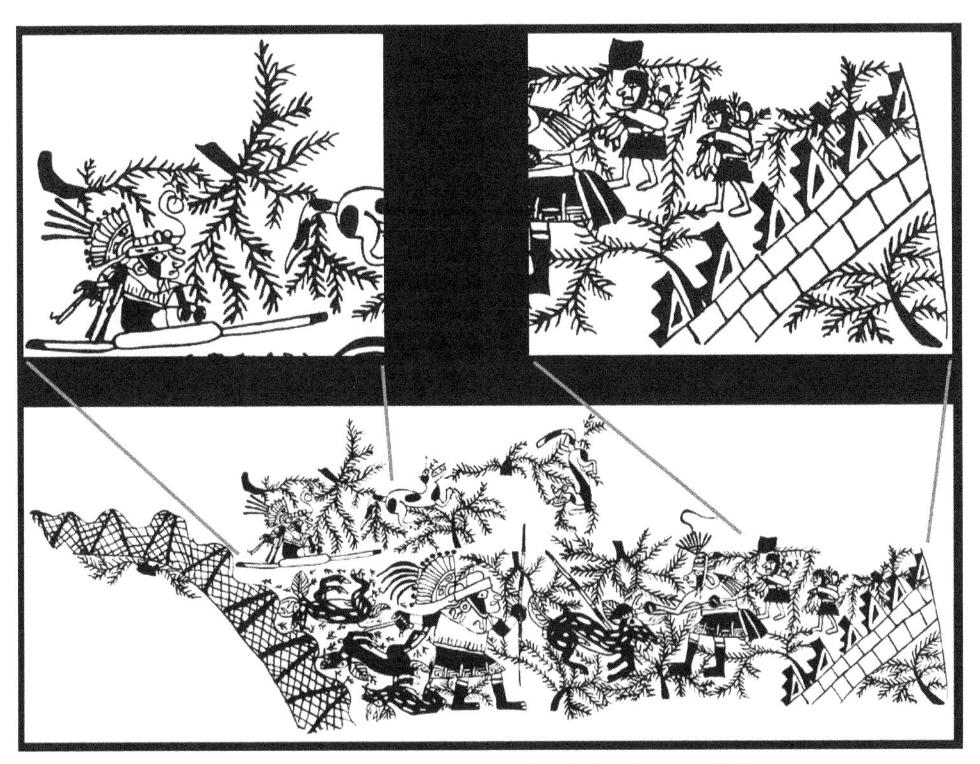

Figure 9.6. Scene from Moche stirrup-spout vessel with deer hunt, including a personage on a litter (*upper left*) and two human beings carrying jars decorated with tree branches (*upper right*). Donna McClelland, PH.PC.001, Christopher B. Donnan and Donna McClelland Moche Archive, 1963–2011, Image Collections and Fieldwork Archives, Dumbarton Oaks, Trustees for Harvard University, Washington, D.C. (after Donnan and McClelland 1999: fig. 6.57).

Ucayali River also gave *Anadenanthera* to their dogs prior to hunting. In this scene, to the right, next to a wall with stepped designs, walk two women (?) carrying jars with domed lids and attached branches that correspond in shape to those trees identified as *Anadenanthera* on vessels with deer hunt representations.

In the second of these vessels (figure 9.7), the two female figures are associated with seven jars with domed lids and attached *Anadenanthera* branches. The domed lids of two of the vessels are replaced by deer heads; the deer's nose attachment is similar to the one seen on the individual seated on the litter in the previous case (see figure 9.6). The deer heads substituting for the neck and lid of the jars suggest *Anadenanthera* as an ingredient of the liquid contained in these vessels. In the register above, an important personage and attendants are armed with spear throwers.

Figure 9.7. Scene from Moche stirrup-spout vessel with jars and deer heads. Donna McClelland, PH.PC.001, Christopher B. Donnan and Donna McClelland Moche Archive, 1963–2011, Image Collections and Fieldwork Archives, Dumbarton Oaks, Trustees for Harvard University, Washington, D.C. (after Donnan and McClelland 1999: fig. 4.50).

The third of these stirrup-spout vessels (figure 9.8) depicts a mutilated human being bound to a tree stump. The mutilated individual stands over a painted scene with elements similar to those on the second described vessel. On the lower register of the painted scene, a woman sits tending to jars with *Anadenanthera* branches while above her an individual standing on a platform and surrounded by armed attendants is offered a drinking cup.

Moche iconography related to the deer hunt provides rare evidence for the use of visionary potions by pre-Columbian inhabitants of South America. The constant association and identification of the deer with fruiting *Anadenanthera* trees and its association with these ceramic vessels and dippers underscore the possibility of oral administration among the Moche. This is further supported by a scene where the drink contained in the jars is offered to an important personage (figure 9.8).

Knobloch (2000), in her study of Wari ceramics found at the site of Conchopata, near Ayacucho, presents suggestive evidence for potions containing *Anadenanthera* seeds. She has identified an icon as a probable representation of *Anadenanthera* flowers, leaves, and seedpods (figure 9.9). She based her identification on a relatively realistic image painted on a Conchopata vessel. Numerous snuff trays from San Pedro de Atacama include the *Anadenanthera* icon. A stone snuff tray fragment from Tiahuanaco is inscribed with four undulating *Anadenanthera* icons. These icons are frequent in Tiwanaku iconography and are prominent on the Ponce monolith. Given the apparent absence of snuffing paraphernalia

Figure 9.8. Detail from Moche stirrup-spout vessel with personage being offered a drinking cup surrounded by armed individuals. (Line drawing by Donna Torres.)

in the Wari area, Knobloch (2000: 397–98) suggests that *Anadenanthera colubrina* could have been ingested as a drink. Citing Polo de Ondegardo (1916, 3: 29–30), she proposes that *A. colubrina* was added to chicha and was likely the beverage held by the large urns and jars found at Conchopata.

Several authors (Goldstein 2005: 208–10; Janusek 2004: 224; Moseley et al. 2005: 17267, figs. 5–6) have reported clear evidence of extensive chicha production at the archaeological sites of Tiahuanaco, Lukurmata, and Moquegua. Apparently, these archaic chichas, as reported in early colonial documents, might have contained vegetable admixtures to the fermented corn, molle (*Schinus molle*), or algarrobo (*Prosopis* spp.) base. Further knowledge of the components of archaeological chicha will contribute to the understanding of the origins and development of pharmacologically complex potions such as ayahuasca, yagé, and vino de cebil.

Ceramic fragment from Conchopata (after Knoblock 2000: Fig. 2)

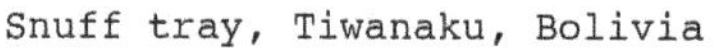

Snuff tray, Tiwanaku, Bolivia

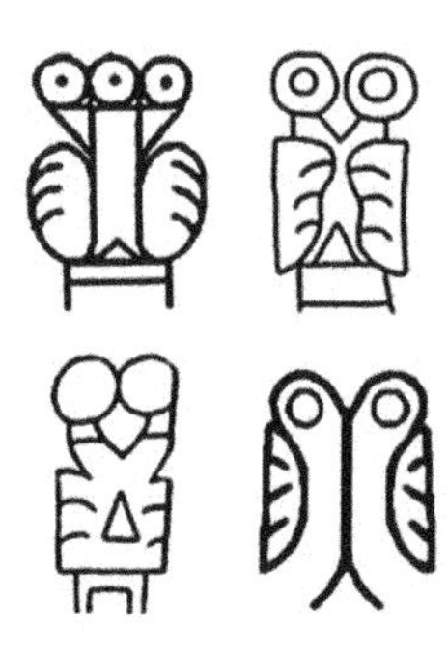

Details from snuff trays, San Pedro de Atacama, Chile

Figure 9.9. Diverse representations of the *Anadenanthera* icon: *top*, ceramic fragment from Conchopata (photo courtesy of Patricia Knobloch); *bottom left*, snuff tray, Tiwanaku, Bolivia; *bottom right*, details from snuff trays, San Pedro de Atacama, Chile.

Conclusions

The evidence suggests multiple origin locations for ayahuasca, yagé, and analogous potions, rather than a center from which a fixed recipe diffused. The presence of diverse potions with varying ingredients also supports this argument. In the Río Negro basin and in the middle to upper tributaries of the Orinoco, the simultaneous consumption of caapi and yopo could be seen as ayahuasca analogues. The Piaroa chew caapi stems for two to three hours prior to snuff inhalation to enhance and prolong the visionary state. When the Piaroa desire a particularly strong snuff experience, a potion with *Banisteriopsis* as the sole ingredient is ingested prior to the use of snuff (Rodd 2002, 2008). For the tropical grasslands (llanos) of the Orinoco basin in Colombia and Venezuela, the chewing and drinking of caapi prior to inhalation of powdered *Anadenanthera* seeds was a frequent modality for enhancement of the bufotenine present in the seeds. Concomitant use, as seen among the Piaroa and the Guahibo, could likely be a precursor to the invention of a complex potion such as ayahuasca or yagé, and it clearly indicates a knowledge of issues of plant synergy.

In the Andes, the addition of *A. colubrina* to a fermented sprouted corn, molle, or algarrobo base was another modality for tryptamine/β-carboline synergy. Bufotenine retains about one-third of its activity when ingested orally (Ott 2001: 279). Its potency as a smoke or snuff was well-known, a factor that could suggest to a user to seek ways to enhance its oral activity. Issues of plant availability could also motivate a search for more efficient ways to prepare and ingest psychoactive plants. A clear example can be seen in the preference for smoking, a somewhat wasteful method, in northwestern Argentina circa AD 300–900, where *A. colubrina* is abundant, and the emphasis on snuffing, a less wasteful means of ingestion, in San Pedro de Atacama, where *A. colubrina* is not present. Snuffing provides a more efficient and economical use of available seeds. The absence of *A. colubrina* on the western slopes of the Andes could have motivated a search for more effective ways of consumption and of enhancing and prolonging the oral activity of bufotenine.

The problem to be resolved in proposing chicha with an admixture of *Anadenanthera* seeds, as well as other plants, as a precedent for modern ayahuasca and yagé is whether there are β-carboline alkaloids present in the brew that could potentiate the psychoactive tryptamines. Ethanol is metabolized into several β-carbolines. It is converted by alcohol dehydrogenase into acetaldehyde. That compound readily reacts with tryptamines and catecholamines (epinephrine, norepinephrine, and dopamine) to produce both β-carbolines and isoquinolines. Drinking chicha could possibly potentiate, via these endogenous β-carbolines, any tryptamines ingested subsequently. It is also quite reasonable to speculate that within the plants used in the fermentation process, there is alcohol dehydrogenase (a widespread, common enzyme, found not only in mammals but also virtually everywhere in plants). This enzyme could then convert some of the ethanol produced during fermentation into β-carbolines and thus potentiate the tryptamines present when *Anadenanthera* seeds are added (Dennis McKenna, pers. comm., April 2012). This model would have to be tested in order to support a thesis of ancient Andean chicha-making traditions as precursors of ayahuasca and yagé.

As to the origins of present-day recipes for ayahuasca and yagé, I would suggest that northwestern Amazonia (see figure 9.1) might be the location of origin and that development occurred during the late pre-conquest period, contemporary with the period of Inca expansion (ca. AD 1350–1535). This region is a crossroads for exchange between the highlands and the tropical forest since pre-Columbian times; it is also an area relatively close to the Andean foothills. For example, connections between the Chavín culture (ca. 300–900 BC) and the Amazon are clear (Lathrap 1971). Sculpture in the Chavín style has been found in the upper drainage of the Marañon River, indicating accessibility and ideological exchange with the lowlands to the east of Chavín (Burger 2008: 163; Morales Chocano 2008: 148). Another example of Andean contact with the Amazon area is visible in the culture of San Agustín, circa 100 BC–AD 500, located on the eastern slopes of the Colombian Massif. San Agustín is characterized by the presence of numerous monumental stone sculptures. There are details in the sculpture that clearly connect San Agustín with Amazonian cultures. The Caquetá River and tributaries provide low passes that serve as a direct route to the Amazon River. Stone sculptures in the San Agustín style have been found in the upper Caquetá River region (Friede 1946: 196; Silva Celis 1963: 397). These two examples of pre-Columbian cultures relatively close to the area where the development of ayahuasca probably took place suggest the possibility of Andean contributions to the development of Amazonian visionary potions.

Concomitant practices such as those of the Piaroa and the Guahibo, including the chewing and drinking of caapi to prepare for snuffing sessions, combined with knowledge of fermented drinks with the addition of vilca seeds, as well as other unknown plant ingredients, could have motivated a search of the local flora to create the numerous potions and plant combinations referred to today as ayahuasca and yagé. These two potions are evidence of a dynamic pharmacopoeia, constantly being invented and reinvented in search of access to alternative states of consciousness.

Additional evidence for the recent invention of ayahuasca (*Banisteriopsis* plus *Psychotria viridis*) is apparent in its distribution pattern in the Peruvian Amazon. From northwestern Amazonia the use of ayahuasca may have spread following routes of colonial/missionary expansion (Shepard 2014: 16). Brabec de Mori (2011) proposes, first, an expansion from the Tukano or their predecessors to Kichwa speakers related to Jesuit missions in Ecuador and Peru; second, to the Quechua de Lamas (in Lamas province) and Shawi people (in Loreto province); and third, up the Ucayali and to the Brazilian state of Acre, probably associated with the movements of rubber workers (Brabec de Mori 2011: 42). In its movement to the southwest, ayahuasca reached the Shipibo about two centuries ago (Brabec de Mori 2014: 207). Gow (2015: 57) demonstrates how the Piro of the Urubamba River in Peru may have known the existence of ayahuasca circa 1880, although they did not incorporate it into their shamanic techniques until much later, probably circa 1930. Gow (2015: 45) further proposes that ayahuasca is a recent introduction to shamanic and pharmacological practices of indigenous populations of the southwestern Amazon (Gow 2015: 45). The recent distribution of ayahuasca in western Amazonia supports a date for the creation of ayahuasca sometime circa AD 1550–1650.

Archaeological evidence for ancient use of visionary potions is difficult to document. The information provided by Cobo, Ondegardo, and others implies that chicha was employed in the Central Andes during the Late Horizon (ca. AD 1350–1535) as a basic or primary beverage to which psychoactive plants, including vilca, were added. Moche and Wari iconography provide suggestive evidence of such use in Peru, circa AD 300–900. Consequently, it is probable that potions and brews analogous to ayahuasca were in use in the Central Andes and adjacent coast circa AD 500.

The evidence suggests multiple origin locations interacting with each other to create a variety of plant combinations and methods of administration (drinking, smoking, snuffing, enemas) appropriate to location, not a fixed recipe that diffused out from a single center. Instead, a concept related to issues of plant interaction with the intention of modulating states of consciousness was conceived, enabling the creation of visionary preparations not limited by regional plant availability.

Acknowledgments

I am indebted to Carlo Brescia, Jace Callaway, Luis Eduardo Luna, Dennis McKenna, Jonathan Ott, and Giorgio Samorini for generously sharing their knowledge of ayahuasca botany, pharmacology, and history.

References Cited

Aguado, P. de. 1956. *Recopilación historical.* 4 vols. Bogotá: Biblioteca de la Presidencia de Colombia.

Aguerre, A., A. F. Distel, and C. Aschero. 1975. Comentarios sobre nuevas fechas en la cronología arqueológica precerámica de la Provincia de Jujuy. *Relaciones Sociedad Argentina de Antropología,* n.s., 9: 211–214.

América Indígena. 1986. *Chamanismo y uso de plantas del género* Banisteriopsis *en la hoya amazónica.* Proceedings of a symposium organized by Luis Eduardo Luna, XLV Congreso Internacional de Americanistas, Bogotá, July 7–11, 1985. *América Indígena* 46 (1). Mexico City: Instituto Indigenista Interamericano.

Angelo, D., and J. Capriles. 2000. La importancia de las plantas psicotrópicas para la economía de intercambio y relaciones de interacción en el Altiplano Sur Andino. *Complutum* (Universidad Complutense de Madrid) 11: 275–84.

Aschero, C., and H. Yacobaccio. 1994. 20 años después: Inca Cueva 7 reinterpretado. Resúmenes del XI Congreso de Nacional de Arqueología Argentina, San Rafael, Argentina.

Beyer, S. V. 2009. *Singing to the Plants: A Guide to Mestizo Shamanism in the Upper Amazon.* Albuquerque: University of New Mexico Press.

Beyer, S. V. 2012. On the Origins of Ayahuasca. *Singing to the Plants: Steve Beyer's Blog on Ayahuasca and the Amazon,* April 25. www.singingtotheplants.com/2012/04/on-origins-of-ayahuasca/.

Bird, J. 1948. Preceramic Cultures in Chicama and Virú. In *A Reappraisal of Peruvian Archaeology,* ed. W. C. Bennett, 21–28. Memoirs of the Society for American Archaeology no. 4. Menasha, Wis.: Society for American Archaeology and Institute of Andean Research.

Bondeson, W. E. 1972. Tobacco from a Tiahuanacoid Culture Period. In *A Medicine-Man's Implements and Plants in a Tiahuanacoid Tomb in Highland Bolivia,* by S. H. Wassén, 177–84. Etnologiska Studier 32. Gothenburg, Sweden: Göteborgs Etnografiska Museum.

Brabec de Mori, B. 2011. Tracing Hallucinations: Contributing to a Critical Ethnohistory of Ayahuasca Usage in the Peruvian Amazon. In *The Internationalization of Ayahuasca,* ed. B. C. Labate and H. Jungaberle, 23–47. Performances: Intercultural Studies on Ritual, Play and Theatre / Performanzen: Interkulturelle Studien zu Ritual, Spiel und Theater Series 16. Berlin: LIT Verlag.

Brabec de Mori, B. 2014. From the Natives Point of View: How Shipibo-Kanibo Experience and Interpret Ayahuasca Drinking with "Gringos." In *Ayahuasca Shamanism in the Amazon and Beyond,* ed. B. C. Labate and C. Cavnar, 206–30. Oxford: Oxford University Press.

Bruhn, J. G., B. Holmstedt, and J.-E. Lindgren. 1995. Natema, the Hallucinogenic Drink of the Jivaro Indians of Ecuador: An Ethnopharmacological Study of Rafael Karsten's Collection from 1917. *Acta Americana* (Swedish Americanist Society, Uppsala) 3 (2): 161–80.

Burger, R. L. 2008. The Original Context of the Yauya Stela. In *Chavín Art, Architecture and Culture,* ed. W. Conklin and J. Quilter, 163–79. Los Angeles: Cotsen Institute of Archaeology, University of California.

Burroughs, W., A. Ginsberg, and O. Harris. 2006. *The Yage Letters Redux.* San Francisco, Calif.: City Lights Books.

Califano, M. 1976. El chamanismo Mataco. *Scripta Ethnologica* 3 (2): 7–60.

Chantre y Herrera, J. 1901. *Historia de las misiones de la Compañía de Jesús en el Marañón español.* Madrid: Imprenta de A. Avrial.

Cobo, B. 1964. *Historia del Nuevo Mundo.* Biblioteca de Autores Españoles 91, 92. Madrid: Ediciones Atlas.

Da Mota, C. N. 1997. *Jurema's Children in the Forest of Spirits: Healing and Ritual among Two Brazilian Indigenous Groups*. London: Intermediate Technology Publications.
Donnan, C. B. 1976. *Moche Art and Iconography*. UCLA Latin American Center Publications. Los Angeles: University of California.
Donnan, C. B. 1982. La caza del venado en el arte Mochica. *Revista del Museo Nacional* (Lima) 46: 235–51.
Donnan, C. B., and D. McClelland. 1999. *Moche Fineline Painting: Its Evolution and Its Artists*. Los Angeles: Fowler Museum of Cultural History, University of California.
Duviols, P. 1967. Un inédit de Cristóbal de Albornoz: "La instrucción para descubrir todas las guacas del Pirú y sus camayos y haziendas." *Journal de la Societé des Americanistes* (Musée de l'Homme) 55 (2): 497–510.
Duviols, P. 2003. *Procesos y visitas de idolatrías: Cajatambo, siglo XVII*. Travaux de l'Institut Français d'Études Andines 94. Lima: Pontificia Universidad Católica del Perú.
Fernández Distel, A. 1980. Hallazgo de pipas en complejos precerámicos del borde de la Puna Jujeña (Republica Argentina) y el empleo de alucinógenos por parte de las mismas culturas. *Estudios Arqueológicos* (Universidad de Chile, Antofagasta) 5: 55–75.
Friede, J. 1946. Migraciones indígenas en El Valle del Alto Magdalena. In *Compilación de apuntes arqueológicos, etnológicos, geográficos y estadísticos del municipio de San Agustín*, ed. T. López M., 193–2013. San Agustín, Colombia: Coopgráficas.
Furst, P. T. 1974. Hallucinogens in Precolumbian Art. In *Art and Environment in Native America*, ed. M. E. King and I. R. Traylor, 50–101. Lubbock: Museum of Texas Technological University.
Goldstein, P. S. 2005. *Andean Diaspora: The Tiwanaku Colonies and the Origins of South American Empire*. Gainesville: University Press of Florida.
Gonçalves de Lima, O. 1946. Observações sobre o "vinho da *Jurema*" utilizado pelos indios Pancaru de Tacaratu (Pernambuco). *Arquivos* 4: 46–50.
Gow, P. 2015. Methods of Tobacco Use among Two Arawakan-Speaking Peoples in Southwestern Amazonia: A Case Study of Structural Diffusion. In *The Master Plant: Tobacco in Lowland South America*, ed. A. Russell and E. Rahman, 45–61. London: Bloomsbury Academic.
Gragson, T. L. 1997. The Use of Underground Plant Organs and Its Relation to Habitat Selection among the Pumé Indians of Venezuela. *Economic Botany* 51 (4): 377–84.
Guamán Pomo de Ayala, G. 1980. *El primer nueva corónica y buen gobierno*. Ed. J. V. Murra and R. Adorno, trans. J. L. Urioste. Colección América Nuestra-América Antigua. Mexico City: Siglo Veintiuno.
Holmstedt, B., and J. E. Lindgren. 1967. Chemical Constituents and Pharmacology of South American Snuffs. In *Ethnopharmacologic Search for Psychoactive Drugs*, ed. D. H. Efron, B. Holmstedt, and N. S. Kline, 339–73. Public Health Service Publication 1645. Washington, D.C.: U.S. Department of Health, Education, and Welfare.
Isbell, B. J. 1978. *To Defend Ourselves: Ecology and Ritual in an Andean Village*. Austin: Institute of Latin American Studies, University of Texas.

Janusek, J. W. 2004. *Identity and Power in the Ancient Andes: Tiwanaku Cities through Time*. New York: Routledge.

Knobloch, P. J. 2000. Wari Ritual Power at Conchopata: An Interpretation of *Anadenanthera colubrina* Iconography. *Latin American Antiquity* 11 (4): 387–402.

Koch-Grünberg, T. 2005. *Dois anos entre os indígenas: Viagens no noroeste do Brasil (1903/1905)*. Manaus, Brazil: EDUA (Editora da Universidade Federal do Amazonas) and FSDB (Facultade Salesian Don Bosco). Originally published in 1909–10 in 2 vols. under the title *Zwei Jahre unter den Indianern: Reisen in nordwest-Brasilien 1903/1905* (Berlin: Ernst Wasmuth).

Labate, B. C., and C. Cavnar, eds. 2014. *Ayahuasca Shamanism in the Amazon and Beyond*. Oxford Ritual Studies. Oxford: Oxford University Press.

Lathrap, D. W. 1971. The Tropical Forest and the Cultural Context of Chavín. In *Dumbarton Oaks Conference on Chavín*, ed. E. Benson, 73–100. Washington, D.C.: Dumbarton Oaks Research Library and Collection.

Luna, L. E. 1986. *Vegetalismo—Shamanism among the Mestizo Population of the Peruvian Amazon*. Stockholm Studies in Comparative Religion 27. Stockholm: Almqvist and Wiksell International.

Magnin, J. 1988. *Breve descripcion de la Provincia de Quito, en la América meridional, y de sus misiones de sucumbíos de religiosos de S. Franc[isc]o, y de Maynas de P.P. de la Comp[añi]a de JHS a las orillas del gran río Marañón, hecha para el mapa que se hizo el año 1740*. In *Noticias auténticas del famoso río Marañón y misión apostólica de la Compañía de Jesús de la Provincia de Quito en los dilatados bosques de dicho río, escribialas por los años de 1738 un misionero de la misma compañía*, ed. J. P. Chaumeil, 463–92. Colección Monumenta Amazónica, Serie B. Iquitos: Instituto de Investigaciones Científicas de la Amazonía Peruana.

Maroni, P. 1988. *Noticias auténticas del famoso río Marañón y misión apostólica de la Compañía de Jesús de la Provincia de Quito en los dilatados bosques de dicho río, escribialas por los años de 1738 un misionero de la misma compañía*, ed. J. P. Chaumeil, 4–325. Colección Monumenta Amazónica, Serie B. Iquitos: Instituto de Investigaciones Científicas de la Amazonía Peruana.

Medeiros, G. 2006. L'usage rituel de la Jurema chez les Indigènes du Brésil colonial et les dynamiques des frontières territoriales du Nord-Est au XVIIIe siècle. In *Colloque Internationale "Las sociedades fronteirizas del Mediterráneo al Atlántico (ss. XVI–XVII),"* ed. M. Bertrand and N. Planas, 1–20. Madrid: Casa de Velazquez.

Monterio de Noronha, J. A. 2006. *Roteiro da viagem da cidade do Pará até as últimas colônias do sertão da província (1768)*. Documenta Uspiana 1. São Paulo: Editora da Universidade de São Paulo.

Morales Chocano, D. 2008. The Importance of Pacopampa Architecture and Iconography in the Central Andean Formative. In *Chavín Art, Architecture and Culture*, ed. W. Conklin and J. Quilter, 143–60. Los Angeles: Cotsen Institute of Archaeology, University of California.

Moseley, M. E., D. J. Nash, P. R. Williams, S. D. deFrance, A. Miranda, and M. Ruales. 2005. Burning Down the Brewery: Establishing and Evacuating an Ancient Imperial Colony at Cerro Baúl, Peru. *Proceedings of the National Academy of Sciences of the United States* 102 (48): 17264–71.

Ogalde, J. P., B. T. Arriaza, and E. C. Soto. 2009. Identification of Psychoactive Alkaloids in Ancient Andean Human Hair by Gas Chromatography/Mass Spectrometry. *Journal of Archaeological Science* 36: 467–72.
Ondegardo, J. Polo de. 1916. Informaciones acerca de la religión y gobierno de los Incas. In *Colección de libros y documentos referentes a la historia del Perú*, vols. 3 and 4. Lima: H. H. Urteaga.
Ott, J. 1994. *Ayahuasca Analogues: Pangaean Entheogens.* Kennewick, Wash.: Natural Products Company.
Ott, J. 1996. *Pharmacotheon: Entheogenic Drugs, Their Plant Sources and History.* Kennewick, Wash.: Natural Products Company.
Ott, J. 1998. Pharmahuasca, Anahuasca and Vinho da Jurema: Human Pharmacology of Oral DMT Plus Harmine. *Yearbook for Ethnomedicine and the Study of Consciousness* 7: 251–71 (double issue of *Yearbook for Ethnomedicine* 6 and 7, 1997/98). Berlin: Verlag für Wissenschaft und Bildung.
Ott, J. 2001. Pharmañopo-Psychonautics: Human Intranasal, Sublingual, Intrarectal, Pulmonary and Oral Pharmacology of Bufotenine. *Journal of Psychoactive Drugs* 33 (3): 273–81.
Oyuela-Caycedo, A., and N. C. Kawa. 2015. A Deep History of Tobacco in Lowland South America. In *The Master Plant: Tobacco in Lowland South America*, ed. A. Russell and E. Rahman, 27–44. London: Bloomsbury Academic.
Pané, R. 1999. *An Account of the Antiquities of the Indians.* Durham, N.C.: Duke University Press. Spanish version, *Relación acerca de las antigüedades de los Indios* (Mexico City: Siglo Veintiuno Editores).
Pérez Gollán, J. A., and I. Gordillo. 1994. *Vilca/Uturuncu:* Hacia una arqueología del uso de alucinógenos en las sociedades prehispánicas de los Andes del Sur. *Cuicuilco* 1 (1): 99–140.
Pinkley, H. V. 1969a. Etymology of *Psychotria* in View of a New Use of the Genus. *Rhodora* 71: 535–40.
Pinkley, H. V. 1969b. Plant Admixtures to Ayahuasca, the South American Hallucinogenic Drink. *Lloydia* 32: 305–14.
Prance, G. T. 1972. Ethnobotanical Notes from Amazonian Brazil. *Economic Botany* 26 (3): 221–37.
Reichel-Dolmatoff, G. 1944. La cultura material de los indios Guahibo. *Revista del Instituto Etnológico Nacional* 1 (2): 437–506.
Reichel-Dolmatoff, G. 1978. *Beyond the Milky Way: Hallucinatory Imagery of the Tukano Indians.* Los Angeles: Latin American Center Publications, University of California.
Reis Altschul, S. von. 1964. A Taxonomic Study of the Genus *Anadenanthera. Contributions from the Gray Herbarium of Harvard University* 193: 3–65.
Reis Altschul, S. von. 1972. *The Genus* Anadenanthera *in Amerindian Cultures.* Cambridge, Mass.: Botanical Museum, Harvard University.
Rocha, J. 1905. *Memorandum de viaje (regiones Amazónicas).* Bogotá: Casa Editorial de *El Mercurio.*
Rodd, R. 2002. Snuff Synergy: Preparation, Use and Pharmacology of *Yopo* and *Banisteriopsis caapi* among the Piaroa of Southern Venezuela. *Journal of Psychoactive Drugs* 34 (3): 273–79.

Rodd, R. 2008. Reassessing the Cultural and Psychopharmacological Significance of *Banisteriopsis caapi*: Preparation, Classification and Use among the Piaroa of Southern Venezuela. *Journal of Psychoactive Drugs* 40 (3): 301–7.

Samorini, G. 2016. *Jurema, la pianta della visione: Dai culti del Brasile alla psiconautica di frontiera*. Milan: ShaKe Edizioni.

Sampaio-Silva, O. 1997. *Tuxá: Índios do Nordeste*. São Paulo: Annablume Editora.

Schleiffer, H. 1974. *Sacred Narcotic Plants of the New World Indians: An Anthology of Texts from the Sixteenth Century to Date.* New York: Hafner Press, Macmillan Publishing.

Schultes, R. E. 1957. The Identity of the Malpighiaceous Narcotics of South America. *Botanical Museum Leaflets* 18 (1): 1–56.

Schultes, R. E., and A. Hofmann. 1980. *The Botany and Chemistry of Hallucinogens.* Springfield, Ill.: Charles C. Thomas.

Shepard, G. H., Jr. 2014. Will the Real Shaman Please Stand Up? The Recent Adoption of Ayahuasca among Indigenous Groups of the Peruvian Amazon. In *Ayahuasca Shamanism in the Amazon and Beyond*, ed. B. C. Labate and C. Cavnar, 16–39. Oxford: Oxford University Press.

Silva Célis, E. 1963. Movimiento de la civilización agustiniana por el Alto Amazonas. *Revista Colombiana de Antropología* 13: 389–400.

Simson, A. 1886. *Travels in the Wilds of Ecuador and the Exploration of the Putumayo River*. London: Sampson Low, Marston, Searle, and Rivington.

Spruce, R. 1873. On Some Remarkable Narcotics of the Amazon Valley and Orinoco. *Ocean Highways: The Geographical Review* (London), n.s., 1: 184–93.

Spruce, R. (1908) 1970. *Notes of a Botanist in the Amazon and the Andes.* New York: Johnson Reprint.

Torres, C. M. 1998. Psychoactive Substances in the Archaeology of Northern Chile and Northwest Argentina. *Chungará* 30 (1): 49–63.

Trout, K. 2008. Old Hair and Tryptamines. *Entheogen Review* 16 (4): 146–49.

Vega, G. de la. (1609) 1970. *Royal Commentaries of the Incas, and General History of Peru*. Part 1. Trans. H. V. Livermore. Austin: University of Texas Press.

Wassén, S. H. 1965. Introduction to *The Use of Some Specific Kinds of South American Indian Snuff and Related Paraphernalia*, 7–114. Etnologiska Studier 28. Gothenburg, Sweden: Göteborgs Etnografiska Museum.

Wassén, S. H. 1967. Anthropological Survey of the Use of South American Snuffs. In *Ethnopharmacologic Search for Psychoactive Drugs*, ed. D. H. Efron, B. Holmstedt, and N. S. Kline, 233–89. Public Health Service Publication 1645. Washington, D.C.: U.S. Department of Health, Education, and Welfare.

Wassén, S. H. 1972. *A Medicine-Man's Implements and Plants in a Tiahuanacoid Tomb in Highland Bolivia*, 7–114. Etnologiska Studier 32. Gothenburg, Sweden: Göteborgs Etnografiska Museum.

10

A Synonym for Sacred

Vilca Use in the Preconquest Andes

MATTHEW P. SAYRE

The many reasons why people seek to alter their daily lives and reach for something beyond their normal experience vary as greatly as do the means by which they seek to do so (Bell 1992, 1997; Geertz 1973). Intoxication has many quotidian and ritual manifestations, and this volume considers these divergent aspects of past plant use and emphasizes that intoxicants should be understood as broader elements of social life as opposed to simply an attempt to flee the social realm. In many modern states, intoxication is often understood to be the result of the overconsumption of alcohol (Dietler 2006) or a temporary escape from regimented life and a behavior solely suited for informal events (Douglas 1987). Intoxication, however, can also be codified and mandated. In fact, religions often contain practices that alter the mind without the use of pharmacopeia (Bell 1992, 1997; Rappaport 1999). For example, the physical processes of fasting, praying, and chanting over extended periods of time can lead to altered states capable of producing visions (Luhrmann 2012). The combination of physical exertion and movement, as well as the previously mentioned instances of "natural" mind-altering activities, may have been combined with sacred plant consumption in some instances.

Plants can occupy critical roles in religious practice and discourse and change behavioral practice when they are consumed for their consciousness-altering qualities (Schultes et al. 2001). In many ancient societies, plants capable of producing visions were used in medicinal or religious practice (Burger 1992; Rafferty and Mann 2004; Sayre and Bruno 2017; Wilbert 1987). While all plants can be toxic, those with the special ability to temporarily alter the mental state can acquire particular resonance and power. These plants may have been considered conduits to the gods or gods in their own right (Schultes et al. 2001).

The widespread use of mind-altering plants in preconquest South America is well documented (Burger 1992; Cobo [1653] 1997; Schultes et al. 2001). According to Schultes et al. (2001: 30), there are more than 130 hallucinogenic plants used in the New World, as compared to only 50 in the Old World. There is no botanical reason to assume that this is a natural difference; rather, there appears to have been a more concerted search for these traits on the part of the pre-Columbian societies of the Americas.

This expansive pre-Columbian experimentation with and mastery of the diverse uses of the local flora does not mean that certain plants were not more favored than others. Rather, increased paleoethnobotanical research appears to indicate that certain plants were widely used and traded because of their unique or mind-altering characteristics (Hastorf 2003). Thus, although there was a widespread pharmacopeia available to local peoples, certain plants were found to be more useful for trade and use. This chapter presents evidence that one plant in particular, *vilca* (*Anadenanthera* sp.), was the most widely traded and consumed in the preconquest Andes.

This chapter considers the role that vilca, in particular, filled in preconquest rituals in the Andes, with a special focus placed on its use at the site of Chavín de Huántar in Peru, a ceremonial center that was clearly associated with the use of mind-altering plants (Burger 1992; Rick 2008; Sayre 2014). The greater consideration of how widespread vilca use was in the ancient Andes is an important question that also elucidates broader activities such as trade routes, procurement strategies, and similarities in ritual activities across time and space. Vilca use in the past is addressed through two central means. The first point is methodological; it is an examination of how context can determine the relevance of a find. In this instance, I examine the physical nature of material remains and where they were or could be recovered. The second is a historio-cultural point about the formal space of the temple where particular activities occurred. In this instance, priests and sacred plants are contextualized as being in codified in/out relations that vary based on relationships with ritual participants. These concerns shape how we understand vilca use in the ancient Andes.

Vilca Growth and Use in the Ancient Americas

The vilca plant (*Anadenanthera colubrina*) is also known as yopo or cebil outside of the Central Andes (figure 10.1). Additionally, a separate species (*Anadenanthera peregrina*) was often used in the northern tropical regions of the continent; this species later spread to the islands of the Caribbean (see Kaye, chapter 6, this volume). The Taínos of the Bahamas appear in the earliest reference to smoking tobacco and inhaling the powder of vilca seeds (Las Casas 1909, cited in Torres and Repke 2006). The contemporary use of *Anadenanthera* is also practiced by groups such as the Yanomamo, the Uwa-Tunebo, and the Otomac, among others in the Orinoco area of northern South America.

The importance of this plant can also be traced through the relatively widespread use of it as a place-name or toponym (figure 10.2). As mentioned previously, the vilca plant is also known as yopo outside of the

Figure 10.1. *Anadenanthera colubrina* tree and seedpods.

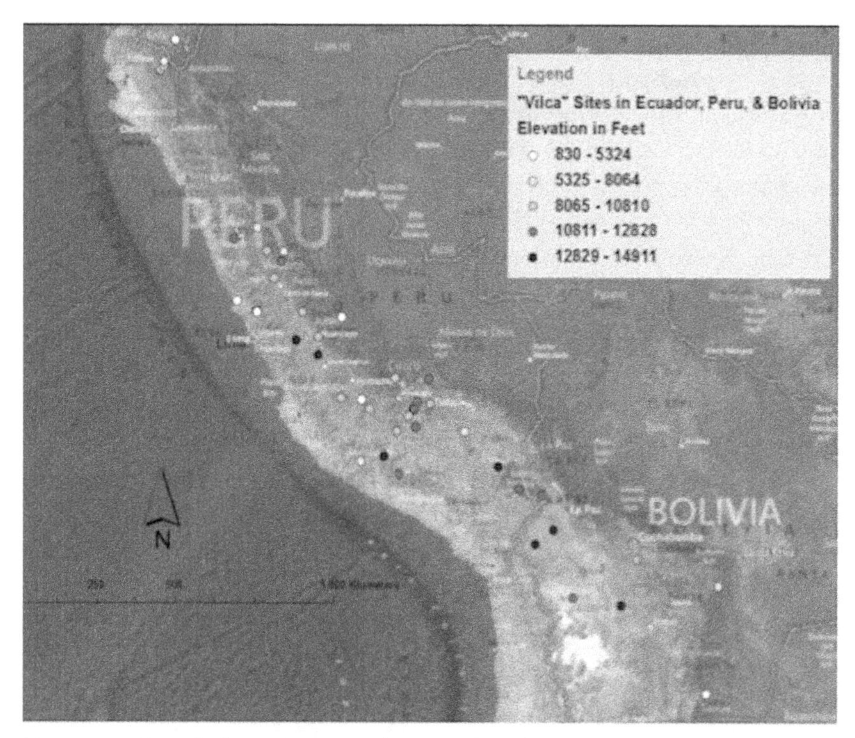

Figure 10.2. Map of vilca toponyms in the Central Andes. (Courtesy of Jeff Stup.)

Central Andes. Searches for yopo-derived toponyms did not reveal regular place-name associations; by contrast, vilca regularly features in Quechua- and Aymara-language toponyms.

The common occurrence of vilca place-names across the Central Andes would seem to correlate primarily with the use of this plant. However, the term *vilca* does not solely refer to the plant, so the toponyms may also have other connotations: The exact sense of *vilca* in the manuscript (Salomon and Urioste 1991) is uncertain but perhaps related to a contemporaneous Aymara word meaning both "sun" and "shrine" (Bertonio [1612] 1956: 386). Internal evidence (chap. 31, sec. 417) suggests that in the Huarochiri context it means a person who has entered into the society of *huacas* by achievement or marriage. In the Tratado (Arguedas and Duviols 1966: 209), the word *vilca* is translated as "a very important *cacique*" (*cacique muy principal*; see also Zuidema 1973: 19). In Huanchor village in 1621, the founding hero Huanchor was mummified and housed underneath a huaca called *Huanchorvilca* (Arguedas and Duviols 1966: 264). Overall, the implication seems to be that a vilca is a human being who partakes of a huaca's status (Salomon and Urioste 1991: 46).

The antiquity of vilca plant use is the subject of ongoing research. The presence of mortars and snuffing trays was documented in the early Spanish chronicles, as was the need to remove these activities from the natives' ritual practices:

> They have another kind of *huacas* that are called *vilcas*. . . . They heal and purge themselves with it and are also buried with it in most provinces of this kingdom. It should be noted that some wood or stone carvings resembling sheep, and with a hole as in an inkwell (which is where this *vilca* is pulverized), must be found and destroyed. This is called *vilcana*, and it is adored and revered. These *vilcanas* are made out of many different beautiful stones and strong woods. They have, in addition to this *vilca*, many other types of *vilcas*, especially purgatives. (Cristóbal de Albornoz, written ca. 1580 [Duviols 1967], cited in Torres and Repke 2006: 28)

These vilcas and vilcanas were noted to be like huacas, or sacred stones/places that were considered to have great power and received offerings. The Spanish priests had multiple agendas, but one of them was diverting offerings from the old gods to the new churches being built. In addition, plants that could change consciousness and perception were associated with past ritual activity and were not well-known in Catholic practice, so these practices were also the subject of extirpation.

Chavín's Place in the Ancient Andes

Chavín de Huántar has often been portrayed as the emblematic site of the Early Horizon/Formative period in the Central Andes (Burger 1992; Kaulicke and Onuki 2010). The central Peruvian site is approximately equidistant from the Pacific coast and the Amazonian jungle. This early temple, occupied circa 1200–500 BCE (Rick et al. 2011), is one of the earliest examples of complex ceremonial architecture in the highlands. As Burger (1985) and Williams Leon (1985) noted, there were clear antecedents, such as Cardal and Garagay, on the coast for many of the architectural forms constructed at Chavín. The site is considered a core site of the Early Horizon, now commonly referred to as the Formative period, owing in part to the importance of its iconography (Burger 1992). The staff god and some of the core Chavín imagery may appear earlier at other sites west and south of Chavín, suggesting that this site is more of a culmination of the Early Horizon phase than the instigator of it (Shady Solis and Leyva 2003).

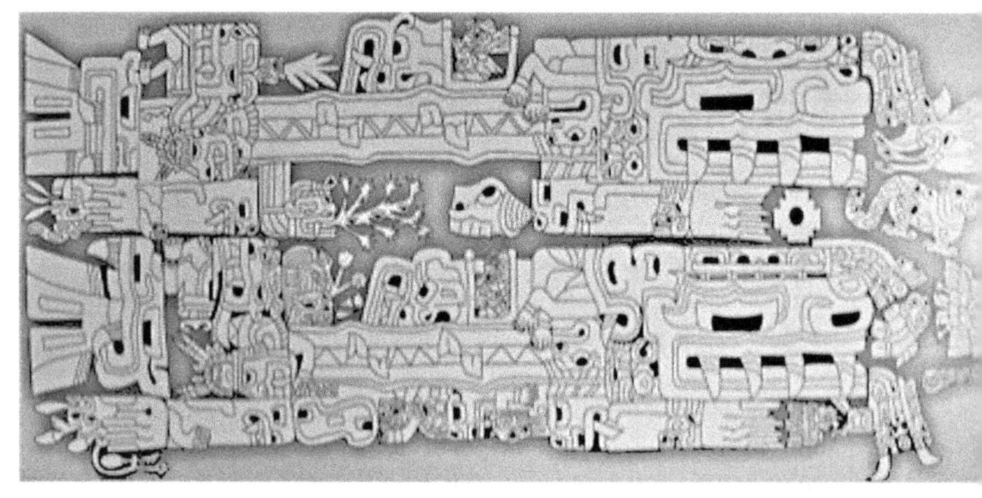

Figure 10.3. Tello Obelisk plant images. Museo Nacional Chavín de Huántar, Chavín de Huántar, Peru. (Photograph by M. Sayre.)

The Formative in the Central Andes was a period when hierarchical social organization was becoming entrenched (Lumbreras 1989). This temporal reality, when combined with the elaborate planning evident in the construction of the site, could lead to the conclusion that this was an early polity engaged in capturing labor or surplus production. Alternatively, the site is sometimes presumed to have been a peaceful pilgrimage center that attracted devotees from across the Central Andes (Burger 1992). It also was located within a relatively short distance of trade routes that extended from the coast or the eastern jungles. In conjunction with its preeminent status in Andean archaeology and a corpus of studies of its elaborate iconography, there have been many inferences concerning resource use at Chavín.

Chavín has long attracted the gaze of archaeobotanists, drawn by its iconic imagery of lowland plants featured on the Tello Obelisk (figure 10.3). This image appears to depict yuca or cassava (*Manihot esculenta*), achira (*Canna edulis*), peanuts (*Arachis hypogea*), chile peppers (*Capsicum* sp.), and bottle gourds (*Lagenaria* sp.) (Burger 1992; Lathrap 1973). Interestingly, some scholars have suggested that the iconography depicted sacred plants/hallucinogens used at the site.

The psychoactive substances that were possibly ritually consumed at the site include San Pedro cactus (*Trichocereus pachanoi*), whose active alkaloid is mescaline; *huacacachu* or *floribunda* (*Brugmansia* sp.), with many tropane alkaloids; ayahuasca (*Banisteriopsis caapi*, along with other ingredients), with indole alkaloids; vilca or cebil (*Anadenanthera colubrina*), with bufotenine and indole alkaloids; *epená* (*Virola theiodora*), with indole alkaloids; and tobacco (*Nicotiana tabacum*), with nicotine (Burger 1992, 2011; Cordy-Collins 1980; Peñaloza 1984; Schultes et al. 2001; Torres 2008). However, among these species, the only one unequivocally depicted on the iconography is San Pedro cactus, a plant of local highland origins; on this, many scholars refer to the work of Cordy-Collins (1980) and Sharon (2000). Cordy-Collins's analysis of the shamanic textiles revealed that many of the elements of Chavín iconography, interpreted as depicting shamans on trancelike voyages, were repeated on coastal textiles. This work established the broad scale use of San Pedro on the Peruvian coast.

Peñaloza (1984) completed a unique interpretation of the Tello Obelisk in which she hypothesized that all of the plants depicted on the obelisk were hallucinogens used in rituals at the site. While it has often been noted that there are images of shamans and San Pedro on Chavín's iconography, Peñaloza's research opens up the question of whether Lathrap and others may have misidentified some of the botanical elements on the Tello Obelisk. This possibility deserves consideration, as the Chavinos clearly were not obsessed with realism in their depictions of the natural world: plants and animals often had their exact forms distorted to emphasize talons, fangs, leaves, and other enigmatic or powerful elements. Although the core of Peñaloza's hypothesis is plausible, her emphasis on angel's trumpets (*Brugmansia* sp.) may be misplaced, as this plant may not have been extensively used in ayahuasca until after the conquest (Torres and Repke 2006). Regular consumption of San Pedro cactus and vilca—two plants more readily available in the highland Central Andes—at the site seems more probable. These two plants would produce vastly different bodily experiences that could last short periods of time or persist much longer: the inclusion of vilca in chicha (beer commonly prepared from maize) was reportedly a practice in Inca times (Torres and Repke 2006), and this process could have enhanced the effects of both the alcohol and the hallucinogen.

Chavín's iconography and stone sculpture include other references to sacred plants. Direct depictions of this important plant include images of a priest marching with a San Pedro cactus (figure 10.4), as well as a tenon head with the same cactus protruding from its head. Also, many of the tenon heads have been interpreted as depicting human faces in various states of transformation into animal-like beings. These faces in metamorphosis are thought to represent religious practitioners entering

Figure 10.4. Priest carrying San Pedro cactus, from the Circular Plaza. (Photograph courtesy of Nick Weiland.)

a dream or hallucinogenic state in which they could interact with other supernatural beings in a different world (Burger 1992; Torres 2008).

Chavín has clear evidence for the use of certain hallucinogenic plants, but the physical evidence for the use of some of these plants and compounds is not always clear. A significant portion of the literature on the use of hallucinogens in South America focuses on the use of ayahuasca, known as the magic drink of the Amazon (Schultes et al. 2001). While this potent combination of plants (traditionally *Banisteriopsis* sp. and at least two other ingredients, such as *Brugmansia* sp.) is capable of producing intense visions, it can also cause permanent damage to the cerebral system. The connections between ayahuasca and its use in rituals at Chavín and other early temples frequently relied on ethnographic analogies to native Colombian tribal practices documented by Reichel-Dolmatoff (1975, 1978). Recent work has begun to question whether ayahuasca was used in preconquest times (Torres and Repke 2006). There is little to no evidence for its use in the early chronicles, and as a result, all claims to its use in the archaeological past should prompt questions about the nature of the evidence.

Torres (2008: 239) has presented four types of evidence for the use of psychoactive plants at Chavín de Huántar: (1) remains of psychoactive plants; (2) implements related to use of psychoactive materials; (3) representations of psychoactive plants; and (4) depictions of the use of psychoactive materials. His excellent review of the major iconographic evidence at Chavín for the use of sacred plants is a starting point for much of this discussion.

These conjectures, including interpretations of shamanic transformation in the sculptural remains, have ensured that discussions of sacred plant use in the Americas almost always reference Chavín without acknowledging that, as of yet, there has been no direct botanical evidence of these practices. Recent work by Rick (2008) and Torres (2008) has suggested that shamanic practices were deployed at the site, although the appropriateness of the term *shamanism* has been contested, given that, as in South America, it is usually reserved for societies, unlike Chavín, without monumental architecture (Moore 2005: 116).

The next sections present evidence about Andean religious practices as well as botanical data. The data vary from physical remains to iconographic representations of plants and are analyzed in conjunction with a discussion of theoretical and methodological possibilities. These topics help illuminate how intoxicating rites, particularly those involving vilca and the use of mind-altering plants at Andean sites, may have been experienced or practiced at Chavín. The pattern of alternating constricting and intimate spaces with open and communal spaces helps reveal whether certain sectors of the monument were intended for public or private events. The transition between spaces is analyzed in conjunction with the possible use of distinct sacred plants in these different realms. In addition to variations in consumption practices, there likely were also associated differences in the quantities and relative status of the people involved.

Priests, Diseases, and Curing

The distance between modern peoples and the subjects they are trying to interrogate can be difficult to breach. One telling example of this is when modern scholars attempt to imagine a world in which the germ theory of disease was not the dominant paradigm. In the West, germ theory was not acknowledged until the late nineteenth century, and Western medicine until the twentieth century was not capable of fighting most bacterial or viral infections. The only sources for combating these diseases were plant remedies or combinations of spiritual beliefs and quixotic cures (Latour 1993).

The belief in "bad vapors" or "bad air" was an initial attempt at modeling how disease could spread invisibly between patients. While certain non-Western texts, such as the Atharvaveda, do describe living organisms as being capable of infecting humans, this line of thought was not always the dominant discourse in the preindustrial world (Zysk 1985).

Bad spirits could be considered the causes of disease. The modern-day *mesa* ceremonies on the Peruvian coast involving San Pedro use can provide a corollary for this concept. In this instance, San Pedro is imbibed to grant the healer insight into the life of the patient so that the healer can see who or what may be responsible for his/her maladies. This is a cultural practice in which disease and suffering are thought to be caused by bad thoughts, poor choices, and willful competition. These bad airs and sicknesses can essentially be counterattacked with ceremonies conducted under the influence of San Pedro (Sharon 2000).

Archaeological Evidence and Botanical Data

The paleoethnobotanical identification of intoxicating plants is rare and methodologically complex. Some of the plants (for example, epená and vilca) leave chemical signatures that are quite similar (Torres et al. 1991). Projects associated with Hastorf's work at Chiripa in Bolivia have attempted to discern whether phytoliths can be used to investigate the trade and use of sacred plants (Logan 2006). This work has determined that there may be diagnostic phytoliths (microscopic plant silica that preserve over long periods of time) capable of revealing these practices, but as of yet, the archaeological record has not readily revealed the presence of hallucinogenic plants.

In my own work at Chavín, I have collected samples of scrapings from the insides of bone tubes for gas chromatography–mass spectrometry (GCMS) analysis, but they unfortunately were too small for analysis. While Torres and colleagues (2001) had samples weighing 10 grams in Atacama, in my case, the samples gathered from possible snuff tubes have not been found in conjunction with larger pieces of botanical material, and this lack of material has made it difficult to test for active chemical

Table 10.1. Sacred plants with diagnostic phytoliths

Scientific name	Common name	Plant family	Plant part tested[a]
Anadenanthera colubrina	Vilca	Fabaceae	Seed, pod
Banisteriopsis caapi	Ayahuasca	Malpighiaceae	Bark, leaf
Datura inoxia	Thorn-apple	Solanaceae	Seed, leaf

Source: Logan 2006.
Note: [a] Plant parts that contain diagnostic phytoliths.

compounds. The preservation conditions at arid San Pedro de Atacama were clearly superior to those of the wet/dry-season climate of Chavín. Future work is needed to accurately estimate what size the samples need to be in order to search for the key alkaloids present in vilca and other sacred plants.

Bone tubes and snuffing trays found at Chavín were likely used for the consumption of mind-altering biotica but could instead have been decorative elements or had multiple uses that we have not yet considered. The tubes were commonly constructed from bird bones, which are naturally hollow; however, others were carved from larger bones. Bone tubes were found by Tello, Lumbreras, Burger, Rick, Mesia, and Sayre, among others (Burger 2011; Mesia 2007; Sayre 2010). In many instances, they were carved with natural imagery and stylistic elements commonly found on ceramics from the site. The snuffing trays discussed by Burger (1992) and others appear to be constructed from whalebone, and it is difficult to see them as having some use other than for grinding and consuming plants. These obviously exotic goods were brought to the site from the coast, although recent evidence from the La Banda region has not determined whether these materials were brought to the site fully constructed or the materials were worked into their particular forms at the site. Additionally, there is the possibility that snuffing tubes were made from natural plant reeds, which would not easily preserve in the botanical record.

The iconographic evidence for San Pedro use has been further clarified by recent research (Rick 2008). The lower remnant of the image from the plaque of the shamanic figure (see figure 10.4) removed any doubts that remained about whether the image depicted a being carrying a cactus or a staff (a symbol of power recurrent in Chavín iconography), as it clearly represents the former.

In excavations conducted at the site to date, there have been no San Pedro seeds found; however, there are seeds from other members of the family Cactaceae (Sayre 2010). Macrobotanical evidence is not necessarily the clearest indication of sacred plant use, since certain plants native

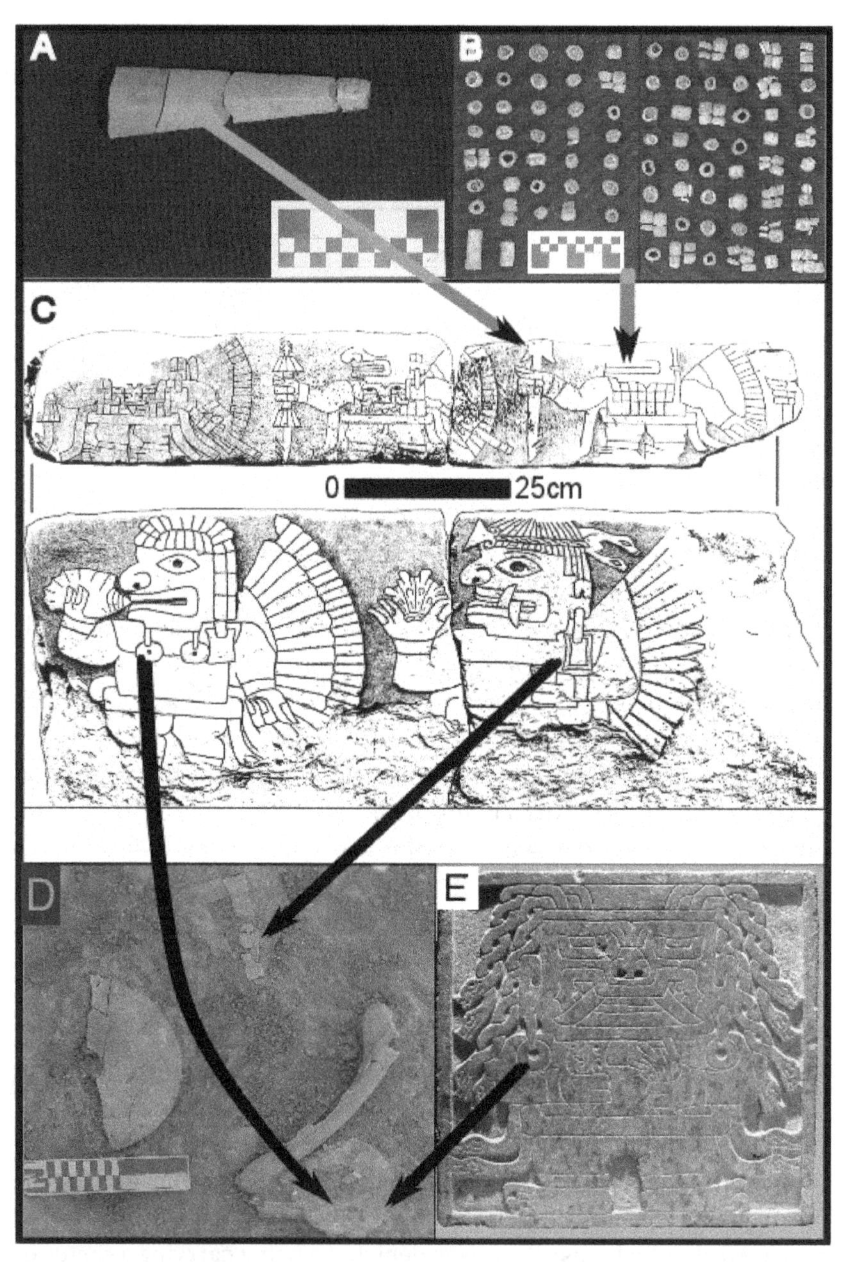

Figure 10.5. La Banda artifacts in relation to iconography of priests (*C*) from the monumental center: *A*, lithic artifact from La Banda sector; *B*, bone beads from La Banda sector; *C*, iconography depicting priests in procession; *D*, artifacts from La Banda sector made from marine mammal bone; *E*, iconography from site depicting ear spools. (Drawing courtesy of J. Rick; photographs by the author.)

to the region, notably San Pedro, may enter the archaeological record as environmental indicators rather than as products of ritual practice. The presence of San Pedro seeds would not be indicative of use of the cactus in hallucinogenic drinks, as this part of the plant is not used in the preparation of the cactus beverage; instead, the stalk is the central element used in the preparation of the beverage, and it is cooked along with other herbs, many of which are noted for their biomedical properties (Schultes et al. 2001: 168). In addition, varieties of *Brugmansia* species are not uncommonly added to the beverage. However, the four-sided varieties are rare and were highly prized by humans (Sharon 2000), so physical evidence of those exact remains may be taken as more convincing evidence for human usage.

There are certainly rare instances when human beings are found in direct association with sacred plants and their associated paraphernalia. The Atacama case was an example of Pompeii-like activity preservation (Torres et al. 1991). In that instance, the burial of a person dressed in shamanic or priestly garb was found with a bag containing vilca seeds and snuff trays. The excellent preservation of these remains, found in the Atacama desert, is highly unusual and cannot be expected for studies in less arid regions.

In the La Banda sector, excavations of the domestic region (located across the Mosna River from the main temple at Chavín), we found evidence of priestly dwellings (Sayre 2010). Within these spaces there were hearths, a central formal patio, and walled corridors. In one of the major rooms off of the main patio, there was abundant evidence for the production of ceremonial goods for use by priests. Ear spools, ceremonial projectile points, bone beads, and shells were found in this unit (K-13), and these finds can be seen on the iconography from the ceremonial center (figure 10.5). There were also more than twenty tubes made from bird bone, four possible tablets or spatulas made from camelid and cervid long bones, and eight spoons from camelid skull and long bones (Rosenfeld, pers. comm., 2012). Of course, many of these artifacts could have had multiple uses, but their presence, interpreted in light of the vilca snuff kits excavated in San Pedro de Atacama, is significant (Torres et al. 1991).

These finds lead to a dichotomous and unexpected result. The temple iconography appears to have clear and direct connections to some of the physical remains found in the La Banda region. Yet if San Pedro seeds had been directly recovered from this area, that would not be clear evidence for the use of this plant in the preparation of a hallucinogenic beverage, because, as mentioned above, the plant is common in the region but the seeds are not used in the beverage. Thus, what seems to be direct data (as opposed to indirect iconographic data) may actually be weaker data. In contrast, vilca macrobotanical remains, because of their relatively contained distribution, do provide clear evidence for the exchange of a hallucinogenic plant, but the iconographic depictions of the plant are more abstract than those of San Pedro (Burger 2011). The artifactual correlates found for images in the iconographic record should redirect analysis away from the constant search for one-to-one material correlates and toward a more nuanced research into all categories of evidence.

Experience: Inclusive and Exclusive

The difficulties in determining botanical practices do not limit the questions that the possible use of these plants provokes, such as How were these practices experienced spatially? Who was allowed to use these plants? Where and when were they provided? and Who carried them to Chavín?

The architecture of the main temple area in Chavín leads to the possibility that the open spaces may have been used for the consumption of chicha by large numbers of people, while the galleries and enclosed spaces, such as the Lanzón Gallery, may have been where hallucinogens were consumed by small numbers of participants in conjunction with priests. The large and open spaces appear to lead toward smaller enclosed spaces that become more common over time (Kembel 2008; Rick 2008).

Research conducted outside of the ceremonial core (Burger 1984; Contreras 2007; Mesia 2007; Sayre 2010) has revealed evidence of domestic deposits and, in limited cases, direct support for houses and other domestic structures (figure 10.6). These remains rarely contain evidence of ritual deposits, and there have been few instances of caches of elaborate artifacts found outside of the ceremonial center itself. The people living in the regions immediately surrounding the temple presumably created a mental division between sacred and profane space. The excavated domestic areas all have easy access to the temple itself and may have actually been the living spaces of people who controlled or managed the temple. While there has been conjecture about the nature of Chavín's political organization (Lumbreras 2007; Rick 2008), precisely how profound the differences were between members of different status groups remains unclear. Burger (1984) proposed that there was an upper and a lower class, but attempts at proving this divide in other domestic regions of the site have been less than convincing.

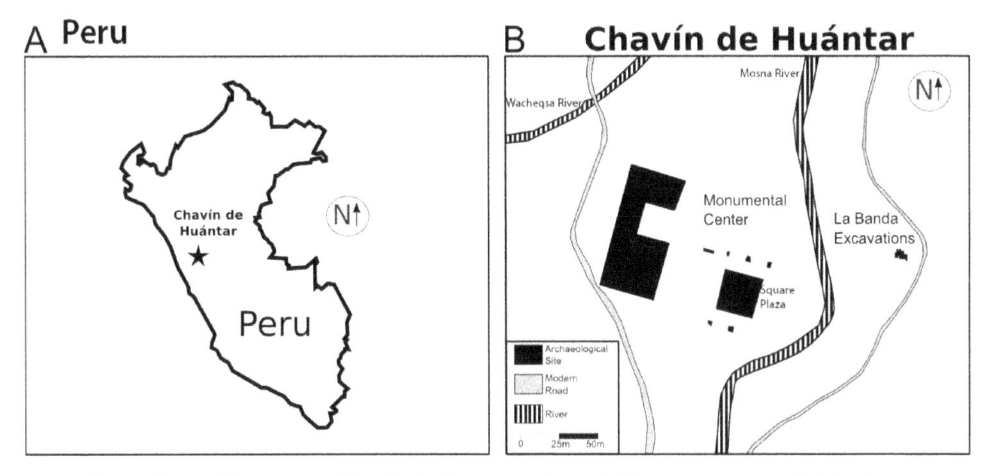

Figure 10.6. *A*, Location of Chavín de Huántar in Peru. *B*, Site map showing La Banda sector excavations to the east of the main temple.

The clear indication is that the occupants of the shelters and dwelling spaces immediately surrounding the temple had access to the sacred region and that they participated or managed rites in that space. These people would have left their place of dwelling, crossed a liminal space, and entered the temple (Rowe 1963). The classic division between the ritual and the domestic would not have been absolute, but the material remains excavated to date do lead us to the conclusion that there was some sense of difference between the areas and a need to conduct oneself differently in the temple. The people who constructed, cleaned, and worshipped at the temple of Chavín almost certainly did not actually reside in the temple itself. Over the course of decades of research, there has been little evidence of domestic debris within the ceremonial center or in the immediate areas surrounding the temple (Burger 1992; Lumbreras 2007; Tello 1943). While offerings of food and drink have been found (Lumbreras 1989), these were considered to be evidence of rites and singular activities rather than remains of quotidian practices. The area where participants entered the temple and the movement across its space may provide insight into the structure of local rituals, as well as providing evidence of when and where certain sacred plants may have been used.

The procession route of participants in temple rites seems fairly clear (Rick 2008: 24). The recent discovery of the formal entrance to the circular plaza revealed numerous visual elements that would have both included and excluded participants in the rites (Rick, pers. comm., 2011). The ceremonial core of the site is separated by many architectural structures (figure 10.6). The square plaza is a large open-air space that could have contained well over two thousand people—although there is debate about whether this was actually a public space. This was likely the space of initial events that would have led from there to more-contained and limited spaces. The next probable space for ritual activities would be in front of the black and white portal, an area where standing participants could have gazed up to see priests descending on hanging staircases, which ended in midair, down from the temple's roof. From there, likely a limited number of people would have followed the stairway to the north of them up and then down into the circular plaza. Here their view of the rest of the monument would have been limited, and they would have seen only the staircases back to the areas from which they had come or up into the Lanzón Gallery and over to the other main galleries (Rick 2008). Finally, there are other galleries and structures in the West Field, but the use and layout of these spaces are not well understood. The general pathway described here begins in a large communal setting and heads into increasingly constricted and singular spaces where small numbers of individuals could have been led and instructed by priests of the temple (Rick 2008).

Processions would have passed through the Atrium on their way to the Circular Plaza to the east. Both of these spaces were surrounded by walls and other structures that limited sight lines, and they were bounded by entrances to the underground galleries (Rick 2008). Flotation samples from the Atrium yielded sprouted maize, suggesting that maize chicha may have been consumed in that area (Sayre 2010: 122).

That the galleries themselves are capable of producing altered states and that the mazes were difficult to navigate are noteworthy. The Chavín mazes may have been confusing for both fasting participants and those under the influence of sacred plants. The confined labyrinths of the chambers in the main temples would have provided a claustrophobic environment where the music provided by the shell trumpets, *pututus*, would have reverberated off the walls and in the minds of the inhabitants (Kolar 2017; Rick 2008). In the larger galleries, new research demonstrated that there are architectural acoustic mechanisms that link the pututus with the sounding oracle, or the Lanzon (Kolar et al. 2012).

The priests shown in figure 10.5 may have been some of many who engaged in formal processions both for the masses and for the select few who were invited into the galleries. These priests portrayed in the site's iconography were not necessarily solely mediating human concerns with the divine; they may actually have been channeling the divine and embodying divine beings during important rites. This increased connection would have provided more incentives for pilgrims to the site to interact with temple priests.

Conclusions

As mentioned earlier, Torres (2008: 239) presented four types of evidence for the use of psychoactive plants at Chavín de Huántar: psychoactive plant remains, implements related to the use of psychoactive materials, representations of psychoactive plants, and depictions of the use of psychoactive materials. This hierarchy of evidence indicates that chemical analysis may reveal much about when and where sacred plants were used at Chavín. However, to date, the insufficiency of organic material associated with the paraphernalia has prevented any successful chemical residue analysis. That being said, the material remains recovered to date make it clear that the iconography and other seemingly more inference-dependent forms of evidence may have material correlates in the archaeological record (figure 10.5). My research in La Banda has documented direct connections between the site's iconography and artifacts recovered in the ground (Sayre et al. 2016). There are also remains of snuff tubes, and these tools are primarily associated with the use of vilca. These findings should cause researchers to question the assumed reliability of different forms of evidence. In this case, we have seen that the iconographic representations can be real and that the presence of "real" San Pedro seeds, from a locally occurring plant whose seeds are not used in the production of the mind-altering beverage, could lead to false conclusions.

Most of the intoxicants (other than San Pedro) described in this paper would have come from outside of Chavín's immediate sphere. This is also true of vilca. The production and use of these plants would have led to increased trade or travel of gift-bearing peoples. These same people surely carried these plants along with their sustenance. When trade or exchange of the sacred plants by people interested in participating in Chavín's sacred world occurred, the bearers of these plants would have had to interact with the local power structure.

Mind-altering plants did not commonly have widespread distributions in the preconquest Americas. Tobacco (*Nicotiana tabacum*) and maize (*Zea mays*), the latter of which was commonly fermented, were widely distributed. But other plants that could likely adapt to a variety of environments, such as coca (*Erythroxylum* sp.), were not known to have spread out of South America into Central America (Plowman and Hensold 2004). The widespread distribution of vilca and its lack of clear economic uses other than those discussed in this chapter lead to a unique consideration. This plant was widely acknowledged to provide visions, and it appears to have been easily transported. And as Torres's discussion of the use of yopo in this volume (chapter 9) demonstrates, these *Anadenanthera* species were cultivated and traded widely across the Americas, affirming their importance in rituals and curing practices in many lands and cultural traditions, not solely those that referred to it as *vilca*.

This volume should serve to contextualize our exoticization of the past and also to exoticize our daily existence. Tobacco in ancient South America (Wilbert 1987) would never have been assumed to be a habitual product consumed twenty or more times a day, nor would hallucinogenic plants be primarily conceived as a means of relating to music. The experience of consuming psychoactive plants in ancient times would have been a social activity—part of broader rituals that occurred at restricted moments in time, invoking disparate realms of religious practice—and one that was constrained and ruled by local practices.

References Cited

Arguedas, J. M., trans., and P. Duviols, ed. 1966. *Dioses y hombres de Huaorichirí: Narración quechua recogido por Francisco Avila* [1598]. Lima: Instituto Francés de Estudios Andinos, Instituto de Estudios Peruanos.

Bell, C. M. 1992. *Ritual Theory, Ritual Practice*. New York: Oxford University Press.

Bell, C. M. 1997. *Ritual: Perspectives and Dimensions*. New York: Oxford University Press.

Bertonio, L. (1612) 1956. *Vocabulario de la lengua aymara*. La Paz, Bolivia: Don Bosco.

Burger, R. 1984. *The Prehistoric Occupation of Chavín de Huántar, Peru*. University of California Publications in Anthropology. Berkeley: University of California Press.

Burger, R. 1985. Concluding Remarks: Early Peruvian Civilization and Its Relationship to the Chavín Horizon. In *Early Ceremonial Architecture in the Andes*, ed. C. B. Donnan, 262–89. Washington, D.C.: Dumbarton Oaks.

Burger, R. 1992. *Chavin and the Origins of Andean Civilization*. London: Thames and Hudson.

Burger, R. 2011. What Kind of Hallucinogenic Snuff Was Used at Chavín de Huántar? An Iconographic Identification. *Ñawpa Pacha* 31 (2): 123–40.

Cobo, B. (1653) 1997. *Inca Religion and Customs*. Trans. R. Hamilton. Austin: University of Texas Press.

Contreras, D. A. 2007. Sociopolitical and Geomorphologic Dynamics at Chavín de Huántar, Peru. PhD diss., Stanford University.

Cordy-Collins, A. 1980. An Artistic Record of the Chavín Hallucinatory Experience. *Masterkey for Indian Lore and History* 54 (3): 84–93.

Dietler, M. 2006. Alcohol: Anthropological/Archaeological Perspectives. *Annual Review of Anthropology* 35: 229–49.
Douglas, M. 1987. *Constructive Drinking: Perspectives on Drink from Anthropology.* International Commission on Anthropology of Food and Food Problems. Editions de la Masion des Sciences de L'homme. Cambridge: Cambridge University Press.
Duviols, P. 1967. Un inédit de Cristóbal de Albornoz: La instrucción para descubrir todas las guacas del Pirú y sus camoyos y haziendas. *Journal de la Societé des Americanistes* 55 (2): 497–510.
Geertz, C. 1973. *The Interpretation of Cultures: Selected Essays.* New York: Basic Books.
Hastorf, C. 2003. Andean Luxury Foods: Special Food for the Ancestors, Deities and the Elite. *Antiquity* 77 (297): 545–54.
Kaulicke, P., and Y. Onuki. 2010. *Las cronologías del formativo: 50 años de investigaciones japonesas en perspectiva.* Lima: Fondo Editorial Pontificia Universidad Católica del Perú.
Kembel, S. 2008. The Architecture of the Monumental Center of Chavín de Huántar: Sequence, Transformation, and Chronology. In *Chavín: Art, Architecture, and Culture*, ed. W. J. Conklin and J. Quilter, 35–81. Monograph 61. Los Angeles: Cotsen Institute of Archaeology.
Kolar, Miriam A. 2017. Sensing Sonically at Andean Formative Chavín de Huántar, Perú. *Time and Mind* 10 (1): 39–59.
Kolar, M. A., J. W. Rick, P. R. Cook, and J. S. Abel. 2012. A Multidisciplinary Methodology for Studying Ancient Auditory Environments. Paper presented at the AAAS Annual Meeting, Vancouver, Canada.
Las Casas, B. de. 1909. *Apologetica historia de Las Indias.* Historiadores de Indias 1. Madrid: Nueva Biblioteca de Autores Españoles.
Lathrap, D. W. 1973. Gifts of the Cayman: Some Thoughts on the Subsistence Basis of Chavín. In *Variation in Anthropology: Essays in Honor of John McGregor*, ed. D. W. Lathrap and J. Douglas, 91–105. Urbana: Illinois Archaeological Survey.
Latour, B. 1993. *We Have Never Been Modern.* Cambridge, Mass.: Harvard University Press.
Logan, A. L. 2006. The Application of Phytolith and Starch Grain Analysis to Understanding Formative Period Subsistence, Ritual, and Trade on the Taraco Peninsula, Highland Bolivia. Master's thesis, University of Missouri, Columbia.
Luhrmann, T. M. 2012. *When God Talks Back: Understanding the American Evangelical Relationship with God.* New York: Alfred A. Knopf.
Lumbreras, L. G. 1989. *Chavín de Huántar en el nacimiento de la civilización Andina.* Lima: Instituto Andino de Estudios Arqueologicos.
Lumbreras, L. G. 2007. *Chavín: Excavaciones arqueológicas.* Lima: Universidad Alas Peruanas (UAP).
Mesia, C. 2007. Intrasite Spatial Organization at Chavín de Huántar during the Andean Formative: Three Dimensional Modeling, Stratigraphy and Ceramics. PhD diss., Stanford University.
Moore, J. D. 2005. *Cultural Landscapes in the Ancient Andes: Archaeologies of Place.* Gainesville: University Press of Florida.

Peñaloza, E. Mulvany de. 1984. Motivos fitomorfos de alucinógenos en Chavín. *Chungará* 12: 57–80.

Plowman, T., and N. Hensold. 2004. Names, Types, and Distribution of Neotropical Species of *Erythroxylum* (Erythroxylaceae). *Brittonia* 56 (1): 1–53.

Rafferty, S. M., and R. Mann. 2004. *Smoking and Culture: The Archaeology of Tobacco Pipes in Eastern North America*. Knoxville: University of Tennessee Press.

Rappaport, R. A. 1999. *Ritual and Religion in the Making of Humanity*. Cambridge Studies in Social and Cultural Anthropology. Cambridge: Cambridge University Press.

Reichel-Dolmatoff, G. 1975. *The Shaman and the Jaguar: A Study of Narcotic Drugs among the Indians of Colombia*. Philadelphia: Temple University Press.

Reichel-Dolmatoff, G. 1978. *Beyond the Milky Way: Hallucinatory Imagery of the Tukano Indians*. UCLA Latin American Studies. Los Angeles: UCLA Latin American Center Publications.

Rick, J. W. 2008. Context, Construction, and Ritual in the Development of Authority at Chavín de Huántar. In *Chavín: Art, Architecture, and Culture*, ed. W. J. Conklin and J. Quilter, 3–34. Monograph 61. Los Angeles: Cotsen Institute of Archaeology.

Rick, J. W., R. Rick, S. Kembel, D. Contreras, M. Sayre, and J. Wolf. 2011. *La cronología de Chavín de Huántar y sus implicancias para el Periodo Formativo*. Boletín de Arqueología. Lima: Fondo Editorial Pontificia Universidad Católica del Perú.

Rowe, J. H. 1963. Urban Settlements in Ancient Peru. *Ñawpa Pacha* 1: 1–27.

Salomon, F., and G. L. Urioste. 1991. *The Huarochiri Manuscript: A Testament of Ancient and Colonial Andean Religion*. Austin: University of Texas Press.

Sayre, M. 2010. Life across the River: Agricultural, Ritual, and Production Practices at Chavín de Huántar, Perú. PhD diss., University of California–Berkeley.

Sayre, M. 2014. Ceremonial Plants in the Andean Region. In *Plants and People: Choices and Diversity through Time*, vol. 1, ed. A. Chevalier, E. Marinova, and L. Peña-Chocarro, 368–73. Earth Series 1. Oxford, U.K.: Oxbow Books.

Sayre, M., and M. Bruno, eds. 2017. *Social Perspectives on Ancient Lives from Paleoethnobotanical Data*. Cham, Switzerland: Springer.

Sayre, M., M. J. Miller, and S. Rosenfeld. 2016. Isotopic Evidence for the Trade and Production of Exotic Marine Mammal Bone Artifacts at Chavín de Huántar, Peru. *Archaeological and Anthropological Sciences* 8 (2): 403–17.

Schultes, R. E., A. Hofmann, and C. Rätsch. 2001. *Plants of the Gods: Their Sacred, Healing, and Hallucinogenic Powers*. Rev. ed. . Rochester, N.Y.: Healing Arts Press.

Shady Solis, R., and C. Leyva. 2003. *La ciudad sagrada de Caral-Supe: Los origenes de la civilizacion andina y la formacion del estado pristino en el antiguo Peru*. Proyecto Especial Arqueologico Caral-Supe. Lima: Instituto Nacional de Cultura.

Sharon, D. 2000. *Shamanism and the Sacred Cactus: Ethnoarchaeological Evidence for San Pedro Use in Northern Peru*. San Diego Museum Papers 37. San Diego, Calif.: San Diego Museum of Man.

Tello, J. C. 1943. Discovery of the Chavín Culture in Peru. *American Antiquity* 9 (1): 135–60.

Torres, C. M. 2008. Chavin's Psychoactive Pharmacopeia: The Iconographic Evidence. In *Chavín: Art, Architecture, and Culture*, ed. W. J. Conklin and J. Quilter, 239–59. Monograph 61. Los Angeles: Cotsen Institute of Archaeology.

Torres, C. M., and D. B. Repke. 2006. *Anadenanthera: Visionary Plant of Ancient South America.* New York: Haworth Herbal Press.
Torres, C. M., D. B. Repke, K. Chan, D. McKenna, A. Llagostera, and R. E. Schultes. 1991. Snuff Powders from Pre-Hispanic San Pedro de Atacama: Chemical and Contextual Analysis. *Current Anthropology* 32 (5): 640–49.
Wilbert, J. 1987. *Tobacco and Shamanism in South America.* New Haven, Conn.: Yale University Press.
Williams Leon, C. 1985. A Scheme of the Early Monumental Architecture of the Central Coast of Peru. In *Early Ceremonial Architecture in the Andes,* ed. C. B. Donnan, 227–40. Washington, D.C.: Dumbarton Oaks Research Library and Collection.
Zuidema, T. 1973. Kinship and Ancestorcult in Three Peruvian Communities: Hernández Príncipe's Account of 1622. *Bulletin de l'Institut Français d'Etudes Andines* 2 (1): 16–33.
Zysk, K. G. 1985. *Religious Healing in the Veda, with Translations and Annotations of Medical Hymns from the *Rgveda and the Atharvaveda and Renderings from the Corresponding Ritual Texts.* Transactions of the American Philosophical Society. Philadelphia: American Philosophical Society.

11

Ingredients Matter

Maize versus Molle Brewing in Ancient Andean Feasting

JUSTIN JENNINGS AND LIDIO M. VALDEZ

As in many other regions of the world, beer is an essential part of the feasts that structure South American societies. The Napo Runa of the Ecuadorian Amazon, for example, drink copious amounts of manioc beer at special events, and the beverage is strongly linked to female sexuality (Uzendoski 2004: 889). During carnival, drunken Bolivian miners gather around a statue of El Tío, the god of the mines, to festoon him with garlands, place food on his throne, and soak the ground with beer and rum (Bonilla 2006: 336). Seventh-Day Adventists in Peru have sworn off alcohol but not drinking—they drink glass after glass of Coca-Cola in a sequence that mimics the one traditionally used for beer drinking (Allen 2009: 43–45).

The production, exchange, and consumption of beer have long been important in the Andes, and drinking traditions can be effectively traced back among the cultures of the ancient Andes (Jennings and Bowser 2009). We know most about the Inca, whose empire was premised in part on using fermented beverages to signal royal generosity (Murra 1960; Ramírez 2005). Building on long-standing traditions of reciprocity, the ruler hosted feasts to recompense people for their service to the state. The millions of liters of beer brewed under the auspices of the Inca emperor indebted his subjects to him by the sheer quantity of drinks provided (Bray 2003: 18–19; Hastorf and Johannessen 1993: 118–19; Moore 1989: 685; Morris 1979: 32). The importance of fermented beverages might be best emphasized by the native reaction to another drink. Bernabe Cobo ([1653] 1979: 27) noted that that "water is their worst enemy; they never drink it pure unless they are unable to obtain their beverages, and there is no worse torment for them than being compelled to drink water."

When the Spaniards arrived in the region at the beginning of the sixteenth century, they observed people consuming fermented beverages made from a wide variety of plants (Cutler and Cárdenas 1947; Goldstein et al. 2009: 138; Nuñez del Prado 1973: 26; Steward and Faron 1959: 142); they adopted the word *chicha* as a general term for these beverages (e.g., Betanzos [1551] 1924: 199–200; Sarmiento de Gamboa [1572] 1999: 30). The chicha consumed at Inca events was often made of maize, but alcoholic beverages made from other plants, such as molle, were also served at the feasts that the Inca and earlier cultures used to form social alliances, fulfill reciprocal obligations, create social debt, collect tribute, and advertise social differences (Gero 1990, 1992; Goldstein 2003, 2005; Hastorf 1991; Lau 2002; Moore 1989; Segura Llanos 2001; Shimada 1994).

Hosting a feast in the Andes and elsewhere creates and maintains social capital, the durable network of relationships between peoples and resources that are integral to political economies (Hayden 2001). A host's generosity, measured in no small part by the amount of alcoholic beverages offered, generates a group of indebted participants that the host can later call on for assistance. Yet at the same time, a host is indebted to all of those who helped in preparing the feast. The demands of mass-producing beer for an event are shaped in part by the biochemical demands of the fermentation of different plants. The ways that one makes maize beer are different from the ways that one brews beer from the seeds of an acacia tree, for instance. These differences, therefore, have wide implications on the time, labor, tools, and resources that must be mustered at each stage of production to brew the massive quantities of beer consumed at a feast (e.g., Jennings 2005; Jennings and Chatfield 2009; Jennings et al. 2005).

This chapter explores the implications of the differences in how fermented beverages are currently made from maize kernels versus molle fruits in the Andes. We begin our chapter by discussing the biochemistry of fermenting and follow with a description of how maize beer and molle beer are produced. We then discuss the differences between molle and maize brewing, before paying particular attention to the demands a host would face trying to mass-produce each type of beer for an event. We conclude our chapter by exploring the implications of our findings for interpretations of the Wari political economy during the Middle Horizon period (AD 600–1000). Some researchers have suggested that molle beer was widely consumed in some Wari settlements (Goldstein et al. 2009;

Sayre et al. 2012), and thus the way in which molle beer was made would have had a significant impact on how Wari leaders marshaled social capital. Although the ways that both maize beer and molle beer were made in the past have undoubtedly changed (e.g., Hayashida 2009), we suggest that contemporary brewing recipes can nonetheless provide a sense of the barriers that would be faced by those seeking to use these beverages to build social capital.

Fermentation and Operational Chains

Fermentation is a biological process that transforms a food into carbon dioxide and alcohol through the actions of yeasts or other microbial cells. The process of transforming a raw material into alcohol can take up to two phases. In the first phase, called saccharification, the nonfermentable starches are broken down into sugars by amylases and other enzymes. In the second phase, fermentation, a variety of bacteria, fungi, and molds convert the sugars into alcohol and carbon dioxide (Soni and Sandhu 1999). Alcohol made from grains or other starchy substances, such as rice, millet, sorghum, beets, manioc, and maize, must be saccharified before fermentation can occur. Honey, plums, grapes, and other substances composed of simple sugars, however, only need to be fermented to produce alcohol.

Starch is a complex sugar (polysaccharide) that comes in two main chemical fractions, amylopectin and amylose (Hornsey 1999: 4). To break starch into sugar requires the action of several enzymes, such as α-amylase, β-amylase, and starch phosphorylase, which are collectively known as diastase (Goyal 1999: 91). In beer making, saccharification usually begins with the grinding up of starch grains, after which the granules are put in water. As the water is heated, the hydrogen bonds within the starch molecules weaken, water is absorbed, the starches unwind, and the granules swell. The diastase needed to break down the hydrolyzed starch grains is already present if the grains were first allowed to germinate; alternatively, the diastase is introduced at this stage in production by the addition into the mixture of human saliva, fungus, animal bones, or other additives (see Vencl 1994).

The starch/water mixture, often called mash, is then usually boiled after enzyme activity converts most of the starches into simple sugars. Boiling terminates all enzyme activity, sterilizes the mash, and allows for the completion of chemical reactions that lower the liquid's pH. The sterile, slightly acidic malt provides an environment conducive to the growth of the microbes necessary for fermentation (Hornsey 1999: 86; Soni and Sandhu 1999: 38).

While saccharification is an essential process for only those beers made from starches, fermentation is a necessary step in the production of all alcoholic beverages. Fermentation occurs in anaerobic conditions when certain microbes (especially the yeasts of the *Saccharomyces* species) convert simple sugars into the biochemical energy that the microbe needs to survive and reproduce. One of the primary metabolic pathways used by these organisms produces ethanol (consumable alcohol) and carbon dioxide (Goyal 1999: 116–18; Soni and Sandhu 1999: 33–37). Microbes can be introduced in a variety of ways as the mash cools down: the mash can be left to ferment by contact with airborne yeasts, a starter might be thrown in, or the mash can begin fermentation through contact with spoons or vessels used for making previous batches of beer. There is often a lag phase of a few hours as the microbe grows in the solution and adjusts to the new medium. As the population expands, fermentation rates increase rapidly and lead to the release of CO_2, an increase in the concentration of ethanol, a lowering of pH, and a rise in temperature (Soni and Sandhu 1999: 38–41).

The fermentation process eventually ends because the microbes that begin the process are tolerant of only a limited range of conditions. One of these conditions is the percentage of alcohol, and the tolerance of these microbes to alcohol varies considerably from organism to organism. For example, common brewer's yeast (*Saccharomyces cerevisiae* var. *carlsbergensis*) stops fermentation at about 6 percent ethanol by volume, while typical wine yeasts (*Saccharomyces cerevisiae* var. *ellipsoideus*) stop fermentation at about 12 percent by volume (Soni and Sandhu 1999: 40). A new species of yeast (*Candida thea* sp. nov.) extracted from pre-Columbian fermentation vessels in Ecuador has a tolerance of only 4 percent ethanol by volume (Chang et al. 2012; Fields 2012).

Alcoholic beverages tend to spoil largely because of exposure to bacteria (especially from the *Acetobacter* genus) that convert the ethanol to acetic and lactic acid and also produce other flavors and odors that are unacceptable to consumers (Adams 1985: 1; Haggblade and Holzapfel 1989: 247; Jackson 1999: 618, 2003: 252–53). Spoilage can often occur within a few days, but it can be inhibited significantly by high acidity, low sugar content, high alcohol content, low storage temperatures, and the absence of air (Joshi et al. 1999: 721–26). Just left out on the counter, most alcoholic beverages will last little more than a week. Yet a properly stored, dry red wine, for example, might be palpable decades after it was corked.

As the first author has argued elsewhere (Jennings et al. 2005), the process of alcohol production can be conceived of as an operational chain through which raw materials are transformed into a finished product (e.g., Leroi-Gourhan 1943, 1945). Each stage of production is a technical sequence—a bundle of actions, instruments, and agents that produce a particular result (Miracle 2002: 67; Narotzky 1997: 19). On the one hand, operational sequences are constrained by the properties of the material being processed (Edmonds 1990: 57; Mahias 1993: 162; Narotzky 1997: 19). In the case of alcohol production, the biochemical reactions that convert starches into sugar, sugar into alcohol, and alcohol into vinegar dictate many of the steps in the manufacturing process. On the other hand, operational chains for making alcohol are formed by knowledgeable actors who adapt sequences to achieve particular aims (Lemonnier 1993: 2–3; Narotzky 1997: 18). A brewer can stop fermentation early, for example, or use a different size of strainer to adjust the thickness of the mash. The interaction between the raw materials and the producers is what shapes the operational chain of how a beverage is created (e.g., Bray 1984; Latour 1996).

The ways that maize and molle beer are made are by necessity distinct from one another because the starches in maize kernels must be saccharified before fermentation, while the sugars in molle fruits do not. This biochemical distinction, when combined with variation in other aspects of the plants and their life cycles, creates differences in the recipes of these two beverages that are then further accentuated by the technological choices made by the brewers. The impact of the differences between the recipes in an extra hour to boil water or an added hand to transfer liquid between pots is amplified at feasts because of the amounts of alcohol that must be produced.

Andean ethnographers have often remarked on the copious amounts of alcohol served at public events. Failing to provide enough liquor disgraces the host, and guests are usually encouraged to drink heavily (Bunker 1987; Doughty 1971; Holmberg 1971; Isbell 1978). Participants, for example, will often drink more than 12 liters of maize beer at an event (Jennings 2005: 249). With consumption demands so high, it is easy to see how the differences in the operational chains of molle and maize beer could have far-reaching impacts on the political economy of the Andes, both today and in the pre-Columbian era.

Maize Beer Making

Derived from the manipulation of seven taxa of wild grasses referred to as teosinte, maize (*Zea mays*) is a domesticated cereal crop that has been grown in the Andes for at least six thousand years (Athens et al. 2016). The size and structure of maize cobs have radically changed over this period, ultimately leading to the "easily harvestable, abundantly yielding" varieties of corn with which we are familiar today (Iltis 2006: 22). Maize in the Andes grows during the rainy season, which begins as early as September and often lasts into June. Although a farmer can often grow two crops per year on the coast, only one crop is usually possible in the sierra (Grobman et al. 1961: 29). Maize can be planted alone, but cultivating maize together with beans, squash, quinoa, *achita, kawya,* and, at times, potatoes is a common practice (Valdez 1997: 66).

There is a rich literature describing the importance of maize and maize beer in the period directly preceding the Spanish Conquest (e.g., Goodman-Elgar 2009; Murra 1980; Staller 2006). Detailed brewing descriptions were recorded by the eighteenth century, and these descriptions are broadly similar to those described up to the present day (Anonymous [1720] 1961: 13; Camino 1987: 39–42; Gómez Huamán 1966: 43–44; Hayashida 2008: 163–67; Hocquenghem and Monzon 1995: 112; Llano Restrepo and Campuzano Cifuentes 1994: 24–25; Perlov 2009: 56–58; Ruiz [1788] 1998: 81; Tschiffely 1933: 48–49; Wiener [1880] 1993: 731–32). Drawing from these accounts, we can elucidate the operational chains used to make maize beer through either masticating maize flour or allowing the maize to germinate and then grinding it into flour. Both methods were likely used in the prehistoric Andes (Cutler and Cárdenas 1947: 34; Moore 1989: 686).

The first step in maize beer brewing begins when the maize is ripe at the end of the rainy season. To harvest the maize, farmers first cut the stalks a few centimeters off the ground, then leave the stalks to dry for a few days in the fields (Grobman et al. 1961: 29). The maize ear is then husked, also often in the field, before being brought back to the home (figure 11.1). In many cases, this harvest work can be conducted by the extended family, but on occasion, a small group of kin members or laborers with reciprocal ties may be called in to help (Guillet 1992: 73; Mayer 2002: 114–15). The harvested maize is allowed to dry for several days before it is stored (for up to a year).

The more arduous tasks of maize beer production take place in and around the house. After the kernels are removed from the cob, the brewer

Figure 11.1. Maize harvest in Huanta, Ayacucho Valley, Peru.

must choose whether the maize will be masticated or germinated to break down the starches. Cutler and Cárdenas (1947: 41) vividly describe the mastication method:

> The maize grains are usually ground by hand, often with a half-moon-shaped stone rocker (*maran uña*) on a flat stone (*maran*) as has been done for centuries. The flour is then mixed with saliva. On some of the larger haciendas it is still the custom to have women and children gather in groups to do this. The flour is moistened very slightly with water, rolled into a ball of convenient size and popped into the mouth. It is thoroughly worked with the tongue until well mixed with saliva, after which it is pressed against the roof of the mouth to form a single mass, then shoved forward with the tongue and removed with the fingers. . . . [T]he salivated morsels are dried in the sun and sacked for storage and shipment. They roughly resemble sets of false upper teeth.

The germination method, though more complicated and time-consuming, is less labor-intensive. This process begins with the soaking of maize kernels in large open-mouthed vessels filled with water (Valdez 2012). The maize is removed from the jars after 12–18 hours and then piled together in a dark, dank place inside the home or, more typically, placed between

Figure 11.2. Lithograph depicting women brewing maize beer in the city of Arequipa, Peru (Marcoy 1873: 56).

layers of leaves on one side of the house patio. The maize kernels begin to sprout after three to five days, and during this time water is often poured on the layer twice a day to keep it moist. After the maize has sprouted, it is sometimes heaped into a pile, covered with a cloth or more leaves, and allowed to sit for two more days. The germinated maize is then spread out under the sun in a thin layer to dry for two to five days, depending on weather conditions. The germinated and dried maize kernels, called *qora* (Valdez et al. 2010a: 217), are arduously crushed and ground into flour by household members using rocker grinders and grinding stones (Nicholson 1960: 295; Sillar 2000: 109–10; Valdez 2006: 69).

For the remainder of the brewing process, the maize beer recipe is the same. The flour is placed into a large open-mouthed pot filled with water, and the mixture is boiled at a low temperature over the fire (figure 11.2). Depending on the recipe, this mixture is alternately heated and cooled over the course of one to three days (Cutler and Cárdenas 1947: 45–47; Gillin 1947; Manrique Chávez 1997: 308–9; Nicholson 1960: 296). Water is constantly added during the process as evaporation takes place. During this phase of the process, certain parts of the mixture are removed to make other products. In some cases, the mixture is allowed to completely cool in order for it to separate into three layers. The uppermost liquid layer is transferred into another pot for subsequent fermentation; the middle, jelly-like layer is very sweet, and a portion is often added to

Figure 11.3. A husband and wife stand among their jars (sinkas) of fermenting maize beer in Cahuana, Cotahuasi Valley, Peru.

the liquid that will be fermented; and the grainy third layer is usually fed to pigs or other animals (Cutler and Cárdenas 1947: 45–46).

In other cases, the mixture is not allowed to cool completely and instead is strained through a cloth or basketry sieve into another pot. The maize beer in the second pot is often boiled again and further refined by separation or sieving. Small amounts of flavoring ingredients, such as sugar, cinnamon, orange leaves, peanuts, and sesame seeds, are sometimes added to the mixture at this point (Cavero Carrasco 1986: 116; Cutler and Cárdenas 1947: 47). The mixture is then transferred into narrow-necked jars to cool and ferment (figure 11.3). Because the jars are not washed between batches of maize beer, fermentation is initiated from the preexisting yeasts in the jars. These jars are called *sinkas*, or drunken jars, because they are repeatedly used for brewing beer.

The liquid ferments quickly, and it can begin to bubble violently after a few hours. The fermentation occurs in one to six days, depending on elevation and environment (Cutler and Cárdenas 1947: 47), although three to four days is more typical. Maize beer does not store well and tends to sour in less than seven days. Therefore, the brew needs to be consumed soon after it completes fermentation (Cutler and Cárdenas 1947:

47; Moore 1989: 688; Nicholson 1960: 297). Maize beer's alcohol content by volume is generally low (less than 5 percent) but can vary between 1 percent and 12 percent, depending on the method of production (Cavero Carrasco 1986: 17; Fields 2012; Moore 1989: 685; Steinkraus 1979: 42; Vázquez 1967: 267). Approximately 5 kilograms of maize would be required to produce the 12 liters of beer often consumed by each adult at a feast (Jennings 2005: 248–49). Based on this number, a hectare of maize plants could easily meet the consumption demands of an event serving 200 guests (Jennings 2005: 250).

Molle Beer Making

Schinus molle is a woody tree that is native to both the western and eastern sides of the Andes Mountains. The tree can grow up to 15 meters high and boasts long, slender leaves on thin branches. *S. molle* fruits are found at the end of these branches clustered together into panicles (figure 11.4). The tiny fruits are drupes with a papery purplish-red exocarp covering the seeds (Barkley 1944; Goldstein and Coleman 2004; Kramer 1957). Molle trees flower early in the rainy season (October), and the fruits mature by early in the dry season (late May to early June). The trees often

Figure 11.4. Molle berries on branches before harvest.

produce fruits in abundance during years of poor maize harvests (Valdez 2012). Molle beer, made from the fruits of the tree, was enjoyed by some of the first Spanish chroniclers. Pedro Cieza de León ([1540] 1959: 115, [1552] 1962: 275), for example, described the beverage as "very good," and Garcilaso de la Vega ([1609] 1966: 504) noted that the beer was "delightful" and "full of flavor."

Despite this early recognition of molle beer, there have been only a few, brief written accounts of molle beer production. Garcilaso de la Vega made the earliest observation, noting that "they prepare the beverage from these berries by gently rubbing them with their hands in hot water until it has yielded all its sweetness . . . [and then] they pass that water through a sieve and store for three or four days until it is ready to drink" ([1609] 1945: 182 [trans. by Jennings]). Kramer made similar observations in the 1950s. He suggested that the molle fruits were soaked in warm water before the brewer squeezed out the seeds. The water that held the fruits was then strained and left to ferment for "some days" (Kramer 1957: 322). In a more recent article, Goldstein and Coleman (2004: 526–27) offer a slightly different recipe that involves first extracting the seeds and then boiling the seeds in a pot of water for a half hour. The water is then poured through a sieve into a jar, which is covered with a wet cloth while the contents are allowed to ferment for a week. Boiling is not necessary for making molle beer (e.g., Cook and Glowacki 2003: 180; León 2008: 120–21; Valdez et al. 2010b: 30) but would make the beer safer to drink.

Valdez, the second author of this chapter, grew up in the department of Ayacucho and was often involved in making molle beer. His experiences have provided us with a richer description of the steps used to make molle beer in this region (Valdez 2012). To harvest molle fruits in Ayacucho, a considerable number of workers, of both sexes and all ages, are needed. Assistance usually comes from kin members and neighbors called together through reciprocal relationships; many of the participants also bring the large blankets needed for the harvest. Individuals own trees. Consequently, those wishing to make large amounts of beer must not only harvest their own molle trees but also make special requests to kin members and neighbors in order to harvest their molle trees.

Around a dozen people are required to effectively harvest a sufficient number of molle trees. The harvest begins with a man climbing up a tree carrying a long stick (about 4 meters in length) with a hook on one end. The man moves to a branch, while the people below the branch pair up to grab the blankets on each end and extend them side by side on the ground. As soon as the blankets are extended, the man above begins hitting the branch with his stick to create a shower of molle fruits that land on the blankets. Once a branch is finished, the group moves on to the other branches to repeat the same action until the whole tree is completely harvested. As the group moves from one tree to the next, the molle fruits accumulate quickly. In most cases, a group can gather enough fruits for a smaller-scale feast in a single morning.

To make molle beer, the fruits must first be separated from the small branches, leaves, and panicles that also fall into the extended blankets. This is done by winnowing in the afternoon, when the wind is often stronger. The fruits are then stepped on in order to remove the papery exocarp. A portion of the harvest group often begins this process the same day after lunch, and it is finished over the next couple of days by a smaller group composed of members and relatives of the household that sponsored the molle harvest. We must emphasize that all these activities take place in fields near the molle trees. Once this initial process is completed, the fruits are taken back to the house and are stored in large baskets that are kept dry and covered with blankets to avoid spoilage. Though one can make beer from fruits stored for more than a year, the product is considered to be of lower quality.

Brewing molle beer involves all members of a household, regardless of age and sex. The most important equipment for the preparation of molle beer is a large, open-mouthed vessel that typically sits on a platform outside on the patio (figure 11.5). The vessel is tied securely to a post to help prevent accidental breakage or spillage. Known as the *aqa maqma*, the vessel has a single, small hole that is located about 6 centimeters above its base (Valdez 2012). A leaf of an *Agave americana*, placed right below this hole, is used as a trough to drain the contents of the aqa maqma into a smaller, open-mouthed vessel situated on the ground below the platform.

Before brewing begins, a family member securely closes the aqa maqma's hole with a maize cob. The vessel is then filled halfway with molle fruits, and water is added to bring the mixture to the top of the jar (younger family members are responsible for fetching the needed water). The fruits are soaked for about four hours to release the sugars (also see Kramer 1957: 322; León 2008: 121; Valdez 2012). The hole of the aqa maqma is then opened to enable the sweetened water to be drained from the brewing jar and placed into the smaller, open-mouthed vessel. To ensure that the seeds remain in the vessel, a thin stick is introduced sideways into the hole as soon as the cob is removed. If the molle fruits were harvested recently, then the same seeds may be soaked again, for a second batch of beer. If the seeds are from older fruits, then the vessel will be

Figure 11.5. Pouring molle berries into an open-mouthed vessel (aqa maqma), Huanta, Ayacucho Valley, Peru.

completely emptied before it is filled again with new molle fruits to repeat the procedure. The spent seeds are dried and kept near the kitchen to be used to complement firewood while cooking.

The sweetened water, called *molle upi,* is transferred into smaller, narrow-necked vessels for fermentation (figure 11.6). These vessels are usually sinkas, or drunken jars, that have been previously used for the purpose of fermenting molle beer. These vessels are therefore impregnated with yeasts and are not washed or used for other purposes. In those cases when a fermenting jar is new, placing a few cups of old molle beer

Figure 11.6. Pouring *molle upi* into a fermenting narrow-necked vessel (*urpu*), Huanta, Ayacucho Valley, Peru.

to the new jars is customary (also see Meyerson 1990: 50), or some of the current batch of molle upi is transferred from one of the sinkas into the new jar after a few hours of fermentation. The fermenting jars are placed indoors, securely seated over a dry floor and often near walls for support. The fermentation process takes only a few days in sinkas and up to a week in new vessels if old beer is not added. The presence of white foam on the mouth of the fermenting jar indicates that the beer has fermented. Literally, the jar is said to be drunk.

A well-fermented molle beer is refreshing and pleasant (also see Arnold 1985: 150; Kramer 1957: 322). The quality of the drink is heavily influenced by the freshness of the berries—using recently harvested fruits will result in a better beverage than one made with fruits that were kept in storage for longer periods of time. The beer is slightly bitter, turning increasingly bitter and more alcoholic as time goes by, and it is essentially undrinkable after five days. Molle beer is stronger than maize beer and may perhaps fall into the 6–9 percent alcohol by total volume that is typical of some wines and hard apple ciders. Though fruit production varies enormously based on the age of the tree, rainfall, and other factors, the fruits of dozens of trees would be needed to produce the beer required by 200 people at a normal feast.

To gain a better understanding of the amount of fruit needed to prepare molle beer, Valdez recently participated in the harvesting of 2 kilograms of fruits following the traditional method described above. The molle fruits were soaked in 5 liters of water for four hours. The dry fruits absorbed 2 liters of this water and produced 3 liters of sweetened water (molle upi). Finally, the molle fruits were soaked for a second time in 2.5 liters of water. An additional 2 liters of sweetened water was gathered four hours later. In sum, 2 kilograms of molle fruits—harvested with little effort—is enough to produce a total of 5 liters of molle upi in a single day that can be fermented. Two days later, the beverage was fully fermented and drinkable.

Comparing Maize and Molle Brewing

A cursory inspection of the operational chains of maize and molle brewing highlights what has long been known in many Andean communities: molle beer is much easier to make (figure 11.7). Largely because of the required conversion of starches into sugar during maize brewing, maize beer is a more complicated process (Valdez 2012). As figure 11.7 shows, at least eleven steps must be undertaken to make maize beer, while only six steps are required to make molle beer. Maize brewing is also more time-consuming and more arduous; it requires grinding and greater amounts of firewood and water. Even straining the maize mash takes more time and exertion. Measured simply in terms of the effort required to produce a liter of each alcoholic beverage, there seem to be very few incentives for making maize beer.

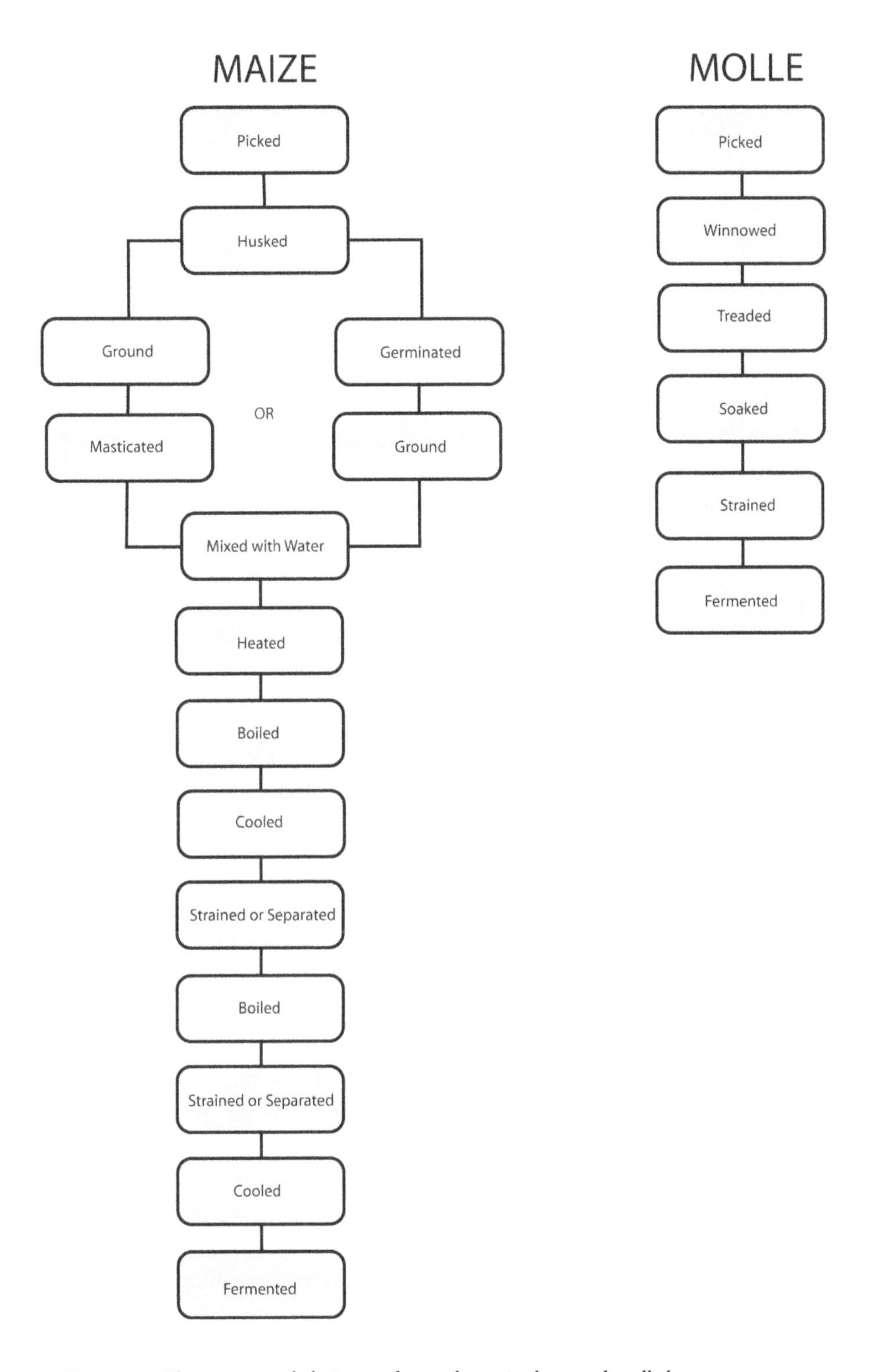

Figure 11.7. The operational chains used to make maize beer and molle beer.

The higher investments in maize beer make it a more prestigious drink, and thus a host might choose to serve the beverage just because it is harder to make. Yet brewing with maize confers other advantages, especially as the scale of production increases. A comparison of the plants, labor, time, fuel, water, and culinary equipment used in molle and maize beer making provides a sense of the challenges faced by those trying to build social capital by serving these beverages for feasts.

MOLLE FRUITS AND MAIZE EARS

We begin our comparison of molle and maize brewing by considering the impact of the basic characteristics of the two plants on the production process. Because maize is an annual plant, farmers select the types and amounts that they want to grow each year. Crop yields vary widely depending on growing conditions—a severe drought might mean no harvest at all, but farmers can adjust what they sow at the beginning of the rainy season based on their anticipated needs for the coming year. Because maize is seen largely as a food crop (Valdez et al. 2010a: 206), a lower than expected harvest will largely preclude maize from being used for beer making: if a family must choose between food and a fermented beverage, then they will choose food.

Depending on molle trees for making beer is therefore less risky. Although yields will fluctuate from year to year, the trees reliably yield at least some fruits each year, and these fruits are not eaten as food (though they can be exchanged for potatoes and other crops). Yet a host's hands are tied in terms of the ultimate number of available molle trees that can be harvested for an event. Taking many years to mature, the trees are planted for the benefit of the next generation and are inherited as part of property holdings.

To amass sufficient maize for a feast, a host must therefore obtain the yield from 1–2 hectares of agricultural land (e.g., Jennings 2005: 250). This can be done by arranging to plant more maize than other crops on one's fields and on the fields of a few friends and close kin. Needed maize can also be secured through exchange for coca leaves and other products. To amass sufficient molle fruit for a feast, the same host would need access to dozens of molle trees. Because the trees are individually owned and spread across the community, he or she would need the support of a much broader group of people to produce the same amount of molle beer for an event. A host must either get permission to gather the fruits from various trees or have the beer produced by different households and then brought to the feast.

Another critical difference between the plants is the longer shelf life of maize. Both maize ears and molle fruits can be stored for about a year in ideal conditions, but the sugars in molle fruits break down more quickly than do the starches in the maize kernels. When fresh, a molle fruit can be used to brew two batches of beer. Only a single batch, however, can be brewed from these same berries if used a few months later. There is no such productivity decline in the maize kernels. A host, therefore, has an incentive to time a feast soon after the molle harvest to capitalize on the greater potency of the fruits. In contrast, a host serving maize beer is much less dependent on the timing of the harvest. As long as the kernels remain dry, protected from insects, and free of rot (often quite difficult, especially at lower elevations), they can be used to make beer at any point over the next year or so with little loss of potency.

LABOR

The labor demands of maize and molle brewing are quite distinct. Maize cultivation is an ongoing commitment. Every year, farmers need to sow the saved-back kernels, weed the fields, water the plants, and keep animals at bay. Irrigation can be particularly labor-intensive, as canals need to be routinely maintained. Much of this work is done within the household, but other activities demand the cooperation of the entire community. At harvest time, a handful of laborers need to cut the maize stalks down and then return a few days later to gather and shuck the ears. Although these actions can be done with family members, the work needs to be completed at a time when everyone is also trying to harvest their own crops.

A larger group of a dozen or more people is brought together in the morning of the molle fruit harvest, but this group shrinks in size by the afternoon as the multiday process of winnowing and treading begins. The harvest time is the only time during molle beer production when labor demands extend beyond the family unit. Fortunately, for the prospective host, the molle fruit harvest usually take place after maize and other crops have been harvested. A host who hopes to serve molle beer can therefore wait until others in the community are available to help. Molle brewing requires little effort after winnowing and treading: the berries are simply placed in water, strained, and fermented. After the fruits are taken home, a single family could theoretically do all of the work needed to brew sufficient molle beer for a 200-person feast. In practice, however, a household's production would be limited by the culinary equipment at a family's disposal.

For maize brewing, the labor demands escalate further after the harvest. Grinding is backbreaking, and adding one's saliva to a pile of maize flour is a more intensive task than one might think. The heating, cooling, straining, and separating involved in maize beer production is also difficult work, as pots are stirred, poured out, and filled repeatedly with water. A lone woman with the occasional help of other family members can often manage the regular consumption needs of a household (Jennings and Chatfield 2009: 211), but a household would not come close to producing enough maize beer for a large feast. To host 200 people, a host would need to have more than a dozen dedicated brewers or rely on the household production of a wide group of households across a community (Jennings 2005: 251–52). This work, however, could be broken up into stages over the course of weeks or even months.

TIME

The production of maize beer is much more time-consuming than producing molle beer (Valdez 2012). If maize beer is made through the mastication method, at least a week has to elapse from when the corn is ground to when fermentation is complete. The germination method adds another week to the process because the brewer needs to wait for the corn to sprout. Most of this time is not spent dedicated to beer making—during the day, a man might spend only a few moments watering a bed of maize or a woman might occasionally peek at the contents of a fermenting jar—but there are many moments of intense labor during this period that demand the attention of multiple family members. For molle beer, in contrast, the time from when the fruits are soaked to when the beer is done fermenting may be as little as three days. Brewing is done in half a day, with the remaining time needed for fermentation.

There is a considerable difference between the beverages in the amount of time that individuals need to invest over the course of brewing. Once the molle fruits are brought back home, the cumulative amount of time spent performing a dedicated beer-making task would usually be less than an hour (though see below for a discussion on obtaining water and fuel for brewing both beverages). It takes only a few minutes to mix the fruit and water together in the aqa maqma, another couple of minutes to drain the molle upi into fermenting jars, and then whatever time is required to move and cover the fermenting jars (Valdez 2012). Maize brewers, in contrast, must be prepared to dedicate many more hours to production. Just the grinding of maize can take two or three days of work by several individuals if someone intends to brew a large batch of beer.

There are also many hours of labor required over the next several days to ensure that the manufacturing process is done in an efficient and timely manner (e.g., Hayashida 2008: 169–70). A woman can often spare a few moments to attend to other activities, but she, along with other members of her family, needs to be present and vigilant during much of the one to three days spent heating, cooling, and straining the liquid.

WATER AND FUEL

Some of the largest labor and time commitments in beer making are the acquisition of water and fuel. In communities without running water, water needs to be brought back to the house from the nearest river, spring, or other water source, which might be a few minutes' walk from the home or farther. In molle beer making, enough water is needed to fill the aqa maqma just once. Maize brewers, however, need more water, and they need it several times in the production sequence. Someone needs to fill the vessels (which are often the same size [see below] as the aqa maqma used to make molle beer) with water when brewing is initiated, but then more water must be added as it boils off during brewing. Because this water demand occurs in the midst of all of the other labor commitments of maize beer making, fetching water often entails the participation of other family members.

Families that rely on firewood, brush, and dung for fuel have to make further commitments in time and labor for maize brewing (e.g., Hayashida 2008: 169–70). Because fuel sources are often in short supply around communities, people commonly have to walk several kilometers over rugged terrain to find what they need to feed their fires (e.g., Arnold 1993: 65–66). In the production of maize beer, water needs to be brought to a slow boil at least once during the process. Heating is not a requirement in molle beer production, although warming the water might help to reduce the time needed for the fruits to soak (alternatively, the water might just be left in the sun to warm up for a few hours before brewing). Molle brewing has the additional benefit of producing fuel—the spent seeds when dried are oily and burn almost instantly. A family making maize beer will therefore need to send members out to gather fuel for the fire, while a rival family making molle beer would actually end up with a fuel as a brewing by-product.

BREWING EQUIPMENT

Although there are critical differences in the operational chains used to make maize and molle beer, the equipment used to produce the beverages is nearly identical. In both processes, brewing occurs in wide-mouthed jars and fermenting takes place using narrow-necked jars. These jars are common in the Andes and usually make up a large part of the culinary equipment kept in a home (e.g., Arnold 1993; Camino 1987; Litto 1976; Ravines and Villiger 1989; Valdez 2012). Wide-mouthed jars are multipurpose vessels that are also used for storage and, more rarely, cooking. Though the aqa maqma with its small hole is dedicated to molle brewing, wide-mouthed jars as a form are not diagnostic of beer making. In contrast, narrow-necked jars (*urpu*) are usually dedicated to fermenting, and often they are used for only one kind of beer; molle beer is particularly notorious for leaving behind a strong flavor in fermenting jars.

Maize beer brewing requires equipment that is not necessary for those making molle beer. Yet these pieces of equipment, such as grinding stones, stirring spoons, and dippers, are common household implements that are not uniquely used in beer making (e.g., Hayashida 2008: 168). Strainers are more indicative of beer making, and they may be ceramic (now sometimes plastic) colanders, baskets, or sheets of cloth (Franquemont et al. 1990: 76; Hayashida 2008: 171). Straining, though, is a necessary step for making either maize or molle beer. Molle fruits are easier to strain—hence Ayacucho brewers' use of a stick to partially cover the hole in the aqa maqma (Valdez 2012)—but colanders, cloth, and other sieves can also be used to strain out the molle fruits before the liquid is transferred to fermenting jars (Goldstein and Coleman 2004: 527; Kramer 1957: 322).

Feasting, Social Capital, and Beer

The operational chains used to produce maize and molle beer impact the ways in which these beverages can be mass-produced for a feast. Each step in the chain requires investment in raw materials, time, labor, and/or equipment that often necessitates the assistance of family members, kin, and other groups. As additional people are involved in preparing for an event, the logistics of feasting preparation become more complicated. A host must often work closely with many people to prepare a feast, and any social capital that is gained at the event is diffused across this broader community. The wide network of relationships required to host a feast therefore usually acts as a leveling mechanism that severely limits the amount of social capital that can be amassed by the host (e.g., Jennings and Chatfield 2009: 221). To gain more social capital, therefore, the host may seek to limit the investments by decreasing preparation time, the amount of raw materials, equipment use, and the number of workers.

Molle beer requires fewer investments to brew than does maize beer, in terms of time, labor, fuel, water, and equipment. With help from a dozen people over the course of a day, and perhaps borrowing some pots from friends and neighbors, a host's family could brew the beer required for a feast in a few days. Though this ease of production would make molle beer attractive to a host, molle brewing offers only limited opportunities for a host to make significant investment savings. Using bigger pots, for example, would offer some saving, but a brewer using additional smaller pots would only have to work a few extra moments to fill them. Heating the water might decrease the time needed to soak the berries but might only save half an hour of time.

The biggest drawback to using molle beer to build social capital is that a host requires the cooperation of much of the village to harvest the necessary number of molle trees. Because molle trees are individually owned, the social capital that the host acquires through the feast is dissipated to a significant degree by his or her debt to the people who offered the fruit from their trees. This is not to suggest that farmers routinely deny access to their trees. In most cases, cooperation is easily obtained. There are often more than enough molle trees to support an event, and friends and neighbors are usually happy to give permission for a host to organize a harvest of the trees on their property. Yet it is *their* fruit that supports the party, and access to this fruit can be denied if tensions rise in a community. In sum, molle beer is ideal for feasting because of its ease of brewing, but its ability to be used to build social capital is limited without direct access to the trees that provide the fruit.

A host serving maize beer has the advantage of more easily assembling a large amount of maize from only a few producers. He or she can work with family members to sow additional maize in anticipation of an event taking place later in the year and is perhaps more flexible in scheduling when an event would occur. Yet this host is faced with meeting the far greater demands of maize brewing. In most cases, a wide swath of the community needs to be encouraged to invest the time and energy to produce beer for an event. Just as in molle brewing, the social capital achieved through hosting a feast serving maize beer would therefore be spread across a wide group of producers. Maize beer's more complicated and intensive operational chain, however, provides a host significant opportunities to lower investment costs.

The labor costs of making maize beer can be dramatically lowered by centralizing production and brewing using bigger pots (Jennings 2005: 250–52; Jennings and Chatfield 2009: 218). These changes offer considerable economy of scale and in some cases could decrease by half the number of people-hours required to produce a liter of beer (Hayashida 2008: 170). Further shifts in production, such as decreasing overall cooking time, expending less effort on grinding (by producing coarser-grained flour), and using only coarse sieves, can be made to decrease investments (see Hayashida 2008). Many of these changes may be difficult to make in the context of a feast, however, because the altered taste of the beer may not be as palatable to guests, and some changes may be seen, at least initially, as inappropriate and thus inhospitable. The largest barrier to significant shifts in production, though, might be the resistance of households in communities where beer is overwhelmingly produced in the home. Centralizing production means the loss of considerable social capital for those used to brewing beer in their home for a feast (Jennings and Chatfield 2009: 221).

Andean communities are structured around reciprocal ties (Mayer 2002). Drinking plays a prevalent role in maintaining these ties (Allen 2009), with weddings, the construction of houses, annual rituals, and other activities often celebrated with feasts where maize, molle, and other beers are consumed. In many cases, these feasts are organized through a cargo system that requires every married adult in the community to sponsor at least one event. These events are not meant to build the social capital of the host at the expense of others. The whole community provides food and fermented beverages for the feast, and then for the next event another member of the community will take on the cargo. Because making both molle and maize beer often requires extensive community involvement, both drinks can be used to strengthen a village's reciprocal ties (Valdez 2012). The two beverages, however, offer different possibilities for those groups, like the Incas, that want to build social capital by putting feast goers in their debt.

Implications for Ancient Andean Political Economy: A Wari Example

The differences in the operational chains used to make maize and molle beer are particularly relevant for our understanding of the Wari state (AD 600–1000). Centered in the Ayacucho Valley, where the second author was raised, the Wari state had broad stylistic influence and founded numerous distant colonies across Peru (Schreiber 1992). Feasting was likely essential to Wari political economy in both its core and its colonies (Cook and Glowacki 2003; Nash 2011). Though maize beer was likely also consumed at these feasts, molle beer is seen to have "played a critical role in Wari commensal practice" (Sayre et al. 2012: 233; also see Goldstein et al. 2009). Molle trees and molle-related toponyms are sometimes found near Wari sites (Williams 2009: 211), and seeds and other parts of the plant have been documented in high concentrations at the Wari centers of Conchopata, Cerro Baúl, and Cerro Mejía (Goldstein et al. 2009; Nash 2011; Sayre et al. 2012).

Paleobotanical researchers at these three Wari sites found molle remains in a wide variety of contexts, ranging from garbage pits to floors and hearths. Seeds are much more common than stems—more than 90 percent of the molle remains at Cerro Baúl are seeds, suggesting that initial processing likely occurred near the trees. Molle remains are often found in kitchens or in contexts containing the likely detritus of feasting events (Goldstein et al. 2009: 150–51; Sayre et al. 2012: 239, 245). At Cerro Baúl and Cerro Mejía, molle seeds are concentrated in and around spaces associated with elites (Goldstein et al. 2009: 152; Nash 2011: 238). Paleobotanists have also recovered maize remains at these sites, but at lower densities (Goldstein et al. 2009: 144; Sayre et al. 2012: 239, 245). The presence of maize cobs and kernels at the sites suggests that the ears were processed in the home, and the discovery of germinated and ground maize at Cerro Baúl supports earlier suggestions that maize beer may have also been brewed there (Moseley et al. 2005: 17267; Nash 2011: 242).

Of particular interest for our discussion is the existence of a possible brewery at Cerro Baúl (Moseley et al. 2005). A hall associated with one of the largest patios at the site (8 × 15 meters), the possible brewery contains the remains of at least ten hearths. Excavators suggest that the building was deliberately set on fire just before the site was abandoned. The contents within the brewery and associated structures have been used to reconstruct the feast that was associated with this final event. The remains of large jars were found in the hearths, and molle and maize remains were found in pits adjacent to these. Interestingly, the context was the only one at Cerro Baúl where the number of stems (n = 4,337) was nearly equivalent to the number of seeds (n = 5,525) (Goldstein et al. 2009). Analysis of the grinding stones found in the brewery suggests that they were used to grind chili peppers, potatoes, and other plants (Sayre et al. 2012: 242).

Our analysis of the operational chains of molle and maize beer adds a note of caution to suggestions that molle beer was the preferred beverage at Wari sites. The argument for a concentration of molle beer is based in large part on the prevalence of molle seeds in particular contexts at these sites. Yet humans and animals often consume the mash and other by-products of maize brewing, whereas the spent molle seeds are inedible. Because maize consumption was quite high during the Middle Horizon at least in Ayacucho (Finucane 2009; Finucane et al. 2006), the abundance of molle remains may simply reflect a lack of consumption of molle seeds. Another concern is that molle seeds are often used to fuel fires—a greater association with kitchen contexts at Wari sites might therefore reflect at least in part molle's use as a fuel rather as a beverage. Finally, the presence of fermenting and brewing vessels does little to support an argument for molle brewing, given the nearly identical nature of the equipment used to make both beers. Because heating is not required for molle beer, the hearths at the brewery and other locations at these sites could, if anything, be used to argue for maize beer production (Valdez 2012). Although agreeing with these authors that molle beer was likely served at Wari sites, we suggest that determining the prevalence of particular beverages at feasts requires further research.

The scholars working at these sites acknowledge that maize, molle, and likely other types of beer were made at Wari sites (Nash 2011: 238; Sayre et al. 2012: 249), yet they suggest that molle beer was the preferred beverage of Wari elites and that this beverage was fundamental to the "small-scale feasts and meetings that were an important element of Wari's administration strategies" (Nash 2011: 238 [trans. by Jennings]). If molle beer was indeed central to Wari political economy, then what can we learn from how molle brewing's operational chain departs from that of maize?

One obvious point is that Wari administrators chose to rely on a beverage that was much easier to make. Hosting a feast would require considerably less labor and fewer material inputs. Although some scholars continue to insist that the Wari state relied on large-scale feasts that served hundreds of people (e.g., Schreiber and Edwards 2010: 157), the extant architectural and material evidence suggests that the number of guests at most events likely measured in the low dozens. One or two households could brew the amount of molle beer needed for these small-scale feasts once the fruits were gathered, and a standard size and scheduling of events would work well with the more regular yields of a group of molle trees. Mass-producing molle beer for smaller feasts would not require the dramatic shifts in labor regimes that are required to produce maize beer for larger events (e.g., Hastorf 1991).

A reliance on molle beer does, however, require regular access to harvests from molle trees. It is unclear how Wari administrators would have controlled the use of trees scattered across the countryside. The ubiquity of both molle stems and fruits across Cerro Baúl and Cerro Mejía suggests that most people had access to the trees, and the fruits could conceivably have been taken to the elites living at Cerro Baúl as tribute with some frequency (Goldstein et al. 2009: 157). Perhaps the molle trees around Wari colonies were seen as the property of the state or there were sumptuary laws restricting consumption. In the case of Cerro Baúl, it is also possible that molle trees may have even been planted when colonists first arrived in the upper Moquegua Valley. However the fruits may have been obtained, a reliance on molle beer would suggest that Wari sites were often able to exert extensive control over this important local resource (though Costion's [2012] evidence for molle brewing at the local site of Yahuay Alta suggests residents had regular access to trees a few kilometers away from Cerro Baúl).

A different procurement strategy occurred at the event that culminated in the abandonment of Cerro Baúl's brewery. In this case, the gathered fruits and stems seem to have been processed on-site, rather than in the fields. Although Goldstein and colleagues (2009: 157) interpret this as evidence for "more elite control over the collection" of fruits, it can also potentially be viewed as a breakdown in the relationships with those who had previously brought the fruit up the steep sides of the site. The inherent weakness of a political economy built on mass production of molle is its dependence on a diffused resource that is difficult to monitor; any perceived slippage in power could jeopardize the state's control of the fruits. In contrast, maize brewing depends primarily on marshalling sufficient labor. Though producing maize beer is more difficult, controlling production is far easier. Instead of stopping a farmer from shaking the branch of a tree, an administrator can check up on a handful of brewers grinding maize in an adjacent room.

Ingredients Matter

When the Spaniards first arrived in the Andes, they were amazed at the wide array of plants that were used to make fermented beverages. They often used the word *chicha* for all of these beverages, and archaeologists have tended to follow the same custom in using *chicha* as an overarching term. Making chicha from peanuts, however, is a different process than making manioc chicha. The characteristics of the plants, when combined with the technical choices made by brewers, create distinct operational chains for each of the beers that could be served at a feast. Knowing the kind of chicha served at an event can therefore provide us with considerable insight into the functioning of ancient Andean political economies.

Yet identifying archaeologically the kind of beers served at an event can be difficult. Many of the plants used to make beer are also food crops, and brewing often occurs in spaces where other domestic tasks are performed. Only some brewing equipment is specialized, and this specialized equipment is rarely unique to a specific kind of beer. Careful attention to archaeological signatures for the operational chain of a beverage may only go so far as to affirm the possibility that a particular plant could have been used to make beer (Valdez 2012; but see Parker and McCool 2015). For more confidence, we need to expand our search for the chemical signatures in human bone of the consumption of certain plants (e.g., Finucane 2009; Hastorf 1991) and the changes in plant morphology associated with the fermentation process (e.g. Dozier and Jennings, in press). Perhaps most important, we need to employ tools like gas chromatography/mass spectrometry and lipid analysis to directly test for plant remains and yeasts in fermenting vessels (e.g., Chang et al. 2012).

We hope that our discussion of the operational chains used to make molle and maize beer adds a greater sense of urgency to the study of alcoholic beverages in the Andes and elsewhere. Although the nuances of the recipes have undoubtedly changed, we suggest that contemporary brewing practices can help us understand the distinct barriers and opportunities faced by a host attempting to mass-produce a particular kind of beer for a feast. Those who sought to use feasts for political gain had a wide array of choices for what was served at an event. By carefully tracing the operational chains involved in the mass production of food and beverages, we can hope to uncover the wide-ranging political, social, and economic impacts of ancient feasts.

References Cited

Adams, M. R. 1985. Vinegar. In *Microbiology of Fermented Foods*, ed. B. J. Wood, 1–44. New York: Elsevier Applied Science.

Allen, C. J. 2009. "Let's Drink Together, My Dear!": Persistent Ceremonies in a Changing Community. In *Drink, Power, and Society in the Andes*, ed. J. Jennings and B. Bowser, 28–48. Gainesville: University Press of Florida.

Anonymous. (1720) 1961. Información anónima sobre la vida y costumbres del pueblo de Virú, Provincia de Trujillo, Departamento de la Libertad, con un recetario crio-

llo del maestro barbero Don Feliciano de Bergara, Siglo XVIII, Año 1720. *Revista del Archivo Nacional del Perú* 25 (1): 5–25.
Arnold, D. E. 1985. *Ceramic Theory and Cultural Process.* Cambridge: Cambridge University Press.
Arnold, D. E. 1993. *Ecology and Ceramic Production in an Andean Community.* Cambridge: Cambridge University Press.
Athens, J. S., J. V. Ward, D. M. Pearsall, K. Chandler-Ezell, D. W. Blinn, and A. E. Morrison. 2016. Early Prehistoric Maize in Northern Highland Ecuador. *Latin American Antiquity* 27 (1): 3–21.
Barkley, F. A. 1944. *Schinus* L. *Brittonia* 5 (2): 160–98.
Betanzos, J. (1551) 1924. *Suma y narración de los Incas.* Colección Librería de Documentos y Referencias de Historia del Perú 8. Lima. Reprint, 2015; CreateSpace Independent Publishing Platform.
Bonilla, H. 2006. Religious Practices in the Andes and Their Relevance to Political Struggle and Development: The Case of El Tío and Miners in Bolivia. *Mountain Research and Development* 26 (4): 336–42.
Bray, F. 1984. *Biology and Biological Technology,* pt. 2, *Agriculture.* Science and Civilisation in China 6, ed. J. Needham. New York: Cambridge University Press.
Bray, T. L. 2003. Inka Pottery as Culinary Equipment: Food, Feasting, and Gender in Imperial Design. *Latin American Antiquity* 14 (1): 3–28.
Bunker, S. G. 1987. Ritual, Respect and Refusal: Drinking Behaviour in an Andean Village. *Human Organization* 46: 334–42.
Camino, L. 1984. Tarika, un centro alfarero. *Boletín de Lima* 6 (35): 49–54.
Camino, L. 1987. *Chicha de maíz: Bebida y vida del pueblo Catacaos.* Piura, Peru: Centro de Investigación y Promoción del Campesinado–Piura.
Cavero Carrasco, R. 1986. *Maíz, chicha y religiosidad andina.* Ayacucho, Peru: Universidad Nacional de San Cristóbal de Huamanga.
Chang, C., Y. Lin, S. Chen, E. Carvaja Barriaga, P. Portero Barahona, C. J. Bond, I. N. Roberts, and C. Lee. 2012. *Candida thea* sp. nov.: A New Anamorphic Beverage-Associated Member of the *Lodderomyces* Clade. *International Journal of Food Microbiology* 153: 10–14.
Cieza de León, P. (1540) 1959. *The Incas.* Norman: University of Oklahoma Press.
Cieza de León, P. (1552) 1962. *La crónica del Perú.* Madrid: Ediciones Espasa-Calpe.
Cobo, B. (1653) 1956. Historia del Nuevo Mundo. In *Obras del Padre Bernabé Cobo,* pt. 1, 8–427. Biblioteca de Autores Españoles 91. Madrid: Ediciones Atlas.
Cobo, B. (1653) 1979. *History of the Inca Empire.* Austin: University of Texas Press.
Cook, A. G., and M. Glowacki. 2003. Pots, Politics, and Power: Huari Ceramic Assemblages and Imperial Administration. In *The Archaeology and Politics of Food and Feasting in Early States and Empires,* ed. T. L. Bray, 173–202. New York: Kluwer Academic/Plenum.
Costion, K. 2012. Huaracane Production and Consumption of Chicha de Molle at Yahuay Alta: An Example of Indigenous Agency in a Colonial Landscape. Paper presented at the 77th Annual Meeting of the Society for American Archaeology, Memphis.
Cutler, H. C., and M. Cárdenas. 1947. Chicha, a Native South American Beer. *Botanical Museum Leaflets* (Harvard University) 13 (3): 33–60.

Doughty, P. L. 1971. The Social Uses of Alcoholic Beverages in a Peruvian Community. *Human Organization* 30 (2): 187–97.

Dozier, C. A., and J. Jennings. In press. Identification of *Chicha de Maiz* in the Pre-Columbian Andes through Starch Analysis. In *Andean Foodways: Interdisciplinary Approaches to Pre-Columbian, Colonial, Contemporary Food and Culture*, ed. J. E. Staller. Tuscaloosa: University of Alabama Press.

Edmonds, M. 1990. Description, Understanding, and the *Chaine Operatoire*. *Archaeological Review from Cambridge* 9 (1): 55–70.

Fields, R. D. 2012. Raising the Dead: New Species of Life Resurrected from Ancient Andean Tomb. *Scientific American*, February 19. www.scientificamerican.com/article.cfm?id=new-species-resurrected-ancient-andean-tomb.

Finucane, B. C. 2009. Maize and Sociopolitical Complexity in the Ayacucho Valley, Peru. *Current Anthropology* 50: 535–45.

Finucane, B. C., P. M. Agurto, and W. H. Isbell. 2006. Human and Animal Diet at Conchopata, Peru: Stable Isotope Evidence for Maize Agriculture and Animal Management Practices during the Middle Horizon. *Journal of Archaeological Science* 33: 1766–76.

Franquemont, C., T. Plowman, E. Franquemont, S. King, C. Niezgoda, W. Davis, and C. Sperling. 1990. *The Ethnobotany of Chinchero, an Andean Community in Southern Peru*. Fieldiana 24. Chicago: Field Museum of Natural History.

Garcilaso de la Vega, I. (1609) 1945. *Obras completas del Inca Garcilaso de la Vega*. Santiago del Estero: Editorial Sopena Argentina.

Garcilaso de la Vega, I. (1609) 1966. *Royal Commentaries of the Incas and General History of Peru*. Pt. 1. Austin: University of Texas Press.

Gero, J. M. 1990. Pottery, Power, and . . . Parties! *Archaeology* 43 (2): 52–56.

Gero, J. M. 1992. Feasts and Females: Gender Ideology and Political Meals in the Andes. *Norwegian Archaeological Review* 25: 15–30.

Gillin, J. P. 1947. *Moche, A Peruvian Coastal Community*. Washington, D.C.: Smithsonian Institution, Institute of Social Anthropology.

Goldstein, D., and R. C. Coleman. 2004. *Schinus molle* L. (Anacardiaceae) Chicha Production in the Central Andes. *Economic Botany* 58 (4): 523–29.

Goldstein, D., R. C. Coleman Goldstein, and P. R. Williams. 2009. You Are What You Drink: A Sociocultural Reconstruction of Pre-Hispanic Fermented Beverage Use at Cerro Baúl, Moquegua, Peru. In *Drink, Power, and Society in the Andes*, ed. J. Jennings and B. Bowser, 133–66. Gainesville: University Press of Florida.

Goldstein, P. 2003. From Stew-Eaters to Maize-Drinkers: The *Chicha* Economy and the Tiwanaku Expansion. In *The Archaeology and Politics of Food and Feasting in Early States and Empires*, ed. T. L. Bray, 143–72. New York: Kluwer Academia/Plenum.

Goldstein, P. 2005. *Andean Diaspora: The Tiwanaku Colonies and the Origins of South American Empire*. Gainesville: University Press of Florida.

Gómez Huamán, N. 1966. Importancia social de la chicha como bebida popular en Huamanga. *Wamani* 1 (1): 33–57.

Goodman-Elgar, M. 2009. Places to Partake: *Chicha* in the Andean Landscape. In *Drink, Power, and Society in the Andes*, ed. J. Jennings and B. Bowser, 75–107. Gainesville: University Press of Florida.

Goyal, R. K. 1999. Biochemistry of Fermentation. In *Biotechnology: Food Fermentation*, ed. V. K. Joshi and A. Pandey, 87–171. Calcutta: Educational Publishers and Distributors.

Grobman, A., W. Salhuana, and R. Sevilla. 1961. *Races of Maize in Peru: Their Origins, Evolution, and Classification*. Publication 915. Washington, D.C.: National Academy of Sciences, National Research Council.

Guillet, D. W. 1992. *Covering Ground: Communal Water Management and the State in the Peruvian Highlands*. Ann Arbor: University of Michigan Press.

Haggblade, S., and W. H. Holzapfel. 1989. Industrialization of Indigenous Beer Brewing. In *Industrialization of Indigenous Fermented Foods*, ed. K. H. Steinkraus, 191–283. New York: Marcel Dekker.

Hastorf, C. A. 1991. Gender, Space, and Food in Prehistory. In *Engendering Archaeology: Women and Prehistory*, ed. J. M. Gero and M. W. Conkey, 132–59. Cambridge, U.K.: Blackwell.

Hastorf, C. A., and S. Johannessen. 1993. Pre-Hispanic Political Change and the Role of Maize in the Central Andes of Peru. *American Anthropologist* 95 (1): 115–38.

Hayashida, F. 2008. Ancient Beer and Modern Brewers: Ethnoarchaeological Observations of Chicha Production in Two Regions of the North Coast of Peru. *Journal of Anthropological Archaeology* 27 (2): 161–74.

Hayashida, F. 2009. *Chicha* Histories: Pre-Hispanic Brewing in the Andes and the Use of Ethnographic and Historic Analogues. In *Drink, Power, and Society in the Andes*, ed. J. Jennings and B. Bowser, 232–56. Gainesville: University Press of Florida.

Hayden, B. 2001. Fabulous Feasts: A Prolegomenon to the Importance of Feasting. In *Feasts: Archaeological and Ethnographic Perspectives on Food, Politics, and Power*, ed. M. Dietler and B. Hayden, 23–64. Washington, D.C.: Smithsonian Institution Press.

Hocquenghem, A. M., and S. Monzon. 1995. *La cocina Piurana: Ensayo de antropología de la alimentación*. Lima: Instituto de Estudios Peruanos.

Holmberg, A. 1971. The Rhythm of Drinking in a Peruvian Coastal Mestizo Community. *Human Organization* 30 (2): 198–202.

Hornsey, I. S. 1999. *Brewing*. Cambridge, U.K.: Royal Society of Chemists.

Iltis, H. H. 2006. Origins of Polystichy in Maize. In *Histories of Maize: Multidisciplinary Approaches to the Prehistory, Linguistics, Biogeography, Domestication, and Evolution of Maize*, ed. J. E. Staller, R. H. Tykot, and B. F. Benz, 22–54. Burlington, Vt.: Elsevier.

Isbell, B. J. 1978. *To Defend Ourselves: Ecology and Ritual in an Andean Village*. Prospect Heights, Ill.: Waveland Press.

Jackson, R. S. 1999. Grape-Based Fermentation Products. In *Biotechnology: Food Fermentation*, ed. V. K. Joshi and A. Pandey, 583–646. Calcutta: Educational Publishers and Distributors.

Jackson, R. S. 2003. Modern Biotechnology of Winemaking. In *Wine: A Scientific Exploration*, ed. M. Sandler and R. Pinder, 228–59. New York: Taylor and Francis.

Jennings, J. 2005. La Chichera y El Patrón: Chicha and the Energetics of Feasting in the Prehistoric Andes. In *Foundations of Power in the Prehispanic Andes*, ed. C. A. Conlee, D. Ogburn, and K. Vaughn, 241–59. Archaeological Publications of the

American Anthropological Association 14. Washington, D.C.: American Anthropological Association.
Jennings, J., and B. Bowser, eds. 2009. *Drink, Power, and Society in the Andes.* Gainesville: University Press of Florida.
Jennings, J., and M. Chatfield. 2009. Pots, Brewers, and Hosts: Women's Power and the Limits of Central Andean Feasting. In *Drink, Power, and Society in the Andes,* ed. J. Jennings and B. Bowser, 200–231. Gainesville: University Press of Florida.
Jennings, J., K. Antrobus, S. J. Atencio, E. Glavich, R. Johnson, G. Loffler, and C. Luu. 2005. "Drinking Beer Is a Blissful Mood": Alcohol Production, Operational Chains, and Feasting in the Ancient World. *Current Anthropology* 46 (2): 275–303.
Joshi, V. K., D. K. Sandhu, and N. S. Thakur. 1999. Fruit-Based Alcoholic Beverages. In *Biotechnology: Food Fermentation,* ed. V. K. Joshi and A. Pandey, 647–744. Calcutta: Educational Publishers and Distributors.
Kramer, F. L. 1957. The Pepper Tree, *Schinus molle* L. *Economic Botany* 2 (4): 322–26.
Latour, B. 1996. *Aramis, or the Love of Technology.* Cambridge, Mass.: Harvard University Press.
Lau, G. 2002. Feasting and Ancestor Veneration at Chinchawas, North Highlands of Ancash, Peru. *Latin American Antiquity* 13 (3): 279–304.
Lemonnier, P. 1993. Introduction. In *Technological Choices: Transformation in Material Cultures since the Neolithic,* ed. P. Lemonnier, 1–35. New York: Routledge.
León, R. 2008. *Chicha peruana, una bebida, una cultura.* Lima: Universidad San Martín de Porres.
Leroi-Gourhan, A. 1943. *Evolution et techniques: L'Homme et la matière.* Paris: Albin Michel.
Leroi-Gourham, A. 1945. *Evolution et techniques: Milieu et technique.* Paris: Albin Michel.
Litto, G. 1976. *South American Folk Pottery.* New York: Watson-Guptill.
Llano Restrepo, M., and M. Campuzano Cifuentes. 1994. *La chicha, una bebida fermentada a través de la historia.* Bogotá: Instituto Colombiano de Antropología, Bogotá.
Mahias, M. C. 1993. Pottery Techniques in India: Technical Variants and Social Choice. In *Technological Choices: Transformation in Material Cultures since the Neolithic,* ed. P. Lemonnier, 157–80. New York: Routledge.
Manrique Chávez, A. 1997. *El maíz en el Perú.* Lima: Consejo Nacional de Ciencia y Tecnología.
Marcoy, P. 1873. *A Journey across South America.* London: Blackie and Son.
Mayer, E. 2002. *The Articulated Peasant: Household Economies in the Andes.* Boulder, Colo.: Westview Press.
Meyerson, J. 1990. *Tambo: Life in an Andean Village.* Austin: University of Texas Press.
Miracle, P. 2002. Mesolithic Meals from Mesolithic Middens. In *Consuming Passions and Patterns of Consumption,* ed. P. Miracle and N. Milner, 65–88. Cambridge, U.K.: McDonald Institute of Archaeology.
Moore, J. 1989. Pre-Hispanic Beer in Coastal Peru: Technology and Social Context of Prehistoric Production. *American Anthropologist* 91 (3): 682–95.

Morris, C. 1979. Maize Beer in the Economics, Politics, and Religion of the Inca Empire. In *Fermented Food Beverages in Nutrition*, ed. C. F. Gastineau, W. J. Darby, and T. B. Turner, 21–34. New York: Academic Press.
Moseley, M. E., D. J. Nash, P. R. Williams, S. D. deFrance, A. Miranda, and M. Ruales. 2005. Burning Down the Brewery: Establishing and Evacuating an Ancient Imperial Colony at Cerro Baúl, Peru. *Proceedings of the National Academy of Sciences* 102 (48): 17264–71.
Murra, J. V. 1960. Rite and Crop in the Inca State. In *Culture in History: Essays in Honor of Paul Radin*, ed. S. Diamond, 393–407. New York: Columbia University Press.
Murra, J. V. 1980. *The Economic Organization of the Inka State*. Greenwich, Conn.: JAI Press.
Narotzky, S. 1997. *New Directions in Economic Anthropology*. Chicago: Pluto.
Nash, D. 2011. Fiestas y la economía política Wari en Moquegua, Perú. *Chungara* 43 (2): 221–42.
Nicholson, G. E. 1960. Chicha Maize Types and Chicha Manufacture in Peru. *Economic Botany* 14 (4): 290–99.
Nuñez del Prado, O. 1973. *Kuyo Chico: Applied Anthropology in an Andean Community*. Chicago: University of Chicago Press.
Parker, B. J., and W. McCool. 2015. Indices of Household Maize Beer Production in the Andes. *Journal of Anthropological Research* 71 (3): 359–400.
Perlov, D. 2009. Working through Daughters: Strategies for Gaining and Maintaining Social Power among the Chicheras of Highland Bolivia. In *Drink, Power, and Society in the Andes*, ed. J. Jennings and B. Bowser, 49–74. Gainesville: University Press of Florida.
Ramírez, S. E. 2005. *To Feed and Be Fed: The Cosmological Bases of Authority and Identity in the Andes*. Stanford: Stanford University Press.
Ravines, R., and F. Villiger, eds. 1989. *La cerámica tradicional del Perú*. Lima: Editorial Los Pinos.
Ruiz, H. (1788) 1998. *The Journals of Hipólito Ruiz*. Ed. R. E. Schultes. Portland, Ore.: Timber Press.
Sarmiento de Gamboa, P. (1572) 1999. *History of the Incas*. Mineola, N.Y.: Dover Books.
Sayre, M., D. Goldstein, W. Whitehead, and P. R. Williams. 2012. A Marked Preference: *Chicha de Molle* and Wari State Consumption Practices. *Ñawpa Pacha* 32 (2): 231–58.
Schreiber, K. J. 1992. *Wari Imperialism in Middle Horizon Peru*. Anthropological Papers 87. Ann Arbor: University of Michigan.
Schreiber, K. J., and M. J. Edwards. 2010. Los centros administrativos huari y las manifestaciones físicas del poder imperial. In *Señores de los imperios del sol*, ed. K. Makowski, 152–61. Lima: Banco de Credito.
Segura Llanos, R. 2001. *Rito y economía en Cajamarquilla: Investigaciones arqueológicas en el conjunto arquitectónico Julio C. Tello*. Lima: Fondo Editorial de la Pontificia Universidad Católica del Perú.
Shimada, I. 1994. *Pampa Grande and the Mochica Culture*. Austin: University of Texas Press.

Sillar, B. 2000. *Shaping Culture, Making Pots and Constructing Households: An Ethnoarchaeological Study of Pottery Production, Trade, and Use in the Andes.* BAR International Series 883. Oxford: British Archaeological Reports.

Soni, S. K., and D. K. Sandhu. 1999. Microbiology of Fermentation. In *Biotechnology: Food Fermentation*, ed. V. K. Joshi and A. Pandey, 25–85. Calcutta: Educational Publishers and Distributors.

Staller, J. E. 2006. The Social, Symbolic, and Economic Significance of *Zea mays* L. in the Late Horizon Period. In *Histories of Maize: Multidisciplinary Approaches to the Prehistory, Linguistics, Biogeography, Domestication, and Evolution of Maize*, ed. J. E. Staller, R. H. Tykot, and B. F. Benz, 449–67. Burlington, Vt.: Elsevier.

Steinkraus, K. H. 1979. Nutritionally Significant Indigenous Foods Involving an Alcoholic Fermentation. In *Fermented Food Beverages in Nutrition*, ed. C. F. Gastineau, W. J. Darby, and T. B. Turner, 35–59. New York: Academic Press.

Steward, J. H., and L. C. Faron. 1959. *Native Peoples of South America.* New York: McGraw-Hill.

Tschiffely, A. F. 1933. *Tschiffely's Ride: Ten Thousand Miles in the Saddle from Southern Cross to Pole Star.* New York: Simon and Schuster.

Uzendoski, M. A. 2004. Manioc Beer and Meat: Value, Reproduction, and Cosmic Substance among the Napo Runa of the Ecuadorian Amazon. *Journal of the Royal Anthropological Institute* 10: 883–902.

Valdez, L. M. 1997. Ecology and Ceramic Production in an Andean Community: A Reconsideration of the Evidence. *Journal of Anthropological Research* 53: 65–85.

Valdez, L. M. 2006. Maize Beer Production in Middle Horizon Peru. *Journal of Anthropological Research* 62: 53–80.

Valdez, L. M. 2012. Molle Beer Production in a Peruvian Highland Valley. *Journal of Anthropological Research* 68 (1): 71–93.

Valdez, L. M., K. J. Bettcher, and J. E. Valdez. 2010a. El centro especializado Wari de Marayniyoq, Ayacucho, Perú. In *Arqueología en el Perú: Nuevos aportes para el estudio de las sociedades Andinas prehispánicas*, ed. R. Romero Velarde and T. P. Swendsen, 205–28. Lima: Anheb Impresiones.

Valdez, L. M., K. J. Bettcher, and J. E. Valdez. 2010b. Production of Maize Beer at a Wari Site in the Ayacucho Valley, Peru. *Arqueología Iberoamericana* 5: 23–35.

Vázquez, M. C. 1967. La chicha en los países andinos. *América Indígena* 27 (2): 264–82.

Vencl, S. 1994. The Archaeology of Thirst. *Journal of European Archaeology* 2 (2): 299–326.

Wiener, C. (1880) 1993. *Perú y Bolivia, relato de viaje.* Lima: Instituto Francés de Estudios Andinos.

Williams, P. R. 2009. Wari and Tiwanaku Borderlands. In *Tiwanaku: Papers of the 2005 Mayer Center Symposium at the Denver Art Museum*, ed. M. Young-Sánchez, 211–24. Denver: Denver Art Museum.

CONTRIBUTORS

Zuzana Chovanec is an adjunct faculty member in the Division of Liberal Arts and Communication at Tulsa Community College and a volunteer research associate of anthropology at the State University of New York at Albany. She specializes in organic residue analysis, human-environment interactions, and the eastern Mediterranean. Her research has focused on the prehistoric Bronze Age on Cyprus and the use of prestigious products, including psychoactive substances, medicines, and perfumes. Her current projects pertain to the role of the opium poppy in the Mediterranean basin and the influence of the natural world on Bronze and Iron Age art in Cyprus.

Robert C. Clarke is the author of several *Cannabis* science books and has traveled extensively throughout Eurasia exploring the evolution of human-cannabis relationships and documenting traditional *Cannabis* production and use. Rob's breeding interests include selecting and preserving landrace varieties and developing drug cultivars. Presently, Rob serves as an executive director of BioAgronomics Group consultants and is affiliated with the Phylos Bioscience Cannabis Evolution Project.

Scott M. Fitzpatrick is professor of archaeology and associate director of the Museum of Natural and Cultural History at the University of Oregon. He specializes in the prehistory of island and coastal regions, particularly the Pacific and Caribbean, with research focusing primarily on colonization events, seafaring capabilities, exchange systems, and historical ecology. He has active field projects on islands in Micronesia, the Caribbean, the Florida Keys, and the Oregon coast and has published more than one hundred peer-reviewed book chapters and journal articles. Dr. Fitzpatrick is the founding coeditor of the *Journal of Island and Coastal Archaeology* and an associate editor for *Archaeology in Oceania*, and he serves on the editorial boards for two other journals.

Justin Jennings is curator of New World archaeology at the Royal Ontario Museum and associate professor of anthropology at the University of Toronto. A specialist in the Pre-Columbian Andes, he focuses on village life, urbanism, cultural horizons, and the emergence and maintenance of social inequality in South America and other regions of the world. One research interest that crosscuts these themes is alcohol production and its relationship to changing feasting regimes. Dr. Jennings has published widely for scholarly and general audiences; his most recent book is *Killing Civilization: A Reassessment of Early Urbanism and Its Consequences.*

Quetta Kaye received her PhD from the University of London in 2010. She has been involved with Caribbean archaeology since excavating in Barbados in 1993 and then as a codirector of the Carriacou Archaeology Field Project from 2003 until she retired from active fieldwork in 2015. Dr. Kaye has been the secretary of the International Association for Caribbean Archaeology since 2003. Areas of research interest include the prehistory of the Caribbean and the circum-Caribbean area, the ancient use of hallucinogens and altered states of consciousness, and archaeobotanical and chemical analysis of prehistoric materials for evidence of intoxicants.

Jennifer Loughmiller-Cardinal is part-time professor at the State University of New York at New Paltz in the Anthropology Department and a graduate student at SUNY Albany in the Chemistry Department. Jennifer specializes in Classic period Mayan archaeology, especially focusing on pottery use and function, archaeometry (food residues), ritual behavior, epigraphy and iconography, and linguistics. She is currently working on several projects in both Mesoamerica and South America, analyzing elite burial goods and identifying ritual foodstuffs.

Mark D. Merlin is professor in the Botany Department at the University of Hawai'i at Manoa. He is the author of *Man and Marijuana: Some Aspects of the Ancient Relationships* and *On the Trail of the Ancient Opium Poppy* and a coauthor of *Kava: The Pacific Drug* and *Cannabis: Evolution and Ethnobotany*. He was also lead author for six textbooks on traditional ethnobotany in Micronesia. Dr. Merlin's educational guidebooks for the native and naturalized flora of the Hawaiian Islands have been in print and used widely for over forty years.

Thomas J. Pluckhahn is professor in the Department of Anthropology at the University of South Florida. He earned his PhD from the University of Georgia in 2002. He is the author of *Kolomoki: Settlement, Ceremony, and Status in the Deep South, A.D. 350 to 750* and the coauthor (with Victor D.

Thompson) of *The Archaeology of Village Life at Crystal River*, as well as numerous journal articles and book chapters. He specializes in the archaeology of households, settlements, and landscapes, focusing particularly on the U.S. Southeast.

Sean M. Rafferty is associate professor of anthropology at the State University of New York at Albany. He specializes in the prehistory of eastern North America, with research focusing primarily on ritual practices, the use of intoxicants, and residue analysis. He has a long-term field project in the Schoharie Valley of New York State. Dr. Rafferty is the editor of the journal *Northeast Anthropology*.

Matthew P. Sayre is associate professor and the chair of the Department of Anthropology and Sociology at the University of South Dakota. He is also active in the development of the new Sustainability Department. His research focuses on the past ecological, ritual, and production practices of people in the Andean region of South America. He has worked at the UNESCO World Heritage site of Chavín de Huántar, Peru, over the past decade and leads a field project focused on the domestic settlements in the La Banda sector of the site. He also conducts archaeological research on the Middle Horizon of the Central Andes as well as on current climate change issues through his work with traditional farmers in the Potato Park of Cuzco, Peru. His recent book (coedited with Maria Bruno), *Social Perspectives on Ancient Lives from Paleoethnobotanical Data*, is a collection of theoretically informed studies of plant use in past societies.

Daniel M. Seinfeld works in cultural resource management and teaches graduate courses in archaeology and material culture in the Department of Art History at Florida State University. He has conducted research projects in the southeastern United States and Mesoamerica on topics including mound building, maize use, residue analysis, ancient intoxicant use, and the chemistry of glass trade beads. In addition to his research, he also works in NAGPRA compliance and laws ensuring the respectful treatment of unmarked graves.

Victor D. Thompson is professor of anthropology and director of the Center for Archaeological Sciences at the University of Georgia. His primary interests are in the Native American societies that occupied the coastal and wetland areas of the American Southeast. The majority of his work has taken place in Florida and along the Georgia coast. He is the author, coauthor, and coeditor of numerous publications published by the University Press of Florida, the American Museum of Natural History, *American Antiquity*,

Journal of Archaeological Science, *Archaeological Prospection*, and *World Archaeology*, among others. He is the founding editor for the series History and Ecology in Island and Coastal Societies, published by the University Press of Florida. He is the current associate editor for book reviews for *American Antiquity*.

Constantino Manuel Torres is professor emeritus of the Art and Art History Department at Florida International University in Miami. He has conducted research on ancient cultures of the South-Central Andes since 1982. His work has concentrated on the San Pedro de Atacama oasis, Chile, and the use of *Anadenanthera*-based snuffs. His books include *Anadenanthera: Visionary Plant of Ancient South America* (coauthored with David Repke), a comprehensive and detailed study of this plant in continuous use for the past four thousand years. He has published numerous peer-reviewed articles and book chapters. On two occasions he has been an invited presenter to the Dumbarton Oaks Round Table, and he participated in a symposium on the art of the South-Central Andes at the Center for Advanced Studies in the Visual Arts of the National Gallery, Washington, D.C.; he has also been the recipient of three Fulbright Fellowships. His recent research on *Anadenanthera* preparations has led to the study of ayahuasca analogues in South American antiquity.

Lidio M. Valdez is assistant professor in the Department of Anthropology, Economics and Political Science at MacEwan University (Canada) and is a specialist in the archaeology of the Central Andes, with particular interest in the study of complexity, conflict, mortuary patterns, settlement studies, and ceramic analysis. For more than three decades, Dr. Valdez has carried out field research in the Peruvian central highland valley of Ayacucho, investigating the Early Intermediate, Middle Horizon, and Late Horizon periods. At the same time he has carried out field research on the south coast of Peru, investigating the same time periods. Results of his studies have been published in a variety of scholarly journals, including *Current Anthropology*, *Journal of Anthropological Research*, *World Archaeology*, *Latin American Antiquity*, and *American Antiquity*.

INDEX

Page numbers in *italics* refer to illustrations.

Printed in the USA
CPSIA information can be obtained
at www.ICGtesting.com
CBHW072034271124
17878CB00006B/59